LAUREL

"THE WISEST, SANEST, SOUNDEST, MOST UNDER-STANDING AND COMPASSIONATE TREATMENT OF AMERICAN WOMAN'S GREATEST PROBLEM."
—Ashley Montagu

"Betty Friedan has been and remains a bridge between conservative and radical elements in feminism, and an ardent advocate of harmony and humane values."
—Marilyn French, *Esquire*

THE FEMININE MYSTIQUE
Betty Friedan

"A HIGHLY READABLE, PROVOCATIVE BOOK."
—*The New York Times Book Review*

"Written with a passionate drive . . . it will leave you with some haunting facts as well as a few hair-raising stories. That *The Feminine Mystique* is at the same time a scholarly work, appropriate for serious study, only adds to its usefulness."
—*Saturday Review*

"THE MOST IMPORTANT BOOK OF THE TWENTIETH CENTURY . . . BETTY FRIEDAN IS TO WOMEN WHAT MARTIN LUTHER KING WAS TO BLACKS."
—Barbara Seaman, author of *Free and Female*

Also by Betty Friedan

"IT CHANGED MY LIFE"
THE SECOND STAGE
THE FOUNTAIN OF AGE

The Feminine Mystique

by Betty Friedan

With a New Introduction and Epilogue
by the Author

LAUREL

A LAUREL BOOK
Published by
Dell Publishing
a division of
Bantam Doubleday Dell Publishing Group, Inc.
1540 Broadway
New York, New York 10036

For all the new women,
and the new men

Contents

Twenty Years After

 It is twenty years now since *The Feminine Mystique* was published. I am still awed by the revolution that book helped spark. It's a mystery to me that I was able to put it together, at the time it was needed, and that women, and men, even now stop me on the street, and remember where they were when they read it—"in the maternity ward, with my third kid, and then I decided to go to law school."

I keep being surprised as the changes which the women's movement set in motion continue to play themselves out in our lives—the enormous and mundane, subtle and not-so-subtle, delightful, painful, immediate, far-reaching, paradoxical, inexorable and probably irreversible changes in women's lives, and men's. Firewomen, chairpersons, housespouses, the gender gap, Ms., palimony, take-out food, woman priests, woman rabbis, woman prime ministers out-*macho*ing male dictators in miniwars, women's studies, women's history, double burden, dressing for success, more women now going to college than men, assertiveness training, male consciousness raising, role strain, role reversal, networking, sexism, displaced homemakers, equal pay for work of comparable value, marriage contracts, child custody for men, first babies at forty, the two-paycheck family, the single-parent family, Victor-Victoria, Tootsie . . . Who could have predicted some of these? Not I, certainly.

It's hard enough for me, both personally and politically, to cope with the realities of our revolution, as its daughters and sons take its terms for granted and face new problems, new pressures, new choices and conflicts, and the need for new dreams. It's hard to go on *evolving*, as we all must, just to keep up with a revolution as big as this, when some who now follow, or fight, or study it, or seek power through it, seem to want to lock it in place forever, as an unchanging ism.

Early last year, I fled to Harvard as a Fellow of the Institute of Politics of the Kennedy School of Government, pursuing with relief a new scholarly quest, retreating (or so I thought) from feminist power struggles, disheartened less by the attacks of our enemies—who are clearly losing even the political war they seemed temporarily to have won—than by the fury of some of my sister feminists because I said the women's movement had to move anew, was already moving into a second stage, which can't be seen in terms of women alone or women against men. We have transcended our necessary reaction against the feminine mystique, I said in my book *The Second Stage*, and we have come about as far as we can with a male model of equality. I said that we need a model of equality encompassing female experience, female values that men now begin to share. As our revolution coincides with larger economic upheavals, I said, we must come to new terms with family and with work. Some didn't like my saying that.

I've sometimes wondered how Karl Marx would have handled the reality of "thesis, antithesis, synthesis" as his revolution hardened into ism, and became the stuff of daily life. He wouldn't have been a Marxist? Well, I am not Karl Marx, and ours is not that kind of bloody revolution, and I am still a feminist. We are in the second stage now, whether or not anyone wants to admit it. But I am sick and tired of the new spate of media pronouncements claiming that the women's movement is finished and the revolution is lost because the "postfeminist generation" is moving from a different place.

Of course the postfeminist generation is in a different place. The women's movement put it there. I speak now as if of ancient history, lecturing to the young in schools from the University of New Hampshire to San Diego State about what it was like when women lived their lives—and were counseled, studied, treated, taught—according to that feminine mystique which defined woman only as husband's wife, children's mother, server of physical needs of husband, children, home, and never as person defining herself by her own actions in society. Their *mothers* were the ones who rejected the feminine mystique and went back to school and went to work and otherwise started to change their lives twenty years ago. I do not find it a cause for feminist grief that members of this new generation simply take the personhood of women for granted. If they take women's rights and the opportunities we fought for too much for granted—if they are worried now about jobs, difficult choices about having children, how to pay for a house with or without two incomes, and double burdens they can't refuse even if sometimes they'd like to—that's a mark of how far our revolution has come, and a summons to its own next stage.

As far as I'm concerned, the daughters have to move on; they don't have to say thank you—though it's nice when they do. It's also nice that so many now study women's history in college, even in high school. But I am impatient to get those "women's studies" integrated into history, and into every subject, as it's taught from grade school on. I still remember how surprised I was, taking the bus in from my suburban dream house in Rockland County to the New York Public Library when I was writing my book, twenty-odd years ago, to uncover the women's history that had been buried by the feminine mystique in the 1940's and 1950's, and to realize that Mary Wollstonecraft, Elizabeth Cady Stanton, Margaret Fuller, Lucy Stone, Susan B. Anthony, and Charlotte Perkins Gilman—whom most educated women like myself had never studied then, even at Smith—had taken that passionate journey ahead of me. Will our memory be buried in another generation as theirs was? Will some future great-granddaughter have to invent feminism once more from scratch, starting over again? I doubt it. I think the consciousness of woman as person, the differences made already by the rights and opportunities won—endangered, incomplete as they still are —go too broad and deep into life now, and are too buttressed by economic necessity, to be easily erased or reversed. Our daughters are busy now with living the new complexities we opened. But just let somebody seriously try to take those rights away!

Emily, my own daughter-the-doctor, went from taking it all for granted in college ("I'm not a feminist, I'm a person; it's not necessary to fight for women anymore") to fervent feminism after one year in medical school: "There are so many of us now, they don't dare do it openly the way they used to, so you think there's something wrong with you. It's worse, now that it's so subtle." But it's not worse that women are 30 per cent of the medical-school class, rather than 3 per cent.

After organizing the women in her medical school on the unfinished business of sex discrimination, my daughter began to concern herself with fundamental issues in the practice of medicine itself. and in her own life. She did not want to climb the professi al ladder as a specialist or a research star. She wanted to go into family practice, to deal with the patient as a whole person in the concrete family setting, not as a specimen of isolated symptoms. Her current problem has to do with the eight hundred miles separating her hospital residency and his, and with how they can live together as they'd like when their equally rigid hospital schedules don't give either one of them more than thirty-six hours off, most weeks. Neither of them would consider asking the other to sacrifice his or her own goals for the sake of their relationship, which somehow survives those obstacles of distance and time. Trade-offs, second-stage flexibility, aren't easy to work out when the institutions themselves still gear their professional training in terms of men of the past whose wives took care of the details of life, and followed along. My daughter-the-doctor will not be, and will not have, such a wife.

My daughter-in-law, Helen, is technically, at the moment, mostly a housewife. The baby was not exactly planned. There were difficult choices to be made, since both she and Jonathan, my younger son, had just finished college, after having dropped out for some years. One day last summer, when they'd brought the baby out to my house in Sag Harbor, Helen overheard me on the phone discussing how to stop new attacks on the Supreme Court decision asserting women's right to legal medical abortion. "The right to abortion is very important to me," said this post-feminist mother, nursing her baby. "It's important knowing that we had the baby because we chose to."

I relish their mutual joy, their new confident maturity and sense of themselves in their chosen parenthood—which Jonathan has truly shared from their first decision to use a nurse-midwife and a birthing center instead of a traditional hospital. Watching him skillfully maneuver Rafael into his snowsuit and throw him gleefully over his shoulder, into that snuggly backpack, I sense that he gets at least as much of his male identity from being a father as from being an engineer. But Helen is unmistakably the mother. She does not let any male doctor-as-God tell her what to do with her baby the way we let Dr. Spock tell us. She worked until the very end of pregnancy, switching from nursery-school teaching to word-processing to make more money, then concentrated on mothering for a year, and now has a flexible, part-time job where she can take the baby along. Being a feminist is to her something you don't need to think about very much, like being an American. The very language of her dreams, as she shares them with us at breakfast, is feminist. She knows who she is as a woman.

And I, as a grandmother at last, am the envy of my friends, whose doctor/lawyer/banker daughters are too caught up in their careers to yet carry on the gene pool. With my beautiful, incredible grandbaby—such a beaming, bright bundle of energy, smiling at me with his father's big ears and dimples and his own deep blue eyes, so familiar, so intensely alive, so awesome a miracle—I exult in the generation of life, though I have been too busy this year to baby-sit much.

This year, a number of my "family of friends" had their first babies at thirty-five, at forty, some undergoing rather scary, unexpected complications at birth. Other friends made me fear for their sanity as they suddenly became obsessed, in their mid-forties, after twenty years of brilliant career, with the wish to have a child, and underwent surgical procedures, miscarried, eventually came to terms with the finality of the biological clock. The power of this desire to have a child—when women no longer need to have a child to define themselves as women, to have status, economic support, and identity in society—seems to be as great as or even greater than ever. Choice has liberated an exultant motherhood, beyond mystique. It has also liberated women to be generative in other ways, without at all now feeling like freaks. Gloria Steinem, for instance, and Germaine Greer have been fine role models for that pattern.

But there is unfinished business here, to make such choices real for many women. Now that economic necessity dictates that most women must continue to work after they become mothers (nearly half of the women with children under six now work, compared with less than one-fifth in 1960; and so do nearly two-thirds of the women with kids over six), someone is going to have to battle in a new and serious way for institutions that will help the new family. A new economic-political basis must be found for the maternity leave, paternity leave, parental sick leave, parental sabbaticals, reduced schedules, flextime, job sharing, and child-care supports that don't now exist. But who will take up this battle, and how will it be fought, in a time when jobs themselves are so scarce that people must take what they can get, when budgets for social programs that already exist are being cut down?

It is crucial for feminists to understand the power of that choice to have children, and to keep fighting for the right to abortion. But they must give new priority to a child-care crusade and to restructuring work. If these issues are not addressed soon, we can fear a new feminine mystique, invoked to send women home again to have babies instead of competing for dwindling jobs. During this time of deepening recession-depression, President Reagan, who has declared a new campaign against abortion, has also suggested that there wouldn't be any unemployment if women would stop looking for jobs.

It's necessary to think beyond the win/lose, zero-sum, black-and-white, either/or male model even to understand what really happened with ERA.

Until the final hours of June 30, 1982—when after sixty years of battle, after passage of the amendment by Congress and its ratification by thirty-five of the thirty-eight needed states, the legislatures of Illinois, Flordia, Oklahoma, North Carolina, Missouri, and Virginia, with the advice and consent of President Reagan and the Republican party in power, and no strong opposition from Democratic bosses, allowed the Equal Rights Amendment to die—American politicians must still have been blinded by the feminine mystique. They still thought women voted only as men's wives.

Because those involved were only women, the politicians didn't count it as politically *real* somehow that 450 organizations representing 50 million Americans stood united in support of ERA, with nearly 70 per cent of the adult population behind them, according to the polls. There was a larger national consensus for ERA, historians now say, than for any previous constitutional amendment. The politicians didn't take it in right away, that in the last months NOW alone was raising a million dollars a month from women giving fifteen, twenty-five, or fifty dollars from their paychecks or grocery money for that constitutional guarantee of equal rights which they now realized they needed, as unemployment and divorce rates rose, and Reagan gutted sex-discrimination laws. That was more money than the Democratic party was raising.

Not until the 1982 elections did political analysts begin to take seriously the "gender gap," which had in fact been building for some years. Month after month, women had been indicating their sharp disapproval of President Reagan. By 1982 the Gallup poll found that just 36 per cent of women approved of Reagan's job performance, as compared to 47 per cent of men. And, it was suddenly realized, women were now voting in higher proportions than men.

This new manifestation of women's political power goes beyond first-stage feminism, with its emphasis on electing women over men, and beyond women's rights, though it was surely that battle for our own rights that gave us, finally, the independence to use the vote as we ourselves defined our larger interests.

The gender gap was fueled, it seemed, not only by the outrage at Reagan and Republican enmity to ERA and abortion but by women's great outrage at Reaganomics and at a national budget that destroyed services essential to the health and life of the old, the poor, children, students, the handicapped, and the environment while diverting increasing billions into nuclear missiles and tax savings for the rich. The callousness to the human suffering of unemployment and to the danger to future life of nuclear build-up seems to have outraged women, above all. (Paradoxically, those years of serious feminist battle for equal rights brought traditional feminine values off the pedestal of the mystique into the political mainstream.)

And so it didn't matter that Ed Koch, in his race for the New York gubernatorial nomination, said the proper words about women's rights, when he'd been so opportunistic about Reaganomics. It didn't matter that Cong. Margaret Heckler (R., Mass.) and Cong. Millicent Fenwick (R., N.J.) were women and had been for ERA; they went along with Reagan's budget and missiles, and in 1982 they were defeated. Political analysts now agree that women were crucial to the election of Mario Cuomo as governor of New York, and to the defeat or near-defeat in Texas, New Jersey, Missouri, and elsewhere of favorites who had been insensitive to women's basic concerns. At any rate, it is clear now that women's rights and women's issues are no longer minor political sidenotes, worth a patronizing sentence on the sixth page of a political speech or tea and cookies in the White House rose garden. President Reagan has just named not one but two women to the Cabinet—Elizabeth Dole as secretary of transportation and Margaret Heckler as secretary of health and human services. Getting into position for 1984, Walter Mondale and other Democrats often begin their speeches with passionate pledges to equal rights. An extraordinary meeting of leaders of women's groups, church groups, unions, and civil rights organizations was held in New York City to plan a child-care crusade for 1983.

ERA was reintroduced in Congress in 1983, and I say there will be an equal rights amendment in the Constitution by the end of the decade, after we get the government turned around.

A few months ago, I was invited to Rome by women leaders of the ruling Christian Democratic party. The idea was to speak to them, along with leading Italian feminist, socialist, and communist women, about the second stage. My book of that title had just come out in Italy, but I don't think they had really read it.

Evidently the Christian Democrats realized they had made a big political mistake by supporting a referendum that would have taken away Italian women's right to abortion. Despite orders from the pulpit from their priests, in the same week that someone tried to shoot the Pope, the women of Italy had voted in overwhelming numbers in that referendum that they would not give up the right to abortion. Up until then, the supposed conservatism of women had been taken for granted by right-wing politicians of Europe, whom it had helped keep in power. Now, it appeared, I was being brought over by the Christian Democrats in their effort to show a conciliatory position toward feminism. Someone must have told them I "believed in the family."

To my horror, I heard them introducing me as a "repentant feminist" (*femminista penitènte*). I had to clear that up, of course. I had to go back to the feminine mystique, and that necessary, wonderful first stage of women's liberation in Italy, when they had marched in the thousands and voted in the millions for women's rights to divorce and to abortion. In their country, as in mine, I said, reactionary forces were still trying to take those rights away, as the holding of the abortion referendum demonstrated.

Of course, I said, I respect those who, out of religious or other personal conviction, would not choose to use that right. "The value is life," I said, "the life of the woman, and the right of the child to be wanted in life. Abortion is simply a necessity for some when birth control fails.

"But that issue is behind you now, as I hope it will be soon for us," I continued. "We must all move into the second stage, where we face new problems of economic survival, personal survival, and family survival. We must surmount the dangers of nuclear war, terrorism, and economic chaos, and continue to be able to choose to bear children."

I don't know if that's what the Christian Democrats quite expected. The other feminist leaders present, and the socialist and communist women, picked up my second-stage suggestions about the need for new child-care supports and for new kinds of communal housing for working parents and divorced or widowed men and women who now live too much alone. But the new complexities, transcending the feminine mystique and first-stage feminism, can't be contained within the doctrinaire positions of either Right or Left.

I went from Rome to Paris, where Yvette Roudy, who originally translated *The Feminine Mystique* into French, is now President Mitterrand's minister for women's rights. She is no token undersecretary, but holds a full cabinet ministry for women's affairs. Yvette told me of her ministry's efforts, in all the regions and departments of France, to protect women's rights in jobs, education, marriage, and divorce; to give them training for new, nontraditional work; and to help them start businesses. As unemployment mounts, she is fighting socialist and communist leaders for a six-hour day for everyone rather than part-time jobs which women alone would take—and which she feels would set them back. As we walked through the lofty arches of the splendid building that houses her offices, I was proudly shown a "gallery of honor," where after Colette and Susan B. Anthony there was a larger-than-life portrait that was supposed to be me. "That's not me!" I said. The artist had painted us all to be pretty. Like taking the warts off Napoleon's nose. Oh, well . . .

Is this new burst of women's power in France and Italy merely a belated epilogue to that same women's movement that they say has crested and is on its way out over here, or a preview of greater power to come? The fact is, women are given credit for having put Mitterand in power in France, as we did Cuomo in New York State.

How are we going to maintain and express that new political power as women when the post-feminist generation moves from a different place? In Britain, under that arch-conservative female prime minister Margaret Thatcher and in socialist Denmark, Norway, and Sweden, early in 1983, I found my aging feminist friends seriously worried about the emergence of a new feminine mystique as unemployment mounts. When young women getting out of school can't find good jobs, it's easier to believe, once again, that just having babies will take care of their lives. Teenage pregnancy is on the rise again. I remember an earlier attempt by underground feminists in Czechoslovakia to get my help in warning against the feminine mystique reemerging under communism. After they had disbanded their feminist organizations, the commissars started complaining that there were too many women in office, hospital, and teaching jobs—their maternity leaves were disrupting production schedules and professional discipline. "Pay the men more, and let the women stay home and take care of the children." It would be dangerous now to relax the vigilance of feminist organization.

I'm worried now about the new polarizations hinted at by recent polls, cutting across the gender gap, as sharp differences emerge between the married and the unmarried, those with children and those with none, the young and the old, the ones with jobs and the unemployed.

While the new census shows that in the 1980's the great majority of young adult Americans (90 per cent) are continuing to marry, and remarry, and have children within marriage, they are having fewer children and having them later than they used to. But more people are living alone than ever before in history, a 75 per cent increase since 1970. There is now a significant new minority (10 per cent) who will never marry—a 100 per cent increase in a decade. There is also a 100 per cent increase in single-parent households, nine out of ten of which are headed by women. A fourth of all households now contain no children. "Non-family households" have risen by 89 per cent. But the divorce rate now seems to be leveling off, at about 50 per cent. The need, or the choice, to marry, or to remain married, takes on new existential and economic importance, for women as for men, for families in poverty today tend in overwhelming majority to be those headed by women, followed by those headed by men, where there is no second income. But the fact that in the United States today women earn an average of only fifty-nine cents for every dollar men earn still cuts through our illusion of equality. Most of those who use food stamps, welfare, aid for dependent children, and public housing, and receive minimal old-age Social Security payments, turn out to be women; women are also less likely than men to have a spouse to carry the burden if they are laid off the job.

Will the married be the new elite, and those living alone the underclass? Will men and women who make that cherished costly choice to have children become the permanent second class while the single-minded take power?

How can trade-offs within marriage be measured? He makes more than she does, but he feels less strain now because he's no longer carrying it all. She makes less but also feels less stress if she is just "helping"; does the job have to be as central to her identity as it is to his? She feels bitter if he is laid off and she has to carry the whole breadwinning burden, as well as take care of the house and kids, if he still just "helps." He certainly doesn't spend as much time on housework and the kids as she does; he doesn't feel that burden of responsibility for the kids that a mother never quite escapes. But how much of that power does she really want to give up?

Now that we've broken through those rigidly polarized male and female sex roles, will we settle for a diversity of patterns of sharing among women and men, which may change over time; will we cease to apply linear yardstick and time-clock measures of equality? As we are already coming to terms, in American life if not in the ideology of Right or Left, with a diversity of patterns that can be called family, changing over time for all of us, instead of that single static image enshrined in the feminine mystique.

Am I wrong to try to redefine our concept of "family" to link the interests of the old and single with the interests of those in the child-bearing years—when both share a need for new kinds of housing and communal services, which neither group may have the power or numbers to obtain, struggling alone or at cross purposes. Aging suburbanites who now defeat school budgets might join with young parents if new uses of those underused buildings for elders' needs were linked to child-care needs. Those who can't afford to stop working at sixty or sixty-five might welcome jobs that wouldn't demand a rigid 9-to-5 schedule. The option of shorter hours for those who wish them would not solve the unemployment problem, but it would provide more jobs for more people.

The implications of all this go far beyond what we thought of as feminism or the women's movement. Many of those blue-collar jobs from which men are being laid off will not be restored. In our changing technological economy, most men in the future are going to be working at the same kind of service jobs most women hold now—notably jobs involving health, food, recreation, and computers and business machines. They are the only new jobs that have emerged in our economy in the last ten years. Up until now, service jobs have paid less because they were women's work. In Canada, not just the women's movement but the large labor unions are now raising the issue of equal pay for work of comparable value. If the unions do not organize the women and men doing this service work, and do not confront the "quality of work life" concerns—flextime, parental leave, child care—which are no longer just women's, they may lose their clout. And corporate management is being brought to these concerns in the interests of productivity, as in competition with Japan.

For competition itself is forcing American business and professions to evolve beyond the feminine mystique; capitalism somehow manages to adapt to, or co-opt, feminism. The sexual sell rages on, with men as sex objects now as well as women. Men may not be doing as much housework as women, but women are now doing less; the latest studies show the total amount of time Americans spend on housework is going down. Housework is finally contracting to fill the time available; maybe advertisers can no longer make busy American women feel guilty if their sheets are not snowy white. But they may make more money selling time-saving appliances, take-out food—and "dress-for-success" clothes, cars, and magazines—to "working women," that new majority without whose purchasing power the American economy would now collapse.

And as women take control of their bodies, their selves, even as patients, male psychiatrists, obstetricians, and gynecologists are being forced off their godlike pedestals to treat women and other patients as people, or lose them to female therapists.

My friends now in their fifties and sixties who fought the battles—the first woman to have a seat on the Stock Exchange, the first female network vice-president, the first executive vice-president of a major agency, the nuns who became college presidents and doffed their meek habits, the housewives who survived their own divorces and became labor arbitrators, the invisible women passed over for corporate promotion, university tenure or union leadership, who brought and won class-action suits—are facing now the frontiers of age.

There are new questions to be asked, beyond success, beyond marriage and divorce, as we face husbands' strokes and retirement, and our years to come, living alone. Those are the questions that are now my personal and professional concern. Feelings of déjà vu wash over me as I hear geriatric experts talk about the aged with the same patronizing, "compassionate" denial of their personhood that I heard when the experts talked about women twenty years ago.

Much is being said among American women today about the strange dearth of vital men. I go into a town to lecture, and I hear about all the wonderful, dynamic women who have emerged in every field in that town. But frequently, whatever the age of the woman, she says, "There don't seem to be any men. The men seem so dull and gray now. They're dreary, they're flat, they complain, they're tired." And if they're my age, they're dead.

It has more mysterious ramification than we've yet faced—the fact that women are living much longer and aging more vitally than men. The latest census figures show that American women have a life expectancy of 77.8 compared with 69.9 for American men, an eight-year difference compared with just two years in 1900 and five in 1950. Despite the vogue of "dressing for success" and the proliferation of courses teaching women how to get into the executive suite by becoming more like men, women don't seem to be falling into the "superwoman" trap so easily any more. Gloomy predictions notwithstanding, they are not alllowing themselves to be forced into Type A behavior patterns as they take on more demanding jobs in business and the professions. There are no hard data indicating that women succumb any earlier or any more often than formerly to heart attacks, stroke, ulcer, or other stress syndromes. (The one exception is lung cancer—women are smoking more, where men are cutting it out.)

On the contrary, data just published by Rosalind Barnett and Grace Baruch of the Wellesley Center for Research on Women show that women between the ages of thirty-five and fifty-five who combine work, marriage, and motherhood do the best of all women their age in general psychological well-being. They have more control over their lives, which now seems essential to health; they are able to satisfy their needs for achievement and mastery as well as for pleasure and intimacy; and they use the flexibility that comes with combining roles to slough off the dreary, most burdensome part of either role. They are thus less at risk than the housewife whose whole identity is tied up with life at home, which she can never completely control, or the man whose whole identity is tied up with success in the job, where he is not the boss. Most women who now work outside the home do not, it seems, look to the job for their whole identity, as men used to do. (Most women also don't have a "wife" to take care of the details of life.)

And these women do not show the depression, deterioration,

and traumatic crises at mid-life and beyond as much as women used to, in the time of the feminine mystique, and men still do. So far, women are not beginning to die like men. As a matter of fact, I was asked to address the Western Gerontological Association this spring on "Why Can't Men Age More Like Women?"

The very scales of human achievement, of moral values and mental development, have up until now been defined by men in terms of male experience. The highest peak of moral development was some abstract concept of justice, in terms of which philosophers and psychologists from Plato to Freud and beyond found women wanting.

In 1971, a Harvard psychologist named Carol Gilligan began measuring women and men according to a scale based on female experience as well as male, and found a level of moral development beyond abstract justice. The research translated and tested the abstract concept of justice against the concrete experience of daily life in its actual human complexity. On this scale, women reached levels of moral development men did not seem even to conceive of. *In a Different Voice*, she called the book reporting this study.

What new dimensions will emerge, in every field, when women begin to find that different voice, their own voice, and use it in medicine, law, theology, architecture, in all the arts and all the sciences? And when the very scales of measurement of economic and aesthetic and moral and sexual value, and the rubrics of analysis of thought itself, are defined by that voice, in new and equal counterpoint to the one that has defined history up until now?

I got a curious insight into all this during my year as a fellow at Harvard. I immersed myself in the study of evolution, for I become increasingly convinced that the whole process—breaking through the feminine mystique, and the women's movement for equality, and the transition to this second stage, as female values begin to be shared by the male—is not really a revolution at all, but simply a stage in human evolution, necessary for survival.

In that bastion of male excellence, Harvard, women are now

admitted on equal terms with men, if not yet in equal numbers. During my year there I was asked to meet with the women at the law school, women medical students and interns, the women's groups at the divinity and architecture schools. These women were awesome in their competence, but they made me uneasy. They seemed too neat somehow, too controlled—constricted, almost subdued, and slightly juiceless.

A dean of one of the professional schools said, "We take in the most brilliant women, of course. Their record of achievement is breath-taking, as are their scores on the admission tests. But for some reason, they don't do as well as they should when they get here. Can you explain it?"

"Not without interviewing them," I said, "but I have a hunch it's because your structure—your whole ambiance—is so masculine; it alienates them somehow, though they may not be aware of it. Something around here must not elicit the best of female energy. But if that's so, you'd better find it out. Because it's also having an influence on the men that may not be conducive to the kind of leadership needed now in the professions."

So just before I left, I ran a seminar on "Masculinism at Harvard," sponsored by the Institute of Politics. The seminar made Harvard officials so nervous that it was closed to the public and the press. Women, a few men from the law school, and the rest raised questions about the viciously competitive win/lose adversary models they were learning in their case studies, and whether, in fact, a different voice was needed now in law, in business, and in medicine. Among the men, mainly it was older professors, like David Riesman and David McClelland, and some of the young professors, like Stephen Jay Gould, who seem to be wise in a new way, who wanted to talk about such things. But the women, who had seemed to me so strangely subdued, kept nodding their heads. They knew exactly what it was—masculinism— and maybe even what it was doing to them.

It is not easy for a woman to transcend or question the masculinism of a powerful, successful male institution. The first women there will necessarily try to succeed according to the male model. Since it has to be somewhat alien to her, even if she tries harder, she may or may not do as well as the men do, but she probably will not do as well as she herself could, doing it her own way. For women may have to reach a point of critical mass in any institution to raise that different voice, and the institution may have to face its own critical crisis to hear it.

It is not easy to question the masculinism of a powerful and successful nation, until perhaps its most thoughtful men and women sense that it may be coming too close to economic collapse or nuclear extinction for such questions not to be asked. The political gender gap surfaced first in the 1980's as women parted company with men on the basic issue of war and peace. But there were a lot of men among the half million people who marched into Central Park last year for a nuclear freeze.

In Indianapolis in October 1982, at the first NOW convention after the defeat of ERA, in the midst of the infighting and battling for power (only to be expected in a movement of women, who have been too powerless too long; only to be expected, now that women's power can be as important to the election of a senator, a governor, the next president of the United States, as labor, or perhaps even business itself), the foremothers were asking each other which issue would emerge next to hold it all together, mobilize women's passions, like ERA. I've heard such discussions often in these last months, from thoughtful students, from tired women, and even from men, looking from the wreckage of their own beleaguered movement—liberal politics, civil rights, labor, environmental protection—and wondering where the kind of life-changing political passion that has fueled the women's movement these last years will come from next. What will be the issue? Equal pay for work of comparable value? Child care? Displaced homemakers? Rape? Lesbian rights? Discrimination in social security, insurance, and pensions?

So diverse have the choices and patterns of women's lives become that there is no single issue now that could hold us all together as firmly as the battle for our constitutional equal rights. Now that women's rights are in danger and women's outrage has taken concrete political form, equal rights is no longer a separate women's issue. It is now an issue that can elect a president; it is an issue that the major political parties are now sprinting to catch up with. I'm not sure there is, or has to be, a separate, single women's issue in the next stage. I think women's most basic issues now converge with men's, the basic issues of war and peace and economic survival, of quality of life for young and old. But when that different voice, now emerging from women in politics and other fields, also begins to be heard among men, the result will be a different politics.

Are men changing? Those young men, like my son, who carry their little babies so proudly in their backpacks to the supermarket? Those men now suffering the mid-life crises? If men are not to die in their forties and fifties (cardiac arrest, the leading killer, now strikes down eight times as many men as women), they must develop the flexibility and the sensitivity to their own feelings and others'—the attunement to life—that have been considered up to now feminine.

Crazy? Well, who would have thought that the biggest movie hit of 1983 would be a picture called *Tootsie*, in which a male actor impersonates a woman so he can get in a soap opera, as a hospital administrator? (Back in those days of the feminine mystique, actresses used to complain that there were no good parts for women, only patient housewives, waving goodbye.) And he becomes a better man as a woman than he ever was as a man. Men love the movie, and so do women, even though some doctrinaire feminists claim it's *macho* for a man to make a hit playing a woman. But then the women say, pointedly, how much more attractive Dustin Hoffman is as a woman than when he goes back to being a man, as if the only choice is *macho* or wimp. . . . That gutsy voice makes the woman he plays more attractive to men as well as to other women. The sensitivity he acquires, sharing woman's experience, makes him a much better, stronger, more tender man. It is a wonderful, heart-easing, surprising movie. And not even a suggestive snigger of sick sex. Somehow, putting together the male and female halves of our being seems to clean up the sexual act.

We have clearly now broken through and beyond the *mas-*

culine mystique, for man and woman to find such joyous adventure in being a woman. Which is not the same at all as going back to the feminine mystique. It is the next clue in the human mystery. To be continued . . .

Sag Harbor, New York
February 1983

Introduction

to the Tenth Anniversary Edition

It is a decade now since the publication of *The Feminine Mystique,* and until I started writing the book, I wasn't even conscious of the woman problem. Locked as we all were then in that mystique, which kept us passive and apart, and kept us from seeing our real problems and possibilities, I, like other women, thought there was something wrong with *me* because I didn't have an orgasm waxing the kitchen floor. I was a freak, writing that book—not that I waxed any floor, I must admit, in the throes of finishing it in 1963.

Each of us thought she was a freak ten years ago if she didn't experience that mysterious orgastic fulfillment the commercials promised when waxing the kitchen floor. However much we enjoyed being Junior's and Janey's or Emily's mother, or B.J.'s wife, if we still had ambitions, ideas about ourselves as people in our own right—well, we were simply freaks, neurotics, and we confessed our sin or neurosis to priest or psychoanalyst, and tried hard to adjust. We didn't admit it to each other if we felt there should be more in life than peanut-butter sandwiches with the kids, if throwing powder into the washing machine didn't make us relive our wedding night, if getting the socks or shirts pure white was not exactly a peak experience, even if we did feel guilty about the tattletale gray.

Some of us (in 1963, nearly half of all women in the United

States) were already committing the unpardonable sin of working outside the home to help pay the mortgage or grocery bill. Those who did felt guilty, too—about betraying their femininity, undermining their husbands' masculinity, and neglecting their children by daring to work for money at all, no matter how much it was needed. They couldn't admit, even to themselves, that they resented being paid half what a man would have been paid for the job, or always being passed over for promotion, or writing the paper for which *he* got the degree and the raise.

A suburban neighbor of mine named Gertie was having coffee with me when the census taker came as I was writing *The Feminine Mystique*. "Occupation?" the census taker asked. "Housewife," I said. Gertie, who had cheered me on in my efforts at writing and selling magazine articles, shook her head sadly. "You should take yourself more seriously," she said. I hesitated, and then said to the census taker, "Actually, I'm a writer." But, of course, I then was, and still am, like all married women in America, no matter what *else* we do between 9 and 5, a housewife. Of course single women didn't put down "housewife" when the census taker came around, but even here society was less interested in what these women were doing as persons in the world than in asking, "Why isn't a nice girl like you married?" And so they, too, were not encouraged to take themselves seriously.

It seems such a precarious accident that I ever wrote the book at all—but, in another way, my whole life had prepared me to write that book. All the pieces finally came together. In 1957, getting strangely bored with writing articles about breast feeding and the like for *Redbook* and the *Ladies' Home Journal*, I put an unconscionable amount of time into a questionnaire for my fellow Smith graduates of the class of 1942, thinking I was going to disprove the current notion that education had fitted us ill for our role as women. But the questionnaire raised more questions than it answered for me—education had *not* exactly geared us to the role women were trying to play, it seemed. The suspicion arose as to whether it was the education or the role that was wrong. *McCall's* commissioned an article based on my Smith alumnae questionnaire, but the then male publisher of *McCall's*, during that great era of togetherness, turned the piece down in horror, despite underground efforts of female editors. The male *McCall's* editors said it couldn't be true.

I was next commissioned to do the article for *Ladies' Home Journal*. That time I took it back, because they rewrote it to say just the opposite of what, in fact, I was trying to say. I tried it again for *Redbook*. Each time I was interviewing more women, psychologists, sociologists, marriage counselors, and the like and getting more and more sure I was on the track of something. But what? I needed a name for whatever it was that kept us from using our rights, that made us feel guilty about anything we did *not* as our husbands' wives, our children's mothers, but as people ourselves. I needed a name to describe that guilt. Unlike the guilt women used to feel about sexual needs, the guilt they felt now was about needs that didn't fit the sexual definition of women, the mystique of feminine fulfillment—the feminine mystique.

The editor of *Redbook* told my agent, "Betty has gone off her rocker. She has always done a good job for us, but this time only the most neurotic housewife could identify." I opened my agent's letter on the subway as I was taking the kids to the pediatrician. I got off the subway to call my agent and told her, "I'll have to write a book to get this into print." What I was writing threatened the very foundations of the women's magazine world—the feminine mystique.

When Norton contracted for the book, I thought it would take a year to finish it; it took five. I wouldn't have even started it if the New York Public Library had not, at just the right time, opened the Frederick Lewis Allen Room, where writers working on a book could get a desk, six months at a time, rent free. I got a baby-sitter three days a week and took the bus from Rockland County to the city and somehow managed to prolong the six months to two years in the Allen Room, enduring much joking from other writers at lunch when it came out that I was writing a book about women. Then, somehow, the book took me over, obsessed me, wanted to write itself, and I took my papers home and wrote on the dining-room table, the living-room couch, on a neighbor's dock on the river, and kept on writing it in my mind when I stopped to take the kids somewhere or make dinner, and went back to it after they were in bed.

I have never experienced anything as powerful, truly mystical, as the forces that seemed to take me over when I was writing *The Feminine Mystique.* The book came from somewhere deep within me and all my experience came together in it: my mother's discontent, my own training in Gestalt and Freudian psychology, the fellowship I felt guilty about giving up, the stint as a reporter which taught me how to follow clues to the hidden economic underside of reality, my exodus to the suburbs and all the hours with other mothers shopping at supermarkets, taking the children swimming, coffee klatches. Even the years of writing for women's magazines when it was unquestioned gospel that women could identify with *nothing* beyond the home—not politics, not art, not science, not events large or small, war or peace, in the United States or the world, unless it could be approached through female experience as a wife or mother or translated into domestic detail! I could no longer write within that framework. The book I was now writing challenged the very definition of that universe— what I chose to call the feminine mystique. Giving it a name, I knew that it was not the only possible universe for women at all but an unnatural confining of our energies and vision. But as I began following leads and clues from women's words and my own feelings, across psychology, sociology, and recent history, tracing back—through the pages of the magazines for which I'd written—why and how it happened, what it was really doing to women, to their children, even to sex, the implications became apparent and they were fantastic. I was surprised myself at what I was writing, where it was leading. After I finished each chapter, a part of me would wonder, Am I crazy? But there was also a growing feeling of calm, strong, gut-sureness as the clues fitted together, which must be the same kind of feeling a scientist has when he or she zeroes in on a discovery in one of those true-science detective stories.

Only this was not just abstract and conceptual. It meant that

I and every other woman I knew had been living a lie, and all the doctors who treated us and the experts who studied us were perpetuating that lie, and our homes and schools and churches and politics and professions were built around that lie. If women were really *people*—no more, no less—then all the things that kept them from being full people in our society would have to be changed. And women, once they broke through the feminine mystique and took themselves seriously as people, would see their place on a false pedestal, even their glorification as sexual objects, for the putdown it was.

Yet if I had realized how fantastically fast that would really happen—already in less than ten years' time—maybe I would have been so scared I might have stopped writing. It's frightening when you're starting on a new road that no one has been on before. You don't know how far it's going to take you until you look back and realize how far, how very far you've gone. When the first woman asked me, in 1963, to autograph *The Feminine Mystique*, saying what by now hundreds—thousands, I guess—of women have said to me, "It changed my whole life," I wrote, "Courage to us all on the new road." Because there is no turning back on that road. It has to change your whole life; it certainly changed mine.

BETTY FRIEDAN

New York, 1973

Preface and
Acknowledgments

 Gradually, without seeing it clearly for quite a while, I came to realize that something is very wrong with the way American women are trying to live their lives today. I sensed it first as a question mark in my own life, as a wife and mother of three small children, half-guiltily, and therefore half-heartedly, almost in spite of myself, using my abilities and education in work that took me away from home. It was this personal question mark that led me, in 1957, to spend a great deal of time doing an intensive questionnaire of my college classmates, fifteen years after our graduation from Smith. The answers given by 200 women to those intimate open-ended questions made me realize that what was wrong could not be related to education in the way it was then believed to be. The problems and satisfaction of their lives, and mine, and the way our education had contributed to them, simply did not fit the image of the modern American woman as she was written about in women's magazines, studied and analyzed in classrooms and clinics, praised and damned in a ceaseless barrage of words ever since the end of World War II. There was a strange discrepancy between the reality of our lives as women and the image to which we were trying to conform, the image that I came to call the feminine mystique. I wondered if other women faced this schizophrenic split, and what it meant.

And so I began to hunt down the origins of the feminine

mystique, and its effect on women who lived by it, or grew up
under it. My methods were simply those of a reporter on the
trail of a story, except I soon discovered that this was no ordinary story. For the startling pattern that began to emerge, as
one clue led me to another in far-flung fields of modern thought
and life, defied not only the conventional image but basic psychological assumptions about women. I found a few pieces of the
puzzle in previous studies of women; but not many, for women
in the past have been studied in terms of the feminine mystique.
The Mellon study of Vassar women was provocative, Simone de
Beauvoir's insights into French women, the work of Mirra Komarovsky, A. H. Maslow, Alva Myrdal. I found even more provocative the growing body of new psychological thought on
the question of man's identity, whose implications for women
seem not to have been realized. I found further evidence by questioning those who treat women's ills and problems. And
I traced the growth of the mystique by talking to editors of
women's magazines, advertising motivational researchers, and theoretical experts on women in the fields of psychology, psychoanalysis, anthropology, sociology, and family-life education. But
the puzzle did not begin to fit together until I interviewed at
some depth, from two hours to two days each, eighty women
at certain crucial points in their life cycle—high school and college girls facing or evading the question of who they were; young
housewives and mothers for whom, if the mystique were right,
there should be no such question and who thus had no name for
the problem troubling them; and women who faced a jumping-off
point at forty. These women, some tortured, some serene, gave
me the final clues, and the most damning indictment of the feminine mystique.

I could not, however, have written this book without the assistance of many experts, both eminent theoreticians and practical
workers in the field, and, indeed, without the cooperation of many
who themselves believe and have helped perpetrate the feminine
mystique. I was helped by many present and former editors of
women's magazines, including Peggy Bell, John English, Bruce
Gould, Mary Ann Guitar, James Skardon, Nancy Lynch,

Geraldine Rhoads, Robert Stein, Neal Stuart and Polly Weaver; by Ernest Dichter and the staff of the Institute for Motivational Research; and by Marion Skedgell, former editor of the Viking Press, who gave me her data from an unfinished study of fiction heroines. Among behavioral scientists, theoreticians and therapists in the field, I owe a great debt to William Menaker and John Landgraf of New York University, A. H. Maslow of Brandeis, John Dollard of Yale, William J. Goode of Columbia; to Margaret Mead; to Paul Vahanian of Teachers College, Elsa Siipola Israel and Eli Chinoy of Smith. And to Dr. Andras Angyal, psychoanalyst of Boston, Dr. Nathan Ackerman of New York, Dr. Louis English and Dr. Margaret Lawrence of the Rockland County Mental Health Center; to many mental health workers in Westchester County, including Mrs. Emily Gould, Dr. Gerald Fountain, Dr. Henrietta Glatzer and Marjorie Ilgenfritz of the Guidance Center of New Rochelle and the Rev. Edgar Jackson; Dr. Richard Gordon and Katherine Gordon of Bergen County, New Jersey; the late Dr. Abraham Stone, Dr. Lena Levine and Fred Jaffe of the Planned Parenthood Association, the staff of the James Jackson Putnam Center in Boston, Dr. Doris Menzer and Dr. Somers Sturges of the Peter Bent Brigham Hospital, Alice King of the Alumnae Advisory Center and Dr. Lester Evans of the Commonwealth Fund. I am also grateful to those educators valiantly fighting the feminine mystique, who gave me helpful insights: Laura Bornholdt of Wellesley, Mary Bunting of Radcliffe, Marjorie Nicolson of Columbia, Esther Lloyd-Jones of Teachers College, Millicent McIntosh of Barnard, Esther Raushenbush of Sarah Lawrence, Thomas Mendenhall of Smith, Daniel Aaron and many other members of the Smith faculty. I am above all grateful to the women who shared their problems and feelings with me, beginning with the 200 women of Smith, 1942, and Marion Ingersoll Howell and Anne Mather Montero, who worked with me on the alumnae questionnaire that started my search.

Without that superb institution, the Frederick Lewis Allen Room of the New York Public Library and its provision to a writer of quiet work space and continuous access to research sources, this particular mother of three might never have started a book, much less finished it. The same might be said of the sensitive support of my publisher, George P. Brockway, my editor, Burton Beals, and my agent, Martha Winston. In a larger sense, this book might never have been written if I had not had a most unusual education in psychology, from Kurt Koffka, Harold Israel, Elsa Siipola and James Gibson at Smith; from Kurt Lewin, Tamara Dembo, and the others of their group then at Iowa; and from E. C. Tolman, Jean Macfarlane, Nevitt Sanford and Erik Erikson at Berkeley—a liberal education, in the best sense, which was meant to be used, though I have not used it as I originally planned.

The insights, interpretations both of theory and fact, and the implicit values of this book are inevitably my own. But whether or not the answers I present here are final—and there are many questions which social scientists must probe further—the dilemma of the American woman is real. At the present time, many experts, finally forced to recognize this problem, are redoubling their efforts to adjust women to it in terms of the feminine mystique. My answers may disturb the experts and women alike, for they imply social change. But there would be no sense in my writing this book at all if I did not believe that women can affect society, as well as be affected by it; that, in the end, a woman, as a man, has the power to choose, and to make her own heaven or hell.

Grandview, New York
June 1957–July 1962

1 The Problem That
Has No Name

 The problem lay buried, unspoken, for many years in the minds of American women. It was a strange stirring, a sense of dissatisfaction, a yearning that women suffered in the middle of the twentieth century in the United States. Each suburban wife struggled with it alone. As she made the beds, shopped for groceries, matched slipcover material, ate peanut butter sandwiches with her children, chauffeured Cub Scouts and Brownies, lay beside her husband at night—she was afraid to ask even of herself the silent question—"Is this all?"

For over fifteen years there was no word of this yearning in the millions of words written about women, for women, in all the columns, books and articles by experts telling women their role was to seek fulfillment as wives and mothers. Over and over women heard in voices of tradition and of Freudian sophistication that they could desire no greater destiny than to glory in their own femininity. Experts told them how to catch a man and keep him, how to breastfeed children and handle their toilet training, how to cope with sibling rivalry and adolescent rebellion; how to buy a dishwasher, bake bread, cook gourmet snails, and build a swimming pool with their own hands; how to dress, look, and act more feminine and make marriage more exciting; how to keep their husbands from dying young and their sons from growing into delinquents. They were taught to pity the neurotic, unfeminine, unhappy women who wanted to be poets or physicists or presidents. They learned that truly feminine women do not want careers, higher education, political rights—the independence and the opportunities that the old-fashioned feminists fought for. Some women, in their forties and fifties, still remembered painfully giving up those dreams, but most of the younger women no longer even thought about them. A thousand expert voices applauded their femininity, their adjustment, their new maturity. All they had to do was devote their lives from earliest girlhood to finding a husband and bearing children.

By the end of the nineteen-fifties, the average marriage age of women in America dropped to 20, and was still dropping, into the teens. Fourteen million girls were engaged by 17. The proportion of women attending college in comparison with men dropped from 47 per cent in 1920 to 35 per cent in 1958. A century earlier, women had fought for higher education; now girls went to college to get a husband. By the mid-fifties, 60 per cent dropped out of college to marry, or because they were afraid too much education would be a marriage bar. Colleges built dormitories for "married students," but the students were almost always the husbands. A new degree was instituted for the wives —"Ph.T." (Putting Husband Through).

Then American girls began getting married in high school. And the women's magazines, deploring the unhappy statistics about these young marriages, urged that courses on marriage, and marriage counselors, be installed in the high schools. Girls started going steady at twelve and thirteen, in junior high. Manufacturers put out brassieres with false bosoms of foam rubber for little girls of ten. And an advertisement for a child's dress, sizes 3–6x, in the *New York Times* in the fall of 1960, said: "She Too Can Join the Man-Trap Set."

By the end of the fifties, the United States birthrate was overtaking India's. The birth-control movement, renamed Planned Parenthood, was asked to find a method whereby women who had been advised that a third or fourth baby would be born dead or defective might have it anyhow. Statisticians were especially astounded at the fantastic increase in the number of babies among college women. Where once they had two children, now they had four, five, six. Women who had once wanted careers were now making careers out of having babies. So rejoiced *Life* magazine in a 1956 paean to the movement of American women back to the home.

In a New York hospital, a woman had a nervous breakdown when she found she could not breastfeed her baby. In other hospitals, women dying of cancer refused a drug which research had proved might save their lives: its side effects were said to be unfeminine. "If I have only one life, let me live it as a blonde," a larger-than-life-sized picture of a pretty, vacuous woman proclaimed from newspaper, magazine, and drugstore ads. And across America, three out of every ten women dyed their hair blonde. They ate a chalk called Metrecal, instead of food, to shrink to the size of the thin young models. Department-store buyers reported that American women, since 1939, had become three and four sizes smaller. "Women are out to fit the clothes, instead of vice-versa," one buyer said.

Interior decorators were designing kitchens with mosaic murals and original paintings, for kitchens were once again the center of women's lives. Home sewing became a million-dollar industry. Many women no longer left their homes, except to shop, chauffeur their children, or attend a social engagement with their husbands. Girls were growing up in America without ever having jobs outside the home. In the late fifties, a sociological phenomenon was suddenly remarked: a third of American women now worked, but most were no longer young and very few were pursuing careers. They were married women who held part-time jobs, selling or secretarial, to put their husbands through school, their sons through college, or to help pay the mortgage. Or they were widows supporting families. Fewer and fewer women were entering professional work. The shortages in the nursing, social work, and teaching professions caused crises in almost every American city. Concerned over the Soviet Union's lead in the space race, scientists noted that America's greatest source of unused brainpower was women. But girls would not study physics: it was "unfeminine." A girl refused a science fellowship at Johns Hopkins to take a job in a real-estate office. All she wanted, she said, was what every other American girl wanted—to get married, have four children and live in a nice house in a nice suburb.

The suburban housewife—she was the dream image of the young American women and the envy, it was said, of women all over the world. The American housewife—freed by science and labor-saving appliances from the drudgery, the dangers of childbirth and the illnesses of her grandmother. She was healthy, beautiful, educated, concerned only about her husband, her children, her home. She had found true feminine fulfillment. As a housewife and mother, she was respected as a full and equal partner to man in his world. She was free to choose automobiles, clothes, appliances, supermarkets; she had everything that women ever dreamed of.

In the fifteen years after World War II, this mystique of feminine fulfillment became the cherished and self-perpetuating core of contemporary American culture. Millions of women lived their lives in the image of those pretty pictures of the American suburban housewife, kissing their husbands goodbye in front of the picture window, depositing their stationwagonsful of children at school, and smiling as they ran the new electric waxer over the spotless kitchen floor. They baked their own bread, sewed their own and their children's clothes, kept their new washing machines and dryers running all day. They changed the sheets on the beds twice a week instead of once, took the rug-hooking class in adult education, and pitied their poor frustrated mothers, who had dreamed of having a career. Their only dream was to be perfect wives and mothers; their highest ambition to have five children and a beautiful house, their only fight to get and keep their husbands. They had no thought for the unfeminine problems of the world outside the home; they wanted the men to make the major decisions. They gloried in their role as women, and wrote proudly on the census blank: "Occupation: housewife."

For over fifteen years, the words written for women, and the words women used when they talked to each other, while their husbands sat on the other side of the room and talked shop or politics or septic tanks, were about problems with their children, or how to keep their husbands happy, or improve their children's school, or cook chicken or make slipcovers. Nobody argued whether women were inferior or superior to men; they were simply different. Words like "emancipation" and "career" sounded strange and embarrassing; no one had used them for years. When a Frenchwoman named Simone de Beauvoir wrote a book called *The Second Sex*, an American critic commented that she obviously "didn't know what life was all about," and besides, she was talking about French women. The "woman problem" in America no longer existed.

If a woman had a problem in the 1950's and 1960's, she knew that something must be wrong with her marriage, or with herself. Other women were satisfied with their lives, she thought. What kind of a woman was she if she did not feel this mysterious fulfillment waxing the kitchen floor? She was so ashamed to admit her dissatisfaction that she never knew how many other women shared it. If she tried to tell her husband, he didn't understand what she was talking about. She did not really understand it herself. For over fifteen years women in America found it harder to talk about this problem than about sex. Even the psychoanalysts had no name for it. When a woman went to a psychiatrist for help, as many women did, she would say, "I'm so ashamed," or "I must be hopelessly neurotic." "I don't know what's wrong with women today," a suburban psychiatrist said uneasily. "I only know something is wrong because most of my patients happen to be women. And their problem isn't sexual." Most women with this problem did not go to see a psychoanalyst, however. "There's nothing wrong really," they kept telling themselves. "There isn't any problem."

But on an April morning in 1959, I heard a mother of four, having coffee with four other mothers in a suburban development fifteen miles from New York, say in a tone of quiet desperation, "the problem." And the others knew, without words, that she was not talking about a problem with her husband, or her children, or her home. Suddenly they realized they all shared the same problem, the problem that has no name. They began, hesitantly, to talk about it. Later, after they had picked up their chil-

dren at nursery school and taken them home to nap, two of the
women cried, in sheer relief, just to know they were not alone.

Gradually I came to realize that the problem that has no name
was shared by countless women in America. As a magazine writer
I often interviewed women about problems with their children, or
their marriages, or their houses, or their communities. But after
a while I began to recognize the telltale signs of this other problem. I saw the same signs in suburban ranch houses and split-levels
on Long Island and in New Jersey and Westchester County;
in colonial houses in a small Massachusetts town; on patios in
Memphis; in suburban and city apartments; in living rooms in
the Midwest. Sometimes I sensed the problem, not as a reporter,
but as a suburban housewife, for during this time I was also bringing up my own three children in Rockland County, New York.
I heard echoes of the problem in college dormitories and semiprivate maternity wards, at PTA meetings and luncheons of the
League of Women Voters, at suburban cocktail parties, in station
wagons waiting for trains, and in snatches of conversation overheard at Schrafft's. The groping words I heard from other
women, on quiet afternoons when children were at school or on
quiet evenings when husbands worked late, I think I understood
first as a woman long before I understood their larger social and
psychological implications.

Just what was this problem that has no name? What were the
words women used when they tried to express it? Sometimes a
woman would say "I feel empty somehow . . . incomplete." Or
she would say, "I feel as if I don't exist." Sometimes she blotted
out the feeling with a tranquilizer. Sometimes she thought the
problem was with her husband, or her children, or that what she
really needed was to redecorate her house, or move to a better
neighborhood, or have an affair, or another baby. Sometimes,
she went to a doctor with symptoms she could hardly describe:
"A tired feeling . . . I get so angry with the children it scares
me . . . I feel like crying without any reason." (A Cleveland
doctor called it "the housewife's syndrome.") A number of
women told me about great bleeding blisters that break out on

their hands and arms. "I call it the housewife's blight," said a family doctor in Pennsylvania. "I see it so often lately in these young women with four, five and six children who bury themselves in their dishpans. But it isn't caused by detergent and it isn't cured by cortisone."

Sometimes a woman would tell me that the feeling gets so strong she runs out of the house and walks through the streets. Or she stays inside her house and cries. Or her children tell her a joke, and she doesn't laugh because she doesn't hear it. I talked to women who had spent years on the analyst's couch, working out their "adjustment to the feminine role," their blocks to "fulfillment as a wife and mother." But the desperate tone in these women's voices, and the look in their eyes, was the same as the tone and the look of other women, who were sure they had no problem, even though they did have a strange feeling of desperation.

A mother of four who left college at nineteen to get married told me:

I've tried everything women are supposed to do—hobbies, gardening, pickling, canning, being very social with my neighbors, joining committees, running PTA teas. I can do it all, and I like it, but it doesn't leave you anything to think about—any feeling of who you are. I never had any career ambitions. All I wanted was to get married and have four children. I love the kids and Bob and my home. There's no problem you can even put a name to. But I'm desperate. I begin to feel I have no personality. I'm a server of food and a putter-on of pants and a bedmaker, somebody who can be called on when you want something. But who am I?

A twenty-three-year-old mother in blue jeans said:

I ask myself why I'm so dissatisfied. I've got my health, fine children, a lovely new home, enough money. My husband has a real future as an electronics engineer. He doesn't have any of these feelings. He says maybe I need a vacation, let's go to New York for a weekend. But that isn't it. I always had this idea we should do everything together. I can't sit down and read a book alone. If the children are napping and I have one hour to myself I just walk through the house waiting for them to wake up. I don't make a move until I know where the rest of the crowd is going. It's as if ever since you were a little girl, there's always been somebody or something that will take care of your life: your parents, or college, or falling in love, or having a child, or moving to a new house. Then you wake up one morning and there's nothing to look forward to.

A young wife in a Long Island development said:

I seem to sleep so much. I don't know why I should be so tired. This house isn't nearly so hard to clean as the cold-water flat we had when I was working. The children are at school all day. It's not the work. I just don't feel alive.

In 1960, the problem that has no name burst like a boil through the image of the happy American housewife. In the television commercials the pretty housewives still beamed over their foaming dishpans and *Time*'s cover story on "The Suburban Wife, an American Phenomenon" protested: "Having too good a time . . . to believe that they should be unhappy." But the actual unhappiness of the American housewife was suddenly being reported— from the *New York Times* and *Newsweek* to *Good Housekeeping* and CBS Television ("The Trapped Housewife"), although almost everybody who talked about it found some superficial reason to dismiss it. It was attributed to incompetent appliance repairmen (*New York Times*), or the distances children must be chauffeured in the suburbs (*Time*), or too much PTA (*Redbook*). Some said it was the old problem—education: more and more women had education, which naturally made them unhappy in their role as housewives. "The road from Freud to Frigidaire, from Sophocles to Spock, has turned out to be a bumpy one," reported the *New York Times* (June 28, 1960). "Many young women—certainly not all—whose education plunged them into a world of ideas feel stifled in their homes. They find their routine lives out of joint with their training. Like shut-ins, they feel left out. In the last year, the problem of the educated housewife has provided the meat of dozens of speeches made by troubled presidents of women's colleges who maintain, in the face of complaints, that sixteen years of academic training is realistic preparation for wifehood and motherhood."

There was much sympathy for the educated housewife. ("Like a two-headed schizophrenic . . . once she wrote a paper on the Graveyard poets; now she writes notes to the milkman. Once she determined the boiling point of sulphuric acid; now she determines her boiling point with the overdue repairman. . . . The housewife often is reduced to screams and tears. . . . No one, it seems, is appreciative, least of all herself, of the kind of person she becomes in the process of turning from poetess into shrew.")

Home economists suggested more realistic preparation for housewives, such as high-school workshops in home appliances. College educators suggested more discussion groups on home management and the family, to prepare women for the adjustment to domestic life. A spate of articles appeared in the mass magazines offering "Fifty-eight Ways to Make Your Marriage More Exciting." No month went by without a new book by a psychiatrist or sexologist offering technical advice on finding greater fulfillment through sex.

A male humorist joked in *Harper's Bazaar* (July, 1960) that the problem could be solved by taking away woman's right to vote. ("In the pre-19th Amendment era, the American woman was placid, sheltered and sure of her role in American society. She left all the political decisions to her husband and he, in turn, left all the family decisions to her. Today a woman has to make both the family *and* the political decisions, and it's too much for her.")

A number of educators suggested seriously that women no longer be admitted to the four-year colleges and universities: in the growing college crisis, the education which girls could not use as housewives was more urgently needed than ever by boys to do the work of the atomic age.

The problem was also dismissed with drastic solutions no one could take seriously. (A woman writer proposed in *Harper's* that women be drafted for compulsory service as nurses' aides and baby-sitters.) And it was smoothed over with the age-old panaceas: "love is their answer," "the only answer is inner help," "the secret of completeness—children," "a private means of intellectual fulfillment," "to cure this toothache of the spirit—the simple formula of handing one's self and one's will over to God." [1]

The problem was dismissed by telling the housewife she doesn't realize how lucky she is—her own boss, no time clock, no junior executive gunning for her job. What if she isn't happy—does she think men are happy in this world? Does she really, secretly, still want to be a man? Doesn't she know yet how lucky she is to be a woman?

The problem was also, and finally, dismissed by shrugging that there are no solutions: this is what being a woman means, and what is wrong with American women that they can't accept their role gracefully? As *Newsweek* put it (March 7, 1960):

She is dissatisfied with a lot that women of other lands can only dream of. Her discontent is deep, pervasive, and impervious to the superficial remedies which are offered at every hand. . . . An army of professional explorers have already charted the major sources of trouble. . . . From the beginning of time, the female cycle has defined and confined woman's role. As Freud was credited with saying: "Anatomy is destiny." Though no group of women has ever pushed these natural restrictions as far as the American wife, it seems that she still cannot accept them with good grace. . . . A young mother with a beautiful family, charm, talent and brains is apt to dismiss her role apologetically. "What do I do?" you hear her say. "Why nothing. I'm just a housewife." A good education, it seems, has given this paragon among women an understanding of the value of everything except her own worth . . .

And so she must accept the fact that "American women's unhappiness is merely the most recently won of women's rights," and adjust and say with the happy housewife found by *Newsweek*: "We ought to salute the wonderful freedom we all have and be proud of our lives today. I have had college and I've worked, but being a housewife is the most rewarding and satisfying role. . . . My mother was never included in my father's business affairs . . . she couldn't get out of the house and away from us children. But I am an equal to my husband; I can go along with him on business trips and to social business affairs."

The alternative offered was a choice that few women would contemplate. In the sympathetic words of the *New York Times*:

"All admit to being deeply frustrated at times by the lack of privacy, the physical burden, the routine of family life, the confinement of it. However, none would give up her home and family if she had the choice to make again." *Redbook* commented: "Few women would want to thumb their noses at husbands, children and community and go off on their own. Those who do may be talented individuals, but they rarely are successful women."

The year American women's discontent boiled over, it was also reported (*Look*) that the more than 21,000,000 American women who are single, widowed, or divorced do not cease even after fifty their frenzied, desperate search for a man. And the search begins early—for seventy per cent of all American women now marry before they are twenty-four. A pretty twenty-five-year-old secretary took thirty-five different jobs in six months in the futile hope of finding a husband. Women were moving from one political club to another, taking evening courses in accounting or sailing, learning to play golf or ski, joining a number of churches in succession, going to bars alone, in their ceaseless search for a man.

Of the growing thousands of women currently getting private psychiatric help in the United States, the married ones were reported dissatisfied with their marriages, the unmarried ones suffering from anxiety and, finally, depression. Strangely, a number of psychiatrists stated that, in their experience, unmarried women patients were happier than married ones. So the door of all those pretty suburban houses opened a crack to permit a glimpse of uncounted thousands of American housewives who suffered alone from a problem that suddenly everyone was talking about, and beginning to take for granted, as one of those unreal problems in American life that can never be solved—like the hydrogen bomb. By 1962 the plight of the trapped American housewife had become a national parlor game. Whole issues of magazines, newspaper columns, books learned and frivolous, educational conferences and television panels were devoted to the problem.

Even so, most men, and some women, still did not know that

this problem was real. But those who had faced it honestly knew that all the superficial remedies, the sympathetic advice, the scolding words and the cheering words were somehow drowning the problem in unreality. A bitter laugh was beginning to be heard from American women. They were admired, envied, pitied, theorized over until they were sick of it, offered drastic solutions or silly choices that no one could take seriously. They got all kinds of advice from the growing armies of marriage and child-guidance counselors, psychotherapists, and armchair psychologists, on how to adjust to their role as housewives. No other road to fulfillment was offered to American women in the middle of the twentieth century. Most adjusted to their role and suffered or ignored the problem that has no name. It can be less painful, for a woman, not to hear the strange, dissatisfied voice stirring within her.

It is no longer possible to ignore that voice, to dismiss the desperation of so many American women. This is not what being a woman means, no matter what the experts say. For human suffering there is a reason; perhaps the reason has not been found because the right questions have not been asked, or pressed far enough. I do not accept the answer that there is no problem because American women have luxuries that women in other times and lands never dreamed of; part of the strange newness of the problem is that it cannot be understood in terms of the age-old material problems of man: poverty, sickness, hunger, cold. The women who suffer this problem have a hunger that food cannot fill. It persists in women whose husbands are struggling internes and law clerks, or prosperous doctors and lawyers; in wives of workers and executives who make $5,000 a year or $50,000. It is not caused by lack of material advantages; it may not even be felt by women preoccupied with desperate problems of hunger, poverty or illness. And women who think it will be solved by more money, a bigger house, a second car, moving to a better suburb, often discover it gets worse.

It is no longer possible today to blame the problem on loss of femininity: to say that education and independence and equality with men have made American women unfeminine. I have heard so many women try to deny this dissatisfied voice within themselves because it does not fit the pretty picture of femininity the experts have given them. I think, in fact, that this is the first clue to the mystery: the problem cannot be understood in the generally accepted terms by which scientists have studied women, doctors have treated them, counselors have advised them, and writers have written about them. Women who suffer this problem, in whom this voice is stirring, have lived their whole lives in the pursuit of feminine fulfillment. They are not career women (although career women may have other problems); they are women whose greatest ambition has been marriage and children. For the oldest of these women, these daughters of the American middle class, no other dream was possible. The ones in their forties and fifties who once had other dreams gave them up and threw themselves joyously into life as housewives. For the youngest, the new wives and mothers, this was the only dream. They are the ones who quit high school and college to marry, or marked time in some job in which they had no real interest until they married. These women are very "feminine" in the usual sense, and yet they still suffer the problem.

Are the women who finished college, the women who once had dreams beyond housewifery, the ones who suffer the most? According to the experts they are, but listen to these four women:

My days are all busy, and dull, too. All I ever do is mess around. I get up at eight—I make breakfast, so I do the dishes, have lunch, do some more dishes and some laundry and cleaning in the afternoon. Then it's supper dishes and I get to sit down a few minutes before the children have to be sent to bed. . . . That's all there is to my day. It's just like any other wife's day. Humdrum. The biggest time, I am chasing kids.

Ye Gods, what do I do with my time? Well, I get up at six. I get my son dressed and then give him breakfast. After that I wash dishes and bathe and feed the baby. Then I get lunch and while the children nap, I sew or mend or iron and do all the other things I can't get done before noon. Then I cook supper for the family and my husband watches TV while I do the dishes. After I get the children to bed, I set my hair and then I go to bed.

The problem is always being the children's mommy, or the minister's wife and never being myself.

A film made of any typical morning in my house would look like an old Marx Brothers' comedy. I wash the dishes, rush the older children off to school, dash out in the yard to cultivate the chrysanthemums, run back in to make a phone call about a committee meeting, help the youngest child build a blockhouse, spend fifteen minutes skimming the newspapers so I can be well-informed, then scamper down to the washing machines where my thrice-weekly laundry includes enough clothes to keep a primitive village going for an entire year. By noon I'm ready for a padded cell. Very little of what I've done has been really necessary or important. Outside pressures lash me through the day. Yet I look upon myself as one of the more relaxed housewives in the neighborhood. Many of my friends are even more frantic. In the past sixty years we have come full circle and the American housewife is once again trapped in a squirrel cage. If the cage is now a modern plate-glass-and-broadloom ranch house or a convenient modern apartment, the situation is no less painful than when her grandmother sat over an embroidery hoop in her gilt-and-plush parlor and muttered angrily about women's rights.

The first two women never went to college. They live in developments in Levittown, New Jersey, and Tacoma, Washington, and were interviewed by a team of sociologists studying workingmen's wives.[2] The third, a minister's wife, wrote on the fifteenth reunion questionnaire of her college that she never had any career ambitions, but wishes now she had.[3] The fourth, who has a Ph.D. in anthropology, is today a Nebraska housewife with three children.[4] Their words seem to indicate that housewives of all educational levels suffer the same feeling of desperation.

The fact is that no one today is muttering angrily about "women's rights," even though more and more women have gone to college. In a recent study of all the classes that have graduated from Barnard College,[5] a significant minority of earlier graduates blamed their education for making them want "rights," later classes blamed their education for giving them career dreams, but recent graduates blamed the college for making them feel it was not enough simply to be a housewife and mother; they did not want to feel guilty if they did not read books or take part in community activities. But if education is not the cause of the problem, the fact that education somehow festers in these women may be a clue.

If the secret of feminine fulfillment is having children, never have so many women, with the freedom to choose, had so many children, in so few years, so willingly. If the answer is love, never have women searched for love with such determination. And yet there is a growing suspicion that the problem may not be sexual, though it must somehow be related to sex. I have heard from many doctors evidence of new sexual problems between man and wife—sexual hunger in wives so great their husbands cannot satisfy it. "We have made woman a sex creature," said a psychiatrist at the Margaret Sanger marriage counseling clinic. "She has no identity except as a wife and mother. She does not know who she is herself. She waits all day for her husband to come home at night to make her feel alive. And now it is the husband who is not interested. It is terrible for the women, to lie there, night after night, waiting for her husband to make her feel alive." Why is there such a market for books and articles offering sexual advice? The kind of sexual orgasm which Kinsey found in statistical plenitude in the recent generations of American women does not seem to make this problem go away.

On the contrary, new neuroses are being seen among women—and problems as yet unnamed as neuroses—which Freud and his followers did not predict, with physical symptoms, anxieties, and defense mechanisms equal to those caused by sexual repression. And strange new problems are being reported in the growing generations of children whose mothers were always there, driving them around, helping them with their homework—an inability to endure pain or discipline or pursue any self-sustained goal of any sort, a devastating boredom with life. Educators are increasingly uneasy about the dependence, the lack of self-reliance, of the boys and girls who are entering college today. "We fight a continual battle to make our students assume manhood," said a Columbia dean.

A White House conference was held on the physical and muscular deterioration of American children: were they being over-nurtured? Sociologists noted the astounding organization of suburban children's lives: the lessons, parties, entertainments, play and study groups organized for them. A suburban housewife in Portland, Oregon, wondered why the children "need" Brownies and Boy Scouts out here. "This is not the slums. The kids out here have the great outdoors. I think people are so bored, they organize the children, and then try to hook everyone else on it. And the poor kids have no time left just to lie on their beds and daydream."

Can the problem that has no name be somehow related to the domestic routine of the housewife? When a woman tries to put the problem into words, she often merely describes the daily life she leads. What is there in this recital of comfortable domestic detail that could possibly cause such a feeling of desperation? Is she trapped simply by the enormous demands of her role as modern housewife: wife, mistress, mother, nurse, consumer, cook, chauffeur; expert on interior decoration, child care, appliance repair, furniture refinishing, nutrition, and education? Her day is fragmented as she rushes from dishwasher to washing machine to telephone to dryer to station wagon to supermarket, and delivers Johnny to the Little League field, takes Janey to dancing class, gets the lawnmower fixed and meets the 6:45. She can never spend more than 15 minutes on any one thing; she has no time to read books, only magazines; even if she had time, she has lost the power to concentrate. At the end of the day, she is so terribly tired that sometimes her husband has to take over and put the children to bed.

This terrible tiredness took so many women to doctors in the 1950's that one decided to investigate it. He found, surprisingly, that his patients suffering from "housewife's fatigue" slept more than an adult needed to sleep—as much as ten hours a day—and that the actual energy they expended on housework did not tax their capacity. The real problem must be something else, he decided—perhaps boredom. Some doctors told their women patients they must get out of the house for a day, treat themselves to a movie in town. Others prescribed tranquilizers. Many suburban housewives were taking tranquilizers like cough drops. "You wake up in the morning, and you feel as if there's no point in going on another day like this. So you take a tranquilizer because it makes you not care so much that it's pointless."

It is easy to see the concrete details that trap the suburban housewife, the continual demands on her time. But the chains that bind her in her trap are chains in her own mind and spirit. They are chains made up of mistaken ideas and misinterpreted facts, of incomplete truths and unreal choices. They are not easily seen and not easily shaken off.

How can any woman see the whole truth within the bounds of her own life? How can she believe that voice inside herself, when it denies the conventional, accepted truths by which she has been living? And yet the women I have talked to, who are finally listening to that inner voice, seem in some incredible way to be groping through to a truth that has defied the experts.

I think the experts in a great many fields have been holding pieces of that truth under their microscopes for a long time without realizing it. I found pieces of it in certain new research and theoretical developments in psychological, social and biological science whose implications for women seem never to have been examined. I found many clues by talking to suburban doctors, gynecologists, obstetricians, child-guidance clinicians, pediatricians, high-school guidance counselors, college professors, marriage counselors, psychiatrists and ministers—questioning them not on their theories, but on their actual experience in treating American women. I became aware of a growing body of evidence, much of which has not been reported publicly because it does not fit current modes of thought about women—evidence which throws into question the standards of feminine normality, feminine adjustment, feminine fulfillment, and feminine maturity by which most women are still trying to live.

I began to see in a strange new light the American return to early marriage and the large families that are causing the population explosion; the recent movement to natural childbirth and breastfeeding; suburban conformity, and the new neuroses, character pathologies and sexual problems being reported by the doctors. I began to see new dimensions to old problems that have long been taken for granted among women: menstrual difficulties, sexual frigidity, promiscuity, pregnancy fears, childbirth depression, the high incidence of emotional breakdown and suicide among women in their twenties and thirties, the menopause crises, the so-called passivity and immaturity of American men, the discrepancy between women's tested intellectual abilities in childhood and their adult achievement, the changing incidence of adult sexual orgasm in American women, and persistent problems in psychotherapy and in women's education.

If I am right, the problem that has no name stirring in the minds of so many American women today is not a matter of loss of femininity or too much education, or the demands of domesticity. It is far more important than anyone recognizes. It is the key to these other new and old problems which have been torturing women and their husbands and children, and puzzling their doctors and educators for years. It may well be the key to our future as a nation and a culture. We can no longer ignore that voice within women that says: "I want something more than my husband and my children and my home."

2 The Happy Housewife Heroine

 Why have so many American wives suffered this nameless aching dissatisfaction for so many years, each one thinking she was alone? "I've got tears in my eyes with sheer relief that my own inner turmoil is shared with other women," a young Connecticut mother wrote me when I first began to put this problem into words.[1] A woman from a town in Ohio wrote: "The times when I felt that the only answer was to consult a psychiatrist, times of anger, bitterness and general frustration too numerous to even mention, I had no idea that hundreds of other women were feeling the same way. I felt so completely alone." A Houston, Texas, housewife wrote: "It has been the feeling of being almost alone with my problem that has made it so hard. I thank God for my family, home and the chance to care for them, but my life couldn't stop there. It is an awakening to know that I'm not an oddity and can stop being ashamed of wanting something more."

That painful guilty silence, and that tremendous relief when a feeling is finally out in the open, are familiar psychological signs. What need, what part of themselves, could so many women today be repressing? In this age after Freud, sex is immediately suspect. But this new stirring in women does not seem to be sex; it is, in fact, much harder for women to talk about than sex. Could there be another need, a part of themselves they have buried as deeply as the Victorian women buried sex?

If there is, a woman might not know what it was, any more than the Victorian woman knew she had sexual needs. The image of a good woman by which Victorian ladies lived simply left out sex. Does the image by which modern American women live also leave something out, the proud and public image of the high-school girl going steady, the college girl in love, the suburban housewife with an up-and-coming husband and a station wagon full of children? This image—created by the women's magazines, by advertisements, television, movies, novels, columns and books by experts on marriage and the family, child psychology, sexual adjustment and by the popularizers of sociology and psychoanalysis—shapes women's lives today and mirrors their dreams. It may give a clue to the problem that has no name, as a dream gives a clue to a wish unnamed by the dreamer. In the mind's ear, a geiger counter clicks when the image shows too sharp a discrepancy from reality. A geiger counter clicked in my own inner ear when I could not fit the quiet desperation of so many women into the picture of the modern American housewife that I myself was helping to create, writing for the women's magazines. What is missing from the image which shapes the American woman's pursuit of fulfillment as a wife and mother? What is missing from the image that mirrors and creates the identity of women in America today?

In the early 1960's *McCall's* has been the fastest growing of the women's magazines. Its contents are a fairly accurate representation of the image of the American woman presented, and in part created, by the large-circulation magazines. Here are the complete editorial contents of a typical issue of *McCall's* (July, 1960):

1. A lead article on "increasing baldness in women," caused by too much brushing and dyeing.
2. A long poem in primer-size type about a child, called "A Boy Is A Boy."
3. A short story about how a teenager who doesn't go to college gets a man away from a bright college girl.
4. A short story about the minute sensations of a baby throwing

his bottle out of the crib.

5. The first of a two-part intimate "up-to-date" account by the Duke of Windsor on "How the Duchess and I now live and spend our time. The influence of clothes on me and vice versa."

6. A short story about a nineteen-year-old girl sent to a charm school to learn how to bat her eyelashes and lose at tennis. ("You're nineteen, and by normal American standards, I now am entitled to have you taken off my hands, legally and financially, by some beardless youth who will spirit you away to a one-and-a-half-room apartment in the Village while he learns the chicanery of selling bonds. And no beardless youth is going to do that as long as you volley to his backhand.")

7. The story of a honeymoon couple commuting between separate bedrooms after an argument over gambling at Las Vegas.

8. An article on "how to overcome an inferiority complex."

9. A story called "Wedding Day."

10. The story of a teenager's mother who learns how to dance rock-and-roll.

11. Six pages of glamorous pictures of models in maternity clothes.

12. Four glamorous pages on "reduce the way the models do."

13. An article on airline delays.

14. Patterns for home sewing.

15. Patterns with which to make "Folding Screens—Bewitching Magic."

16. An article called "An Encyclopedic Approach to Finding a Second Husband."

17. A "barbecue bonanza," dedicated "to the Great American Mister who stands, chef's cap on head, fork in hand, on terrace or back porch, in patio or backyard anywhere in the land, watching his roast turning on the spit. And to his wife, without whom (sometimes) the barbecue could never be the smashing summer success it undoubtedly is . . ."

There were also the regular front-of-the-book "service" columns on new drug and medicine developments, child-care facts, columns by Clare Luce and by Eleanor Roosevelt, and "Pats and Pans," a column of readers' letters.

The image of woman that emerges from this big, pretty magazine is young and frivolous, almost childlike; fluffy and feminine; passive; gaily content in a world of bedroom and kitchen, sex, babies, and home. The magazine surely does not leave out sex; the only passion, the only pursuit, the only goal a woman is permitted is the pursuit of a man. It is crammed full of food, clothing, cosmetics, furniture, and the physical bodies of young women, but where is the world of thought and ideas, the life of the mind and spirit? In the magazine image, women do no work except housework and work to keep their bodies beautiful and to get and keep a man.

This was the image of the American woman in the year Castro led a revolution in Cuba and men were trained to travel into outer space; the year that the African continent brought forth new nations, and a plane whose speed is greater than the speed of sound broke up a Summit Conference; the year artists picketed a great museum in protest against the hegemony of abstract art; physicists explored the concept of anti-matter; astronomers, because of new radio telescopes, had to alter their concepts of the expanding universe; biologists made a breakthrough in the fundamental chemistry of life; and Negro youth in Southern schools forced the United States, for the first time since the Civil War, to face a moment of democratic truth. But this magazine, published for over 5,000,000 American women, almost all of whom have been through high school and nearly half to college, contained almost no mention of the world beyond the home. In the second half of the twentieth century in America, woman's world was confined to her own body and beauty, the charming of man, the bearing of babies, and the physical care and serving of husband, children, and home. And this was no anomaly of a single issue of a single women's magazine.

I sat one night at a meeting of magazine writers, mostly men, who work for all kinds of magazines, including women's magazines. The main speaker was a leader of the desegregation battle.

Before he spoke, another man outlined the needs of the large women's magazine he edited:

Our readers are housewives, full time. They're not interested in the broad public issues of the day. They are not interested in national or international affairs. They are only interested in the family and the home. They aren't interested in politics, unless it's related to an immediate need in the home, like the price of coffee. Humor? Has to be gentle, they don't get satire. Travel? We have almost completely dropped it. Education? That's a problem. Their own education level is going up. They've generally all had a high-school education and many, college. They're tremendously interested in education for their children—fourth-grade arithmetic. You just can't write about ideas or broad issues of the day for women. That's why we're publishing 90 per cent service now and 10 per cent general interest.

Another editor agreed, adding plaintively: "Can't you give us something else besides 'there's death in your medicine cabinet'? Can't any of you dream up a new crisis for women? We're always interested in sex, of course."

At this point, the writers and editors spent an hour listening to Thurgood Marshall on the inside story of the desegregation battle, and its possible effect on the presidential election. "Too bad I can't run that story," one editor said. "But you just can't link it to woman's world."

As I listened to them, a German phrase echoed in my mind—"*Kinder, Kuche, Kirche*," the slogan by which the Nazis decreed that women must once again be confined to their biological role. But this was not Nazi Germany. This was America. The whole world lies open to American women. Why, then, does the image deny the world? Why does it limit women to "one passion, one role, one occupation?" Not long ago, women dreamed and fought for equality, their own place in the world. What happened to their dreams; when did women decide to give up the world and go back home?

A geologist brings up a core of mud from the bottom of the ocean and sees layers of sediment as sharp as a razor blade deposited over the years—clues to changes in the geological evolution of the earth so vast that they would go unnoticed during the lifespan of a single man. I sat for many days in the New York Public Library, going back through bound volumes of American women's magazines for the last twenty years. I found a change in the image of the American woman, and in the boundaries of the woman's world, as sharp and puzzling as the changes revealed in cores of ocean sediment.

In 1939, the heroines of women's magazine stories were not always young, but in a certain sense they were younger than their fictional counterparts today. They were young in the same way that the American hero has always been young: they were New Women, creating with a gay determined spirit a new identity for women—a life of their own. There was an aura about them of becoming, of moving into a future that was going to be different from the past. The majority of heroines in the four major women's magazines (then *Ladies' Home Journal, McCall's, Good Housekeeping, Woman's Home Companion*) were career women— happily, proudly, adventurously, attractively career women— who loved and were loved by men. And the spirit, courage, independence, determination—the strength of character they showed in their work as nurses, teachers, artists, actresses, copywriters, saleswomen—were part of their charm. There was a definite aura that their individuality was something to be admired, not unattractive to men, that men were drawn to them as much for their spirit and character as for their looks.

These were the mass women's magazines—in their heyday. The stories were conventional: girl-meets-boy or girl-gets-boy. But very often this was not the major theme of the story. These heroines were usually marching toward some goal or vision of their own, struggling with some problem of work or the world, when they found their man. And this New Woman, less fluffily feminine, so independent and determined to find a new life of her own, was the heroine of a different kind of love story. She was less aggressive in pursuit of a man. Her passionate involvement with the world, her own sense of herself as an individual, her self-reliance, gave a different flavor to her relationship with the man.

The heroine and hero of one of these stories meet and fall in love at an ad agency where they both work. "I don't want to put you in a garden behind a wall," the hero says. "I want you to walk with me hand in hand, and together we could accomplish whatever we wanted to" ("A Dream to Share," *Redbook*, January, 1939).

These New Women were almost never housewives; in fact, the stories usually ended before they had children. They were young because the future was open. But they seemed, in another sense, much older, more mature than the childlike, kittenish young housewife heroines today. One, for example, is a nurse ("Mother-in-Law," *Ladies' Home Journal*, June, 1939). "She was, he thought, very lovely. She hadn't an ounce of picture book prettiness, but there was strength in her hands, pride in her carriage and nobility in the lift of her chin, in her blue eyes. She had been on her own ever since she left training, nine years ago. She had earned her way, she need consider nothing but her heart."

One heroine runs away from home when her mother insists she must make her debut instead of going on an expedition as a geologist. Her passionate determination to live her own life does not keep this New Woman from loving a man, but it makes her rebel from her parents; just as the young hero often must leave home to grow up. "You've got more courage than any girl I ever saw. You have what it takes," says the boy who helps her get away ("Have a Good Time, Dear," *Ladies' Home Journal*, May, 1939).

Often, there was a conflict between some commitment to her work and the man. But the moral, in 1939, was that if she kept her commitment to herself, she did not lose the man, if he was the right man. A young widow ("Between the Dark and the Daylight," *Ladies' Home Journal*, February, 1939) sits in her office, debating whether to stay and correct the important mistake she has made on the job, or keep her date with a man. She thinks back on her marriage, her baby, her husband's death . . . "the time afterward which held the struggle for clear judgment, not being afraid of new and better jobs, of having confidence in one's decisions." How can the boss expect her to give up her date! But she stays on the job. "They'd put their life's blood into this campaign. She couldn't let him down." She finds her man, too—the boss!

These stories may not have been great literature. But the identity of their heroines seemed to say something about the housewives who, then as now, read the women's magazines. These magazines were not written for career women. The New Woman heroines were the ideal of yesterday's housewives; they reflected the dreams, mirrored the yearning for identity and the sense of possibility that existed for women then. And if women could not have these dreams for themselves, they wanted their daughters to have them. They wanted their daughters to be more than housewives, to go out in the world that had been denied them.

It is like remembering a long-forgotten dream, to recapture the memory of what a career meant to women before "career woman" became a dirty word in America. Jobs meant money, of course, at the end of the depression. But the readers of these magazines were not the women who got the jobs; career meant more than job. It seemed to mean doing something, being somebody yourself, not just existing in and through others.

I found the last clear note of the passionate search for individual identity that a career seems to have symbolized in the pre-1950 decades in a story called "Sarah and the Seaplane" (*Ladies' Home Journal*, February, 1949). Sarah, who for nineteen years has played the part of docile daughter, is secretly learning to fly. She misses her flying lesson to accompany her mother on a round of social calls. An elderly doctor houseguest says: "My dear Sarah, every day, all the time, you are committing suicide. It's a greater crime than not pleasing others, not doing justice to yourself." Sensing some secret, he asks if she is in love. "She found it difficult to answer. In love? In love with the good-natured, the beautiful Henry [the flying teacher]? In love with the flashing water and the lift of wings at the instant of freedom, and the vision of the smiling, limitless world? 'Yes,' she answered, 'I think I am.'"

The next morning, Sarah solos. Henry "stepped away, slamming the cabin door shut, and swung the ship about for her. She was alone. There was a heady moment when everything she had learned left her, when she had to adjust herself to be alone, entirely alone in the familiar cabin. Then she drew a deep breath and suddenly a wonderful sense of competence made her sit erect and smiling. She was alone! She was answerable to herself alone, and she was sufficient.

" 'I can do it!' she told herself aloud. . . . The wind flew back from the floats in glittering streaks, and then effortlessly the ship lifted itself free and soared." Even her mother can't stop her now from getting her flying license. She is not "afraid of discovering my own way of life." In bed that night she smiles sleepily, remembering how Henry had said, "You're my girl."

"Henry's girl! She smiled. No, she was not Henry's girl. She was Sarah. And that was sufficient. And with such a late start it would be some time before she got to know herself. Half in a dream now, she wondered if at the end of that time she would need someone else and who it would be."

And then suddenly the image blurs. The New Woman, soaring free, hesitates in midflight, shivers in all that blue sunlight and rushes back to the cozy walls of home. In the same year that Sarah soloed, the *Ladies' Home Journal* printed the prototype of the innumerable paeans to "Occupation: Housewife" that started to appear in the women's magazines, paeans that resounded throughout the fifties. They usually begin with a woman complaining that when she has to write "housewife" on the census blank, she gets an inferiority complex. ("When I write it I realize that here I am, a middle-aged woman, with a university education, and I've never made anything out of my life. I'm just a housewife.") Then the author of the paean, who somehow never is a housewife (in this case, Dorothy Thompson, newspaper woman, foreign correspondent, famous columnist, in *Ladies' Home Journal*, March, 1949), roars with laughter. The trouble with you, she scolds, is you don't realize you are expert in a dozen careers, simultaneously. "You might write: business manager, cook, nurse, chauffeur, dressmaker, interior decorator, accountant, caterer, teacher, private secretary—or just put down philanthropist. . . . All your life you have been giving away your energies, your skills, your talents, your services, for love." But still, the housewife complains, I'm nearly fifty and I've never done what I hoped to do in my youth—music—I've wasted my college education.

Ho-ho, laughs Miss Thompson, aren't your children musical because of you, and all those struggling years while your husband was finishing his great work, didn't you keep a charming home on $3,000 a year, and make all your children's clothes and your own, and paper the living room yourself, and watch the markets like a hawk for bargains? And in time off, didn't you type and proofread your husband's manuscripts, plan festivals to make up the church deficit, play piano duets with the children to make practicing more fun, read their books in high school to follow their study? "But all this vicarious living—through others," the housewife sighs. "As vicarious as Napoleon Bonaparte," Miss Thompson scoffs, "or a Queen. I simply refuse to share your self-pity. You are one of the most successful women I know."

As for not earning any money, the argument goes, let the housewife compute the cost of her services. Women can save more money by their managerial talents inside the home than they can bring into it by outside work. As for woman's spirit being broken by the boredom of household tasks, maybe the genius of some women has been thwarted, but "a world full of feminine genius, but poor in children, would come rapidly to an end. . . . Great men have great mothers."

And the American housewife is reminded that Catholic countries in the Middle Ages "elevated the gentle and inconspicuous Mary into the Queen of Heaven, and built their loveliest cathedrals to 'Notre Dame—Our Lady.' . . . The homemaker, the nurturer, the creator of children's environment is the constant recreator of culture, civilization, and virtue. Assuming that she is doing well that great managerial task and creative activity, let her write her occupation proudly: 'housewife.' "

In 1949, the *Ladies' Home Journal* also ran Margaret Mead's *Male and Female*. All the magazines were echoing Farnham and Lundberg's *Modern Woman: The Lost Sex*, which came out in 1942, with its warning that careers and higher education were leading to the "masculinization of women with enormously dangerous consequences to the home, the children dependent on it and to the ability of the woman, as well as her husband, to obtain sexual gratification."

And so the feminine mystique began to spread through the land, grafted onto old prejudices and comfortable conventions which so easily give the past a stranglehold on the future. Behind the new mystique were concepts and theories deceptive in their sophistication and their assumption of accepted truth. These theories were supposedly so complex that they were inaccessible to all but a few initiates, and therefore irrefutable. It will be necessary to break through this wall of mystery and look more closely at these complex concepts, these accepted truths, to understand fully what has happened to American women.

The feminine mystique says that the highest value and the only commitment for women is the fulfillment of their own femininity. It says that the great mistake of Western culture, through most of its history, has been the undervaluation of this femininity. It says this femininity is so mysterious and intuitive and close to the creation and origin of life that man-made science may never be able to understand it. But however special and different, it is in no way inferior to the nature of man; it may even in certain respects be superior. The mistake, says the mystique, the root of women's troubles in the past is that women envied men, women tried to be like men, instead of accepting their own nature, which can find fulfillment only in sexual passivity, male domination, and nurturing maternal love.

But the new image this mystique gives to American women is the old image: "Occupation: housewife." The new mystique makes the housewife-mothers, who never had a chance to be anything else, the model for all women; it presupposes that history has reached a final and glorious end in the here and now, as far as women are concerned. Beneath the sophisticated trappings, it simply makes certain concrete, finite, domestic aspects of feminine existence—as it was lived by women whose lives were confined, by necessity, to cooking, cleaning, washing, bearing children—into a religion, a pattern by which all women must now live or deny their femininity.

Fulfillment as a woman had only one definition for American women after 1949—the housewife-mother. As swiftly as in a dream, the image of the American woman as a changing, growing individual in a changing world was shattered. Her solo flight to find her own identity was forgotten in the rush for the security of togetherness. Her limitless world shrunk to the cozy walls of home.

The transformation, reflected in the pages of the women's magazines, was sharply visible in 1949 and progressive through the fifties. "Femininity Begins at Home," "It's a Man's World Maybe," "Have Babies While You're Young," "How to Snare a Male," "Should I Stop Work When We Marry?" "Are You Training Your Daughter to be a Wife?" "Careers at Home," "Do Women Have to Talk So Much?" "Why GI's Prefer Those German Girls," "What Women Can Learn from Mother Eve," "Really a Man's World, Politics," "How to Hold On to a Happy Marriage," "Don't Be Afraid to Marry Young," "The Doctor Talks about Breast-Feeding," "Our Baby was Born at Home," "Cooking to Me is Poetry," "The Business of Running a Home."

By the end of 1949, only one out of three heroines in the women's magazines was a career woman—and she was shown in the act of renouncing her career and discovering that what she really wanted to be was a housewife. In 1958, and again in 1959, I went through issue after issue of the three major women's magazines (the fourth, *Woman's Home Companion*, had died) without finding a single heroine who had a career, a commitment to any work, art, profession, or mission in the world, other than "Occupation: housewife." Only one in a hundred heroines had a job; even the young unmarried heroines no longer worked except at snaring a husband.[2]

These new happy housewife heroines seem strangely younger than the spirited career girls of the thirties and forties. They seem to get younger all the time—in looks, and a childlike kind of dependence. They have no vision of the future, except to have a baby. The only active growing figure in their world is the child. The housewife heroines are forever young, because their own image *ends* in childbirth. Like Peter Pan, they must remain young

while their children grow up with the world. They must keep on
having babies, because the feminine mystique says there is no
other way for a woman to be a heroine. Here is a typical specimen
from a story called "The Sandwich Maker" (*Ladies' Home Journal*, April, 1959). She took home economics in college, learned
how to cook, never held a job, and still plays the child bride,
though she now has three children of her own. Her problem is
money. "Oh, nothing boring, like taxes or reciprocal trade agree-
ments, or foreign aid programs. I leave all that economic jazz to
my constitutionally elected representative in Washington, heaven
help him."

The problem is her $42.10 allowance. She hates having to ask
her husband for money every time she needs a pair of shoes, but
he won't trust her with a charge account. "Oh, how I yearned for
a little money of my own! Not much, really. A few hundred a
year would have done it. Just enough to meet a friend for lunch
occasionally, to indulge in extravagantly colored stockings, a few
small items, without having to appeal to Charley. But, alas,
Charley was right. I had never earned a dollar in my life, and
had no idea of how money was made. So all I did for a long time
was brood, as I continued with my cooking, cleaning, cooking,
washing, ironing, cooking."

At last the solution comes—she will take orders for sandwiches
from other men at her husband's plant. She earns $52.50 a week,
except that she forgets to count costs, and she doesn't remember
what a gross is so she has to hide 8,640 sandwich bags behind the
furnace. Charley says she's making the sandwiches too fancy. She
explains: "If it's only ham on rye, then I'm just a sandwich maker,
and I'm not interested. But the extras, the special touches—well,
they make it sort of creative." So she chops, wraps, peels, seals,
spreads bread, starting at dawn and never finished, for $9.00 net,
until she is disgusted by the smell of food, and finally staggers
downstairs after a sleepless night to slice a salami for the eight
gaping lunch boxes. "It was too much. Charley came down just
then, and after one quick look at me, ran for a glass of water."
She realizes that she is going to have another baby.

"Charley's first coherent words were 'I'll cancel your lunch orders. You're a mother. That's your job. You don't have to earn money, too.' It was all so beautifully simple! 'Yes, boss,' I murmured obediently, frankly relieved." That night he brings her home a checkbook; he will trust her with a joint account. So she decides just to keep quiet about the 8,640 sandwich bags. Anyhow, she'll have used them up, making sandwiches for four children to take to school, by the time the youngest is ready for college.

The road from Sarah and the seaplane to the sandwich maker was traveled in only ten years. In those ten years, the image of American woman seems to have suffered a schizophrenic split. And the split in the image goes much further than the savage obliteration of career from women's dreams.

In an earlier time, the image of woman was also split in two—the good, pure woman on the pedestal, and the whore of the desires of the flesh. The split in the new image opens a different fissure—the feminine woman, whose goodness includes the desires of the flesh, and the career woman, whose evil includes every desire of the separate self. The new feminine morality story is the exorcising of the forbidden career dream, the heroine's victory over Mephistopheles: the devil, first in the form of a career woman, who threatens to take away the heroine's husband or child, and finally, the devil inside the heroine herself, the dream of independence, the discontent of spirit, and even the feeling of a separate identity that must be exorcised to win or keep the love of husband and child.

In a story in *Redbook* ("A Man Who Acted Like a Husband," November, 1957) the child-bride heroine, "a little freckle-faced brunette" whose nickname is "Junior," is visited by her old college roommate. The roommate Kay is "a man's girl, really, with a good head for business . . . she wore her polished mahogany hair in a high chignon, speared with two chopstick affairs." Kay is not only divorced, but she has also left her child with his grandmother while she works in television. This career-woman-devil tempts Junior with the lure of a job to keep her from breast-feeding her baby. She even restrains the young mother

from going to her baby when he cries at 2 A.M. But she gets her
comeuppance when George, the husband, discovers the crying
baby uncovered, in a freezing wind from an open window, with
blood running down its cheek. Kay, reformed and repentant,
plays hookey from her job to go get her own child and start life
anew. And Junior, gloating at the 2 A.M. feeding—"I'm glad, glad,
glad I'm just a housewife" starts to dream about the baby, growing up to be a housewife, too.

With the career woman out of the way, the housewife with
interests in the community becomes the devil to be exorcised.
Even PTA takes on a suspect connotation, not to mention interest
in some international cause (see "Almost a Love Affair," *McCall's*,
November, 1955). The housewife who simply has a mind of her
own is the next to go. The heroine of "I Didn't Want to Tell
You" (*McCall's*, January, 1958) is shown balancing the checkbook by herself and arguing with her husband about a small
domestic detail. It develops that she is losing her husband to a
"helpless little widow" whose main appeal is that she can't "think
straight" about an insurance policy or mortgage. The betrayed
wife says: "She must have sex appeal and what weapon has a
wife against that?" But her best friend tells her: "You're making
this too simple. You're forgetting how helpless Tania can be, and
how grateful to the man who helps her . . ."

"I couldn't be a clinging vine if I tried," the wife says. "I had a
better than average job after I left college and I was always a
pretty independent person. I'm not a helpless little woman and I
can't pretend to be." But she learns, that night. She hears a noise
that might be a burglar; even though she knows it's only a mouse,
she calls helplessly to her husband, and wins him back. As he comforts her pretended panic, she murmurs that, of course, he was
right in their argument that morning. "She lay still in the soft bed,
smiling in sweet, secret satisfaction, scarcely touched with guilt."

The end of the road, in an almost literal sense, is the disap-
pearance of the heroine altogether, as a separate self and the
subject of her own story. The end of the road is togetherness,
where the woman has no independent self to hide even in guilt;
she exists only for and through her husband and children.

Coined by the publishers of *McCall's* in 1954, the concept "to-getherness" was seized upon avidly as a movement of spiritual significance by advertisers, ministers, newspaper editors. For a time, it was elevated into virtually a national purpose. But very quickly there was sharp social criticism, and bitter jokes about "togetherness" as a substitute for larger human goals—for men. Women were taken to task for making their husbands do house-work, instead of letting them pioneer in the nation and the world. Why, it was asked, should men with the capacities of statesmen, anthropologists, physicists, poets, have to wash dishes and diaper babies on weekday evenings or Saturday mornings when they might use those extra hours to fulfill larger commitments to their society?

Significantly, critics resented only that men were being asked to share "woman's world." Few questioned the boundaries of this world for women. No one seemed to remember that women were once thought to have the capacity and vision of statesmen, poets, and physicists. Few saw the big lie of togetherness for women.

Consider the Easter 1954 issue of *McCall's* which announced the new era of togetherness, sounding the requiem for the days when women fought for and won political equality, and the women's magazines "helped you to carve out large areas of living formerly forbidden to your sex." The new way of life in which "men and women in ever-increasing numbers are marrying at an earlier age, having children at an earlier age, rearing larger families and gaining their deepest satisfaction" from their own homes, is one which "men, women and children are achieving together . . . not as women alone, or men alone, isolated from one another, but as a family, sharing a common experience."

The picture essay detailing that way of life is called "a man's place is in the home." It describes, as the new image and ideal, a New Jersey couple with three children in a gray-shingle split-level house. Ed and Carol have "centered their lives almost com-pletely around their children and their home." They are shown shopping at the supermarket, carpentering, dressing the children, making breakfast together. "Then Ed joins the members of his car pool and heads for the office."

Ed, the husband, chooses the color scheme for the house and makes the major decorating decisions. The chores Ed likes are listed: putter around the house, make things, paint, select furniture, rugs and draperies, dry dishes, read to the children and put them to bed, work in the garden, feed and dress and bathe the children, attend PTA meetings, cook, buy clothes for his wife, buy groceries.

Ed doesn't like these chores: dusting, vacuuming, finishing jobs he's started, hanging draperies, washing pots and pans and dishes, picking up after the children, shoveling snow or mowing the lawn, changing diapers, taking the baby-sitter home, doing the laundry, ironing. Ed, of course, does not do these chores.

For the sake of every member of the family, the family needs a head. This means Father, not Mother. . . . Children of both sexes need to learn, recognize and respect the abilities and functions of each sex. . . . He is not just a substitute mother, even though he's ready and willing to do his share of bathing, feeding, comforting, playing. He is a link with the outside world he works in. If in that world he is interested, courageous, tolerant, constructive, he will pass on these values to his children.

There were many agonized editorial sessions, in those days at *McCall's*. "Suddenly, everybody was looking for this spiritual significance in togetherness, expecting us to make some mysterious religious movement out of the life everyone had been leading for the last five years—crawling into the home, turning their backs on the world—but we never could find a way of showing it that wasn't a monstrosity of dullness," a former *McCall's* editor reminisces. "It always boiled down to, goody, goody, goody, Daddy is out there in the garden barbecuing. We put men in the fashion pictures and the food pictures, and even the perfume pictures. But we were stifled by it editorially.

"We had articles by psychiatrists that we couldn't use because they would have blown it wide open: all those couples propping their whole weight on their kids. But what else could you do with togetherness but child care? We were pathetically grateful to find anything else where we could show father photographed with mother. Sometimes, we used to wonder what would happen to women, with men taking over the decorating, child care, cooking, all the things that used to be hers alone. But we couldn't show women getting out of the home and having a career. The irony is, what we meant to do was to stop editing for women as women, and edit for the men and women together. We wanted to edit for people, not women."

But forbidden to join man in the world, can women be people? Forbidden independence, they finally are swallowed in an image of such passive dependence that they want men to make the decisions, even in the home. The frantic illusion that togetherness can impart a spiritual content to the dullness of domestic routine, the need for a religious movement to make up for the lack of identity, betrays the measure of women's loss and the emptiness of the image. Could making men share the housework compensate women for their loss of the world? Could vacuuming the living-room floor together give the housewife some mysterious new purpose in life?

In 1956, at the peak of togetherness, the bored editors of *McCall's* ran a little article called "The Mother Who Ran Away." To their amazement, it brought the highest readership of any article they had ever run. "It was our moment of truth," said a former editor. "We suddenly realized that all those women at home with their three and a half children were miserably unhappy."

But by then the new image of American woman, "Occupation: housewife," had hardened into a mystique, unquestioned and permitting no questions, shaping the very reality it distorted.

By the time I started writing for women's magazines, in the fifties, it was simply taken for granted by editors, and accepted as an immutable fact of life by writers, that women were not interested in politics, life outside the United States, national issues, art, science, ideas, adventure, education, or even their own communities, except where they could be sold through their emotions as wives and mothers.

Politics, for women, became Mamie's clothes and the Nixons' home life. Out of conscience, a sense of duty, the *Ladies' Home Journal* might run a series like "Political Pilgrim's Progress," showing women trying to improve their children's schools and playgrounds. But even approaching politics through mother love did not really interest women, it was thought in the trade. Everyone knew those readership percentages. An editor of *Redbook* ingeniously tried to bring the bomb down to the feminine level by showing the emotions of a wife whose husband sailed into a contaminated area.

"Women can't take an idea, an issue, pure," men who edited the mass women's magazines agreed. "It has to be translated in terms they can understand as women." This was so well understood by those who wrote for women's magazines that a natural childbirth expert submitted an article to a leading woman's magazine called "How to Have a Baby in an Atom Bomb Shelter." "The article was not well written," an editor told me, "or we might have bought it." According to the mystique, women, in their mysterious femininity, might be interested in the concrete biological details of having a baby in a bomb shelter, but never in the abstract idea of the bomb's power to destroy the human race.

Such a belief, of course, becomes a self-fulfilling prophecy. In 1960, a perceptive social psychologist showed me some sad statistics which seemed to prove unmistakably that American women under thirty-five are not interested in politics. "They may have the vote, but they don't dream about running for office," he told me. "If you write a political piece, they won't read it. You have to translate it into issues they can understand—romance, pregnancy, nursing, home furnishings, clothes. Run an article on the economy, or the race question, civil rights, and you'd think that women had never heard of them."

Maybe they hadn't heard of them. Ideas are not like instincts of the blood that spring into the mind intact. They are communicated by education, by the printed word. The new young housewives, who leave high school or college to marry, do not read books, the psychological surveys say. They only read magazines. Magazines today assume women are not interested in ideas. But going back to the bound volumes in the library, I found in the thirties and forties that the mass-circulation magazines like *Ladies' Home Journal* carried hundreds of articles about the world outside the home. "The first inside story of American diplomatic relations preceding declared war"; "Can the U. S. Have Peace After This War?" by Walter Lippman; "Stalin at Midnight," by Harold Stassen; "General Stilwell Reports on China"; articles about the last days of Czechoslovakia by Vincent Sheean; the persecution of Jews in Germany; the New Deal; Carl Sandburg's account of Lincoln's assassination; Faulkner's stories of Mississippi, and Margaret Sanger's battle for birth control.

In the 1950's they printed virtually no articles except those that serviced women as housewives, or described women as housewives, or permitted a purely feminine identification like the Duchess of Windsor or Princess Margaret. "If we get an article about a woman who does anything adventurous, out of the way, something by herself, you know, we figure she must be terribly aggressive, neurotic," a *Ladies' Home Journal* editor told me. Margaret Sanger would never get in today.

In 1960, I saw statistics that showed that women under thirty-five could not identify with a spirited heroine of a story who worked in an ad agency and persuaded the boy to stay and fight for his principles in the big city instead of running home to the security of a family business. Nor could these new young housewives identify with a young minister, acting on his belief in defiance of convention. But they had no trouble at all identifying with a young man paralyzed at eighteen. ("I regained consciousness to discover that I could not move or even speak. I could wiggle only one finger of one hand." With help from faith and a psychiatrist, "I am now finding reasons to live as fully as possible.")

Does it say something about the new housewife readers that, as any editor can testify, they can identify completely with the victims of blindness, deafness, physical maiming, cerebral palsy, paralysis, cancer, or approaching death? Such articles about people who cannot see or speak or move have been an enduring staple of the women's magazines in the era of "Occupation: housewife." They are told with infinitely realistic detail over and over again, replacing the articles about the nation, the world, ideas, issues, art and science; replacing the stories about adventurous spirited women. And whether the victim is man, woman or child, whether the living death is incurable cancer or creeping paralysis, the housewife reader can identify.

Writing for these magazines, I was continually reminded by editors "that women *have* to identify." Once I wanted to write an article about an artist. So I wrote about her cooking and marketing and falling in love with her husband, and painting a crib for her baby. I had to leave out the hours she spent painting pictures, her serious work—and the way she felt about it. You could sometimes get away with writing about a woman who was not really a housewife, if you made her *sound* like a housewife, if you left out her commitment to the world outside the home, or the private vision of mind or spirit that she pursued. In February, 1949, the *Ladies' Home Journal* ran a feature, "Poet's Kitchen," showing Edna St. Vincent Millay cooking. "Now I expect to hear no more about housework's being beneath anyone, for if one of the greatest poets of our day, and any day, can find beauty in simple household tasks, this is the end of the old controversy."

The one "career woman" who was always welcome in the pages of the women's magazines was the actress. But her image also underwent a remarkable change: from a complex individual of fiery temper, inner depth, and a mysterious blend of spirit and sexuality, to a sexual object, a babyface bride, or a housewife. Think of Greta Garbo, for instance, and Marlene Dietrich, Bette Davis, Rosalind Russell, Katherine Hepburn. Then think of Marilyn Monroe, Debbie Reynolds, Brigitte Bardot, and "I Love Lucy."

When you wrote about an actress for a woman's magazine, you wrote about her as a housewife. You never showed her doing or enjoying her work as an actress, unless she eventually paid for it by losing her husband or her child, or otherwise admitting failure as a woman. A *Redbook* profile of Judy Holliday (June, 1957) described how "a brilliant woman begins to find in her work the joy she never found in life." On the screen, we are told, she plays "with warmth and conviction the part of a mature, intelligent wife and expectant mother, a role unlike anything she had previously attempted." She must find fulfillment in her career because she is divorced from her husband, has "strong feelings of inadequacy as a woman. . . . It is a frustrating irony of Judy's life, that as an actress she has succeeded almost without trying, although, as a woman, she has failed . . ."

Strangely enough, as the feminine mystique spread, denying women careers or any commitment outside the home, the proportion of American women working outside the home increased to one out of three. True, two out of three were still housewives, but why, at the moment when the doors of the world were finally open to all women, should the mystique deny the very dreams that had stirred women for a century?

I found a clue one morning, sitting in the office of a women's magazine editor—a woman who, older than I, remembers the days when the old image was being created, and who had watched it being displaced. The old image of the spirited career girl was largely created by writers and editors who were women, she told me. The new image of woman as housewife-mother has been largely created by writers and editors who are men.

"Most of the material used to come from women writers," she said, almost nostalgically. "As the young men returned from the war, a great many women writers dropped out of the field. The young women started having a lot of children, and stopped writing. The new writers were all men, back from the war, who had been dreaming about home, and a cozy domestic life." One by one, the creators of the gay "career girl" heroines of the thirties began to retire. By the end of the forties, the writers who couldn't get the knack of writing in the new housewife image had left the women's magazine field. The new magazine pros were men, and a few women who could write comfortably according to the housewife formula. Other people began to assemble backstage at the women's magazines: there was a new kind of woman writer who lived in the housewife image, or pretended to; and there was a new kind of woman's editor or publisher, less interested in ideas to reach women's minds and hearts, than in selling them the things that interest advertisers—appliances, detergents, lipstick. Today, the deciding voice on most of these magazines is cast by men. Women often carry out the formulas, women edit the housewife "service" departments, but the formulas themselves, which have dictated the new housewife image, are the product of men's minds.

Also during the forties and fifties, serious fiction writers of either sex disappeared from the mass-circulation women's magazines. In fact, fiction of any quality was almost completely replaced by a different kind of article. No longer the old article about issues or ideas, but the new "service" feature. Sometimes these articles lavished the artistry of a poet and the honesty of a crusading reporter on baking chiffon pies, or buying washing machines, or the miracles paint can do for a living room, or diets, drugs, clothes, and cosmetics to make the body into a vision of physical beauty. Sometimes they dealt with very sophisticated ideas: new developments in psychiatry, child psychology, sex and marriage, medicine. It was assumed that women readers could take these ideas, which appealed to their needs as wives and mothers, but only if they were boiled down to concrete physical details, spelled out in terms of the daily life of an average housewife with concrete do's and don'ts. How to keep your husband happy; how to solve your child's bedwetting; how to keep death out of your medicine cabinet . . .

But here is a curious thing. Within their narrow range, these women's magazine articles, whether straight service to the housewife or a documentary report about the housewife, were almost always superior in quality to women's magazine fiction. They were better written, more honest, more sophisticated. This observation was made over and over again by intelligent readers and puzzled editors, and by writers themselves. "The serious fiction writers have become too internal. They're inaccessible to our readers, so we're left with the formula writers," an editor of *Redbook* said. And yet, in the old days, serious writers like Nancy Hale, even William Faulkner, wrote for the women's magazines and were not considered inaccessible. Perhaps the new image of woman did not permit the internal honesty, the depth of perception, and the human truth essential to good fiction.

At the very least, fiction requires a hero or, understandably for women's magazines, a heroine, who is an "I" in pursuit of some human goal or dream. There is a limit to the number of stories that can be written about a girl in pursuit of a boy, or a housewife in pursuit of a ball of dust under the sofa. Thus the service article takes over, replacing the internal honesty and truth needed in fiction with a richness of honest, objective, concrete, realistic domestic detail—the color of walls or lipstick, the exact temperature of the oven.

Judging from the women's magazines today, it would seem that the concrete details of women's lives are more interesting than their thoughts, their ideas, their dreams. Or does the richness and realism of the detail, the careful description of small events, mask the lack of dreams, the vacuum of ideas, the terrible boredom that has settled over the American housewife?

I sat in the office of another old-timer, one of the few women editors left in the women's magazine world, now so largely dominated by men. She explained her share in creating the feminine mystique. "Many of us were psychoanalyzed," she recalled. "And we began to feel embarrassed about being career women ourselves. There was this terrible fear that we were losing our femininity. We kept looking for ways to help women accept their feminine role."

If the real women editors were not, somehow, able to give up their own careers, all the more reason to "help" other women fulfill themselves as wives and mothers. The few women who still sit in editorial conferences do not bow to the feminine mystique in their own lives. But such is the power of the image they have helped create that many of them feel guilty. And if they have missed out somewhere on love or children, they wonder if their careers were to blame.

Behind her cluttered desk, a *Mademoiselle* editor said uneasily, "The girls we bring in now as college guest editors seem almost to pity us. Because we are career women, I suppose. At a luncheon session with the last bunch, we asked them to go round the table, telling us their own career plans. Not one of the twenty raised her hand. When I remember how I worked to learn this job and loved it—were we all crazy then?"

Coupled with the women editors who sold themselves their

own bill of goods, a new breed of women writers began to write about themselves as if they were "just housewives," reveling in a comic world of children's pranks and eccentric washing machines and Parents' Night at the PTA. "After making the bed of a twelve-year-old boy week after week, climbing Mount Everest would seem a laughable anticlimax," writes Shirley Jackson (*McCall's*, April, 1956). When Shirley Jackson, who all her adult life has been an extremely capable writer, pursuing a craft far more demanding than bedmaking, and Jean Kerr, who is a playwright, and Phyllis McGinley, who is a poet, picture themselves as housewives, they may or may not overlook the housekeeper or maid who really makes the beds. But they implicitly deny the vision, and the satisfying hard work involved in their stories, poems, and plays. They deny the lives they lead, not as housewives, but as individuals.

They are good craftsmen, the best of these Housewife Writers. And some of their work is funny. The things that happen with children, a twelve-year-old boy's first cigarette, the Little League and the kindergarten rhythm band are often funny; they happen in real life to women who are writers as well as women who are just housewives. But there is something about Housewife Writers that isn't funny—like Uncle Tom, or Amos and Andy. "Laugh," the Housewife Writers tell the real housewife, "if you are feeling desperate, empty, bored, trapped in the bedmaking, chauffeuring and dishwashing details. Isn't it funny? We're all in the same trap." Do real housewives then dissipate in laughter their dreams and their sense of desperation? Do they think their frustrated abilities and their limited lives are a joke? Shirley Jackson makes the beds, loves and laughs at her son—and writes another book. Jean Kerr's plays are produced on Broadway. The joke is not on *them*.

Some of the new Housewife Writers *live* the image; *Redbook* tells us that the author of an article on "Breast-Feeding," a woman named Betty Ann Countrywoman, "had planned to be a doctor. But just before her graduation from Radcliffe *cum laude*, she shrank from the thought that such a dedication might shut her off from what she really wanted, which was to marry and have a large family. She enrolled in the Yale University School of Nursing and then became engaged to a young psychiatrist on their first date. Now they have six children, ranging in age from 2 to 13, and Mrs. Countrywoman is instructor in breast-feeding at the Maternity League of Indianapolis" (*Redbook*, June, 1960). She says:

For the mother, breast-feeding becomes a complement to the act of creation. It gives her a heightened sense of fulfillment and allows her to participate in a relationship as close to perfection as any that a woman can hope to achieve. . . . The simple fact of giving birth, however, does not of itself fulfill this need and longing. . . . Motherliness is a way of life. It enables a woman to express her total self with the tender feelings, the protective attitudes, the encompassing love of the motherly woman.

When motherhood, a fulfillment held sacred down the ages, is defined as a total way of life, must women themselves deny the world and the future open to them? Or does the denial of that world *force* them to make motherhood a total way of life? The line between mystique and reality dissolves; real women embody the split in the image. In the spectacular Christmas 1956 issue of *Life*, devoted in full to the "new" American woman, we see, not as women's-magazine villain, but as documentary fact, the typical "career woman—that fatal error that feminism propagated"—seeking "help" from a psychiatrist. She is bright, well-educated, ambitious, attractive; she makes about the same money as her husband; but she is pictured here as "frustrated," so "masculinized" by her career that her castrated, impotent, passive husband is indifferent to her sexually. He refuses to take responsibility and drowns his destroyed masculinity in alcoholism. Then there is the discontented suburban wife who raises hell at the PTA; morbidly depressed, she destroys her children and dominates her husband whom she envies for going out into the business world. "The wife, having worked before marriage, or at least having been educated for some kind of intellectual work, finds herself in the lamentable position of being 'just a housewife.' . . . In her disgruntlement she can work as much damage on the lives of her husband and children (and her own life) as if she were a career woman, and indeed, sometimes more."

And finally, in bright and smiling contrast, are the new house-wife-mothers, who cherish their "differentness," their "unique femininity," the "receptivity and passivity implicit in their sexual nature." Devoted to their own beauty and their ability to bear and nurture children, they are "feminine women, with truly feminine attitudes, admired by men for their miraculous, God-given, sensationally unique ability to wear skirts, with all the implications of that fact." Rejoicing in "the reappearance of the old-fashioned three-to-five-child family in an astonishing quarter, the upper- and upper-middle class suburbs," *Life* says:

> Here, among women who might be best qualified for "careers," there is an increasing emphasis on the nurturing and homemaking values. One might guess . . . that because these women are better informed and more mature than the average, they have been the first to comprehend the penalties of "feminism" and to react against them. . . . Styles in ideas as well as in dress and decoration tend to seep down from such places to the broader population. . . . This is the counter-trend which may eventually demolish the dominant and disruptive trend and make marriage what it should be: a true partnership in which . . . men are men, women are women, and both are quietly, pleasantly, securely confident of which they are—and absolutely delighted to find themselves married to someone of the opposite sex.

Look glowed at about the same time (October 16, 1956):

> The American woman is winning the battle of the sexes. Like a teenager, she is growing up and confounding her critics. . . . No longer a psychological immigrant to man's world, she works, rather casually, as a third of the U. S. labor force, less towards a "big career" than as a way of filling a hope chest or buying a new home freezer. She gracefully concedes the top jobs to men. This wondrous creature also marries younger than ever, bears more babies and looks and acts far more feminine than the "emancipated" girl of the 1920's or even '30's. Steelworker's wife and Junior Leaguer alike do their own housework. . . . Today, if she makes an old-fashioned choice and lovingly tends a garden and a bumper crop of children, she rates louder hosannas than ever before.

In the new America, fact is more important than fiction. The documentary *Life* and *Look* images of real women who devote their lives to children and home are played back as the ideal, the way women should be: this is powerful stuff, not to be shrugged off like the heroines of women's magazine fiction. When a mystique is strong, it makes its own fiction of fact. It feeds on the very facts which might contradict it, and seeps into every corner of the culture, bemusing even the social critics.

Adlai Stevenson, in a commencement address at Smith College in 1955, reprinted in *Woman's Home Companion* (September, 1955), dismissed the desire of educated women to play their own political part in "the crises of the age." Modern woman's participation in politics is through her role as wife and mother, said the spokesman of democratic liberalism: "Women, especially educated women, have a unique opportunity to influence us, man and boy." The only problem is woman's failure to appreciate that her true part in the political crisis is as wife and mother.

Once immersed in the very pressing and particular problems of domesticity, many women feel frustrated and far apart from the great issues and stirring debate for which their education has given them understanding and relish. Once they wrote poetry. Now it's the laundry list. Once they discussed art and philosophy until late in the night. Now they are so tired they fall asleep as soon as the dishes are finished. There is, often, a sense of contraction, of closing horizons and lost opportunities. They had hoped to play their part in the crises of the age. But what they do is wash the diapers.

The point is that whether we talk of Africa, Islam or Asia, women "never had it so good" as you. In short, far from the vocation of marriage and motherhood leading you away from the great issues of our day, it brings you back to their very center and places upon you an infinitely deeper and more intimate responsibility than that borne by the majority of those who hit the headlines and make the news and live in such a turmoil of great issues that they end by being totally unable to distinguish which issues are really great.

Woman's political job is to "inspire in her home a vision of the meaning of life and freedom . . . to help her husband find values that will give purpose to his specialized daily chores . . .

to teach her children the uniqueness of each individual human being."

This assignment for you, as wives and mothers, you can do in the
living room with a baby in your lap or in the kitchen with a can
opener in your hand. If you're clever, maybe you can even practice
your saving arts on that unsuspecting man while he's watching television. I think there is much you can do about our crisis in the humble
role of housewife. I could wish you no better vocation than that.

Thus the logic of the feminine mystique redefined the very
nature of woman's problem. When woman was seen as a human
being of limitless human potential, equal to man, anything that
kept her from realizing her full potential was a problem to be
solved: barriers to higher education and political participation,
discrimination or prejudice in law or morality. But now that
woman is seen only in terms of her sexual role, the barriers to
the realization of her full potential, the prejudices which deny
her full participation in the world, are no longer problems. The
only problems now are those that might disturb her adjustment
as a housewife. So career is a problem, education is a problem,
political interest, even the very admission of women's intelligence
and individuality is a problem. And finally there is the problem that
has no name, a vague undefined wish for "something more" than
washing dishes, ironing, punishing and praising the children. In
the women's magazines, it is solved either by dyeing one's hair
blonde or by having another baby. "Remember, when we were all
children, how we all planned to 'be something?' " says a young
housewife in the *Ladies' Home Journal* (February, 1960). Boast-
ing that she has worn out six copies of Dr. Spock's baby-care
book in seven years, she cries, "I'm lucky! Lucky! I'M SO GLAD
TO BE A WOMAN!"

In one of these stories ("Holiday," *Mademoiselle*, August, 1949)
a desperate young wife is ordered by her doctor to get out of
the house one day a week. She goes shopping, tries on dresses,
looks in the mirror wondering which one her husband, Sam, will
like.

Always Sam, like a Greek chorus in the back of her head. As if she
herself hadn't a definiteness of her own, a clarity that was indisputably

hers. . . . Suddenly she couldn't make the difference between pleated
and gored skirts of sufficient importance to fix her decision. She looked
at herself in the full-length glass, tall, getting thicker around the hips,
the lines of her face beginning to slip. She was twenty-nine, but she
felt middle-aged, as if a great many years had passed and there wasn't
very much yet to come . . . which was ridiculous, for Ellen was only
three. There was her whole future to plan for, and perhaps another
child. It was not a thing to be put off too long.

When the young housewife in "The Man Next to Me" (*Redbook*, November, 1948) discovers that her elaborate dinner party
didn't help her husband get a raise after all, she is in despair.
("You should say I helped. You should say I'm good for something . . . Life was like a puzzle with a piece missing, and the
piece was me, and I couldn't figure my place in it at all.") So
she dyes her hair blonde, and when her husband reacts satisfactorily in bed to the new "blonde me," she "felt a new sense of
peace, as if I'd answered the question within myself."

Over and over again, stories in women's magazines insist that
woman can know fulfillment only at the moment of giving birth
to a child. They deny the years when she can no longer look forward to giving birth, even if she repeats that act over and over
again. In the feminine mystique, there is no other way for a
woman to dream of creation or of the future. There is no way
she can even dream about herself, except as her children's mother,
her husband's wife. And the documentary articles play back new
young housewives, grown up under the mystique, who do not
have even that "question within myself." Says one, described in
"How America Lives" (*Ladies' Home Journal*, June, 1959): "If
he doesn't want me to wear a certain color or a certain kind
of dress, then I truly don't want to, either. The thing is, whatever he has wanted is what I also want. . . . I don't believe in
fifty-fifty marriages." Giving up college and job to marry at
eighteen, with no regrets, she "never tried to enter into the discussion when the men were talking. She never disputed her husband in anything. . . . She spent a great deal of time looking
out the window at the snow, the rain, and the gradual emergence
of the first crocuses. One great time-passer and consolation was

. . . embroidery: tiny stitches in gold-metal or silken thread which require infinite concentration."

There is no problem, in the logic of the feminine mystique, for such a woman who has no wishes of her own, who defines herself only as wife and mother. The problem, if there is one, can only be her children's, or her husband's. It is the husband who complains to the marriage counselor (*Redbook*, June, 1955): "The way I see it, marriage takes two people, each living his own life and then putting them together. Mary seems to think we both ought to live one life: mine." Mary insists on going with him to buy shirts and socks, tells the clerk his size and color. When he comes home at night, she asks with whom he ate lunch, where, what did he talk about? When he protests, she says, "But darling, I want to share your life, be part of all you do, that's all. . . . I want us to be one, the way it says in the marriage service . . ." It doesn't seem reasonable to the husband that "two people can ever be one the way Mary means it. It's just plain ridiculous on the face of it. Besides, I wouldn't like it. I don't want to be so bound to another person that I can't have a thought or an action that's strictly my own."

The answer to "Pete's problem," says Dr. Emily Mudd, the famous marriage counsellor, is to make Mary *feel* she is living his life: invite her to town to lunch with the people in his office once in a while, order his favorite veal dish for her and maybe find her some "healthy physical activity," like swimming, to drain off her excess energy. It is not Mary's problem that she has no life of her own.

The ultimate, in housewife happiness, is finally achieved by the Texas housewife, described in "How America Lives" (*Ladies' Home Journal*, October, 1960), who "sits on a pale aqua satin sofa gazing out her picture window at the street. Even at this hour of the morning (it is barely nine-o'clock), she is wearing rouge, powder and lipstick, and her cotton dress is immaculately fresh." She says proudly: "By 8:30 A.M., when my youngest goes to school, my whole house is clean and neat and I am dressed for the day. I am free to play bridge, attend club meetings, or stay home and read, listen to Beethoven, and just plain loaf."

"Sometimes, she washes and dries her hair before sitting down at a bridge table at 1:30. Mornings she is having bridge at her house are the busiest, for then she must get out the tables, cards, tallies, prepare fresh coffee and organize lunch. . . . During the winter months, she may play as often as four days a week from 9:30 to 3 P.M. . . . Janice is careful to be home, before her sons return from school at 4 P.M."

She is not frustrated, this new young housewife. An honor student at high school, married at eighteen, remarried and pregnant at twenty, she has the house she spent seven years dreaming and planning in detail. She is proud of her efficiency as a housewife, getting it all done by 8:30. She does the major housecleaning on Saturday, when her husband fishes and her sons are busy with Boy Scouts. ("There's nothing else to do. No bridge games. It's a long day for me.")

" 'I love my home,' she says. . . . The pale gray paint in her L-shaped living and dining room is five years old, but still in perfect condition. . . . The pale peach and yellow and aqua damask upholstery looks spotless after eight years' wear. 'Sometimes, I feel I'm too passive, too content,' remarks Janice, fondly, regarding the wristband of large family diamonds she wears even when the watch itself is being repaired. . . . Her favorite possession is her four-poster spool bed with a pink taffeta canopy. 'I feel just like Queen Elizabeth sleeping in that bed,' she says happily. (Her husband sleeps in another room, since he snores.)

" 'I'm so grateful for my blessings,' she says. 'Wonderful husband, handsome sons with dispositions to match, big comfortable house. . . . I'm thankful for my good health and faith in God and such material possessions as two cars, two TV's and two fireplaces.' "

Staring uneasily at this image, I wonder if a few problems are not somehow better than this smiling empty passivity. If they are happy, these young women who live the feminine mystique, then is this the end of the road? Or are the seeds of something worse than frustration inherent in this image? Is there a growing divergence between this image of woman and human reality?

Consider, as a symptom, the increasing emphasis on glamour in the women's magazines: the housewife wearing eye makeup as she vacuums the floor—"The Honor of Being a Woman." Why does "Occupation: housewife" require such insistent glamorizing year after year? The strained glamour is in itself a question mark: the lady doth protest too much.

The image of woman in another era required increasing prudishness to keep denying sex. This new image seems to require increasing mindlessness, increasing emphasis on things: two cars, two TV's, two fireplaces. Whole pages of women's magazines are filled with gargantuan vegetables: beets, cucumbers, green peppers, potatoes, described like a love affair. The very size of their print is raised until it looks like a first-grade primer. The new *McCall's* frankly assumes women are brainless, fluffy kittens; the *Ladies' Home Journal*, feverishly competing, procures rock-and-roller Pat Boone as a counselor to teenagers; *Redbook* and the others enlarge their own type size. Does the size of the print mean that the new young women, whom all the magazines are courting, have only first-grade minds? Or does it try to hide the triviality of the content? Within the confines of what is now accepted as woman's world, an editor may no longer be able to think of anything big to do except blow up a baked potato, or describe a kitchen as if it were the Hall of Mirrors; he is, after all, forbidden by the mystique to deal with a big idea. But does it not occur to any of the men who run the women's magazines that their troubles may stem from the smallness of the image with which they are truncating women's minds?

They are all in trouble today, the mass-circulation magazines, vying fiercely with each other and television to deliver more and more millions of women who will buy the things their advertisers sell. Does this frantic race force the men who make the images to see women only as thing-buyers? Does it force them to compete finally in emptying women's minds of human thought? The fact is, the troubles of the image-makers seem to be increasing in direct proportion to the increasing mindlessness of their image. During the years in which that image has narrowed woman's world down to the home, cut her role back to housewife, five of the mass-circulation magazines geared to women have ceased publication; others are on the brink.

The growing boredom of women with the empty, narrow image of the women's magazines may be the most hopeful sign of the image's divorce from reality. But there are more violent symptoms on the part of women who are committed to that image. In 1960, the editors of a magazine specifically geared to the happy young housewife—or rather to the new young couples (the wives are not considered separate from their husbands and children)—ran an article asking, "Why Young Mothers Feel Trapped" (*Redbook*, September, 1960). As a promotion stunt, they invited young mothers with such a problem to write in the details, for $500. The editors were shocked to receive 24,000 replies. Can an image of woman be cut down to the point where it becomes itself a trap?

At one of the major women's magazines, a woman editor, sensing that American housewives might be desperately in need of something to enlarge their world, tried for some months to convince her male colleagues to introduce a few ideas outside the home into the magazine. "We decided against it," the man who makes the final decisions said. "Women are so completely divorced from the world of ideas in their lives now, they couldn't take it." Perhaps it is irrelevant to ask, who divorced them? Perhaps these Frankensteins no longer have the power to stop the feminine monster they have created.

I helped create this image. I have watched American women for fifteen years try to conform to it. But I can no longer deny my own knowledge of its terrible implications. It is not a harmless image. There may be no psychological terms for the harm it is doing. But what happens when women try to live according to an image that makes them deny their minds? What happens when women grow up in an image that makes them deny the reality of the changing world?

The material details of life, the daily burden of cooking and cleaning, of taking care of the physical needs of husband and children—these did indeed define a woman's world a century ago when Americans were pioneers, and the American frontier lay in conquering the land. But the women who went west with the wagon trains also shared the pioneering purpose. Now the American frontiers are of the mind, and of the spirit. Love and children and home are good, but they are not the whole world, even if most of the words now written for women pretend they are. Why should women accept this picture of a half-life, instead of a share in the whole of human destiny? Why should women try to make housework "something more," instead of moving on the frontiers of their own time, as American women moved beside their husbands on the old frontiers?

A baked potato is not as big as the world, and vacuuming the living room floor—with or without makeup—is not work that takes enough thought or energy to challenge any woman's full capacity. Women are human beings, not stuffed dolls, not animals. Down through the ages man has known that he was set apart from other animals by his mind's power to have an idea, a vision, and shape the future to it. He shares a need for food and sex with other animals, but when he loves, he loves as a man, and when he discovers and creates and shapes a future different from his past, he is a man, a human being.

This is the real mystery: why did so many American women, with the ability and education to discover and create, go back home again, to look for "something more" in housework and rearing children? For, paradoxically, in the same fifteen years in which the spirited New Woman was replaced by the Happy Housewife, the boundaries of the human world have widened, the pace of world change has quickened, and the very nature of human reality has become increasingly free from biological and material necessity. Does the mystique keep American woman from growing with the world? Does it force her to deny reality, as a woman in a mental hospital must deny reality to believe she is a queen? Does it doom women to be displaced persons, if not virtual schizophrenics, in our complex, changing world?

It is more than a strange paradox that as all professions are finally open to women in America, "career woman" has become a dirty word; that as higher education becomes available to any woman with the capacity for it, education for women has become so suspect that more and more drop out of high school and college to marry and have babies; that as so many roles in modern society become theirs for the taking, women so insistently confine themselves to one role. Why, with the removal of all the legal, political, economic, and educational barriers that once kept woman from being man's equal, a person in her own right, an individual free to develop her own potential, should she accept this new image which insists she is not a person but a "woman," by definition barred from the freedom of human existence and a voice in human destiny?

The feminine mystique is so powerful that women grow up no longer knowing that they have the desires and capacities the mystique forbids. But such a mystique does not fasten itself on a whole nation in a few short years, reversing the trends of a century, without cause. What gives the mystique its power? Why did women go home again?

3 The Crisis in Woman's Identity

 I discovered a strange thing, interviewing women of my own generation over the past ten years. When we were growing up, many of us could not see ourselves beyond the age of twenty-one. We had no image of our own future, of ourselves as women.

I remember the stillness of a spring afternoon on the Smith campus in 1942, when I came to a frightening dead end in my own vision of the future. A few days earlier, I had received a notice that I had won a graduate fellowship. During the congratulations, underneath my excitement, I felt a strange uneasiness; there was a question that I did not want to think about.

"Is this really what I want to be?" The question shut me off, cold and alone, from the girls talking and studying on the sunny hillside behind the college house. I thought I was going to be a psychologist. But if I wasn't sure, what did I want to be? I felt the future closing in—and I could not see myself in it at all. I had no image of myself, stretching beyond college. I had come at seventeen from a Midwestern town, an unsure girl; the wide horizons of the world and the life of the mind had been opened to me. I had begun to know who I was and what I wanted to do. I could not go back now. I could not go home again, to the life of my mother and the women of our town, bound to home, bridge, shopping, children, husband, charity, clothes. But now that the time had come to make my own future, to take the deciding step, I suddenly did not know what I wanted to be.

I took the fellowship, but the next spring, under the alien California sun of another campus, the question came again, and I could not put it out of my mind. I had won another fellowship that would have committed me to research for my doctorate, to a career as professional psychologist. "Is this really what I want to be?" The decision now truly terrified me. I lived in a terror of indecision for days, unable to think of anything else.

The question was not important, I told myself. No question was important to me that year but love. We walked in the Berkeley hills and a boy said: "Nothing can come of this, between us. I'll never win a fellowship like yours." Did I think I would be choosing, irrevocably, the cold loneliness of that afternoon if I went on? I gave up the fellowship, in relief. But for years afterward, I could not read a word of the science that once I had thought of as my future life's work; the reminder of its loss was too painful.

I never could explain, hardly knew myself, why I gave up this career. I lived in the present, working on newspapers with no particular plan. I married, had children, lived according to the feminine mystique as a suburban housewife. But still the question haunted me. I could sense no purpose in my life, I could find no peace, until I finally faced it and worked out my own answer.

I discovered, talking to Smith seniors in 1959, that the question is no less terrifying to girls today. Only they answer it now in a way that my generation found, after half a lifetime, not to be an answer at all. These girls, mostly seniors, were sitting in the living room of the college house, having coffee. It was not too different from such an evening when I was a senior, except that many more of the girls wore rings on their left hands. I asked the ones around me what they planned to be. The engaged ones spoke of weddings, apartments, getting a job as a secretary while husband finished school. The others, after a hostile silence, gave vague answers about this job or that, graduate study, but no one had any real plans. A blonde with a ponytail asked me the next day if I had believed the things they had said. "None of it was true," she told me. "We don't like to be asked what we want to do. None of us know. None of us even like to think about it. The ones who are going to be married right away are the lucky ones. They don't have to think about it."

But I noticed that night that many of the engaged girls, sitting silently around the fire while I asked the others about jobs, had also seemed angry about something. "They don't want to think about not going on," my ponytailed informant said. "They know they're not going to use their education. They'll be wives and mothers. You can say you're going to keep on reading and be interested in the community. But that's not the same. You won't really go on. It's a disappointment to know you're going to stop now, and not go on and use it."

In counterpoint, I heard the words of a woman, fifteen years after she left college, a doctor's wife, mother of three, who said over coffee in her New England kitchen:

The tragedy was, nobody ever looked us in the eye and said you have to decide what you want to do with your life, besides being your husband's wife and children's mother. I never thought it through until I was thirty-six, and my husband was so busy with his practice that he couldn't entertain me every night. The three boys were in school all day. I kept on trying to have babies despite an Rh discrepancy. After two miscarriages, they said I must stop. I thought that my own growth and evolution were over. I always knew as a child that I was going to grow up and go to college, and then get married, and that's as far as a girl has to think. After that, your husband determines and fills your life. It wasn't until I got so lonely as the doctor's wife and kept screaming at the kids because they didn't fill my life that I realized I had to make my own life. I still had to decide what I wanted to be. I hadn't finished evolving at all. But it took me ten years to think it through.

The feminine mystique permits, even encourages, women to ignore the question of their identity. The mystique says they can answer the question "Who am I?" by saying "Tom's wife . . . Mary's mother." But I don't think the mystique would have such power over American women if they did not fear to face this terrifying blank which makes them unable to see themselves after twenty-one. The truth is—and how long it has been true, I'm not sure, but it was true in my generation and it is true of girls growing up today—an American woman no longer has a private image to tell her who she is, or can be, or wants to be.

The public image, in the magazines and television commercials, is designed to sell washing machines, cake mixes, deodorants, detergents, rejuvenating face creams, hair tints. But the power of that image, on which companies spend millions of dollars for television time and ad space, comes from this: American women no longer know who they are. They are sorely in need of a new image to help them find their identity. As the motivational researchers keep telling the advertisers, American women are so unsure of who they should be that they look to this glossy public image to decide every detail of their lives. They look for the image they will no longer take from their mothers.

In my generation, many of us knew that we did not want to be like our mothers, even when we loved them. We could not help but see their disappointment. Did we understand, or only resent, the sadness, the emptiness, that made them hold too fast to us, try to live our lives, run our fathers' lives, spend their days shopping or yearning for things that never seemed to satisfy them, no matter how much money they cost? Strangely, many mothers who loved their daughters—and mine was one—did not want their daughters to grow up like them either. They knew we needed something more.

But even if they urged, insisted, fought to help us educate ourselves, even if they talked with yearning of careers that were not open to them, they could not give us an image of what we could be. They could only tell us that their lives were too empty, tied to home; that children, cooking, clothes, bridge, and charities were not enough. A mother might tell her daughter, spell it out, "Don't be just a housewife like me." But that daughter, sensing that her mother was too frustrated to savor the love of her husband and children, might feel: "I will succeed where my mother failed, I will fulfill myself as a woman," and never read the lesson of her mother's life.

Recently, interviewing high-school girls who had started out full of promise and talent, but suddenly stopped their education, I began to see new dimensions to the problem of feminine conformity. These girls, it seemed at first, were merely following the typical curve of feminine adjustment. Earlier interested in geology or poetry, they now were interested only in being popular; to get boys to like them, they had concluded, it was better to be like all the other girls. On closer examination, I found that these girls were so terrified of becoming like their mothers that they could not see themselves at all. They were afraid to grow up. They had to copy in identical detail the composite image of the popular girl—denying what was best in themselves out of fear of femininity as they saw it in their mothers. One of these girls, seventeen years old, told me:

I want so badly to feel like the other girls. I never get over this feeling of being a neophyte, not initiated. When I get up and have to cross a room, it's like I'm a beginner, or have some terrible affliction, and I'll never learn. I go to the local hangout after school and sit there for hours talking about clothes and hairdos and the twist, and I'm not that interested, so it's an effort. But I found out I could make them like me—just do what they do, dress like them, talk like them, not do things that are different. I guess I even started to make myself not different inside.

I used to write poetry. The guidance office says I have this creative ability and I should be at the top of the class and have a great future. But things like that aren't what you need to be popular. The important thing for a girl is to be popular.

Now I go out with boy after boy, and it's such an effort because I'm not myself with them. It makes you feel even more alone. And besides, I'm afraid of where it's going to lead. Pretty soon, all my differences will be smoothed out, and I'll be the kind of girl that could be a housewife.

I don't want to think of growing up. If I had children, I'd want them to stay the same age. If I had to watch them grow up, I'd see myself growing older, and I wouldn't want to. My mother says she can't sleep at night, she's sick with worry over what I might do. When I was little, she wouldn't let me cross the street alone, long after the other kids did.

I can't see myself as being married and having children. It's as if I wouldn't have any personality myself. My mother's like a rock that's been smoothed by the waves, like a void. She's put so much into her family that there's nothing left, and she resents us because she doesn't get enough in return. But sometimes it seems like there's nothing there. My mother doesn't serve any purpose except cleaning the house. She isn't happy, and she doesn't make my father happy. If she didn't care about us children at all, it would have the same effect as caring too much. It makes you want to do the opposite. I don't think it's really love. When I was little and I ran in all excited to tell her I'd learned how to stand on my head, she was never listening.

Lately, I look into the mirror, and I'm so afraid I'm going to look like my mother. It frightens me, to catch myself being like her in gestures or speech or anything. I'm not like her in so many ways, but if I'm like her in this one way, perhaps I'll turn out like my mother after all. And that terrifies me.

And so the seventeen-year-old was so afraid of being a woman like her mother that she turned her back on all the things in herself and all the opportunities that would have made her a different woman, to copy from the outside the "popular" girls. And finally, in panic at losing herself, she turned her back on her own popularity and defied the conventional good behavior that would have won her a college scholarship. For lack of an image that would help her grow up as a woman true to herself, she retreated into the beatnik vacuum.

Another girl, a college junior from South Carolina told me:

I don't want to be interested in a career I'll have to give up.

My mother wanted to be a newspaper reporter from the time she was twelve, and I've seen her frustration for twenty years. I don't want to be interested in world affairs. I don't want to be interested in anything beside my home and being a wonderful wife and mother. Maybe education is a liability. Even the brightest boys at home want just a sweet, pretty girl. Only sometimes I wonder how it would feel to be able to stretch and stretch and stretch, and learn all you want, and not have to hold yourself back.

Her mother, almost all our mothers, were housewives, though many had started or yearned for or regretted giving up careers. Whatever they told us, we, having eyes and ears and mind and heart, knew that their lives were somehow empty. We did not want to be like them, and yet what other model did we have?

The only other kind of women I knew, growing up, were the old-maid high-school teachers; the librarian; the one woman doctor in our town, who cut her hair like a man; and a few of my college professors. None of these women lived in the warm center of life as I had known it at home. Many had not married or had children. I dreaded being like them, even the ones who taught me truly to respect my own mind and use it, to feel that I had a part in the world. I never knew a woman, when I was growing up, who used her mind, played her own part in the world, and also loved, and had children.

I think that this has been the unknown heart of woman's problem in America for a long time, this lack of a private image. Public images that defy reason and have very little to do with women themselves have had the power to shape too much of their lives. These images would not have such power, if women were not suffering a crisis of identity.

The strange, terrifying jumping-off point that American women reach—at eighteen, twenty-one, twenty-five, forty-one—has been noticed for many years by sociologists, psychologists, analysts, educators. But I think it has not been understood for what it is. It has been called a "discontinuity" in cultural conditioning; it has been called woman's "role crisis." It has been blamed on the education which made American girls grow up feeling free and equal to boys—playing baseball, riding bicycles, conquering geometry and college boards, going away to college, going out in the world to get a job, living alone in an apartment in New York or Chicago or San Francisco, testing and discovering their own powers in the world. All this gave girls the feeling they could be and do whatever they wanted to, with the same freedom as boys, the critics said. It did not prepare them for their role as women. The crisis comes when they are forced to adjust to this role. Today's high rate of emotional distress and breakdown among women in their twenties and thirties is usually attributed to this "role crisis." If girls were educated for their role as women, they would not suffer this crisis, the adjusters say.

But I think they have seen only half the truth.

What if the terror a girl faces at twenty-one, when she must decide who she will be, is simply the terror of growing up—growing up, as women were not permitted to grow before? What if the terror a girl faces at twenty-one is the terror of freedom to decide her own life, with no one to order which path she will take, the freedom and the necessity to take paths women before were not able to take? What if those who choose the path of "feminine adjustment"—evading this terror by marrying at eighteen, losing themselves in having babies and the details of housekeeping—are simply refusing to grow up, to face the question of their own identity?

Mine was the first college generation to run head-on into the new mystique of feminine fulfillment. Before then, while most women did indeed end up as housewives and mothers, the point of education was to discover the life of the mind, to pursue truth and to take a place in the world. There was a sense, already dulling when I went to college, that we would be New Women. Our world would be much larger than home. Forty per cent of my college class at Smith had career plans. But I remember how, even then, some of the seniors, suffering the pangs of that bleak fear of the future, envied the few who escaped it by getting married right away.

The ones we envied then are suffering that terror now at forty. "Never have decided what kind of woman I am. Too much personal life in college. Wish I'd studied more science, history, government, gone deeper into philosophy," one wrote on an alumnae questionnaire, fifteen years later. "Still trying to find the rock to build on. Wish I had finished college. I got married instead." "Wish I'd developed a deeper and more creative life of my own and that I hadn't become engaged and married at nineteen. Having expected the ideal in marriage, including a hundred-per-cent devoted husband, it was a shock to find this isn't the way it is," wrote a mother of six.

Many of the younger generation of wives who marry early have never suffered this lonely terror. They thought they did not have to choose, to look into the future and plan what they wanted to do with their lives. They had only to wait to be chosen, marking time passively until the husband, the babies, the new house decided what the rest of their lives would be. They slid easily into their sexual role as women before they knew who they were themselves. It is these women who suffer most the problem that has no name.

It is my thesis that the core of the problem for women today is not sexual but a problem of identity—a stunting or evasion of growth that is perpetuated by the feminine mystique. It is my thesis that as the Victorian culture did not permit women to accept or gratify their basic sexual needs, our culture does not permit women to accept or gratify their basic need to grow and fulfill their potentialities as human beings, a need which is not solely defined by their sexual role.

Biologists have recently discovered a "youth serum" which, if fed to young caterpillars in the larva state, will keep them from ever maturing into moths; they will live out their lives as caterpillars. The expectations of feminine fulfillment that are fed to women by magazines, television, movies, and books that popularize psychological half-truths, and by parents, teachers and counselors who accept the feminine mystique, operate as a kind of youth serum, keeping most women in the state of sexual larvae, preventing them from achieving the maturity of which they are capable. And there is increasing evidence that woman's failure to grow to complete identity has hampered rather than enriched her sexual fulfillment, virtually doomed her to be castrative to her husband and sons, and caused neuroses, or problems as yet unnamed as neuroses, equal to those caused by sexual repression.

There have been identity crises for man at all the crucial turning points in human history, though those who lived through them did not give them that name. It is only in recent years that the theorists of psychology, sociology and theology have isolated this problem, and given it a name. But it is considered a man's problem. It is defined, for man, as the crisis of growing up, of choosing his identity, "the decision as to what one is and is going to be," in the words of the brilliant psychoanalyst Erik H. Erikson:

I have called the major crisis of adolescence the identity crisis; it occurs in that period of the life cycle when each youth must forge for himself some central perspective and direction, some working unity, out of the effective remnants of his childhood and the hopes of his anticipated adulthood; he must detect some meaningful resemblance between what he has come to see in himself and what his sharpened awareness tells him others judge and expect him to be. . . . In some people, in some classes, at some periods in history, the crisis will be minimal; in other people, classes and periods, the crisis will be clearly marked off as a critical period, a kind of "second birth," apt to be aggravated either by widespread neuroticisms or by pervasive ideological unrest.[1]

In this sense, the identity crisis of one man's life may reflect, or set off, a rebirth, or new stage, in the growing up of mankind. "In some periods of his history, and in some phases of his life cycle, man needs a new ideological orientation as surely and sorely as he must have air and food," said Erikson, focusing new light on the crisis of the young Martin Luther, who left a Catholic monastery at the end of the Middle Ages to forge a new identity for himself and Western man.

The search for identity is not new, however, in American thought—though in every generation, each man who writes about it discovers it anew. In America, from the beginning, it has somehow been understood that men must thrust into the future; the pace has always been too rapid for man's identity to stand still. In every generation, many men have suffered misery, unhappiness, and uncertainty because they could not take the image of the man they wanted to be from their fathers. The search for identity of the young man who can't go home again has always been a major theme of American writers. And it has always been considered right in America, good, for men to suffer these agonies of growth, to search for and find their own identities. The farm boy went to the city, the garment-maker's son became a doctor, Abraham Lincoln taught himself to read—these were more than rags-to-riches stories. They were an integral part of the American dream. The problem for many was money, race, color, class, which barred them from choice—not what they would be if they were free to choose.

Even today a young man learns soon enough that he must decide who he wants to be. If he does not decide in junior high, in high school, in college, he must somehow come to terms with it by twenty-five or thirty, or he is lost. But this search for identity is seen as a greater problem now because more and more boys cannot find images in our culture—from their fathers or other men —to help them in their search. The old frontiers have been conquered, and the boundaries of the new are not so clearly marked. More and more young men in America today suffer an identity crisis for want of any image of man worth pursuing, for want of a purpose that truly realizes their human abilities.

But why have theorists not recognized this same identity crisis in women? In terms of the old conventions and the new feminine mystique women are not expected to grow up to find out who they are, to choose their human identity. Anatomy is woman's destiny, say the theorists of femininity; the identity of woman is determined by her biology.

But is it? More and more women are asking themselves this question. As if they were waking from a coma, they ask, "Where am I . . . what am I doing here?" For the first time in their history, women are becoming aware of an identity crisis in their own lives, a crisis which began many generations ago, has grown worse with each succeeding generation, and will not end until they, or their daughters, turn an unknown corner and make of themselves and their lives the new image that so many women now so desperately need.

In a sense that goes beyond any one woman's life, I think this is the crisis of women growing up—a turning point from an immaturity that has been called femininity to full human identity. I think women had to suffer this crisis of identity, which began a hundred years ago, and have to suffer it still today, simply to become fully human.

4 The Passionate Journey

 It was the need for a new identity that started women, a century ago, on that passionate journey, that vilified, misinterpreted journey away from home.

It has been popular in recent years to laugh at feminism as one of history's dirty jokes: to pity, sniggering, those old-fashioned feminists who fought for women's rights to higher education, careers, the vote. They were neurotic victims of penis envy who wanted to be men, it is said now. In battling for women's freedom to participate in the major work and decisions of society as the equals of men, they denied their very nature as women, which fulfills itself only through sexual passivity, acceptance of male domination, and nurturing motherhood.

But if I am not mistaken, it is this first journey which holds the clue to much that has happened to women since. It is one of the strange blind spots of contemporary psychology not to recognize the reality of the passion that moved these women to leave home in search of new identity, or, staying home, to yearn bitterly for something more. Theirs was an act of rebellion, a violent denial of the identity of women as it was then defined. It was the need for a new identity that led those passionate feminists to forge new trails for women. Some of those trails were unexpectedly rough, some were dead ends, and some may have been false, but the need for women to find new trails was real.

The problem of identity was new for women then, truly new.
The feminists were pioneering on the front edge of woman's
evolution. They had to prove that women were human. They
had to shatter, violently if necessary, the decorative Dresden
figurine that represented the ideal woman of the last century.
They had to prove that woman was not a passive, empty mirror,
not a frilly, useless decoration, not a mindless animal, not a thing
to be disposed of by others, incapable of a voice in her own
existence, before they could even begin to fight for the rights
women needed to become the human equals of men.

Changeless woman, childish woman, a woman's place is in the
home, they were told. But man was changing; his place was in
the world and his world was widening. Woman was being left
behind. Anatomy was her destiny; she might die giving birth to
one baby, or live to be thirty-five, giving birth to twelve, while
man controlled his destiny with that part of his anatomy which
no other animal had: his mind.

Women also had minds. They also had the human need to
grow. But the work that fed life and moved it forward was no
longer done at home, and women were not trained to understand
and work in the world. Confined to the home, a child among her
children, passive, no part of her existence under her own control,
a woman could only exist by pleasing man. She was wholly dependent on his protection in a world that she had no share in
making: man's world. She could never grow up to ask the simple
human question, "Who am I? What do I want?"

Even if man loved her as a child, a doll, a decoration; even if
he gave her rubies, satin, velvets; even if she was warm in her
house, safe with her children, would she not yearn for something
more? She was, at that time, so completely defined as object by
man, never herself as subject, "I," that she was not even expected
to enjoy or participate in the act of sex. "He took his pleasure
with her . . . he had his way with her," as the sayings went.
Is it so hard to understand that emancipation, the right to full
humanity, was important enough to generations of women, still
alive or only recently dead, that some fought with their fists, and
went to jail and even died for it? And for the right to human

growth, some women denied their own sex, the desire to love
and be loved by a man, and to bear children.

It is a strangely unquestioned perversion of history that the
passion and fire of the feminist movement came from man-hating,
embittered, sex-starved spinsters, from castrating, unsexed non-
women who burned with such envy for the male organ that they
wanted to take it away from all men, or destroy them, demanding rights only because they lacked the power to love as women.
Mary Wollstonecraft, Angelina Grimké, Ernestine Rose, Margaret Fuller, Elizabeth Cady Stanton, Julia Ward Howe, Margaret Sanger all loved, were loved, and married; many seem to
have been as passionate in their relations with lover and husband,
in an age when passion in woman was as forbidden as intelligence,
as they were in their battle for woman's chance to grow to full
human stature. But if they, and those like Susan Anthony, whom
fortune or bitter experience turned away from marriage, fought
for a chance for woman to fulfill herself, not in relation to man,
but as an individual, it was from a need as real and burning as
the need for love. ("What woman needs," said Margaret Fuller,
"is not as a woman to act or rule, but as a nature to grow, as
an intellect to discern, as a soul to live freely, and unimpeded to
unfold such powers as were given her.")

The feminists had only one model, one image, one vision, of
a full and free human being: man. For until very recently, only
men (though not all men) had the freedom and the education
necessary to realize their full abilities, to pioneer and create and
discover, and map new trails for future generations. Only men
had the vote: the freedom to shape the major decisions of society.
Only men had the freedom to love, and enjoy love, and decide
for themselves in the eyes of their God the problems of right
and wrong. Did women want these freedoms because they wanted
to be men? Or did they want them because they also were human?

That this is what feminism was all about was seen symbolically
by Henrik Ibsen. When he said in the play "A Doll's House," in
1879, that a woman was simply a human being, he struck a new
note in literature. Thousands of women in middle-class Europe
and America, in that Victorian time, saw themselves in Nora.

And in 1960, almost a century later, millions of American housewives, who watched the play on television, also saw themselves
as they heard Nora say:

> You have always been so kind to me. But our home has been nothing
> but a playroom. I have been your doll wife, just as at home I was
> Papa's doll child; and here the children have been my dolls. I thought
> it great fun when you played with me, just as they thought it fun when
> I played with them. That is what our marriage has been, Torvald . . .
> How am I fitted to bring up the children? . . . There is another
> task I must undertake first. I must try and educate myself—you are
> not the man to help me in that. I must do that for myself. And that is
> why I am going to leave you now . . . I must stand quite alone if I
> am to understand myself and everything about me. It is for that reason
> that I cannot remain with you any longer . . .

Her shocked husband reminds Nora that woman's "most sacred
duties" are her duties to her husband and children. "Before all
else, you are a wife and mother," he says. And Nora answers:

> I believe that before all else I am a reasonable human being, just
> as you are—or, at all events, that I must try and become one. I know
> quite well, Torvald, that most people would think you right, and
> that views of that kind are to be found in books; but I can no longer
> content myself with what most people say or with what is found in
> books. I must think over things for myself and get to understand
> them . . .

It is a cliché of our own time that women spent half a century
fighting for "rights," and the next half wondering whether they
wanted them after all. "Rights" have a dull sound to people who
have grown up after they have been won. But like Nora, the
feminists had to win those rights before they could begin to live
and love as human beings. Not very many women then, or even
now, dared to leave the only security they knew—dared to turn
their backs on their homes and husbands to begin Nora's search.
But a great many, then as now, must have found their existence
as housewives so empty that they could no longer savor the love
of husband and children.

Some of them—and even a few men who realized that half the

human race was denied the right to become fully human—set out to change the conditions that held women in bondage. Those conditions were summed up by the first Woman's Rights Convention in Seneca Falls, New York, in 1848, as woman's grievances against man:

He has compelled her to submit to laws in the formation of which she has no voice. . . . He has made her, if married, in the eyes of the law, civilly dead. He has taken from her all right to property, even to the wages she earns . . . In the covenant of marriage, she is compelled to promise obedience to her husband, he becoming to all intents and purposes her master—the law giving him power to deprive her of her liberty, and to administer chastisement. . . . He closes against her all the avenues of wealth and distinction which he considers most honorable to himself. As a teacher of theology, medicine or law, she is not known. He has denied her the facilities for obtaining a thorough education, all colleges being closed against her. . . . He has created a false public sentiment by giving to the world a different code of morals for men and women by which moral delinquencies which exclude women from society are not only tolerated, but deemed of little account to man. He has usurped the prerogative of Jehovah himself, claiming it as his right to assign for her a sphere of action, when that belongs to her conscience and to her God. He has endeavored in every way that he could to destroy her confidence in her own powers, to lessen her self-respect, and to make her willing to lead a dependent and abject life.

It was these conditions, which the feminists set out to abolish a century ago, that made women what they were—"feminine," as it was then, and is still, defined.

It is hardly a coincidence that the struggle to free woman began in America on the heels of the Revolutionary War, and grew strong with the movement to free the slaves.[1] Thomas Paine, the spokesman for the Revolution, was among the first to condemn in 1775 the position of women "even in countries where they may be esteemed the most happy, constrained in their desires in the disposal of their goods, robbed of freedom and will by the laws, the slaves of opinion . . ." During the Revolution, some ten years before Mary Wollstonecraft spearheaded the feminist movement in England, an American woman, Judith Sargent Murray, said woman needed knowledge to envision new goals and grow by reaching for them. In 1837, the year Mount Holyoke opened its doors to give women their first chance at education equal to man's, American women were also holding their first national anti-slavery convention in New York. The women who formally launched the women's rights movement at Seneca Falls met each other when they were refused seats at an anti-slavery convention in London. Shut off behind a curtain in the gallery, Elizabeth Stanton, on her honeymoon, and Lucretia Mott, demure mother of five, decided that it was not only the slaves who needed to be liberated.

Whenever, wherever in the world there has been an upsurge of human freedom, women have won a share of it for themselves. Sex did not fight the French Revolution, free the slaves in America, overthrow the Russian Czar, drive the British out of India; but when the idea of human freedom moves the minds of men, it also moves the minds of women. The cadences of the Seneca Falls Declaration came straight from the Declaration of Independence:

When, in the course of human events, it becomes necessary for one portion of the family of man to assume among the people of the earth a position different from that they have hitherto occupied. . . . We hold these truths to be self-evident: that all men and women are created equal.

Feminism was not a dirty joke. The feminist revolution had to be fought because women quite simply were stopped at a stage of evolution far short of their human capacity. "The domestic function of woman does not exhaust her powers," the Rev. Theodore Parker preached in Boston in 1853. "To make one half the human race consume its energies in the functions of housekeeper, wife and mother is a monstrous waste of the most precious material God ever made." And running like a bright and sometimes dangerous thread through the history of the feminist movement was also the idea that equality for woman was necessary to free both man and woman for true sexual fulfillment.[2] For the degradation of woman also degraded marriage, love, all relations between man and woman. After the sexual revolution, said Robert Dale Owen, "then will the monopoly of sex perish with other unjust monopolies; and women will not be restricted to one virtue, and one passion, and one occupation." [3]

The women and men who started that revolution anticipated "no small amount of misconception, misrepresentation and ridicule." And they got it. The first to speak out in public for women's rights in America—Fanny Wright, daughter of a Scotch nobleman, and Ernestine Rose, daughter of a rabbi—were called respectively, "red harlot of infidelity" and "woman a thousand times below a prostitute." The declaration at Seneca Falls brought such an outcry of "Revolution," "Insurrection Among Women," "The Reign of Petticoats," "Blasphemy," from newspapers and clergymen that the faint-hearted withdrew their signatures. Lurid reports of "free love" and "legalized adultery" competed with phantasies of court sessions, church sermons and surgical operations interrupted while a lady lawyer or minister or doctor hastily presented her husband with a baby.

At every step of the way, the feminists had to fight the conception that they were violating the God-given nature of woman. Clergymen interrupted women's-rights conventions, waving Bibles and quoting from the Scriptures: "Saint Paul said . . . and the head of every woman is man" . . . "Let your women be silent in the churches, for it is not permitted unto them to speak" . . . "And if they will learn anything, let them ask their husbands at home; for it is a shame for women to speak in the church" . . . "But I suffer not a woman to teach, nor to usurp authority over the man, but to be in silence; for Adam was first formed, then Eve" . . . "Saint Peter said: likewise, ye wives, be in subjection to your own husbands" . . .

To give women equal rights would destroy that "milder gentler nature, which not only makes them shrink from, but disqualifies them for the turmoil and battle of public life," a Senator from New Jersey intoned piously in 1866. "They have a higher and a holier mission. It is in retiracy to make the character of coming men. Their mission is at home, by their blandishments, and their love, to assuage the passions of men as they come in from the battle of life, and not themselves by joining in the contest to add fuel to the very flames."

"They do not appear to be satisfied with having unsexed themselves, but they desire to unsex every female in the land," said a New York assemblyman who opposed one of the first petitions for a married woman's right to property and earnings. Since "God created man as the representative of the race," then "took from his side the material for woman's creation" and returned her to his side in matrimony as "one flesh, one being," the assembly smugly denied the petition: "A higher power than that from which emanates legislative enactments has given forth the mandate that man and woman shall not be equal." [4]

The myth that these women were "unnatural monsters" was based on the belief that to destroy the God-given subservience of women would destroy the home and make slaves of men. Such myths arise in every kind of revolution that advances a new portion of the family of man to equality. The image of the feminists as inhuman, fiery man-eaters, whether expressed as an offense against God or in the modern terms of sexual perversion, is not unlike the stereotype of the Negro as a primitive animal or the union member as an anarchist. What the sexual terminology hides is the fact that the feminist movement was a revolution. There were excesses, of course, as in any revolution, but the excesses of the feminists were in themselves a demonstration of the revolution's necessity. They stemmed from, and were a passionate repudiation of, the degrading realities of woman's life, the helpless subservience behind the gentle decorum that made women objects of such thinly veiled contempt to men that they even felt contempt for themselves. Evidently, that contempt and self-contempt were harder to get rid of than the conditions which caused them.

Of course they envied man. Some of the early feminists cut their hair short and wore bloomers, and tried to be like men. From the lives they saw their mothers lead, from their own experience, those passionate women had good reason to reject the conventional image of woman. Some even rejected marriage and motherhood for themselves. But in turning their backs on the old feminine image, in fighting to free themselves and all women, some of them became a different kind of woman. They became complete human beings.

The name of Lucy Stone today brings to mind a man-eating fury, wearing pants, brandishing an umbrella. It took a long time for the man who loved her to persuade her to marry him, and though she loved him and kept his love throughout her long life, she never took his name. When she was born, her gentle mother cried: "Oh, dear! I am sorry it is a girl. A woman's life is so hard." A few hours before the baby came, this mother, on a farm in western Massachusetts in 1818, milked eight cows because a sudden thunderstorm had called all hands into the field: it was more important to save the hay crop than to safeguard a mother on the verge of childbirth. Though this gentle, tired mother carried the endless work of farmhouse and bore nine children, Lucy Stone grew up with the knowledge that "There was only one will in our house, and that was my father's."

She rebelled at being born a girl if that meant being as lowly as the Bible said, as her mother said. She rebelled when she raised her hand at church meeting and, time and again, it was not counted. At a church sewing circle, where she was making a shirt to help a young man through theological seminary, she heard Mary Lyon talk of education for women. She left the shirt unfinished, and at sixteen started teaching school for $1 a week, saving her earnings for nine years, until she had enough to go to college herself. She wanted to train herself "to plead not only for the slave, but for suffering humanity everywhere. Especially do I mean to labor for the elevation of my own sex." But at Oberlin, where she was one of the first women to graduate from the "regular course," she had to practice public speaking secretly in the woods. Even at Oberlin, the girls were forbidden to speak in public.

Washing the men's clothes, caring for their rooms, serving them at table, listening to their orations, but themselves remaining respectfully silent in public assemblages, the Oberlin "co-eds" were being prepared for intelligent motherhood and a properly subservient wifehood.[5]

In appearance, Lucy Stone was a little woman, with a gentle, silvery voice which could quiet a violent mob. She lectured on abolition Saturdays and Sundays, as an agent for the Anti-Slavery Society, and for women's rights the rest of the week on her own —facing down and winning over men who threatened her with clubs, threw prayer books and eggs at her head, and once in mid-winter shoved a hose through a window and turned icy water on her.

In one town, the usual report was circulated that a big, masculine woman, wearing boots, smoking a cigar, swearing like a trooper, had arrived to lecture. The ladies who came to hear this freak expressed their amazement to find Lucy Stone, small and dainty, dressed in a black satin gown with a white lace frill at the neck, "a prototype of womanly grace . . . fresh and fair as the morning." [6]

Her voice so rankled pro-slavery forces that the *Boston Post* published a rude poem promising "fame's loud trumpet shall be blown" for the man who "with a wedding kiss shuts up the mouth of Lucy Stone." Lucy Stone felt that "marriage is to a woman a state of slavery." Even after Henry Blackwell had pursued her from Cincinnati to Massachusetts ("She was born locomotive," he complained), and vowed to "repudiate the supremacy of either woman or man in marriage," and wrote her: "I met you at Niagara and sat at your feet by the whirlpool looking down into the dark waters with a passionate and unshared and unsatisfied yearning in my heart that you will never know, nor understand," and made a public speech in favor of women's rights; even after she admitted that she loved him, and wrote "You can scarcely tell me anything I do not know about the emptiness of a single life," she suffered blinding migraine headaches over the decision to marry him.

At their wedding, the minister Thomas Higginson reported that "the heroic Lucy cried like any village bride." The minister also said: "I never perform the marriage ceremony without a renewed sense of the iniquity of a system by which man and wife are one, and that one is the husband." And he sent to the newspapers, for other couples to copy, the pact which Lucy Stone and Henry Blackwell joined hands to make, before their wedding vows:

> While we acknowledge our mutual affection by publicly assuming the relationship of husband and wife . . . we deem it a duty to declare that this act on our part implies no sanction of, nor promise of voluntary obedience to such of the present laws of marriage as refuse to recognize the wife as an independent, rational being, while they confer upon the husband an injurious and unnatural superiority.[7]

Lucy Stone, her friend, the pretty Reverend Antoinette Brown, (who later married Henry's brother), Margaret Fuller, Angelina Grimké, Abbey Kelley Foster—all resisted early marriage, and did not, in fact, marry until in their battle against slavery and for women's rights they had begun to find an identity as women unknown to their mothers. Some, like Susan Anthony and Elizabeth Blackwell, never married; Lucy Stone kept her own name in more than symbolic fear that to become a wife was to die as a person. The concept known as "femme couverte" (covered woman), written into the law, suspended the "very being or legal existence of a woman" upon marriage. "To a married woman, her new self is her superior, her companion, her master."

If it is true that the feminists were "disappointed women," as their enemies said even then, it was because almost all women living under such conditions had reason to be disappointed. In one of the most moving speeches of her life, Lucy Stone said in 1855:

> From the first years to which my memory stretches, I have been a disappointed woman. When, with my brothers, I reached forth after sources of knowledge, I was reproved with "It isn't fit for you; it doesn't belong to women" . . . In education, in marriage, in religion, in everything, disappointment is the lot of woman. It shall be the business of my life to deepen this disappointment in every woman's heart until she bows down to it no longer.[8]

In her own lifetime, Lucy Stone saw the laws of almost every state radically changed in regard to women, high schools opened

to them and two-thirds of the colleges in the United States. Her
husband and her daughter, Alice Stone Blackwell, devoted their
lives, after her death in 1893, to the unfinished battle for woman's
vote. By the end of her passionate journey, she could say she was
glad to have been born a woman. She wrote her daughter the day
before her seventieth birthday:

I trust my Mother sees and knows how glad I am to have been
born, and at a time when there was so much that needed help at which
I could lend a hand. Dear Old Mother! She had a hard life, and was
sorry she had another girl to share and bear the hard life of a woman.
. . . But I am wholly glad that I came.[9]

In certain men, at certain times in history, the passion for freedom has been as strong or stronger than the familiar passions of
sexual love. That this was so, for many of those women who
fought to free women, seems to be a fact, no matter how the
strength of that other passion is explained. Despite the frowns
and jeers of most of their husbands and fathers, despite the hostility if not outright abuse they got for their "unwomanly" behavior, the feminists continued their crusade. They themselves
were tortured by soul-searching doubts every step of the way.
It was unladylike, friends wrote Mary Lyon, to travel all over
New England with a green velvet bag, collecting money to start
her college for women. "What do I do that is wrong?" she asked.
"I ride in the stage-coach or cars without an escort. . . . My
heart is sick, my soul is pained with this empty gentility, this
genteel nothingness. I am doing a great work, I cannot come
down."

The lovely Angelina Grimké felt as if she would faint, when
she accepted what was meant as a joke and appeared to speak
before the Massachusetts legislature on the anti-slavery petitions,
the first woman ever to appear before a legislative body. A pastoral letter denounced her unwomanly behavior:

We invite your attention to the dangers which at present seem to
threaten the female character with widespread and permanent injury.
. . . The power of woman is her dependence, flowing from the consciousness of that weakness which God has given her for her pro-

tection. . . . But when she assumes the place and tone of man as a
public reformer . . . her character becomes unnatural. If the vine,
whose strength and beauty is to lean on the trellis-work and half conceal its cluster, thinks to assume the independence and overshadowing
nature of the elm, it will not only cease to bear fruit, but fall in shame
and dishonor in the dust.[10]

More than restlessness and frustration made her refuse to be
"shamed into silence," and made New England housewives walk
two, four, six, and eight miles on winter evenings to hear her.

The emotional identification of American women with the battle to free the slaves may or may not testify to the unconscious
foment of their own rebellion. But it is an undeniable fact that,
in organizing, petitioning, and speaking out to free the slaves,
American women learned how to free themselves. In the South,
where slavery kept women at home, and where they did not get
a taste of education or pioneering work or the schooling battles
of society, the old image of femininity reigned intact, and there
were few feminists. In the North, women who took part in the
Underground Railroad, or otherwise worked to free the slaves,
never were the same again. Feminism also went west with the
wagon trains, where the frontier made women almost equal from
the beginning. (Wyoming was the first state to give women the
vote.) Individually, the feminists seem to have had no more nor
less reason than all women of their time to envy or hate man.
But what they did have was self-respect, courage, strength.
Whether they loved or hated man, escaped or suffered humilia-
tion from men in their own lives, they identified with women.
Women who accepted the conditions which degraded them felt
contempt for themselves and all women. The feminists who fought
those conditions freed themselves of that contempt and had less
reason to envy man.

The call to that first Woman's Rights Convention came about
because an educated woman, who had already participated in
shaping society as an abolitionist, came face to face with the
realities of a housewife's drudgery and isolation in a small town.
Like the college graduate with six children in the suburb of today, Elizabeth Cady Stanton, moved by her husband to the small

town of Seneca Falls, was restless in a life of baking, cooking, sewing, washing and caring for each baby. Her husband, an abolitionist leader, was often away on business. She wrote:

> I now understood the practical difficulties most women had to contend with in the isolated household and the impossibility of woman's best development if in contact the chief part of her life with servants and children. . . . The general discontent I felt with woman's portion . . . and the wearied, anxious look of the majority of women, impressed me with the strong feeling that some active measures should be taken. . . . I could not see what to do or where to begin—my only thought was a public meeting for protest and discussion.[11]

She put only one notice in the newspapers, and housewives and daughters who had never known any other kind of life came in wagons from a radius of fifty miles to hear her speak.

However dissimilar their social or psychological roots, all who led the battle for women's rights, early and late, also shared more than common intelligence, fed by more than common education for their time. Otherwise, whatever their emotions, they would not have been able to see through the prejudices which had justified woman's degradation, and to put their dissenting voice into words. Mary Wollstonecraft educated herself and was then educated by that company of English philosophers then preaching the rights of man. Margaret Fuller was taught by her father to read the classics of six languages, and was caught up in the transcendentalist group around Emerson. Elizabeth Cady Stanton's father, a judge, got his daughter the best education then available, and supplemented it by letting her listen to his law cases. Ernestine Rose, the rabbi's daughter who rebelled against her religion's doctrine that decreed woman's inferiority to man, got her education in "free thinking" from the great utopian philosopher Robert Owen. She also defied orthodox religious custom to marry a man she loved. She always insisted, in the bitterest days of the fight for women's rights, that woman's enemy was not man. "We do not fight with man himself, but only with bad principles."

These women were not man-eaters. Julia Ward Howe, brilliant and beautiful daughter of the New York "400" who studied intensively every field that interested her, wrote the "Battle Hymn of the Republic" anonymously, because her husband believed her life should be devoted to him and their six children. She took no part in the suffrage movement until 1868, when she met Lucy Stone, who "had long been the object of one of my imaginary dislikes. As I looked into her sweet, womanly face and heard her earnest voice, I felt that the object of my distaste had been a mere phantom, conjured up by silly and senseless misrepresentations. . . . I could only say, 'I am with you.' " [12]

The irony of that man-eating myth is that the so-called excesses of the feminists arose from their helplessness. When women are considered to have no rights nor to deserve any, what can they do for themselves? At first, it seemed there was nothing they could do but talk. They held women's rights conventions every year after 1848, in small towns and large, national and state conventions, over and over again—in Ohio, Pennsylvania, Indiana, Massachusetts. They could talk till doomsday about the rights they did not have. But how do women get legislators to let them keep their own earnings, or their own children after divorce, when they do not even have a vote? How can they finance or organize a campaign to get the vote when they have no money of their own, nor even the right to own property?

The very sensitivity to opinion which such complete dependence breeds in women made every step out of their genteel prison a painful one. Even when they tried to change conditions that were within their power to change, they met ridicule. The fantastically uncomfortable dress "ladies" wore then was a symbol of their bondage: stays so tightly laced they could hardly breathe, half a dozen skirts and petticoats, weighing ten to twelve pounds, so long they swept up refuse from the street. The specter of the feminists taking the pants off men came partly from the "Bloomer" dress—a tunic, knee-length skirt, ankle length pantaloons. Elizabeth Stanton wore it, eagerly at first, to do her housework in comfort, as a young woman today might wear shorts or slacks. But when the feminists wore the Bloomer dress in public, as a symbol of their emancipation, the rude jokes, from newspaper editors, street corner loafers, and small boys, were unbearable to their feminine sensitivities. "We put the dress on for greater free-

dom, but what is physical freedom compared to mental bondage,"
said Elizabeth Stanton and discarded her "Bloomer" dress. Most,
like Lucy Stone, stopped wearing it for a feminine reason: it was
not very becoming, except to the extremely tiny, pretty Mrs.
Bloomer herself.

Still, that helpless gentility had to be overcome, in the minds of
men, in the minds of other women, in their own minds. When
they decided to petition for married women's rights to own property, half the time even the women slammed doors in their faces
with the smug remark that they had husbands, they needed no
laws to protect them. When Susan Anthony and her women cap-
tains collected 6,000 signatures in ten weeks, the New York State
Assembly received them with roars of laughter. In mockery, the
Assembly recommended that since ladies always get the "choicest
tidbits" at the table, the best seat in the carriage, and their choice
of which side of the bed to lie on, "if there is any inequity or op-
pression the gentlemen are the sufferers." However, they would
waive "redress" except where both husband and wife had signed
the petition. "In such case, they would recommend the parties to
apply for a law authorizing them to change dresses, that the husband may wear the petticoats and the wife the breeches."

The wonder is that the feminists were able to win anything at
all—that they were not embittered shrews but increasingly zestful
women who knew they were making history. There is more spirit
than bitterness in Elizabeth Stanton, having babies into her forties,
writing Susan Anthony that this one truly will be her last, and the
fun is just beginning—"Courage, Susan, we will not reach our
prime until we're fifty." Painfully insecure and self-conscious
about her looks—not because of treatment by men (she had
suitors) but because of a beautiful older sister and mother who
treated a crossed eye as a tragedy—Susan Anthony, of all the
nineteenth-century feminist leaders, was the only one resembling
the myth. She felt betrayed when the others started to marry and
have babies. But despite the chip on her shoulder, she was no bitter
spinster with a cat. Traveling alone from town to town, hammer-
ing up her meeting notices, using her abilities to the fullest as
organizer and lobbyist and lecturer, she made her own way in a

larger and larger world.

In their own lifetime, such women changed the feminine image that had justified woman's degradation. At a meeting while men jeered at trusting the vote to women so helpless that they had to be lifted over mud puddles and handed into carriages, a proud feminist named Sojourner Truth raised her black arm:

Look at my arm! I have ploughed and planted and gathered into barns . . . and ain't I a woman? I could work as much and eat as much as a man—when I could get it—and bear the lash as well . . . I have borne thirteen children and seen most of 'em sold into slavery, and when I cried out with my mother's grief, none but Jesus helped me—and ain't I a woman?

That image of empty gentility was also undermined by the growing thousands of women who worked in the red brick factories: the Lowell mill girls who fought the terrible working conditions which, partly as a result of women's supposed inferiority, were even worse for them than for men. But those women, who after a twelve- or thirteen-hour day in the factory still had household duties, could not take the lead in the passionate journey. Most of the leading feminists were women of the middle class, driven by a complex of motives to educate themselves and smash that empty image.

What drove them on? "Must let out my pent-up energy in some new way," wrote Louisa May Alcott in her journal when she decided to volunteer as a nurse in the Civil War. "A most interesting journey, into a new world, full of stirring sights and sounds, new adventures, and an ever-growing sense of the great task I had undertaken. I said my prayers as I went rushing through the country, white with tents, all alive with patriotism, and already red with blood. A solemn time, but I'm glad to live in it."

What drove them on? Lonely and racked with self-doubt, Elizabeth Blackwell, in that unheard-of, monstrous determination to be a woman doctor, ignored sniggers—and tentative passes—to do her anatomical dissections. She battled for the right to witness the dissection of the reproductive organs, but decided against walking in the commencement procession because it would be unladylike. Shunned even by her fellow physicians, she wrote:

I am woman as well as physician . . . I understand now why this life has never been lived before. It is hard, with no support but a high purpose, to live against every species of social opposition . . . I should like a little fun now and then. Life is altogether too sober.[13]

In the course of a century of struggle, reality gave the lie to the myth that woman would use her rights for vengeful domination of man. As they won the right to equal education, the right to speak out in public and own property, and the right to work at job or profession and control their own earnings, the feminists felt less reason to be bitter against man. But there was one more battle to be fought. As M. Carey Thomas, the brilliant first president of Bryn Mawr, said in 1908:

Women are one-half the world, but until a century ago . . . women lived a twilight life, a half life apart, and looked out and saw men as shadows walking. It was a man's world. The laws were men's laws, the government a man's government, the country a man's country. Now women have won the right to higher education and economic independence. The right to become citizens of the state is the next and inevitable consequence of education and work outside the home. We have gone so far; we must go farther. We cannot go back.[14]

The trouble was, the women's rights movement had become almost too respectable; yet without the right to vote, women could not get any political party to take them seriously. When Elizabeth Stanton's daughter, Harriet Blatch, came home in 1907, the widow of an Englishman, she found the movement in which her mother had raised her in a sterile rut of tea and cookies. She had seen the tactics women used in England to dramatize the issue in a similar stalemate: heckling speakers at public meetings, deliberate provocation of the police, hunger strikes in jail—the kind of dramatic nonviolent resistance Ghandi used in India, or that the Freedom Riders now use in the United States when legal tactics leave segregation intact. The American feminists never had to resort to the extremes of their longer-sinned-against English counterparts. But they did dramatize the vote issue until they aroused an opposition far more powerful than the sexual one.
As the battle to free women was fired by the battle to free the

slaves in the nineteenth century, it was fired in the twentieth by the battles of social reform, of Jane Addams and Hull House, the rise of the union movement, and the great strikes against intolerable working conditions in the factories. For the Triangle Shirtwaist girls, working for as little as $6 a week, as late as 10 o'clock at night, fined for talking, laughing, or singing, equality was a question of more than education or the vote. They held out on picket lines through bitter cold and hungry months; dozens were clubbed by police and dragged off in Black Marias. The new feminists raised money for the strikers' bail and food, as their mothers had helped the Underground Railroad.

Behind the cries of "save femininity," "save the home," could now be glimpsed the influence of political machines, quailing at the very thought of what those reforming women would do if they got the vote. Women, after all, were trying to shut down the saloons. Brewers as well as other business interests, especially those that depended on underpaid labor of children and women, openly lobbied against the woman's suffrage amendment in Washington. "Machine men were plainly uncertain of their ability to control an addition to the electorate which seemed to them relatively unsusceptible to bribery, more militant and bent on disturbing reforms ranging from sewage control to the abolition of child labor and worst of all, 'cleaning up' politics." [15] And Southern congressmen pointed out that suffrage for women also meant Negro women.

The final battle for the vote was fought in the twentieth century by the growing numbers of college-trained women, led by Carrie Chapman Catt, daughter of the Iowa prairie, educated at Iowa State, a teacher and a newspaperwoman, whose husband, a successful engineer, firmly supported her battles. One group that later called itself the Woman's Party made continual headlines with picket lines around the White House. After the outbreak of World War I, there was much hysteria about women who chained themselves to the White House fence. Maltreated by police and courts, they went on hunger strikes in jail and were finally martyred by forced feeding. Many of these women were Quakers and pacifists; but the majority of the feminists supported the war even as they continued their campaign for women's rights. They are hardly accountable for the myth of the man-eating feminist which is prevalent today, a myth that has cropped up continuously from the days of Lucy Stone to the present, whenever anyone has reason to oppose women's move out of the home.

In this final battle, American women over a period of fifty years conducted 56 campaigns of referenda to male voters; 480 campaigns to get legislatures to submit suffrage amendments to voters; 277 campaigns to get state party conventions to include woman's suffrage planks; 30 campaigns to get presidential party conventions to adopt woman's suffrage planks, and 19 campaigns with 19 successive Congresses.[16] Someone had to organize all those parades, speeches, petitions, meetings, lobbying of legislators and Congressmen. The new feminists were no longer a handful of devoted women; thousands, millions of American women with husbands, children, and homes gave as much time as they could spare to the cause. The unpleasant image of the feminists today resembles less the feminists themselves than the image fostered by the interests who so bitterly opposed the vote for women in state after state, lobbying, threatening legislators with business or political ruin, buying votes, even stealing them, until, and even after, 36 states had ratified the amendment.

The ones who fought that battle won more than empty paper rights. They cast off the shadow of contempt and self-contempt that had degraded women for centuries. The joy, the sense of excitement and the personal rewards of that battle are described beautifully by Ida Alexa Ross Wylie, an English feminist:

To my astonishment, I found that women, in spite of knock-knees and the fact that for centuries a respectable woman's leg had not even been mentionable, could at a pinch outrun the average London bobby. Their aim with a little practice became good enough to land ripe vegetables in ministerial eyes, their wits sharp enough to keep Scotland Yard running around in circles and looking very silly. Their capacity for impromptu organization, for secrecy and loyalty, their iconoclastic disregard for class and established order were a revelation to all concerned, but especially themselves. . . .

The day that, with a straight left to the jaw, I sent a fair-sized CID officer into the orchestra pit of the theatre where we were holding one of our belligerent meetings, was the day of my own coming of age. . . . Since I was no genius, the episode could not make me one, but it set me free to be whatever I was to the top of my bent. . . .

For two years of wild and sometimes dangerous adventure, I worked and fought alongside vigorous, happy, well-adjusted women who laughed instead of tittering, who walked freely instead of teetering, who could outfast Ghandi and come out with a grin and a jest. I slept on hard floors between elderly duchesses, stout cooks, and young shop-girls. We were often tired, hurt and frightened. But we were content as we had never been. We shared a joy of life that we had never known. Most of my fellow-fighters were wives and mothers. And strange things happened to their domestic life. Husbands came home at night with a new eagerness. . . . As for children, their attitude changed rapidly from one of affectionate toleration for poor, darling mother to one of wide-eyed wonder. Released from the smother of mother love, for she was too busy to be more than casually concerned with them, they discovered that they liked her. She was a great sport. She had guts. . . . Those women who stood outside the fight—I regret to say the vast majority—and who were being more than usually Little Women, hated the fighters with the venomous rage of envy . . .[17]

Did women really go home again as a reaction to feminism? The fact is that to women born after 1920, feminism was dead history. It ended as a vital movement in America with the winning of that final right: the vote. In the 1930's and 40's, the sort of woman who fought for woman's rights was still concerned with human rights and freedom—for Negroes, for oppressed workers, for victims of Franco's Spain and Hitler's Germany. But no one was much concerned with rights for women: they had all been won. And yet the man-eating myth prevailed. Women who displayed any independence or initiative were called "Lucy Stoners." "Feminist," like "career woman," became a dirty word. The feminists had destroyed the old image of woman, but they could not erase the hostility, the prejudice, the discrimination that still remained. Nor could they paint the new image of what women might become when they grew up under conditions that no longer made them inferior to men, dependent, passive, incapable of thought or decision.

Most of the girls who grew up during the years when the feminists were eliminating the causes of that denigrating "genteel nothingness" got their image of woman from mothers still trapped in it. These mothers were probably the real model for the man-eating myth. The shadow of the contempt and self-contempt which could turn a gentle housewife into a domineering shrew also turned some of their daughters into angry copies of man. The first women in business and the professions were thought to be freaks. Insecure in their new freedom, some perhaps feared to be soft or gentle, love, have children, lest they lose their prized independence, lest they be trapped again as their mothers were. They reinforced the myth.

But the daughters who grew up with the rights the feminists had won could not go back to that old image of genteel nothingness, nor did they have their aunts' or mothers' reasons to be angry copies of man, or fear to love them. They had come unknowing to the turning-point in woman's identity. They had truly outgrown the old image; they were finally free to be what they chose to be. But what choice were they offered? In that corner, the fiery, man-eating feminist, the career woman—loveless, alone. In this corner, the gentle wife and mother—loved and protected by her husband, surrounded by her adoring children. Though many daughters continued on the passionate journey their grandmothers had begun, thousands of others fell out—victims of a mistaken choice.

The reasons for their choice were, of course, more complex than the feminist myth. How did Chinese women, after having their feet bound for many generations, finally discover they could run? The first women whose feet were unbound must have felt such pain that some were afraid to stand, let alone to walk or run. The more they walked, the less their feet hurt. But what would have happened if, before a single generation of Chinese girls had grown up with unbound feet, doctors, hoping to save them pain and distress, told them to bind their feet again? And teachers told them that walking with bound feet was feminine, the only way a woman could walk if she wanted a man to love her? And scholars told them that they would be better mothers if they could not walk too far away from their children? And peddlers, discovering that women who could not walk bought more trinkets, spread fables of the dangers of running and the bliss of being bound? Would many little Chinese girls, then, grow up wanting to have their feet securely bound, never tempted to walk or run?

The real joke that history played on American women is not the one that makes people snigger, with cheap Freudian sophistication, at the dead feminists. It is the joke that Freudian thought played on living women, twisting the memory of the feminists into the man-eating phantom of the feminine mystique, shriveling the very wish to be more than just a wife and mother. Encouraged by the mystique to evade their identity crisis, permitted to escape identity altogether in the name of sexual fulfillment, women once again are living with their feet bound in the old image of glorified femininity. And it is the same old image, despite its shiny new clothes, that trapped women for centuries and made the feminists rebel.

5 The Sexual Solipsism of Sigmund Freud

 It would be half-wrong to say it started with Sigmund Freud. It did not really start, in America, until the 1940's. And then again, it was less a start than the prevention of an end. The old prejudices —women are animals, less than human, unable to think like men, born merely to breed and serve men—were not so easily dispelled by the crusading feminists, by science and education, and by the democratic spirit after all. They merely reappeared in the forties, in Freudian disguise. The feminine mystique derived its power from Freudian thought; for it was an idea born of Freud, which led women, and those who studied them, to misinterpret their mothers' frustrations, and their fathers' and brothers' and husbands' resentments and inadequacies, and their own emotions and possible choices in life. It is a Freudian idea, hardened into apparent fact, that has trapped so many American women today.

The new mystique is much more difficult for the modern woman to question than the old prejudices, partly because the mystique is broadcast by the very agents of education and social science that are supposed to be the chief enemies of prejudice, partly because the very nature of Freudian thought makes it virtually invulnerable to question. How can an educated American woman, who is not herself an analyst, presume to question a

Freudian truth? She knows that Freud's discovery of the unconscious workings of the mind was one of the great breakthroughs in man's pursuit of knowledge. She knows that the science built on that discovery has helped many suffering men and women. She has been taught that only after years of analytic training is one capable of understanding the meaning of Freudian truth. She may even know how the human mind unconsciously resists that truth. How can she presume to tread the sacred ground where only analysts are allowed?

No one can question the basic genius of Freud's discoveries, nor the contribution he has made to our culture. Nor do I question the effectiveness of psychoanalysis as it is practiced today by Freudian or anti-Freudian. But I do question, from my own experience as a woman, and my reporter's knowledge of other women, the application of the Freudian theory of femininity to women today. I question its use, not in therapy, but as it has filtered into the lives of American women through the popular magazines and the opinions and interpretations of so-called experts. I think much of the Freudian theory about women is obsolescent, an obstacle to truth for women in America today, and a major cause of the pervasive problem that has no name.

There are many paradoxes here. Freud's concept of the superego helped to free man of the tyranny of the "shoulds," the tyranny of the past, which prevents the child from becoming an adult. Yet Freudian thought helped create a new superego that paralyzes educated modern American women—a new tyranny of the "shoulds," which chains women to an old image, prohibits choice and growth, and denies them individual identity.

Freudian psychology, with its emphasis on freedom from a repressive morality to achieve sexual fulfillment, was part of the ideology of women's emancipation. The lasting American image of the "emancipated woman" is the flapper of the twenties: burdensome hair shingled off, knees bared, flaunting her new freedom to live in a studio in Greenwich Village or Chicago's near North Side, and drive a car, and drink, and smoke and enjoy sexual adventures—or talk about them. And yet today, for reasons far removed from the life of Freud himself, Freudian thought has become the ideological bulwark of the sexual counter-revolution in America. Without Freud's definition of the sexual nature of woman to give the conventional image of femininity new authority, I do not think several generations of educated, spirited American women would have been so easily diverted from the dawning realization of who they were and what they could be.

The concept "penis envy," which Freud coined to describe a phenomenon he observed in women—that is, in the middle-class women who were his patients in Vienna in the Victorian era—was seized in this country in the 1940's as the literal explanation of all that was wrong with American women. Many who preached the doctrine of endangered femininity, reversing the movement of American women toward independence and identity, never knew its Freudian origin. Many who seized on it—not the few psychoanalysts, but the many popularizers, sociologists, educators, ad-agency manipulators, magazine writers, child experts, marriage counselors, ministers, cocktail-party authorities—could not have known what Freud himself meant by penis envy. One needs only to know what Freud *was* describing, in those Victorian women, to see the fallacy in literally applying his theory of femininity to women today. And one needs only to know *why* he described it in that way to understand that much of it is obsolescent, contradicted by knowledge that is part of every social scientist's thinking today, but was not yet known in Freud's time.

Freud, it is generally agreed, was a most perceptive and accurate observer of important problems of the human personality. But in describing and interpreting those problems, he was a prisoner of his own culture. As he was creating a new framework for our culture, he could not escape the framework of his own. Even his genius could not give him, then, the knowledge of cultural processes which men who are not geniuses grow up with today.

The physicist's relativity, which in recent years has changed our whole approach to scientific knowledge, is harder, and therefore easier to understand than the social scientist's relativity. It is not a slogan, but a fundamental statement about truth to say that no social scientist can completely free himself from the prison of his own culture; he can only interpret what he observes in the scientific framework of his own time. This is true even of the great innovators. They cannot help but translate their revolutionary observations into language and rubrics that have been determined by the progress of science up until their time. Even those discoveries that create new rubrics are relative to the vantage point of their creator.

The knowledge of other cultures, the understanding of cultural relativity, which is part of the framework of social scientists in our own time, was unknown to Freud. Much of what Freud believed to be biological, instinctual, and changeless has been shown by modern research to be a result of specific cultural causes.[1] Much of what Freud described as characteristic of universal human nature was merely characteristic of certain middle-class European men and women at the end of the nineteenth century.

For instance, Freud's theory of the sexual origin of neurosis stems from the fact that many of the patients he first observed suffered from hysteria—and in those cases, he found sexual repression to be the cause. Orthodox Freudians still profess to believe in the sexual origin of all neurosis, and since they look for unconscious sexual memories in their patients, and translate what they hear into sexual symbols, they still manage to find what they are looking for.

But the fact is, cases of hysteria as observed by Freud are much more rare today. In Freud's time, evidently, cultural hypocrisy forced the repression of sex. (Some social theorists even suspect that the very absence of other concerns, in that dying Austrian empire, caused the sexual preoccupation of Freud's patients.[2]) Certainly the fact that his culture denied sex focused Freud's interest on it. He then developed his theory by describing all the stages of growth as sexual, fitting all the phenomena he observed into sexual rubrics.

His attempt to translate all psychological phenomena into sexual terms, and to see all problems of adult personality as the effect of childhood sexual fixations also stemmed, in part, from his own background in medicine, and from the approach to causation implicit in the scientific thought of his time. He had the same diffidence about dealing with psychological phenomena in their own terms which often plagues scientists of human behavior. Something that could be described in physiological terms, linked to an organ of anatomy, seemed more comfortable, solid, real, scientific, as he moved into the unexplored country of the unconscious mind. As his biographer, Ernest Jones, put it, he made a "desperate effort to cling to the safety of cerebral anatomy." [3] Actually, he had the ability to see and describe psychological phenomena so vividly that whether his concepts were given names borrowed from physiology, philosophy or literature—penis envy, ego, Oedipus complex—they seemed to have a concrete physical reality. Psychological facts, as Jones said, were "as real and concrete to him as metals are to a metallurgist." [4] This ability became a source of great confusion as his concepts were passed down by lesser thinkers.

The whole superstructure of Freudian theory rests on the strict determinism that characterized the scientific thinking of the Victorian era. Determinism has been replaced today by a more complex view of cause and effect, in terms of physical processes and phenomena as well as psychological. In the new view, behavioral scientists do not need to borrow language from physiology to explain psychological events, or give them pseudo-reality. Sexual phenomena are no more nor less real than, for instance, the phenomenon of Shakespeare's writing Hamlet, which cannot exactly be "explained" by reducing it to sexual terms. Even Freud himself cannot be explained by his own deterministic, physiological blueprint, though his biographer traces his genius, his "divine passion for knowledge" to an insatiable sexual curiosity, before the age of three, as to what went on between his mother and father in the bedroom.[5]

Today biologists, social scientists, and increasing numbers of psychoanalysts see the need or impulse to human growth as a primary human need, as basic as sex. The "oral" and "anal" stages which Freud described in terms of sexual development—the child gets his sexual pleasure first by mouth, from mother's breast, then from his bowel movements—are now seen as stages of human growth, influenced by cultural circumstances and parental attitudes as well as by sex. When the teeth grow, the mouth can bite as well as suck. Muscle and brain also grow; the child becomes capable of control, mastery, understanding; and his need to grow and learn, at five, twenty-five, or fifty, can be satisfied, denied, repressed, atrophied, evoked or discouraged by his culture as can his sexual needs.

Child specialists today confirm Freud's observation that problems between mother and child in the earliest stages are often played out in terms of eating; later in toilet training. And yet in America in recent years there has been a noticeable decline in children's "eating problems." Has the child's instinctual development changed? Impossible, if by definition, the oral stage is instinctual. Or has the culture removed eating as a focus for early childhood problems—by the American emphasis on permissiveness in child care, or simply by the fact that in our affluent society food has become less a cause for anxiety in mothers? Because of Freud's own influence on our culture, educated parents are usually careful not to put conflict-producing pressures on toilet training. Such conflicts are more likely to occur today as the child learns to talk or read.[6]

In the 1940's, American social scientists and psychoanalysts had already begun to reinterpret Freudian concepts in the light of their growing cultural awareness. But, curiously, this did not prevent their literal application of Freud's theory of femininity to American women.

The fact is that to Freud, even more than to the magazine editor on Madison Avenue today, women were a strange, inferior, less-than-human species. He saw them as childlike dolls, who existed in terms only of man's love, to love man and serve his needs. It was the same kind of unconscious solipsism that made man for many centuries see the sun only as a bright object that revolved around the earth. Freud grew up with this attitude built in by his culture—not only the culture of Victorian Europe, but that Jewish culture in which men said the daily prayer: "I thank Thee, Lord, that Thou hast not created me a woman," and women prayed in submission: "I thank Thee, Lord, that Thou has created me according to Thy will."

Freud's mother was the pretty, docile bride of a man twice her age; his father ruled the family with an autocratic authority traditional in Jewish families during those centuries of persecution when the fathers were seldom able to establish authority in the outside world. His mother adored the young Sigmund, her first son, and thought him mystically destined for greatness; she seemed to exist only to gratify his every wish. His own memories of the sexual jealousy he felt for his father, whose wishes she also gratified, were the basis of his theory of the Oedipus complex. With his wife, as with his mother and sisters, his needs, his desires, his wishes, were the sun around which the household revolved. When the noise of his sisters' practicing the piano interrupted his studies, "the piano disappeared," Anna Freud recalled years later, "and with it all opportunities for his sisters to become musicians."

Freud did not see this attitude as a problem, or cause for any problem, in women. It was woman's nature to be ruled by man, and her sickness to envy him. Freud's letters to Martha, his future wife, written during the four years of their engagement (1882–1886) have the fond, patronizing sound of Torvald in *A Doll's House*, scolding Nora for her pretenses at being human. Freud was beginning to probe the secrets of the human brain in the laboratory at Vienna; Martha was to wait, his "sweet child," in her mother's custody for four years, until he could come and fetch her. From these letters one can see that to him her identity was defined as child-housewife, even when she was no longer a child and not yet a housewife.

Tables and chairs, beds, mirrors, a clock to remind the happy couple of the passage of time, an armchair for an hour's pleasant daydreaming, carpets to help the housewife keep the floors clean, linen tied with pretty ribbons in the cupboard and dresses of the latest fashion and hats with artificial flowers, pictures on the wall, glasses for everyday and others for wine and festive occasions, plates and dishes . . . and the sewing table and the cozy lamp, and everything must be kept in good order or else the housewife who has divided her heart into little bits, one for each piece of furniture, will begin to fret. And this object must bear witness to the serious work that holds the household together, and that object, to a feeling for beauty, to dear friends one likes to remember, to cities one has visited, to hours one wants to recall. . . .

Are we to hang our hearts on such little things? Yes, and without hesitation. . . .

I know, after all, how sweet you are, how you can turn a house into a paradise, how you will share in my interests, how gay yet painstaking you will be. I will let you rule the house as much as you wish, and you will reward me with your sweet love and by rising above all those weaknesses for which women are so often despised. As far as my activities allow, we shall read together what we want to learn, and I will initiate you into things which could not interest a girl as long as she is unfamiliar with her future companion and his occupation . . .[7]

On July 5, 1885, he scolds her for continuing to visit Elise, a friend who evidently is less than demure in her regard for men:

What is the good of your feeling that you are now so mature that this relationship can't do you any harm? . . . You are far too soft, and this is something I have got to correct, for what one of us does will also be charged to the other's account. You are my precious little woman and even if you make a mistake, you are none the less so. . . . But you know all this, my sweet child . . .[8]

The Victorian mixture of chivalry and condescension which is found in Freud's scientific theories about women is explicit in a letter he wrote on November 5, 1883, deriding John Stuart Mills' views on "female emancipation and the woman's question altogether."

In his whole presentation, it never emerges that women are different beings—we will not say lesser, rather the opposite—from men. He finds the suppression of women an analogy to that of Negroes. Any girl, even without a suffrage or legal competence, whose hand a man kisses and for whose love he is prepared to dare all, could have set him right. It is really a stillborn thought to send women into the struggle for existence exactly as man. If, for instance, I imagined my gentle sweet girl as a competitor, it would only end in my telling her, as I did seventeen months ago, that I am fond of her and that I implore her to withdraw from the strife into the calm, uncompetitive activity of my home. It is possible that changes in upbringing may suppress all a woman's tender attributes, needful of protection and yet so victorious, and that she can then earn a livelihood like men. It is also possible that in such an event one would not be justified in mourning the passing away of the most delightful thing the world can offer us—our ideal of womanhood. I believe that all reforming action in law and education would break down in front of the fact that, long before the age at which a man can earn a position in society, Nature has determined woman's destiny through beauty, charm, and sweetness. Law and custom have much to give women that has been withheld from them, but the position of women will surely be what it is: in youth an adored darling and in mature years a loved wife.[9]

Since all of Freud's theories rested, admittedly, on his own penetrating, unending psychoanalysis of himself, and since sexuality was the focus of all his theories, certain paradoxes about his own sexuality seem pertinent. His writings, as many scholars have noted, give much more attention to infantile sexuality than to its mature expression. His chief biographer, Jones, pointed out that he was, even for those times, exceptionally chaste, puritanical and moralistic. In his own life, he was relatively uninterested in sex. There were only the adoring mother of his youth, at sixteen a romance that existed purely in fantasy with a girl named Gisele, and his engagement to Martha at twenty-six. The nine months when they both lived in Vienna were not too happy because she was, evidently, uneasy and afraid of him; but separated by a comfortable distance for four years, there was a "grande passion" of 900 love letters. After their marriage, the passion seems to have quickly disappeared, though his biographers note that he was too rigid a moralist to seek sexual satisfaction outside of marriage. The only woman on whom, as an adult, he ever focused the violent passions of love and hate of which he was capable was Martha, during the early years of their engagement. After that, such emotions were focused on men. As Jones, his respectful biographer, said: "Freud's deviation from the average in this respect, as well as his pronounced mental bisexuality, may well have influenced his theoretical views to some extent." [10]

Less reverent biographers, and even Jones himself, point out that when one considers Freud's theories in terms of his own life, one is reminded of the puritanical old maid who sees sex everywhere.[11] It is interesting to note that his main complaint about his docile hausfrau was that she was not "docile" enough—and yet, in interesting ambivalence, that she was not "at her ease" with him, that she was not able to be a "comrade-in-arms."

But, as Freud was painfully to discover, she was not at heart docile and she had a firmness of character that did not readily lend itself to being molded. Her personality was fully developed and well integrated: it would well deserve the psychoanalyst's highest compliment of being "normal." [12]

One gets a glimpse of Freud's "intention, never to be fulfilled, to mold her to his perfect image," when he wrote her that she must "become quite young, a sweetheart, only a week old, who will quickly lose every trace of tartness." But he then reproaches himself:

The loved one is not to become a toy doll, but a good comrade who still has a sensible word left when the strict master has come to the end of his wisdom. And I have been trying to smash her frankness so that she should reserve opinion until she is sure of mine. [13]

As Jones pointed out, Freud was pained when she did not meet his chief test—"complete identification with himself, his opinions, his feelings, and his intentions. She was not really his unless he could perceive his 'stamp' on her." Freud "even admitted that it was boring if one could find nothing in the other person to put right." And he stresses again that Freud's love "could be set free and displayed only under very favorable conditions. . . . Martha was probably afraid of her masterful lover and she would commonly take refuge in silence." [14]

So, he eventually wrote her, "I renounce what I demanded. I do not need a comrade-in-arms, such as I hoped to make you into. I am strong enough to fight alone. . . . You remain for me a precious sweet, loved one." [15] Thus evidently ended "the only time in his life when such emotions [love and hate] centered on a woman." [16]

The marriage was conventional, but without that passion. As Jones described it:

There can have been few more successful marriages. Martha certainly made an excellent wife and mother. She was an admirable manager—the rare kind of woman who could keep servants indefinitely—but she was never the kind of Hausfrau who put things before people. Her husband's comfort and convenience always ranked first. . . . It was not to be expected that she should follow the roaming flights of his imagination any more than most of the world could.[17]

She was as devoted to his physical needs as the most doting Jewish mother, organizing each meal on a rigid schedule to fit the convenience of "der Papa." But she never dreamed of sharing his life as an equal. Nor did Freud consider her a fit guardian for their children, especially of their education, in case of his death. He himself recalls a dream in which he forgets to call for her at the theater. His associations "imply that forgetting may be permissible in unimportant matters." [18]

That limitless subservience of woman taken for granted by Freud's culture, the very lack of opportunity for independent action or personal identity, seems often to have generated that uneasiness and inhibition in the wife, and that irritation in the husband, which characterized Freud's marriage. As Jones summed it up, Freud's attitude toward women "could probably be called rather old-fashioned, and it would be easy to ascribe this to his social environment and the period in which he grew up rather than to any personal factors."

Whatever his intellectual opinions may have been in the matter, there are many indications in his writing and correspondence of his emotional attitude. It would certainly be going too far to say that he regarded the male sex as the lords of creation, for there was no tinge of arrogance or superiority in his nature, but it might perhaps be fair to describe his view of the female sex as having as their main function to be ministering angels to the needs and comforts of men. His letters and his love choice make it plain that he had only one type of sexual object in his mind, a gentle feminine one. . . .

There is little doubt that Freud found the psychology of women more enigmatic than that of men. He said once to Marie Bonaparte: "The great question that has never been answered and which I have not yet been able to answer, despite my thirty years of research into the feminine soul, is, what does a woman want?" [19]

Jones also remarked:

Freud was also interested in another type of woman, of a more intellectual and perhaps masculine cast. Such women several times played a part in his life, accessory to his men friends though of a finer caliber, but they had no erotic attraction for him.[20]

These women included his sister-in-law, Minna Bernays, much more intelligent and independent than Martha, and later women analysts or adherents of the psychoanalytic movement: Marie Bonaparte, Joan Riviere, Lou Andreas-Salomé. There is no suspicion, however, from either idolators or hostile biographers that he ever sought sexual satisfaction outside his marriage. Thus it would seem that sex was completely divorced from his human passions, which he expressed throughout the productive later years of his long life in his thought and, to a lesser extent, in friendships with men and those women he considered his equals, and thus "masculine." He once said: "I always find it uncanny when I can't understand someone in terms of myself." [21]

Despite the importance of sex in Freud's theory, one gets from his words the impression that the sex act appeared degrading to him; if women themselves were so degraded, in the eyes of man, how could sex appear in any other light? That was not his theory, of course. To Freud, it was the idea of incest with mother or sister that makes man "regard the sex act as something degrading, which soils and contaminates not only the body." [22] In any event, the degradation of women was taken for granted by Freud—and is the key to his theory of femininity. The motive force of woman's personality, in Freud's theory, was her envy of the penis, which causes her to feel as much depreciated in her own eyes "as in the eyes of the boy, and later perhaps of the man," and leads, in normal femininity, to the wish for the penis of her husband, a wish that is never really fulfilled until she possesses a penis through giving birth to a son. In short, she is merely an "homme manqué," a man with something missing. As the eminent psychoanalyst Clara Thompson put it: "Freud never became free from the Victorian attitude toward women. He accepted as an inevitable part of the fate of being a woman the limitation of outlook and life of the Victorian era. . . . The castration complex and penis envy concepts, two of the most basic ideas in his whole thinking, are postulated on the assumption that women are biologically inferior to men." [23]

What did Freud mean by the concept of penis envy? For even those who realize that Freud could not escape his culture do not question that he reported truly what he observed within it. Freud found the phenomenon he called penis envy so unanimous, in middle-class women in Vienna, in that Victorian time, that he based his whole theory of femininity on it. He said, in a lecture on "The Psychology of Women":

In the boy the castration-complex is formed after he has learned from the sight of the female genitals that the sexual organ which he prizes so highly is not a necessary part of every woman's body . . . and thenceforward he comes under the influence of castration-anxiety, which supplies the strongest motive force for his further development. The castration-complex in the girl, as well, is started by the sight of the genital organs of the other sex. She immediately notices the difference and, it must be admitted, its significance. She feels herself at a great disadvantage, and often declares that she would like to have something like that too and falls a victim to penis envy, which leaves ineradicable traces on her development and character-formation, and even in the most favorable instances, is not overcome without a great expenditure of mental energy. That the girl recognizes the fact that she lacks a penis does not mean that she accepts its absence lightly. On the contrary, she clings for a long time to the desire to get something like it, and believes in that possibility for an extraordinary number of years; and even at a time when her knowledge of reality has long since led her to abandon the fulfillment of this desire as being quite unattainable, analysis proves that it still persists in the unconscious, and retains a considerable charge of energy. The desire after all to obtain the penis for which she so much longs may even contribute to the motives that impel a grown-up woman to come to analysis, and what she quite reasonably expects to get from analysis, such as the capacity to pursue an intellectual career, can often be recognized as a sublimated modification of this repressed wish.[24]

"The discovery of her castration is a turning-point in the life of the girl," Freud went on to say. "She is wounded in her self-love by the unfavorable comparison with the boy, who is so much better equipped." Her mother, and all women, are depreciated in her own eyes, as they are depreciated for the same reason in the eyes of man. This either leads to complete sexual inhibition and neurosis, or to a "masculinity complex" in which she refuses to give up "phallic" activity (that is, "activity such as is usually characteristic of the male") or to "normal femininity," in which the girl's own impulses to activity are repressed, and she turns to her father in her wish for the penis. "The feminine situation is, however, only established when the wish for the penis is replaced by the wish for a child—the child taking the place of the penis." When she played with dolls, this "was not really an expression of her femininity," since this was activity, not passivity. The "strongest feminine wish," the desire for a penis, finds real fulfillment only "if the child is a little boy, who brings the longed-for penis with him. . . . The mother can transfer to her son all the ambition she has had to suppress in herself, and she can hope to get from him the satisfaction of all that has remained to her of her masculinity complex." [25]

But her inherent deficiency, and the resultant penis envy, is so hard to overcome that the woman's superego—her conscience, ideals—are never as completely formed as a man's: "women have but little sense of justice, and this is no doubt connected with the preponderance of envy in their mental life." For the same reason, women's interests in society are weaker than those of men, and "their capacity for the sublimation of their instincts is less." Finally, Freud can not refrain from mentioning "an impression which one receives over and over again in analytical work"— that not even psychoanalysis can do much for women, because of the inherent deficiency of femininity.

A man of about thirty seems a youthful, and, in a sense, an incompletely developed individual, of whom we expect that he will be able to make good use of the possibilities of development, which analysis lays open to him. But a woman of about the same age, frequently staggers us by her psychological rigidity and unchangeability. . . . There are no paths open to her for further development; it is as though the whole process had been gone through and remained unaccessible to influence for the future; as though, in fact, the difficult development which leads to femininity had exhausted all the possibilities of the individual . . . even when we are successful in removing the sufferings by solving her neurotic conflict.[26]

What was he really reporting? If one interprets "penis envy" as other Freudian concepts have been reinterpreted, in the light of our new knowledge that what Freud believed to be biological was often a cultural reaction, one sees simply that Victorian culture gave women many reasons to envy men: the same conditions, in fact, that the feminists fought against. If a woman who was denied the freedom, the status and the pleasures that men enjoyed wished secretly that she could have these things, in the shorthand of the dream, she might wish herself a man and see herself with that one thing which made men unequivocally different—the penis. She would, of course, have to learn to keep her envy, her anger, hidden: to play the child, the doll, the toy, for her destiny depended on charming man. But underneath, it might still fester, sickening her for love. If she secretly despised herself, and envied man for all she was not, she might go through the motions of love, or even feel a slavish adoration, but would she be capable of free and joyous love? You cannot explain away woman's envy of man, or her contempt for herself, as mere refusal to accept her sexual deformity, unless you think that a woman, by nature, is a being inferior to man. Then, of course, her wish to be equal is neurotic.

It is recognized now that Freud never gave proper attention, even in man, to growth of the ego or self: "the impulse to master, control or come to self-fulfilling terms with the environment." [27] Analysts who have freed themselves from Freud's bias and joined other behavioral scientists in studying the human need to grow, are beginning to believe that this is the basic human need, and that interference with it, in any dimension, is the source of psychic trouble. The sexual is only one dimension of the human potential. Freud, it must be remembered, thought all neuroses were sexual in origin; he saw women only in terms of their sexual relationship with men. But in all those women in whom he saw sexual problems, there must have been very severe problems of blocked growth, growth short of full human identity—an immature, incomplete self. Society as it was then, by explicit denial of education and independence, prevented women from realizing their full potential, or from attaining those interests and ideals that might have stimulated their growth. Freud reported these deficiencies, but could only explain them as the toll of "penis envy." He saw women's envy of man *only* as sexual sickness. He saw that women who secretly hungered to be man's equal would not enjoy being his object; and in this, he seemed to be describing a fact. But when he dismissed woman's yearning for equality as "penis envy," was he not merely stating his own view that women could never really be man's equal, anymore than she could wear his penis?

Freud was not concerned with changing society, but in helping man, and woman, adjust to it. Thus he tells of a case of a middle-aged spinster whom he succeeded in freeing from a symptom-complex that prevented her from taking any part in life for fifteen years. Freed of these symptoms she "plunged into a whirl of activity in order to develop her talents, which were by no means small, and derive a little appreciation, enjoyment, and success from life before it was too late." But all her attempts ended when she saw that there was no place for her. Since she could no longer relapse into her neurotic symptoms, she began to have accidents; she sprained her ankle, her foot, her hand. When this also was analyzed, "instead of accidents, she contracted on the same occasions slight illnesses, such as catarrh, sore throat, influenzal conditions or rheumatic swellings, until at last, when she made up her mind to resign herself to inactivity, the whole business came to an end." [28]

Even if Freud and his contemporaries considered women inferior by God-given, irrevocable nature, science does not justify such a view today. That inferiority, we now know, was caused by their lack of education, their confinement to the home. Today, when women's equal intelligence has been proved by science, when their equal capacity in every sphere except sheer muscular strength has been demonstrated, a theory explicitly based on woman's natural inferiority would seem as ridiculous as it is hypocritical. But that remains the basis of Freud's theory of women, despite the mask of timeless sexual truth which disguises its elaborations today.

Because Freud's followers could only see woman in the image defined by Freud—inferior, childish, helpless, with no possibility of happiness unless she adjusted to being man's passive object,—they wanted to help women get rid of their suppressed envy, their neurotic desire to be equal. They wanted to help women find sexual fulfillment as women, by affirming their natural inferiority.

But society, which defined that inferiority, had changed drastically by the time Freud's followers transposed bodily to twentieth century America the causes as well as the cures of the condition Freud called penis envy. In the light of our new knowledge of cultural processes and of human growth, one would assume that women who grew up with the rights and freedom and education that Victorian women were denied would be different from the women Freud tried to cure. One would assume that they would have much less reason to envy man. But Freud was interpreted to American woman in such curiously literal terms that the concept of penis envy acquired a mystical life of its own, as if it existed quite independent of the women in whom it had been observed. It was as if Freud's Victorian image of woman became more real than the twentieth-century women to whom it was applied. Freud's theory of femininity was seized in America with such literalness that women today were considered no different than Victorian women. The real injustices life held for women a century ago, compared to men, were dismissed as mere rationalizations of penis envy. And the real opportunities life offered to women now, compared to women then, were forbidden in the name of penis envy.

The literal application of Freudian theory can be seen in these passages from *Modern Woman: The Lost Sex*, by the psychoanalyst Marynia Farnham and the sociologist Ferdinand Lundberg, which was paraphrased ad nauseam in the magazines and in marriage courses, until most of its statements became a part of the conventional, accepted truth of our time. Equating feminism with penis envy, they stated categorically:

Feminism, despite the external validity of its political program and most (not all) of its social program, was at its core a deep illness. . . .

The dominant direction of feminine training and development today
. . . discourages just those traits necessary to the attainment of sexual
pleasure: receptivity and passiveness, a willingness to accept dependence without fear or resentment, with a deep inwardness and readiness
for the final goal of sexual life—impregnation. . . .

It is not in the capacity of the female organism to attain feelings of
well-being by the route of male achievement. . . . It was the error of
the feminists that they attempted to put women on the essentially male
road of exploit, off the female road of nurture. . . .

The psychosocial rule that begins to take form, then, is this: the
more educated the woman is, the greater chance there is of sexual
disorder, more or less severe. The greater the disordered sexuality in
a given group of women, the fewer children do they have. . . . Fate
has granted them the boon importuned by Lady Macbeth; they have
been unsexed, not only in the matter of giving birth, but in their feelings of pleasure.[29]

Thus Freud's popularizers embedded his core of unrecognized
traditional prejudice against women ever deeper in pseudoscientific cement. Freud was well aware of his own tendency to
build an enormous body of deductions from a single fact—a
fertile and creative method, but a two-edged sword, if the significance of that single fact was misinterpreted. Freud wrote Jung
in 1909:

Your surmise that after my departure my errors might be adored as
holy relics amused me enormously, but I don't believe it. On the contrary, I think that my followers will hasten to demolish as swiftly as
possible everything that is not safe and sound in what I leave behind.[30]

But on the subject of women, Freud's followers not only compounded his errors, but in their tortuous attempt to fit their observations of real women into his theoretical framework, closed
questions that he himself had left open. Thus, for instance, Helene
Deutsch, whose definitive two-volume *The Psychology of
Woman—A Psychoanalytical Interpretation* appeared in 1944, is
not able to trace all women's troubles to penis envy as such. So
she does what even Freud found unwise, and equates "femininity"
with "passivity," and "masculinity" with "activity," not only in
the sexual sphere, but in all spheres of life.

While fully recognizing that woman's position is subjected to external influence, I venture to say that the fundamental identities "feminine-passive" and "masculine-active" assert themselves in all known cultures and races, in various forms and various quantitative proportions.

Very often a woman resists this characteristic given her by nature and in spite of certain advantages she derives from it, displays many modes of behavior that suggest that she is not entirely content with her own constitution . . . the expression of this dissatisfaction, combined with attempts to remedy it, result in woman's "masculinity complex." [31]

The "masculinity complex," as Dr. Deutsch refines it, stems directly from the "female castration complex." Thus, anatomy is still destiny, woman is still an "homme manqué." Of course, Dr. Deutsch mentions in passing that "With regard to the girl, however, the environment exerts an inhibiting influence as regards both her aggressions and her activity." So, penis envy, deficient female anatomy, and society "all seem to work together to produce femininity." [32]

"Normal" femininity is achieved, however, only insofar as the woman finally renounces all active goals of her own, all her own "originality," to identify and fulfill herself through the activities and goals of husband, or son. This process can be sublimated in nonsexual ways—as, for instance, the woman who does the basic research for her male superior's discoveries. The daughter who devotes her life to her father is also making a satisfactory feminine "sublimation." Only activity of her own or originality, on a basis of equality, deserves the opprobrium of "masculinity complex." This brilliant feminine follower of Freud states categorically that the women who by 1944 in America had achieved eminence by activity of their own in various fields had done so at the expense of their feminine fulfillment. She will mention no names, but they all suffer from the "masculinity complex."

How could a girl or woman who was not a psychoanalyst discount such ominous pronouncements, which, in the forties, suddenly began to pour out from all the oracles of sophisticated thought?

It would be ridiculous to suggest that the way Freudian theories were used to brainwash two generations of educated American women was part of a psychoanalytic conspiracy. It was done by well-meaning popularizers and inadvertent distorters; by orthodox converts and bandwagon faddists; by those who suffered and those who cured and those who turned suffering to profit; and, above all, by a congruence of forces and needs peculiar to the American people at that particular time. In fact, the literal acceptance in the American culture of Freud's theory of feminine fulfillment was in tragicomic contrast to the personal struggle of many American psychoanalysts to reconcile what they saw in their women patients with Freudian theory. The theory said women should be able to fulfill themselves as wives and mothers if only they could be analyzed out of their "masculine strivings," their "penis envy." But it wasn't as easy as that. "I don't know why American women are so dissatisfied," a Westchester analyst insisted. "Penis envy seems so difficult to eradicate in American women, somehow."

A New York analyst, one of the last trained at Freud's own Psychoanalytic Institute in Vienna, told me:

For twenty years now in analyzing American women, I have found myself again and again in the position of having to superimpose Freud's theory of femininity on the psychic life of my patients in a way that I was not willing to do. I have come to the conclusion that penis envy simply does not exist. I have seen women who are completely expressive, sexually, vaginally, and yet who are not mature, integrated, fulfilled. I had a woman patient on the couch for nearly two years before I could face her real problem—that it was not enough for her to be just a housewife and mother. One day she had a dream that she was teaching a class. I could not dismiss the powerful yearning of this housewife's dream as penis envy. It was the expression of her own need for mature self-fulfillment. I told her: "I can't analyze this dream away. You must do something about it."

This same man teaches the young analysts in his postgraduate clinicum at a leading Eastern university: "If the patient doesn't fit the book, throw away the book, and listen to the patient."

But many analysts threw the book *at* their patients and Freudian theories became accepted fact even among women who never lay down on an analyst's couch, but only knew what they read or heard. To this day, it has not penetrated to the popular culture that the pervasive growing frustration of American women may not be a matter of feminine sexuality. Some analysts, it is true, modified the theories drastically to fit their patients, or even discarded them altogether—but these facts never permeated the public awareness. Freud was accepted so quickly and completely at the end of the forties that for over a decade no one even questioned the race of the educated American woman back to the home. When questions finally had to be asked because something was obviously going wrong, they were asked so completely within the Freudian framework that only one answer was possible: education, freedom, rights are wrong for women.

The uncritical acceptance of Freudian doctrine in America was caused, at least in part, by the very relief it provided from uncomfortable questions about objective realities. After the depression, after the war, Freudian psychology became much more than a science of human behavior, a therapy for the suffering. It became an all-embracing American ideology, a new religion. It filled the vacuum of thought and purpose that existed for many for whom God, or flag, or bank account were no longer sufficient —and yet who were tired of feeling responsible for lynchings and concentration camps and the starving children of India and Africa. It provided a convenient escape from the atom bomb, McCarthy, all the disconcerting problems that might spoil the taste of steaks, and cars and color television and backyard swimming pools. It gave us permission to suppress the troubling questions of the larger world and pursue our own personal pleasures. And if the new psychological religion—which made a virtue of sex, removed all sin from private vice, and cast suspicion on high aspirations of the mind and spirit—had a more devastating personal effect on women than men, nobody planned it that way.

Psychology, long preoccupied with its own scientific inferiority complex, long obsessed with neat little laboratory experiments that gave the illusion of reducing human complexity to the simple measurable behavior of rats in a maze, was transformed into a life-giving crusade that swept across the barren fields of American thought. Freud was the spiritual leader, his theories were the bible. And how exciting and real and important it all was. Its mysterious complexity was part of its charm to bored Americans. And if some of it remained impenetrably mystifying, who would admit that he could not understand it? America became the center of the psychoanalytic movement, as Freudian, Jungian and Adlerian analysts fled from Vienna and Berlin and new schools flourished on the multiplying neuroses, and dollars, of Americans.

But the practice of psychoanalysis as a therapy was not primarily responsible for the feminine mystique. It was the creation of writers and editors in the mass media, ad-agency motivation researchers, and behind them the popularizers and translators of Freudian thought in the colleges and universities. Freudian and pseudo-Freudian theories settled everywhere, like fine volcanic ash. Sociology, anthropology, education, even the study of history and literature became permeated and transfigured by Freudian thought. The most zealous missionaries of the feminine mystique were the functionalists, who seized hasty gulps of predigested Freud to start their new departments of "Marriage and Family Life Education." The functional courses in marriage taught American college girls how to "play the role" of woman —the old role became a new science. Related movements outside the colleges—parent education, child-study groups, prenatal maternity study groups and mental-health education—spread the new psychological superego throughout the land, replacing bridge and canasta as an entertainment for educated young wives. And this Freudian superego worked for growing numbers of young and impressionable American women as Freud said the superego works—to perpetuate the past.

Mankind never lives completely in the present; the ideologies of the supergo perpetuate the past, the traditions of the race and the people, which yield but slowly to the influence of the present and to new developments, and, so long as they work through the superego, play an important part in man's life, quite independently of economic conditions.[33]

The feminine mystique, elevated by Freudian theory into a scientific religion, sounded a single, overprotective, life-restricting, future-denying note for women. Girls who grew up playing baseball, baby-sitting, mastering geometry—almost independent enough, almost resourceful enough, to meet the problems of the fission-fusion era—were told by the most advanced thinkers of our time to go back and live their lives as if they were Noras, restricted to the doll's house by Victorian prejudice. And their own respect and awe for the authority of science—anthropology, sociology, psychology share that authority now—kept them from questioning the feminine mystique.

6 The Functional Freeze, the Feminine Protest, and Margaret Mead

Instead of destroying the old prejudices that restricted women's lives, social science in America merely gave them new authority. By a curious circular process, the insights of psychology and anthropology and sociology, which should have been powerful weapons to free women, somehow canceled each other out, trapping women in dead center.

During the last twenty years, under the catalytic impact of Freudian thought, psychoanalysts, anthropologists, sociologists, social psychologists, and other workers in the behavioral sciences have met in professional seminars and foundation-financed conferences in many university centers. Cross-fertilization seemed to make them all bloom, but some strange hybrids were produced. As psychoanalysts began to reinterpret Freudian concepts like "oral" and "anal" personality in the light of an awareness, borrowed from anthropology, that cultural processes must have been at work in Freud's Vienna, anthropologists set out for the South Sea islands to chart tribal personality according to literal "oral" and "anal" tables. Armed with "psychological hints for ethnological field workers," the anthropologists often found what they were looking for. Instead of translating, sifting, the cultural bias *out* of Freudian theories, Margaret Mead, and the others who pioneered in the fields of culture and personality, compounded the error by fitting their own anthropological observations into Freudian rubric. But none of this might have had the same freezing effect on women if it had not been for a simultaneous aberration of American social scientists called functionalism.

Centering primarily on cultural anthropology and sociology and reaching its extremes in the applied field of family-life education, functionalism began as an attempt to make social science more "scientific" by borrowing from biology the idea of studying institutions as if they were muscles or bones, in terms of their "structure" and "function" in the social body. By studying an institution only in terms of its function within its own society, the social scientists intended to avert unscientific value judgments. In practice, functionalism was less a scientific movement than a scientific word-game. "The function is" was often translated "the function should be"; the social scientists did not recognize their own prejudices in functional disguise any more than the analysts recognized theirs in Freudian disguise. By giving an absolute meaning and a sanctimonious value to the generic term "woman's role," functionalism put American women into a kind of deep freeze —like Sleeping Beauties, waiting for a Prince Charming to waken them, while all around the magic circle the world moved on.

The social scientists, male and female, who, in the name of functionalism, drew this torturously tight circle around American women, also seemed to share a certain attitude which I will call "the feminine protest." If there is such a thing as a masculine protest—the psychoanalytic concept taken over by the functionalists to describe women who envied men and wanted to be men and therefore denied that they were women and became more manly than any man—its counterpart can be seen today in a feminine protest, made by men and women alike, who deny what women really are and make more of "being a woman" than it could ever be. The feminine protest, at its most straightforward, is simply a means of protecting women from the dangers inherent in assuming true equality with men. But why should any social scientist, with godlike manipulative superiority, take it

upon himself—or herself—to protect women from the pains of
growing up?

Protectiveness has often muffled the sound of doors closing
against women; it has often cloaked a very real prejudice, even
when it is offered in the name of science. If an old-fashioned
grandfather frowned at Nora, who is studying calculus because
she wants to be a physicist, and muttered, "Woman's place is in
the home," Nora would laugh impatiently, "Grandpa, this is
1963." But she does not laugh at the urbane pipe-smoking professor of sociology, or the book by Margaret Mead, or the definitive two-volume reference on female sexuality, when they tell
her the same thing. The complex, mysterious language of functionalism, Freudian psychology, and cultural anthropology hides
from her the fact that they say this with not much more basis
than grandpa.

So our Nora would smile at Queen Victoria's letter, written
in 1870: "The Queen is most anxious to enlist everyone who can
speak or write to join in checking this mad, wicked folly of
'Woman's Rights' with all its attendant horrors, on which her
poor feeble sex is bent, forgetting every sense of womanly feeling and propriety. . . . It is a subject which makes the Queen
so furious that she cannot contain herself. God created men and
women different—then let them remain each in their own position."

But she does not smile when she reads in *Marriage for Moderns:*

The sexes are complementary. It is the works of my watch that
move the hands and enable me to tell time. Are the works, therefore,
more important than the case? . . . Neither is superior, neither inferior. Each must be judged in terms of its own functions. Together
they form a functioning unit. So it is with men and women—together
they form a functioning unit. Either alone is in a sense incomplete.
They are complementary. . . . When men and women engage in the
same occupations or perform common functions, the complementary
relationship may break down.[1]

This book was published in 1942. Girls have studied it as a
college text for the past twenty years. Under the guise of sociol-

ogy, or "Marriage and Family Life," or "Life Adjustment," they are offered advice of this sort:

The fact remains, however, that we live in a world of reality, a world of the present and the immediate future, on which there rests the heavy hand of the past, a world in which tradition still holds sway and the mores exert a stronger influence than does the theorist . . . a world in which most men and women do marry and in which most married women are homemakers. To talk about what might be done if tradition and the mores were radically changed or what may come about by the year 2000 may be interesting mental gymnastics, but it does not help the young people of today to adjust to the inevitables of life or raise their marriages to a higher plane of satisfaction.[2]

Of course, this "adjustment to the inevitables of life" denies the speed with which the conditions of life are now changing— and the fact that many girls who so adjust at twenty will still be alive in the year 2000. This functionalist specifically warns against any and all approaches to the "differences between men and women" except "adjustment" to those differences as they now stand. And if, like our Nora, a woman is contemplating a career, he shakes a warning finger.

For the first time in history, American young women in great numbers are being faced with these questions: Shall I voluntarily prepare myself for a lifelong celibate career? Or shall I prepare for a temporary vocation, which I shall give up when I marry and assume the responsibilities of homemaking and motherhood? Or should I attempt to combine homemaking and a career? . . . The great majority of married women are homemakers. . . .
If a woman can find adequate self-expression through a career rather than through marriage, well and good. Many young women, however, overlook the fact that there are numerous careers that do not furnish any medium or offer any opportunity for self-expression. Besides they do not realize that only the minority of women, as the minority of men, have anything particularly worthwhile to express.[3]

And so Nora is left with the cheerful impression that if she chooses a career, she is also choosing celibacy. If she has any illusions about combining marriage and career, the functionalist admonishes her:

How many individuals . . . can successfully pursue two careers simultaneously? Not many. The exceptional person can do it, but the ordinary person cannot. The problem of combining marriage and homemaking with another career is especially difficult, since it is likely that the two pursuits will demand qualities of different types. The former, to be successful, requires self-negation; the latter, self-enhancement. The former demands cooperation; the latter competition. . . . There is greater opportunity for happiness if husband and wife supplement each other than there is when there is duplication of function . . .[4]

And just in case Nora has any doubts about giving up her career ambitions, she is offered this comforting rationalization:

A woman who is an effective homemaker must know something about teaching, interior decoration, cooking, dietetics, consumption, psychology, physiology, social relations, community resources, clothing, household equipment, housing, hygiene and a host of other things. . . . She is a general practitioner rather than a specialist. . . .
The young woman who decides upon homemaking as her career need have no feeling of inferiority. . . . One may say, as some do, "Men can have careers because women make homes." One may say that women are released from the necessity for wage earning and are free to devote their time to the extremely important matter of home-making because men specialize in breadwinning. Or one may say that together the breadwinner and the homemaker form a complementary combination second to none.[5]

This marriage textbook is not the most subtle of its school. It is almost too easy to see that its functional argument is based on no real chain of scientific fact. (It is hardly scientific to say "this is what is, therefore this is what should be.") But this is the essence of functionalism as it came to pervade all of American sociology in this period, whether or not the sociologist called himself a "functionalist." In colleges which would never stoop to the "role-playing lessons" of the so-called functional family course, young women were assigned Talcott Parsons' authoritative "analysis of sex-roles in the social structure of the United States," which contemplates no alternative for a woman other than the role of "housewife," patterned with varying emphasis on "domesticity," "glamour," and "good companionship."

It is perhaps not too much to say that only in very exceptional cases can an adult man be genuinely self-respecting and enjoy a respected status in the eyes of others if he does not "earn a living" in an approved occupational role. . . . In the case of the feminine role the situation is radically different. . . . The woman's fundamental status is that of her husband's wife, the mother of his children . . .[6]

Parsons, a highly respected sociologist and the leading functional theoretician, describes with insight and accuracy the sources of strain in this "segregation of sex roles." He points out that the "domestic" aspect of the housewife role "has declined in importance to the point where it scarcely approaches a full-time occupation for a vigorous person": that the "glamour pattern" is "inevitably associated with a rather early age level" and thus "serious strains result from the problem of adaptation to increasing age," that the "good companion" pattern—which includes "humanistic" cultivation of the arts and community welfare—"suffers from a lack of fully institutionalized status. . . . It is only those with the strongest initiative and intelligence who achieve fully satisfying adaptations in this direction." He states that "it is quite clear that in the adult feminine role there is quite sufficient strain and insecurity so that widespread manifestations are to be expected in the form of neurotic behavior." But Parsons warns:

It is, of course, possible for the adult woman to follow the masculine pattern and seek a career in fields of occupational achievement in direct competition with men of her own class. It is, however, notable that in spite of the very great progress of the emancipation of women from the traditional domestic pattern only a very small fraction have gone very far in this direction. It is also clear that its generalization would only be possible with profound alterations in the structure of the family.

True equality between men and women would not be "functional"; the status quo can be maintained only if the wife and mother is exclusively a homemaker or, at most, has a "job" rather than a "career" which might give her status equal to that of her husband. Thus Parsons finds sexual segregation "functional" in terms of keeping the social structure as it is, which seems to be the functionalist's primary concern.

Absolute equality of opportunity is clearly incompatible with any positive solidarity of the family. . . . Where married women are employed outside the home, it is, for the great majority, in occupations which are not in direct competition for status with those of men of their own class. Women's interests, and the standard of judgment applied to them, run, in our society, far more in the direction of personal adornment. . . . It is suggested that this difference is functionally related to maintaining family solidarity in our class structure.[7]

Even the eminent woman sociologist Mirra Komarovsky, whose functional analysis of how girls learn to "play the role of woman" in our society is brilliant indeed, cannot quite escape the rigid mold functionalism imposes: adjustment to the status quo. For to limit one's field of inquiry to the function of an institution in a given social system, with no alternatives considered, provides an infinite number of rationalizations for all the inequalities and inequities of that system. It is not surprising that social scientists began to mistake their own function as one of helping the individual "adjust" to his "role," in that system.

A social order can function only because the vast majority have somehow adjusted themselves to their place in society and perform the functions expected of them. . . . The differences in the upbringing of the sexes . . . are obviously related to their respective roles in adult life. The future homemaker trains for her role within the home, but the boy prepares for his by being given more independence outside the home, by his taking a "paper route" or a summer job. A provider will profit by independence, dominance, aggressiveness, competitiveness.[8]

The risk of the "traditional upbringing" of girls, as this sociologist sees it, is its possible "failure to develop in the girl the independence, inner resources, and that degree of self-assertion which life will demand of her"—in her role as wife. The functional warning follows:

Even if a parent correctly [sic] considers certain conventional attributes of the feminine role to be worthless, he creates risks for the girl in forcing her to stray too far from the accepted mores of her time. . . . The steps which parents must take to prepare their daughters to meet economic exigencies and familial responsibilities of modern life—these very steps may awaken aspirations and develop habits which conflict with certain features of their feminine roles, as these are defined today. The very education which is to make the college housewife a cultural leaven of her family and her community may develop in her interests which are frustrated by other phases of housewifery. . . . We run the risk of awakening interests and abilities which, again, run counter to the present definition of femininity.[9]

She goes on to cite the recent case of a girl who wanted to be a sociologist. She was engaged to a GI who didn't want his wife to work. The girl herself hoped she wouldn't find a good job in sociology.

An unsatisfactory job would, she felt, make it easier for her to comply eventually with her future husband's wishes. The needs of the country for trained workers, the uncertainty of her own future, her current interests notwithstanding, she took a routine job. Only the future will tell whether her decision was prudent. If her fiance returns from the front, if the marriage takes place, if he is able to provide for the family without her assistance, if her frustrated wishes do not boomerang, then she will not regret her decision. . . .

At the present historical moment, the best adjusted girl is probably one who is intelligent enough to do well in school but not so brilliant as to get all A's . . . capable but not in areas relatively new to women; able to stand on her own two feet and to earn a living, but not so good a living as to compete with men; capable of doing some job well (in case she doesn't marry, or otherwise has to work) but not so identified with a profession as to need it for her happiness.[10]

So, in the name of adjustment to the cultural definition of femininity—in which this brilliant sociologist obviously does not herself believe (that word "correctly" betrays her)—she ends up virtually endorsing the continued *infantilizing* of American woman, except insofar as it has the unintended consequence of making "the transition from the role of daughter to that of the spouse more difficult for her than for the son."

Essentially, it is assumed that to the extent that the woman remains more "infantile," less able to make her own decisions, more dependent upon one or both parents for initiating and channeling behavior and attitudes, more closely attached to them so as to find it difficult to part from them or to face their disapproval . . . or shows any other indices of lack of emotional emancipation—to that extent she may find it more difficult than the man to conform to the cultural norm of primary loyalty to the family she establishes later. It is possible, of course, that the only effect of the greater sheltering is to create in women a generalized dependency which will then be transferred to the husband and which will enable her all the more readily to accept the role of wife in a family which still has many patriarchal features.[11]

She finds evidence in a number of studies that college girls, in fact, are more infantile, dependent and tied to parents than boys, and do not mature, as boys do, by learning to stand alone. But she can find no evidence—in twenty psychiatric texts—that there are, accordingly, more in-law problems with the wife's parents than the husband's. Evidently, only with such evidence could a functionalist comfortably question the deliberate infantilization of American girls!

Functionalism was an easy out for American sociologists. There can be no doubt that they were describing things "as they were," but in so doing, they were relieved of the responsibility of building theory from facts, of probing for deeper truth. They were also relieved of the need to formulate questions and answers that would be inevitably controversial (at a time in academic circles, as in America as a whole, when controversy was not welcome). They assumed an endless present, and based their reasoning on denying the possibility of a future different from the past. Of course, their reasoning would hold up only as long as the future did not change. As C. P. Snow has pointed out, science and scientists are future-minded. Social scientists under the functional banner were so rigidly present-minded that they denied the future; their theories enforced the prejudices of the past, and actually prevented change.

Sociologists themselves have recently come to the conclusion that functionalism was rather "embarrassing" because it really said nothing at all. As Kingsley Davis pointed out in his presidential address on "The Myth of Functional Analysis as a Special Method in Sociology and Anthropology" at the American Sociological Association in 1959:

> For more than thirty years now "functional analysis" has been debated among sociologists and anthropologists. . . . However strategic it may have been in the past, it has now become an impediment rather than a prop to scientific progress. . . . The claim that functionalism cannot handle social change because it posits an integrated static society is true by definition. . . .[12]

Unfortunately, the female objects of functional analysis were profoundly affected by it. At a time of great change for women, at a time when education, science, and social science should have helped women bridge the change, functionalism transformed "what is" for women, or "what was," to "what should be." Those who perpetrated the feminine protest, and made more of being a woman than it can ever be, in the name of functionalism or for whatever complex of personal or intellectual reasons, closed the door of the future on women. In all the concern for adjustment, one truth was forgotten: women were being adjusted to a state inferior to their full capabilities. The functionalists did not wholly accept the Freudian argument that "anatomy is destiny," but they accepted whole-heartedly an equally restrictive definition of woman: woman is what society says she is. And most of the functional anthropologists studied societies in which woman's destiny was defined by anatomy.

The most powerful influence on modern women, in terms both of functionalism and the feminine protest, was Margaret Mead. Her work on culture and personality—book after book, study after study—has had a profound effect on the women in my generation, the one before it, and the generation now growing up. She was, and still is, the symbol of the woman thinker in America. She has written millions of words in the thirty-odd years between *Coming of Age in Samoa* in 1928 and her latest article on American women in the *New York Times Magazine* or *Redbook*. She is studied in college classrooms by girls taking courses in anthropology, sociology, psychology, education, and marriage and family life; in graduate schools by those who will one day teach girls and counsel women; in medical schools by future pediatricians and psychiatrists; even in theological schools by progressive young ministers. And she is read in the women's magazines and the Sunday supplements, where she publishes as readily as in the learned journals, by girls and women of all ages. Margaret Mead is her own best popularizer—and her influence has been felt in almost every layer of American thought.

But her influence, for women, has been a paradox. A mystique takes what it needs from any thinker of the time. The feminine mystique might have taken from Margaret Mead her vision of the infinite variety of sexual patterns and the enormous plasticity of human nature, a vision based on the differences of sex and temperament she found in three primitive societies: the Arapesh, where both men and women were "feminine" and "maternal" in personality and passively sexual, because both were trained to be cooperative, unaggressive, responsive to the needs and demands of others; the Mundugumor, where both husband and wife were violent, aggressive, positively sexed, "masculine"; and the Tchambuli, where the woman was the dominant, impersonal managing partner, and the man the less responsible and emotionally dependent person.

If those temperamental attitudes which we have traditionally regarded as feminine—such as passivity, responsiveness, and a willingness to cherish children—can so easily be set up as the masculine pattern in one tribe, and in another be outlawed for the majority of women as well as for the majority of men, we no longer have any basis for regarding such aspects of behavior as sex-linked. . . . The material suggests that we may say that many, if not all, of the personality traits which we have called masculine or feminine are as lightly linked to sex, as are the clothing, the manners, and the form of head-dress that a society at a given period assigns to either sex.[13]

From such anthropological observations, she might have passed on to the popular culture a truly revolutionary vision of women finally free to realize their full capabilities in a society which replaced arbitrary sexual definitions with a recognition of genuine individual gifts as they occur in either sex. She had such a vision, more than once:

Where writing is accepted as a profession that may be pursued by either sex with perfect suitability, individuals who have the ability to write need not be debarred from it by their sex, nor need they, if they do write, doubt their essential masculinity or femininity . . . and it is here that we can find a ground-plan for building a society that would substitute real differences for arbitrary ones. We must recognize that beneath the superficial classifications of sex and race the same potentialities exist, recurring generation after generation, only to perish because society has no place for them.

Just as society now permits the practice of an art to members of either sex, so it might also permit the development of many contrasting temperamental gifts in each sex. It would abandon its various attempts to make boys fight and to make girls remain passive, or to make all children fight. . . . No child would be relentlessly shaped to one pattern of behavior, but instead there should be many patterns, in a world that had learned to allow to each individual the pattern which was most congenial to his gifts.[14]

But this is not the vision the mystique took from Margaret Mead; nor is it the vision that she continues to offer. Increasingly, in her own pages, her interpretation blurs, is subtly transformed, into a glorification of women in the female role—as defined by their sexual biological function. At times she seems to lose her own anthropological awareness of the malleability of human personality, and to look at anthropological data from the Freudian point of view—sexual biology determines all, anatomy is destiny. At times she seems to be arguing in functional terms, that while woman's potential is as great and various as the unlimited human potential, it is better to preserve the sexual biological limitations established by a culture. At times she says both things in the same page, and even sounds a note of caution, warning of the dangers a woman faces in trying to realize a human potential which her society has defined as masculine.

The difference between the two sexes is one of the important conditions upon which we have built the many varieties of human culture that give human beings dignity and stature. . . . Sometimes one quality has been assigned to one sex, sometimes to the other. Now it is boys who are thought of as infinitely vulnerable and in need of special cherishing care, now it is girls. . . . Some people think of women as too weak to work out of doors, others regard women as the appropriate bearers of heavy burdens "because their heads are stronger than men's." . . . Some religions, including our European traditional religions, have assigned women an inferior role in the religious hierarchy, others have built their whole symbolic relationship with the supernatural world upon male imitations of the natural functions of women. . . . Whether we deal with small matters or with large, with the frivolities of ornament and cosmetics or the sanctities of man's place in the universe, we find this great variety of ways, often flatly contradictory one to the other, in which the roles of the two sexes have been patterned.

But we always find the patterning. We know of no culture that has said, articulately, that there is no difference between men and women except in the way they contribute to the creation of the next generation; that otherwise in all respects they are simply human beings with varying gifts, no one of which can be exclusively assigned to either sex.

Are we dealing with a must that we dare not flout because it is rooted so deep in our biological mammalian nature that to flout it means individual and social disease? Or with a must that, although not so deeply rooted, still is so very socially convenient and so well tried that it would be uneconomical to flout it—a must which says, for example, that it is easier to get children born and bred if we stylize the behavior of the sexes very differently, teaching them to walk and dress and act in contrasting ways and to specialize in different kinds of work? [15]

We must also ask: What are the potentialities of sex differences? . . . If little boys have to meet and assimilate the early shock of knowing that they can never create a baby with the sureness and incontrovertibility that is a woman's birthright, how does this make them more creatively ambitious, as well as more dependent upon achievement? If little girls have a rhythm of growth which means that their own sex appears to them as initially less sure than their brothers, and so gives them a little false flick towards compensatory achievement that almost always dies down before the certainty of maternity, this probably does mean a limitation on their sense of ambition? But what positive potentialities are there also? [16]

In these passages from *Male and Female*, a book which became the cornerstone of the feminine mystique, Margaret Mead betrays her Freudian orientation, even though she cautiously prefaces each statement of apparent scientific fact with the small word "if." But it is a very significant "if." For when sexual differences become the basis of your approach to culture and personality, and when you assume that sexuality is the driving force of human personality (an assumption that you took from Freud), and when, moreover, as an anthropologist, you know that there are no true-for-every-culture sexual differences except those involved in the act of procreation, you will inevitably give that one biological difference, the difference in reproductive role, increasing importance in the determination of woman's personality.

Margaret Mead did not conceal the fact that, after 1931, Freudian rubrics, based on the zones of the body, were part of the equipment she took with her on anthropological field trips.[17] Thus she began to equate "those assertive, creative, productive aspects of life on which the superstructure of a civilization depends" with the penis, and to define feminine creativity in terms of the "passive receptivity" of the uterus.

In discussing men and women, I shall be concerned with the primary differences between them, the difference in their reproductive roles. Out of the bodies fashioned for complementary roles in perpetuating the race, what differences in functioning, in capacities, in sensitivities, in vulnerabilities arise? How is what men can do related to the fact that their reproductive role is over in a single act, what women can do related to the fact that their reproductive role takes nine months of gestation, and until recently many months of breast feeding? What is the contribution of each sex, seen as itself, not as a mere imperfect version of the other?

Living in the modern world, clothed and muffled, forced to convey our sense of our bodies in terms of remote symbols like walking sticks and umbrellas and handbags, it is easy to lose sight of the immediacy of the human body plan. But when one lives among primitive peoples, where women wear only a pair of little grass aprons, and may discard even these to insult each other or to bathe in a group, and men wear only a very lightly fastened G-string of beaten bark . . . and small babies wear nothing at all, the basic communications . . . that are conducted between bodies become very real. In our own society, we have now invented a therapeutic method that can laboriously deduce from the recollections of the neurotic, or the untrammelled phantasies of the psychotic, how the human body, its entrances and exits, originally shaped the growing individual's view of the world.[18]

As a matter of fact, the lens of "anatomy is destiny" seemed to be peculiarly right for viewing the cultures and personalities of Samoa, Manus, Arapesh, Mundugumor, Tchambuli, Iatmul and Bali; right as perhaps it never was right, in that formulation, for Vienna at the end of the nineteenth century or America in the twentieth.

In the primitive civilizations of the South Sea islands, anatomy was still destiny when Margaret Mead first visited them. Freud's theory that the primitive instincts of the body determined adult personality could find convincing demonstration. The complex goals of more advanced civilizations, in which instinct and environment are increasingly controlled and transformed by the human mind, did not then form the irreversible matrix of every human life. It must have been much easier to see biological differences between men and women as the basic force in life in those unclothed primitive peoples. But only if you go to such an island with the Freudian lens in your eye, accepting before you start what certain irreverent anthropologists call the toilet-paper theory of history, will you draw from observations in primitive civilizations of the role of the unclothed body, male or female, a lesson for modern women which assumes that the unclothed body can determine in the same way the course of human life and personality in a complex modern civilization.

Anthropologists today are less inclined to see in primitive civilization a laboratory for the observation of our own civilization, a scale model with all the irrelevancies blotted out; civilization is just not that irrelevant.

Because the human body is the same in primitive South Sea tribes and modern cities, an anthropologist, who starts with a psychological theory that reduces human personality and civilization to bodily analogies, can end up advising modern women to live through their bodies in the same way as the women of the South Seas. The trouble is that Margaret Mead could not recreate a South Sea world for us to live in: a world where having a baby is the pinnacle of human achievement. (If reproduction were the chief and only fact of human life, would all men today suffer from "uterus envy?")

In Bali, little girls between two and three walk much of the time with purposely thrust-out little bellies, and the older women tap them playfully as they pass. "Pregnant," they tease. So the little girl learns that although the signs of her membership in her own sex are slight, her breasts mere tiny buttons no bigger than her brother's, her genitals a simple inconspicuous fold, some day she will be pregnant, some day she will have a baby, and having a baby is, on the whole, one of the most exciting and conspicuous achievements that can be presented to the eyes of small children in these simple worlds, in some of which the largest buildings are only fifteen feet high, the largest boat some twenty feet long. Furthermore, the little girl learns that she will have a baby not because she is strong or energetic or initiating, not because she works and struggles and tries, and in the end succeeds, but simply because she is a girl and not a boy, and girls turn into women, and in the end—if they protect their femininity—have babies.[19]

To an American woman in the twentieth century competing in a field which demands initiative and energy and work and in which men resent her success, to a woman with less will and ability to compete than Margaret Mead, how tempting is her vision of that South Sea world where a woman succeeds and is envied by man just by being a woman.

In our Occidental view of life, woman, fashioned from man's rib, can at the most strive unsuccessfully to imitate man's superior powers and higher vocations. The basic theme of the initiatory cult, however, is that women, by virtue of their ability to make children, hold the secret of life. Man's role is uncertain, undefined, and perhaps unnecessary. By a great effort man has hit upon a method of compensating himself for his basic inferiority. Equipped with various mysterious noise-making instruments, whose potency rests upon their actual forms being unknown to those who hear the sounds—that is, the women and children must never know that they are really bamboo flutes, or hollow logs . . . they can get the male children away from the women, brand them as incomplete and themselves turn boys into men. Women, it is true, make human beings, but only men can make men.[20]

True, this primitive society was a "shaky structure, protected by endless taboos and precautions"—by women's shame, fluttery fear, indulgence of male vanity—and it survived only as long as everyone kept the rules. "The missionary who shows the flutes to the women has broken the culture successfully." [21] But Margaret Mead, who might have shown American men and women "the flutes" of their own arbitrary and shaky taboos, precautions, shames, fears, and indulgence of male vanity, did not use her knowledge in this way. Out of life the way it was—in Samoa, Bali, where all men envied women—she held up an ideal for American women that gave new reality to the shaky structure of sexual prejudice, the feminine mystique.

The language is anthropological, the theory stated as fact is Freudian, but the yearning is for a return to the Garden of Eden: a garden where women need only forget the "divine discontent" born of education to return to a world in which male achievement becomes merely a poor substitute for child-bearing.

The recurrent problem of civilization is to define the male role satisfactorily enough—whether it be to build gardens or raise cattle, kill game or kill enemies, build bridges or handle bank shares—so that the male may, in the course of his life, reach a solid sense of irreversible achievement of which his childhood knowledge of the satisfactions of child-bearing has given him a glimpse. In the case of women, it is only necessary that they be permitted by the given social arrangements to fulfill their biological role, to attain this sense of irreversible achievement. If women are to be restless and questing, even in the face of childbearing, they must be made so through education.[22]

What the feminine mystique took from Margaret Mead was not her vision of woman's great untested human potential, but this glorification of the female sexual function that has indeed been tested, in every culture, but seldom, in civilized cultures, valued as highly as the unlimited potential of human creativity, so far mainly displayed by man. The vision the mystique took from Margaret Mead was of a world where women, by merely being women and bearing children, will earn the same respect accorded men for their creative achievements—as if possession of uterus and breasts bestows on women a glory that men can never know, even though they labor all their lives to create. In such a world, all the other things that a woman can do or be are merely pale substitutes for the conception of a child. Femininity becomes more than its definition by society; it becomes a value which society must protect from the destructive onrush of civilization like the vanishing buffalo.

Margaret Mead's eloquent pages made a great many American women envy the serene femininity of a bare-breasted Samoan, and try to make themselves into languorous savages, breasts unfettered by civilization's brassieres, and brains undisturbed by pallid man-made knowledge of the goals of human progress.

> Woman's biological career-line has a natural climax structure that can be overlaid, muted, muffled and publicly denied, but which remains as an essential element in both sexes' view of themselves. . . . The young Balinese girl to whom one says, "Your name is I Tewa?" and who draws herself up and answers, "I am Men Bawa" (Mother of Bawa) is speaking absolutely. She is the mother of Bawa; Bawa may die tomorrow, but she remains the mother of Bawa; only if he had died unnamed would her neighbors have called her "Men Belasin," "Mother Bereft." Stage after stage in women's life-histories thus stand, irrevocable, indisputable, accomplished. This gives a natural basis for the little girl's emphasis on being rather than on doing. The little boy learns that he must act like a boy, do things, prove that he is a boy, and prove it over and over again, while the little girl learns that she is a girl, and all she has to do is to refrain from acting like a boy.[23]

And so it goes, on and on, until one is inclined to say—so what? You are born, you grow, you are impregnated, you have a child, it grows; this is true of all cultures, recorded or unrecorded, the one we know from life and the recondite ones which only the far-traveled anthropologist knows. But is this all there is to life for a woman today?

It is not to deny the importance of biology to question a definition of woman's nature that is based so completely on her biological difference from man. Female biology, woman's "biological career-line," may be changeless—the same in Stone Age women twenty thousand years ago, and Samoan women on remote islands, and American women in the twentieth century—but the nature of the human relationship to biology *has* changed. Our increasing knowledge, the increasing potency of human intelligence, has given us an awareness of purposes and goals beyond the simple biological needs of hunger, thirst, and sex. Even these simple needs, in men or women today, are not the same as they were in the Stone Age or in the South Sea cultures, because they are now part of a more complex pattern of human life.

As an anthropologist, of course, Margaret Mead knew this. And for all her words glorifying the female role, there are other words picturing the wonders of a world in which women would be able to realize their full capabilities. But this picture is almost invariably overlaid with the therapeutic caution, the manipulative superiority, typical of too many American social scientists. When this caution is combined with perhaps an over-evaluation of the power of social science not merely to interpret culture and personality, but to order our lives, her words acquire the aura of a righteous crusade—a crusade against change. She joins the other functional social scientists in their emphasis on adjusting to society as we find it, on living our lives within the framework of the conventional cultural definitions of the male and female roles. This attitude is explicit in the later pages of *Male and Female.*

Giving each sex its due, a full recognition of its special vulnerabilities and needs for protection, means looking beyond the superficial resemblances during the period of later childhood when both boys and girls, each having laid many of the problems of sex adjustment aside, seem so eager to learn, and so able to learn the same things. . . . But every adjustment that minimizes a difference, a vulnerability, in one sex, a differential strength in the other, diminishes their possibility of complementing each other, and corresponds—symbolically—to sealing off the constructive receptivity of the female and the vigorous outgoing constructive activity of the male, muting them both in the end to a duller version of human life, in which each is denied the fullness of humanity that each might have had.[24]

No human gift is strong enough to flower fully in a person who is threatened with loss of sex membership. . . . No matter with what good will we may embark on a program of actually rearing both men and women to make their full and special contributions in all the complex processes of civilization—medicine and law, education and religion, the arts and sciences—the task will be very difficult. . . .

It is of very doubtful value to enlist the gifts of women if bringing women into fields that have been defined as male frightens the men, unsexes the women, muffles and distorts the contribution the women could make, either because their presence excludes men from the occupation or because it changes the quality of the men who enter it. . . . It is folly to ignore the signs which warn us that the present terms in which women are lured by their own curiosities and drives developed under the same educational system as boys . . . are bad for both men and women.[25]

The role of Margaret Mead as the professional spokesman of femininity would have been less important if American women had taken the example of her own life, instead of listening to what she said in her books. Margaret Mead has lived a life of open challenge, and lived it proudly, if sometimes self-consciously, as a woman. She has moved on the frontiers of thought and added to the superstructure of our knowledge. She has demonstrated feminine capabilities that go far beyond childbirth; she made her way in what was still very much a "man's world" without denying that she was a woman; in fact, she proclaimed in her work a unique woman's knowledge with which no male anthropologist could compete. After so many centuries of unquestioned masculine authority, how natural for someone to proclaim a feminine authority. But the great human visions of stopping wars, curing sickness, teaching races to live together, building new and beautiful structures for people to live in, are more than "other ways of having children."

It is not easy to combat age-old prejudices. As a social scientist, and as a woman, she struck certain blows against the prejudicial image of woman that may long outlast her own life. In her insistence that women are human beings—unique human beings, not men with something missing—she went a step beyond Freud. And yet, because her observations were based on Freud's bodily analogies, she cut down her own vision of women by glorifying the mysterious miracle of femininity, which a woman realizes simply by being female, letting the breasts grow and the menstrual blood flow and the baby suck from the swollen breast. In her warning that women who seek fulfillment beyond their biological role are in danger of becoming desexed witches, she spelled out again an unnecessary choice. She persuaded younger women to give up part of their dearly won humanity rather than lose their femininity. In the end she did the very thing that she warned against, re-creating in her work the vicious circle that she broke in her own life:

> We may go up the scale from simple physical differences through complementary distinctions that overstress the role of sex difference and extend it inappropriately to other aspects of life, to stereotypes of such complex activities as those involved in the formal use of the intellect, in the arts, in government, and in religion.
>
> In all these complex achievements of civilization, those activities which are mankind's glory, and upon which depends our hope of survival in this world that we have built, there has been this tendency to make artificial definitions that limit an activity to one sex, and by denying the actual potentialities of human beings limit not only both men and women, but also equally the development of the activity itself. . . .
>
> Here is a vicious circle to which it is not possible to assign either a beginning or an end, in which men's overestimation of women's roles, or women's overestimation of men's roles leads one sex or the other to arrogate, to neglect, or even to relinquish part of our so dearly won humanity. Those who would break the circle are themselves a product of it, express some of its defects in their every gesture, may be only strong enough to challenge it, not able actually to break it. Yet once identified, once analyzed, it should be possible to create a climate of opinion in which others, a little less the product of the dark past because they have been reared with a light in their hand that can shine backwards as well as forwards, may in turn take the next step.[26]

Perhaps the feminine protest was a necessary step after the masculine protest made by some of the feminists. Margaret Mead was one of the first women to emerge into prominence in American life after rights for women were won. Her mother was a social scientist, her grandmother a teacher; she had private images of women who were fully human, she had education equal to any man's. And she was able to say with conviction: it's good to be a woman, you don't need to copy man, you can respect yourself as a woman. She made a resounding feminine protest, in her life and in her work. And it was a step forward when she influenced emancipated modern women to choose, with free intelligence, to have babies, bear them with a proud awareness that denied pain, nurse them at the breast and devote mind and body to their care. It was a step forward in the passionate jour· ney—and one made possible by it—for educated women to say "yes" to motherhood as a conscious human purpose and not a burden imposed by the flesh. For, of course, the natural child-birth-breastfeeding movement Margaret Mead helped inspire was not at all a return to primitive earth-mother maternity. It appealed to the independent, educated, spirited American woman— and to her counterparts in western Europe and Russia—because it enabled her to experience childbirth not as a mindless female animal, an object manipulated by the obstetrician, but as a whole person, able to control her own body with her aware mind. Perhaps less important than birth control and the other rights which made woman more equal to man, the work of Margaret Mead helped humanize sex. It took a scientific supersaleswoman to re-create in modern American life even a semblance of the conditions under which primitive tribesmen jealously imitated maternity and bled themselves. (The modern husband goes through the breathing exercises with his wife as she prepares for natural childbirth.) But did she oversell women?

It was, perhaps, not her fault that she was taken so literally that procreation became a cult, a career, to the exclusion of every other kind of creative endeavor, until women kept on having babies because they knew no other way to create. She was often quoted out of context by the lesser functionalists and the women's magazines. Those who found in her work confirmation of their own unadmitted prejudices and fears ignored not only the complexity of her total work, but the example of her complex life. With all the difficulties she must have encountered, pioneering as a woman in the realm of abstract thought that was the domain of man (a one-sentence review of *Sex and Temperament* indicates the resentment she often met: "Margaret, have you found a culture yet where the men had the babies?"), she has never re-treated from the hard road to self-realization so few women have traveled since. She told women often enough to stay on that road. If they only heard her other words of warning, and conformed to her glorification of femininity, perhaps it was because they were not as sure of themselves and their human abilities as she was.

Margaret Mead and the lesser functionalists knew the pains, the risks, of breaking through age-old social strictures.[27] This awareness was their justification for qualifying their statements of women's potentiality with the advice that women not com-pete with men, but seek respect for their uniqueness as women. It was hardly revolutionary advice; it did not upset the tradi-tional image of woman any more than Freudian thought upset it. Perhaps it was their intention to subvert the old image; but instead they gave the new mystique its scientific authority.

Ironically, Margaret Mead, in the 1960's, began to voice alarm at the "return of the cavewoman"—the retreat of American women to narrow domesticity, while the world trembled on the brink of technological holocaust. In an excerpt from a book titled *American Women: The Changing Image*, which appeared in the *Saturday Evening Post* (March 3, 1962), she asked:

Why have we returned, despite our advances in technology, to the Stone Age picture? . . . Woman has gone back, each to her separate cave, waiting anxiously for her mate and children to return, guarding her mate jealously against other women, almost totally unaware of any life outside her door. . . . In this retreat into fecundity, it is not the individual woman who is to blame. It is the climate of opinion that has developed in this country . . .

Apparently Margaret Mead does not acknowledge, or perhaps recognize her own role as a major architect of that "climate of opinion." Apparently she has overlooked much of her own work, which helped persuade several generations of able modern Ameri-can women "in desperate cavewoman style, to devote their whole lives to narrow domesticity—first in schoolgirl dreaming and a search for roles which make them appealingly ignorant, then as mothers and then as grandmothers . . . restricting their activities to the preservation of their own private, and often boring existences."

Even though it would seem that Margaret Mead is now trying to get women out of the home, she still ascribes a sexual specialness to everything a woman does. Trying to seduce them into the modern world of science as "the teacher-mothers of infant scientists," she is still translating the new possibilities open to women and the new problems facing them as members of the human race into sexual terms. But now "those roles which have historically belonged to women" are stretched to include political responsibility for nuclear disarmament—"to cherish not just their own but the children of the enemy." Since, beginning with the same premise and examining the same body of anthropological evidence, she now arrives at a slightly different sexual role for women, one might seriously question the basis upon which she decides the roles a woman should play—and finds it so easy to change the rules of the game from one decade to the next.

Other social scientists have arrived at the astonishing conclusion that "being a woman was no more and no less than being human." [28] But a cultural lag is built into the feminine mystique. By the time a few social scientists were discovering the flaws in "woman's role," American educators had seized upon it as a magic sesame. Instead of educating women for the greater maturity required to participate in modern society—with all the problems, conflicts, and hard work involved, for educators as well as women—they began educating them to "play the role of woman."

7 The Sex-Directed
Educators

It must have been going on for ten or fifteen years before the educators even suspected it—the old-fashioned educators, that is. The new sex-directed educators were surprised that anyone should be surprised, shocked that anyone should be shocked.

The shock, the mystery, to the naive who had great hopes for the higher education of women was that more American women than ever before were going to college—but fewer of them were going on from college to become physicists, philosophers, poets, doctors, lawyers, stateswomen, social pioneers, even college professors. Fewer women in recent college graduating classes have gone on to distinguish themselves in a career or profession than those in the classes graduated before World War II, the Great Divide. Fewer and fewer college women were preparing for any career or profession requiring more than the most casual commitment. Two out of three girls who entered college were dropping out before they even finished. In the 1950's, those who stayed, even the most able, showed no signs of wanting to be anything more than suburban housewives and mothers. In fact, to professors at Vassar and Smith and Barnard, resorting to desperate means to arouse students' interest in *anything* college could teach them, the girls seemed suddenly incapable of any ambition, any vision, any passion, except the pursuit of a wedding ring. In this pursuit they seemed almost desperate, as early as freshman year.

Out of loyalty to that more and more futile illusion—the importance of higher education for women—the purist professors kept quiet at first. But the disuse of, the resistance to, higher education by American women finally began to show in the statistics:[1] in the departure of the male presidents, scholars, and educators from women's colleges; in the disillusionment, the mystified frustration or cool cynicism of the ones who stayed; and in the skepticism, finally, in colleges and universities, about the value of a professorial investment in any girl or woman, no matter how apparently able and ambitious. Some women's colleges went out of business; some professors, at coeducational universities, said one out of three college places should no longer be wasted on women; the president of Sarah Lawrence, a women's college with high intellectual values, spoke of opening the place to men; the president of Vassar predicted the end of all the great American women's colleges which pioneered higher education for women.

When I read the first cautious hints of what was happening, in the preliminary report of the psychological-sociological-anthropological Mellon Foundation study of Vassar girls in 1956, I thought, "My, how Vassar must have deteriorated."

Strong commitment to an activity or career other than that of housewife is rare. Many students, perhaps a third, are interested in graduate schooling and in careers, for example, teaching. Few, however, plan to continue with a career if it should conflict with family needs. . . . As compared to previous periods, however, e.g., the "feminist era," few students are interested in the pursuit of demanding careers, such as law or medicine, regardless of personal or social pressures. Similarly, one finds few instances of people like Edna St. Vincent Millay, individuals completely committed to their art by the time of adolescence and resistant to any attempts to tamper with it . . .[2]

A later report elaborated:

Vassar students . . . are further convinced that the wrongs of society will gradually right themselves with little or no direct intervention on the part of women college students. . . . Vassar girls, by and large, do not expect to achieve fame, make an enduring contribution to society, pioneer any frontiers, or otherwise create ripples in the placid order of things. . . . Not only is spinsterhood viewed as a personal tragedy but offspring are considered essential to the full life and the Vassar student believes that she would willingly adopt children, if it were necessary, to create a family. In short, her future identity is largely encompassed by the projected role of wife-mother. . . . In describing the qualities to be found in an ideal husband, the majority of Vassar girls are quite explicit in their preference for the man who will assume the most important role, that is, handle his own career and make the majority of decisions affecting matters outside the home. . . . That the female should attempt, in their thinking, to usurp the prerogatives of the male is a distasteful notion which would seriously disrupt their own projected role of helpmate and faithful complement to the man of the house.[3]

I saw the change, a very real one, when I went back to my own college in 1959, to live for a week with the students in a campus house at Smith, and then went on to interview girls from colleges and universities all over the United States.

A beloved psychology professor, on the eve of his retirement, complained:

They're bright enough. They have to be, to get here at all now. But they just won't let themselves get interested. They seem to feel it will get in their way when they marry the young executive and raise all those children in the suburbs. I couldn't schedule the final seminar for my senior honor students. Too many kitchen showers interfered. None of them considered the seminar sufficiently important to postpone their kitchen showers.

He's exaggerating, I thought.

I picked up a copy of the college newspaper I had once edited. The current student editor described a government class in which fifteen of the twenty girls were knitting "with the stony-faced concentration of Madame Defarge. The instructor, more in challenge than in seriousness, announced that Western civilization is coming to an end. The students turned to their notebooks and wrote 'Western civ—coming to an end,' all without dropping a stitch."

Why do they need such baiting, I wondered, remembering how we used to stand around after class, arguing about what the professor had said—Economic Theory, Political Philosophy, the History of Western Civilization, Sociology 21, Science and the Imagination, even Chaucer. "What courses are people excited about now?" I asked a blonde senior in cap and gown. Nuclear physics, maybe? Modern art? The civilizations of Africa? Looking at me as if I were some prehistoric dinosaur, she said:

Girls don't get excited about things like that anymore. We don't want careers. Our parents expect us to go to college. Everybody goes. You're a social outcast at home if you don't. But a girl who got serious about anything she studied—like wanting to go on and do research— would be peculiar, unfeminine. I guess everybody wants to graduate with a diamond ring on her finger. That's the important thing.

I discovered an unwritten rule barring "shop talk" about courses, intellectual talk, in some college houses. On the campus, the girls looked as if they were in such a hurry, rushing, rushing. Nobody, except a few faculty members, sat around talking in the coffee dives or the corner drugstore. We used to sit for hours arguing what-is-truth, art-for-art's-sake, religion, sex, war and peace, Freud and Marx, and all the things that were wrong with the world. A cool junior told me:

We never waste time like that. We don't have bull sessions about abstract things. Mostly, we talk about our dates. Anyhow, I spend three days a week off campus. There's a boy I'm interested in. I want to be with him.

A dark-eyed senior in a raincoat admitted, as a kind of secret addiction, that she liked to wander around the stacks in the library and "pick up books that interest me."

You learn freshman year to turn up your nose at the library. Lately though—well, it hits you, that you won't be at college next year. Suddenly you wish you'd read more, talked more, taken hard courses you skipped. So you'd know what you're interested in. But I guess those things don't matter when you're married. You're interested in your home and teaching your children how to swim and skate, and at night you talk to your husband. I think we'll be happier than college women used to be.

These girls behaved as if college were an interval to be gotten through impatiently, efficiently, bored but businesslike, so "real" life could begin. And real life was when you married and lived in a suburban house with your husband and children. Was it quite natural, this boredom, this businesslike haste? Was it real, this preoccupation with marriage? The girls who glibly disclaimed any serious interest in their education with talk of "when I'm married" often were not seriously interested in any particular man, I discovered. The ones who were rushing to get their college work done, to spend three days a week off campus, sometimes had no real date they wanted to keep.

In my time, popular girls who spent many weekends at Yale were often just as serious about their work as the "brains." Even if you were temporarily, or quite seriously, in love, during the week at college you lived the life of the mind—and found it absorbing, demanding, sometimes exciting, always real. Could these girls who now must work so much harder, have so much more ability to get into such a college against the growing competition, really be so bored with the life of the mind?

Gradually, I sensed the tension, the almost sullen protest, the deliberate effort—or effort deliberately avoided—behind their cool façades. Their boredom was not quite what it seemed. It was a defense, a refusal to become involved. As a woman who unconsciously thinks sex a sin is not there, is somewhere else, as she goes through the motions of sex, so these girls are somewhere else. They go through the motions, but they defend themselves against the impersonal passions of mind and spirit that college might instill in them—the dangerous nonsexual passions of the intellect.

A pretty sophomore explained to me:

The idea is to be casual, very sophisticated. Don't be too enthusiastic about your work or anything. People who take things too seriously are more or less pitied or laughed at. Like wanting to sing, being so intent about it you make other people uncomfortable. An oddball.

Another girl elaborated:

They might feel sorry for you. I think you can be serious about your work and not be looked down upon as a total intellectual, if you stop now and then and think isn't this too hysterical. Because you do it with tongue in cheek, it's O.K.

A girl with a fraternity pin on her pink sweater said:

Maybe we should take it more seriously. But nobody wants to graduate and get into something where they can't use it. If your husband is going to be an organization man, you can't be too educated. The wife is awfully important for the husband's career. You can't be too interested in art, or something like that.

A girl who had dropped out of honors in history told me:

I loved it. I got so excited about my work I would sometimes go into the library at eight in the morning and not come out till ten at night. I even thought I might want to go on to graduate school or law school and really use my mind. Suddenly, I was afraid of what would happen. I wanted to lead a rich full life. I want to marry, have children, have a nice house. Suddenly I felt, what am I beating my brains out for. So this year I'm trying to lead a well-rounded life. I take courses, but I don't read eight books and still feel like reading the ninth. I stop and go to the movies. The other way was harder, and more exciting. I don't know why I stopped. Maybe I just lost courage.

The phenomenon does not seem confined to any particular college; one finds it among the girls in any college, or department of a college, which still exposes students to the life of the mind. A junior from a Southern university said:

Ever since I was a little girl, science has had a fascination for me. I was going to major in bacteriology and go into cancer research. Now I've switched to home economics. I realized I don't want to go into something that deep. If I went on, I'd have been one of those dedicated people. I got so caught up in the first two years, I never got out of the laboratory. I loved it, but I was missing so many things. If the girls were off swimming in the afternoon, I'd be working on my smears and slides. There aren't any girls in bacteriology here, sixty boys and me in the lab. I couldn't get on with the girls anymore who don't understand science. I'm not so intensely interested in home economics as I was in bacteriology, but I realize it was better for me to change, and get out with people. I realized I shouldn't be that serious. I'll go home and work in a department store until I get married.

The mystery to me is not that these girls defend themselves against an involvement with the life of the mind, but that educators should be mystified by their defense, or blame it on the "student culture," as certain educators do. The one lesson a girl could hardly avoid learning, if she went to college between 1945 and 1960, was *not* to get interested, seriously interested, in anything besides getting married and having children, if she wanted to be normal, happy, adjusted, feminine, have a successful husband, successful children, and a normal, feminine, adjusted, successful sex life. She might have learned some of this lesson at home, and some of it from the other girls in college, but she also learned it, incontrovertibly, from those entrusted with developing her critical, creative intelligence: her college professors.

A subtle and almost unnoticed change had taken place in the academic culture for American women in the last fifteen years: the new sex-direction of their educators. Under the influence of the feminine mystique, some college presidents and professors charged with the education of women had become more concerned with their students' future capacity for sexual orgasm than with their future use of trained intelligence. In fact, some leading educators of women began to concern themselves, conscientiously, with protecting students from the temptation to use their critical, creative intelligence—by the ingenious method of educating it *not* to be critical or creative. Thus higher education added its weight to the process by which American women during this period were shaped increasingly to their biological function, decreasingly to the fulfillment of their individual abilities. Girls who went to college could hardly escape those bits and pieces of Freud and Margaret Mead, or avoid a course in "Marriage and Family Life" with its functional indoctrination on "how to play the role of woman."

The new sex-direction of women's education was not, however, confined to any specific course or academic department. It was implicit in all the social sciences; but more than that, it became a part of education itself, not only because the English professor, or the guidance counselor, or the college president read Freud and Mead, but because education was the prime target of the new mystique—the education of American girls with, or like, boys. If the Freudians and the functionalists were right, educators were guilty of defeminizing American women, of dooming them to frustration as housewives and mothers, or to celibate careers, to life without orgasm. It was a damning indictment; many college presidents and educational theorists confessed their guilt without a murmur and fell into the sex-directed line. There were a few cries of outrage, of course, from the old-fashioned educators who still believed the mind was more important than the marriage bed, but they were often near retirement and soon to be replaced by younger, more thoroughly sex-indoctrinated teachers, or they were so wrapped up in their special subjects that they had little say in over-all school policies.

The general educational climate was ripe for the new sex-directed line, with its emphasis on adjustment. The old aim of education, the development of intelligence through vigorous mastery of the major intellectual disciplines, was already in disfavor among the child-centered educators. Teachers College at Columbia was the natural breeding ground for educational functionalism. As psychology and anthropology and sociology permeated the total scholarly atmosphere, education for femininity also spread from Mills, Stephens and the finishing schools (where its basis was more traditional than theoretical) to the proudest bastions of the women's Ivy League, the colleges which pioneered higher education for women in America, and were noted for their uncompromising intellectual standards.

Instead of opening new horizons and wider worlds to able women, the sex-directed educator moved in to teach them adjustment within the world of home and children. Instead of teaching truths to counter the popular prejudices of the past, or critical ways of thinking against which prejudice cannot survive, the sex-directed educator handed girls a sophisticated soup of uncritical prescriptions and presentiments, far more binding on the mind and prejudicial to the future than all the traditional do's and

don'ts. Most of it was done consciously and for the best of helpful reasons by educators who really believed the mystique as the
social scientists handed it to them. If a male professor or college
president did not find this mystique a positive comfort, a confirmation of his own prejudices, he still had no reason *not* to believe it.

The few college presidents and professors who were women
either fell into line or had their authority—as teachers and as
women—questioned. If they were spinsters, if they had not had
babies, they were forbidden by the mystique to speak as women.
(*Modern Woman: The Lost Sex* would forbid them even to teach.)
The brilliant scholar, who did not marry but inspired many generations of college women to the pursuit of truth, was sullied as
an educator of women. She was not named president of the
women's college whose intellectual tradition she carried to its
highest point; the girls' education was put in the hands of a handsome, husbandly man, more suitable to indoctrinating girls for
their proper feminine role. The scholar often left the woman's
college to head a department in a great university, where the
potential Ph.D's were safely men, for whom the lure of scholarship, the pursuit of truth, was not deemed a deterrent to sexual
fulfillment.

In terms of the new mystique, the woman scholar was suspect,
simply by virtue of being one. She was not just working to support her home; she must have been guilty of an unfeminine commitment, to have kept working in her field all those hard, grind-
ing, ill-paid years to the Ph.D. In self-defense she sometimes
adopted frilly blouses or another innocuous version of the feminine protest. (At psychoanalytic conventions, an observer once
noticed, the lady analysts camouflage themselves with pretty,
flowery, smartly feminine hats that would make the casual suburban housewife look positively masculine.) M.D. or Ph.D., those
hats and frilly blouses say, *let nobody question our femininity*.
But the fact is, their femininity was questioned. One famous
women's college adopted in defense the slogan, "We are not educating women to be scholars; we are educating them to be wives

and mothers." (The girls themselves finally got so tired of repeating this slogan in full that they abbreviated it to "WAM.")

In building the sex-directed curriculum, not everyone went as far as Lynn White, former president of Mills College, but if you started with the premise that women should no longer be educated like men, but for their role as women, you almost had to end with his curriculum—which amounted to replacing college chemistry with a course in advanced cooking.

The sex-directed educator begins by accepting education's responsibility for the frustration, general and sexual, of American women.

On my desk lies a letter from a young mother, a few years out of college:

"I have come to realize that I was educated to be a successful man and must now learn by myself to be a successful woman." The basic irrelevance of much of what passes as women's education in America could not be more compactly phrased. . . . The failure of our educational system to take into account these simple and basic differences between the life patterns of average men and women is at least in part responsible for the deep discontent and restlessness which affects millions of women. . . .

It would seem that if women are to restore their self-respect they must reverse the tactics of the older feminism which indignantly denied inherent differences in the intellectual and emotional tendencies of men and women. Only by recognizing and insisting upon the importance of such differences can women save themselves, in their own eyes, of conviction as inferiors.[4]

The sex-directed educator equates as masculine our "vastly overrated cultural creativity," "our uncritical acceptance of 'progress' as good in itself," "egotistic individualism," "innovation," "abstract construction," "quantitative thinking"—of which, of course, the dread symbol is either communism or the atom bomb. Against these, equated as feminine, are "the sense of persons, of the immediate, of intangible qualitative relationships, an aversion for statistics and quantities," "the intuitive," "the emotional," and all the forces that "cherish" and "conserve" what is "good, true, beautiful, useful, and holy."

A feminized higher education might include sociology, anthropology, psychology. ("These are studies little concerned with the laurel-crowned genius of the strong man," praises the educational protector of femininity. "They are devoted to exploring the quiet and unspectacular forces of society and of the mind. . . . They embrace the feminine preoccupation with conserving and cherishing.") It would hardly include either pure science (since abstract theory and quantitative thinking are unfeminine) or fine art, which is masculine, "flamboyant and abstract." The applied or minor arts, however, are feminine: ceramics, textiles, work shaped more by the hand than the brain. "Women love beauty as much as men do but they want a beauty connected with the processes of living . . . the hand is as remarkable and as worthy of respect as the brain."

The sex-directed educator cites approvingly Cardinal Tisserant's saying, "Women should be educated so that they can argue with their husbands." Let us stop altogether professional training for women, he insists: all women must be educated to be housewives. Even home economics and domestic science, as they are now taught at college, are masculine because "they have been pitched at the level of professional training." [5]

Here is a truly feminine education:

One may prophesy with confidence that as women begin to make their distinctive wishes felt in curricular terms, not merely will every women's college and coeducational institution offer a firm nuclear course in the Family, but from it will radiate curricular series dealing with food and nutrition, textiles and clothing, health and nursing, house planning and interior decoration, garden design and applied botany, and child-development. . . . Would it be impossible to present a beginning course in foods as exciting and as difficult to work up after college, as a course in post-Kantian philosophy would be? . . . Let's abandon talk of proteins, carbohydrates and the like, save inadvertently, as for example, when we point out that a British hyper-boiled Brussel sprout is not merely inferior in flavor and texture, but in vitamine content. Why not study the theory and preparation of a Basque paella, of a well-marinated shish kebob, lamb kidneys sauteed in sherry, an authoritative curry, the use of herbs, even such simple sophistications as serving cold artichokes with fresh milk.[6]

The sex-directed educator is hardly impressed by the argument that a college curriculum should not be contaminated or diluted with subjects like cooking or manual training, which can be taught successfully at the high-school level. Teach them to the girls in high school, and "with greater intensity and imagination" again in college. Boys, also, should get some "family-minded" education, but not in their valuable college time; early high-school manual training is enough to "enable them, in future years to work happily at a bench in the garage or in the garden, surrounded by an admiring circle of children . . . or at the barbecue." [7]

This kind of education, in the name of life-adjustment, became a fact on many campuses, high-school as well as college. It was not dreamed up to turn back the growth of women, but it surely helped. When American educators finally began to investigate the waste of our national resources of creative intelligence, they found that the lost Einsteins, Schweitzers, Roosevelts, Edisons, Fords, Fermis, Frosts were feminine. Of the brightest forty per cent of U.S. high-school graduates, only half went on to college: of the half who stopped, *two out of three were girls.*[8] When Dr. James B. Conant went across the nation to find out what was wrong with the American high school, he discovered too many students were taking easy how-to courses which didn't really stretch their minds. Again, most of those who should have been studying physics, advanced algebra, analytic geometry, four years of language—and were not—were girls. They had the intelligence, the special gift which was not sex-directed, but they also had the sex-directed attitude that such studies were "unfeminine."

Sometimes a girl wanted to take a hard subject, but was advised by a guidance counselor or teacher that it was a waste of time—as, for instance, the girl in a good Eastern high school who wanted to be an architect. Her counselor strongly advised her against applying for admission anywhere in architecture, on the grounds that women are rare in that profession, and she would never get in anyhow. She stubbornly applied to two universities who give degrees in architecture; both, to her amazement, accepted her. Then her counselor told her that even though she had been accepted, there was really no future for women in architecture; she would spend her life in a drafting room. She was advised to go to a junior college where the work would be much easier than in architecture and where she would learn all she needed to know when she married.[9]

The influence of sex-directed education was perhaps even more insidious on the high-school level than it was in the colleges, for many girls who were subjected to it never got to college. I picked up a lesson plan for one of these life-adjustment courses now taught in junior high in the suburban county where I live. Entitled "The Slick Chick," it gives functional "do's and don'ts for dating" to girls of eleven, twelve, thirteen—a kind of early or forced recognition of their sexual function. Though many have nothing yet with which to fill a brassiere, they are told archly not to wear a sweater without one, and to be sure to wear slips so boys can't see through their skirts. It is hardly surprising that by the sophomore year, many bright girls in this high school are more than conscious of their sexual function, bored with all the subjects in school, and have no ambition other than to marry and have babies. One cannot help wondering (especially when some of these girls get pregnant as high-school sophomores and marry at fifteen or sixteen) if they have not been educated for their sexual function too soon, while their other abilities go unrecognized.

This stunting of able girls from nonsexual growth is nationwide. Of the top ten per cent of graduates of Indiana high schools in 1955, only fifteen per cent of the boys did not continue their education: thirty-six per cent of the girls did not go on.[10] In the very years in which higher education has become a necessity for almost everyone who wants a real function in our exploding society, *the proportion of women among college students has declined, year by year*. In the fifties, women also dropped out of college at a faster rate than the men: only thirty-seven per cent of the women graduated, in contrast to fifty-five per cent of the men.[11] By the sixties, an equal proportion of boys was dropping out of college.[12] But, in this era of keen competition for college seats, the one girl who enters college for every two boys is "more highly selected," and less likely to be dropped from college for academic failure. Women drop out, as David Riesman says, either to marry or because they fear too much education is a "marriage bar." The average age of first marriage, in the last fifteen years, has dropped to the youngest in the history of this country, the youngest in any of the countries of the Western world, almost as young as it used to be in the so-called underdeveloped countries. In the new nations of Asia and Africa, with the advent of science and education, the marriage age of women is now rising. Today, thanks in part to the functional sex-direction of women's education, the annual rate of population increase in the United States is among the highest in the world—nearly three times that of the Western European nations, nearly double Japan's, and close on the heels of Africa and India.[13]

The sex-directed educators have played a dual role in this trend: by actively educating girls to their sexual function (which perhaps they would fulfill without such education, in a way less likely to prevent their growth in other directions); and by abdicating their responsibility for the education of women, in the strict intellectual sense. With or without education, women are likely to fulfill their biological role, and experience sexual love and motherhood. But without education, women or men are not likely to develop deep interests that go beyond biology.

Education should, and can, make a person "broad in outlook, and open to new experience, independent and disciplined in his thinking, deeply committed to some productive activity, possessed of convictions based on understanding of the world and on his own integration of personality." [14] The main barrier to such growth in girls is their own rigid preconception of woman's role, which sex-directed educators reinforce, either explicitly or by not facing their own ability, and responsibility, to break through it.

Such a sex-directed impasse is revealed in the massive depths of that thousand-page study, *The American College,* when "motivational factors in college entrance" are analyzed from research among 1,045 boys and 1,925 girls. The study recognizes that it is the need to be independent, and find identity in society not primarily through the sex role but through work, which makes boys grow in college. The girl's evasion of growth in college is explained by the fact that for a girl, identity is exclusively sexual; for the girl, college itself is seen even by these scholars not as the key to larger identity but as a disguised "outlet for sexual impulses."

The identity issue for the boy is primarily an occupational-vocational question, while self-definition for the girl depends more directly on marriage. A number of differences follow from this distinction. The girl's identity centers more exclusively on her sex-role—whose wife will I be, what kind of a family will we have; while the boy's self-definition forms about two nuclei; he will be a husband and father (his sex-role identity) but he will also and centrally be a worker. A related difference follows and has particular importance at adolescence: the occupational identity is by and large an issue of personal choice that can begin early and to which all of the resources of rational and thoughtful planning can be directed. The boy can begin to think and plan for this aspect of identity early. . . . The sexual identity, so critical for feminine development, permits no such conscious or orderly effort. It is a mysterious and romantic issue, freighted with fiction, mystique, illusion. A girl may learn certain surface skills and activities of the feminine role, but she will be thought ungraceful and unfeminine if her efforts toward femininity are too clearly conscious. The real core of feminine settlement—living in intimacy with a beloved man—is a future prospect, for which there is no rehearsal. We find that boys and girls in adolescence have different approaches to the future; boys are actively planning and testing for future work identities, apparently sifting alternatives in an effort to find the role that will fit most comfortably their particular skills and interests, temperamental characteristics and needs. Girls, in contrast, are absorbed much more in phantasy, particularly phantasy about boys and popularity, marriage and love.

The dream of college apparently serves as a substitute for more direct preoccupation with marriage: girls who do not plan to go to college are more explicit in their desire to marry, and have a more developed sense of their own sex role. They are more aware of and more frankly concerned with sexuality. . . . The view of phantasy as an outlet for sexual impulses follows the general psychoanalytic conception that impulses denied direct expression will seek some disguised mode of gratification.[15]

Thus, it did not surprise them that seventy per cent of freshmen women at a Midwestern university answered the question, "What do you hope to get out of college?" with, among other things, "the man for me." They also interpreted answers indicating a wish to "leave home," "travel," and answers relating to potential occupations which were given by half the girls as symbolizing "curiosity about the sexual mysteries."

College and travel are alternatives to a more open interest in sexuality. Girls who complete their schooling with high school are closer to assuming an adult sex role in early marriages, and they have more developed conceptions of their sexual impulses and sex roles. Girls who will enter college, on the other hand, will delay direct realization and settlement of sexual identity, at least for a while. During the interim, sexual energy is converted and gratified through a phantasy system that focuses on college, the glamour of college life, and a sublimation to general sensuous experience.[16]

Why do the educators view girls, and only girls, in such completely sexual terms? Adolescent boys also have sexual urges whose fulfillment may be delayed by college. But for boys, the educators are not concerned with sexual "phantasy"; they are concerned with "reality," and boys are expected to achieve personal autonomy and identity by "committing themselves in the sphere of our culture that is most morally worthwhile—the world of work—in which they will be acknowledged as persons with recognized achievements and potentials." Even if the boys' own vocational images and goals are not realistic in the beginning— and this study showed that they were not—the sex-directed educators recognize, for boys, that motives, goals, interests, childish preconceptions, can change. They also recognize that, for most, the crucial last chance for change is in college. But apparently girls are not expected to change, nor are they given the opportunity. Even at coeducational colleges, very few girls get the same education as boys. Instead of stimulating what psychologists have suggested might be a "latent" desire for autonomy in the girls, the sex-directed educators stimulated their sexual fantasy of fulfilling all desire for achievement, status, and identity vicariously through a man. Instead of challenging the girls' childish, rigid, parochial preconception of woman's role, they cater to it by offering them a potpourri of liberal-arts courses, suitable only for a wifely veneer, or narrow programs such as "institutional dietetics," well beneath their abilities and suitable only for a "stopgap" job between college and marriage.

As educators themselves admit, women's college training does not often equip them to enter the business or professional world at a meaningful level, either at graduation or afterward; it is not geared to career possibilities that would justify the planning and work required for higher professional training. For women, the sex-directed educators say with approval, college is the place to find a man. Presumably, if the campus is "the world's best marriage mart," as one educator remarked, both sexes are affected. On college campuses today, professor and student agree, the girls are the aggressors in the marriage hunt. The boys, married or not, are there to stretch their minds, to find their own identity, to fill out their life plan; the girls are there only to fulfill their sexual function.

Research reveals that ninety per cent or more of the rising number of campus wives who were motivated for marriage by "phantasy and the need to conform" are literally working their husbands' way through college.[17] The girl who quits high school or college to marry and have a baby, or to take a job to work her husband's way through, is stunted from the kind of mental growth and understanding that higher education is supposed to give, as surely as child labor used to stunt the physical growth of children. She is also prevented from realistic preparation and planning for a career or a commitment that will utilize her abilities and will be of some importance to society and herself.

During the period when the sex-directed educators were devoting themselves to women's sexual adjustment and femininity, economists charted a new and revolutionary change in American employment: beneath the ebb and flow of boom and recession, they found an absolute, spiraling decline in employment possibilities for the uneducated and the unskilled. But when the government economists on the "Womanpower" study visited college campuses, they found the girls unaffected by the statistical probability that they will spend twenty-five years or more of their adult lives in jobs outside the home. Even when it is virtually certain that most women will no longer spend their lives as full-time housewives, the sex-directed educators have told them not to plan for a career for fear of hampering their sexual adjustment.

A few years ago, sex-directed education finally infiltrated a famous woman's college, which had been proud in the past of its large share of graduates who went on to play leading roles in education and law and medicine, the arts and sciences, government and social welfare. This college had an ex-feminist woman president, who was perhaps beginning to suffer a slight guilt at the thought of all those women educated like men. A questionnaire, sent to alumnae of all ages, indicated that the great majority were satisfied with their non-sex-directed education; but a minority complained that their education had made them overly conscious of women's rights and equality with men, too interested in careers, possessed of a nagging feeling that they should do something in the community, that they should at least keep on reading, studying, developing their own abilities and interests. Why hadn't they been educated to be happy housewives and mothers?

The guilty woman college president—guilty personally of being a college president, besides having a large number of children and a successful husband; guilty also of having been an ardent feminist in her time and of having advanced a good way in her career before she married; barraged by the therapeutic social scientists who accused her of trying to mold these young girls in her own impossible, unrealistic, outmoded, energetic, self-demanding, visionary, unfeminine image—introduced a functional course in marriage and the family, compulsory for all sophomores.

The circumstances which led to the college's decision, two years later, to *drop* that functional course are shrouded in secrecy. Nobody officially connected with the college will talk. But a neighboring educator, a functionalist crusader himself, said with a certain contempt for naive wrong-thinking that they were evidently shocked over there that the girls who took the functional course got married so quickly. (The class of 1959 at that college included a record number of 75 wives, nearly a quarter of the girls who still remained in the class.) He told me calmly:

Why should it upset them, over there, that the girls got married a little early? There's nothing wrong with early marriage, with the proper preparation. I guess they can't get over the old notion that women should be educated to develop their minds. They deny it, but one can't help suspecting that they still believe in careers for women. Unfortunately, the idea that women go to college to get a husband is anathema to some educators.

At the college in question, "Marriage and the Family" is taught once again as a course in sociology, geared to critical analysis of these changing social institutions, and not to functional action, or group therapy. But in the neighboring institution, my professor-informant is second in command of a booming department of "family-life education," which is currently readying a hundred graduate students to teach functional marriage courses in colleges, state teachers' colleges, junior colleges, community colleges, and high schools across America. One senses that these new sex-directed educators do indeed think of themselves as crusaders —crusaders against the old nontherapeutic, nonfunctional values of the intellect, against the old, demanding, sexless education, which confined itself to the life of the mind and the pursuit of truth, and never even tried to help girls pursue a man, have orgasms, or adjust. As my informant elaborated:

These kids are concerned about dating and sex, how to get along with boys, is it all right to have premarital relations. Maybe a girl is trying to decide about her major; she's thinking about a career, and she's also thinking about marriage. You set up a role-playing situation to help her work it out—so she sees the effect on the children. She sees she need not feel guilty about being just a housewife.

There often is an air of defensiveness, when a sex-directed educator is asked to define, for the uninitiated, the "functional approach." One told a reporter:

It's all very well to talk big talk—intellectual generalizations, abstract concepts, the United Nations—but somewhere we have to start facing these problems of interpersonal relations on a more modest scale. We have to stop being so teacher-centered, and become student-centered. It's not what you think they need, but what they think they need. That's the functional approach. You walk into a class, and your aim is no longer to cover a certain content, but to set up an atmosphere that makes your students feel comfortable and talk freely about interpersonal relations, in basic terms, not highfalutin generalizations.

Kids tend in adolescence to be very idealistic. They think they can acquire a different set of values, marry a boy from a different background, and that it won't matter later on. We make them aware it will matter, so they won't walk so lightly into mixed marriages, and other traps.[18]

The reporter asked why "Mate Selection," "Adjustment to Marriage" and "Education for Family Living" are taught in colleges at all, if the teacher is committed not to teach, if no material is to be learned or covered, and if the only aim is to help the student understand personal problems and emotions. After surveying a number of marriage courses for *Mademoiselle,* she concluded: "Only in America would you overhear one undergraduate say to another with total ingenuousness, 'You should have been in class today. We talked about male role-playing and a couple of people really opened up and got personal.' "

The point of role-playing, a technique adapted from group therapy, is to get students to understand problems "on a feeling level." Emotions more heady than those of the usual college classroom are undoubtedly stirred up when the professor invites them to "role-play" the feelings of "a boy and a girl on their wedding night."

There is a pseudotherapeutic air, as the professor listens patiently to endless self-conscious student speeches about personal feelings ("verbalizing") in the hopes of sparking a "group insight." But though the functional course is not group therapy, it is certainly an indoctrination of opinions and values through manipulation of the students' emotions; and in this manipulative disguise, it is no longer subject to the critical thinking demanded in other academic disciplines.

The students take as gospel the bits and pieces assigned in text books that explain Freud or quote Margaret Mead; they do not have the frame of reference that comes from the actual study of psychology or anthropology. In fact, by explicitly banning the usual critical attitudes of college study, these pseudoscientific marriage courses give what is often no more than popular opinion, the fiat of scientific law. The opinion may be currently fashionable, or already outdated, in psychiatric circles, but it is often merely a prejudice, buttressed by psychological or sociological jargon and well-chosen statistics to give the appearance of unquestionable scientific truth.

The discussion on premarital intercourse usually leads to the scientific conclusion that it is wrong. One professor builds up his case against sexual intercourse before marriage with statistics chosen to demonstrate that premarital sexual experience tends to make marital adjustment more difficult. The student will not know of the other statistics which refute this point; if the professor knows of them, he can in the functional marriage course feel free to disregard them as unfunctional. ("Ours is a sick society. The students need some accurate definitive kind of knowledge.") It is functional "knowledge" that "only the exceptional woman can make a go of a commitment to a career." Of course, since most women in the past have not had careers, the few who did were all "exceptional"—as a mixed marriage is "exceptional," and premarital intercourse for a girl is exceptional. All are phenomena of less than 51 per cent. The whole point of functional education often seems to be: what 51 per cent of the population does today, 100 per cent should do tomorrow.

So the sex-directed educator promotes a girl's adjustment by dissuading her from any but the "normal" commitment to marriage and the family. One such educator goes farther than imaginary role-playing; she brings real ex-working mothers to class to talk about their guilt at leaving their children in the morning. Somehow, the students seldom hear about a woman who has successfully broken convention—the young woman doctor whose sister handled her practice when her babies were born, the mother who adjusted her babies' sleeping hours to her work schedule without problems, the happy Protestant girl who married a Catholic, the sexually serene wife whose premarital experience did not seem to hurt her marriage. "Exceptional" cases are of no practical concern to the functionalist, though he often acknowledges scrupulously that there *are* exceptions. (The "exceptional child," in educational jargon, bears a connotation of handicap: the blind, the crippled, the retarded, the genius, the defier of convention—anyone who is different from the crowd, in any way unique—bears a common shame; he is "exceptional.") Somehow, the student gets the point that she does not want to be the "exceptional woman."

Conformity is built into life-adjustment education in many ways. There is little or no intellectual challenge or discipline involved in merely learning to adjust. The marriage course is the easiest course on almost every campus, no matter how anxiously professors try to toughen it by assigning heavy reading and weekly reports. No one expects that case histories (which when read for no serious use are not much more than psychiatric soap operas), role-playing, talking about sex in class, or writing personal papers will lead to critical thinking; that's not the point of functional preparation for marriage.

This is not to say that the study of a social science, as such, produces conformity in woman or man. This is hardly the effect when it is studied critically and motivated by the usual aims of intellectual discipline, or when it is mastered for professional use. But for girls forbidden both professional and intellectual commitment by the new mystique, the study of sociology, anthropology, psychology is often merely "functional." And in the functional course itself, the girls take those bits and pieces from Freud and Mead, the sexual statistics, the role-playing insights, not only literally and out of context, but personally—to be acted upon in their own lives. That, after all, is the whole point of life-adjustment education. It can happen among adolescents in almost any course that involves basic emotional material. It will certainly happen when the material is deliberately used not to build critical knowledge but to stir up personal emotions. Therapy, in the orthodox psychoanalytic tradition, requires the suppression of critical thinking (intellectual resistance) for the proper emotions to come out and be worked through. In therapy, this may work. But does education work, mixed up with therapy? One course could hardly be crucial, in any man or woman's life, but when it is decided that the very aim of woman's education should not be intellectual growth, but sexual adjustment, certain questions could be very crucial.

One might ask: if an education geared to the growth of the human mind weakens femininity, will an education geared to femininity weaken the growth of the mind? What is femininity, if it can be destroyed by an education which makes the mind grow, or induced by not letting the mind grow?

One might even ask a question in Freudian terms: what happens when sex becomes not only id for women, but ego and superego as well; when education, instead of developing the self, is concentrated on developing the sexual functions? What happens when education gives new authority to the feminine "shoulds"—which already have the authority of tradition, convention, prejudice, popular opinion—instead of giving women the power of critical thought, the independence and autonomy to question blind authority, new or old? At Pembroke, the women's college at Brown University in Providence, R.I., a guest psychoanalyst was recently invited to lead a buzz session on "what it means to be a woman." The students seemed disconcerted when the guest analyst, Dr. Margaret Lawrence, said, in simple, un-Freudian English, that it was rather silly to tell women today that their main place is in the home, when most of the work women used to do is now done outside the home, and everyone else in the family spends most of his time outside the house. Hadn't they better be educated to join the rest of the family, out there in the world?

This, somehow, was not what the girls expected to hear from a lady psychoanalyst. Unlike the usual functional, sex-directed lesson, it upset a conventional feminine "should." It also implied that they should begin to make certain decisions of their own, about their education and their future.

The functional lesson is much more soothing to the unsure sophomore who has not yet quite made the break from childhood. It does not defy the comfortable, safe conventions; it gives her sophisticated words for accepting her parents' view, the popular view, without having to figure out views of her own. It also reassures her that she doesn't have to work in college; that she can be lazy, follow impulse. She doesn't have to postpone present pleasure for future goals; she doesn't have to read eight books for a history paper, take the tough physics course. It might give her a masculinity complex. After all, didn't the book say:

> Woman's intellectuality is to a large extent paid for by the loss of valuable feminine qualities. . . . All observations point to the fact that the intellectual woman is masculinized; in her warm, intuitive knowledge has yielded to cold unproductive thinking.[19]

A girl doesn't have to be very lazy, very unsure, to take the hint. Thinking, after all, is hard work. In fact, she would have to do some very cold hard thinking about her own warm, intuitive knowledge to challenge this authoritative statement.

It is no wonder that several generations of American college girls of fine mind and fiery spirit took the message of the sex-directed educators, and fled college and career to marry and have babies before they became so "intellectual" that, heaven forbid, they wouldn't be able to enjoy sex "in a feminine way."

Even without the help of sex-directed educators, the girl growing up with brains and spirit in America learns soon enough to watch her step, "to be like all the others," not to be herself. She learns not to work too hard, think too often, ask too many questions. In high schools, in coeducational colleges, girls are reluctant to speak out in class for fear of being typed as "brains." This phenomenon has been borne out by many studies;[20] any bright girl or woman can document it from personal experience. Bryn Mawr girls have a special term for the way they talk when boys are

around, compared to the real talk they can permit themselves
when they are not afraid to let their intelligence show. In the
coeducational colleges, girls are regarded by others—and think of
themselves—primarily in terms of their sexual function as dates,
future wives. They "seek my security in him" instead of finding
themselves, and each act of self-betrayal tips the scale further
away from identity to passive self-contempt.

There are exceptions, of course. The Mellon study found that
some Vassar seniors, as compared with freshmen, showed an
enormous growth in four years—the kind of growth toward
identity and self-realization which scientists now know takes
place in people in their twenties and even thirties, forties, and
fifties, long after the period of physical growth is over. But many
girls showed no signs of growth. These were the ones who resisted, successfully, involvement with ideas, the academic work
of the college, the intellectual disciplines, the larger values. They
resisted intellectual development, self-development, in favor of
being "feminine," not too brainy, not too interested, not too different from the other girls. It was not that their actual sexual
interests interfered; in fact, the psychologists got the impression
that with many of these girls, "interest in men and marriage is a
kind of defense against intellectual development." For such girls,
even sex is not real, merely a kind of conformity. The sex-directed
educator would find no fault in this kind of adjustment. But in
view of other evidence, one might ask: could such an adjustment
mask a failure to grow that becomes finally a human deformity?

Several years ago a team of California psychologists who had
been following the development of 140 bright youngsters noticed
a sudden sharp drop in IQ curves in some of the teenage records.
When they investigated this, they found that while most of the
youngsters' curves remained at the same high level, year after
year, those whose curves dropped were all girls. The drop had
nothing to do with the physiological changes of adolescence; it
was not found in all girls. But in the records of those girls whose
intelligence dropped were found repeated statements to the effect
that "it isn't too smart for a girl to be smart." In a very real sense,
these girls were arrested in their mental growth, at age fourteen
or fifteen, by conformity to the feminine image.[21]

The fact is, girls today and those responsible for their education do face a choice. They must decide between adjustment, conformity, avoidance of conflict, therapy—or individuality, human identity, education in the truest sense, with all its pains of growth. But they do not have to face the mistaken choice painted by the sex-directed educators, with their dire warnings against loss of femininity and sexual frustration. For the perceptive psychologist who studied the Vassar girls uncovered some startling new evidence about the students who chose to become truly involved with their education. It seems that those seniors who showed the greatest signs of growth were more "masculine" in the sense of being less passive and conventional; but they were more "feminine" in inner emotional life, and the ability to gratify it. They also scored higher, far higher than as freshmen, on certain scales commonly supposed to measure neuroses. The psychologist commented: "We have come to regard elevations on such scales as evidence that education is taking place." [22] He found girls with conflicts showed more growth than the adjusted ones, who had no wish to become independent. The least adjusted were also the more developed—"already prepared for even further changes and more independence." In summing up the Vassar study, its director could not avoid the psychological paradox: education for women does make them less feminine, less adjusted—but it makes them grow.

Being less "feminine" is closely related to being more educated and more mature. . . . It is interesting to note, however, that Feminine Sensitivity, which may well have sources in physiology and in early identifications, does not decrease during the four years; "feminine" interests and feminine role behavior, i.e., conventionality and passivity, can be understood as later and more superficial acquisitions, and, hence, more susceptible to decrease as the individual becomes more mature and more educated. . . .

One might say that if we were interested in stability alone, we would do well to plan a program to keep freshmen as they are, rather than to try to increase their education, their maturity and their flexibility with regard to sex-role behavior. Seniors are more unstable because there is more to be stabilized, less certain of their identities because more possibilities are open to them.[23]

At graduation, such women were, however, only at a "halfway point" in their growth to autonomy. Their fate depended on "whether they now enter a situation in which they can continue to grow or whether they find some quick but regressive means for relieving the stress." The flight into marriage is the easiest, quickest way to relieve that stress. To the educator, bent on women's growth to autonomy, such a marriage is "regressive." To the sex-directed educator, it is femininity fulfilled.

A therapist at another college told me of girls who had never committed themselves, either to their work or any other activity of the college and who felt that they would "go to pieces" when their parents refused to let them leave college to marry the boys in whom they found "security." When these girls, with help, finally applied themselves to work—or even began to feel a sense of self by taking part in an activity such as student government or the school newspaper—they lost their desperate need for "security." They finished college, worked, went out with more mature young men, and are now marrying on quite a different emotional basis.

Unlike the sex-directed educator, this professional therapist felt that the girl who suffers almost to the point of breakdown in the senior year, and who faces a personal decision about her own future—faces even an irreconcilable conflict between the values and interests and abilities her education has given her, and the conventional role of housewife—is still "healthier" than the adjusted, calm, stable girl in whom education did not "take" at all and who steps smoothly from her role as parents' child to husband's wife, conventionally feminine, without ever waking up to painful individual identity.

And yet the fact is, today most girls do not let their education "take"; they stop themselves before getting this close to identity. I could see this in the girls at Smith, and the girls I interviewed from other colleges. It was clear in the Vassar research. The Vassar study showed that just as girls begin to feel the conflicts, the growing pains of identity, they stop growing. They more or less consciously stop their own growth to play the feminine role. Or, to put it in another way, they evade further experiences con-

recently when Russians orbited moons and men in space, asked whether adjustment should be education's aim. In fact, the sex-directed educators, so bent on women's feminine adjustment, could gaily cite the most ominous facts about American house-wives—their emptiness, idleness, boredom, alcoholism, drug ad-diction, disintegration to fat, disease, and despair after forty, when their sexual function has been filled—without deviating a bit from their crusade to educate all women to this sole end.

So the sex-directed educator disposes of the thirty years women are likely to live after forty with three blithe proposals:

1. A course in "Law and Order for the Housewife" to enable her to deal, as a widow, with insurances, taxes, wills, investments.

2. Men might retire earlier to help keep their wives company.

3. A brief fling in "volunteer community services, politics, the arts or the like"—though, since the woman will be untrained the main value will be personal therapy. "To choose only one example, a woman who wants some really novel experience may start a campaign to rid her city or country of that nauseous eczema of our modern world, the billboard.

"The billboards will remain and multiply like bacteria infesting the landscape, but at least she will have had a vigorous adult education course in local politics. Then she can relax and devote herself to the alumnae activities of the institution from which she graduated. Many a woman approaching middle years has found new vigor and enthu-siasm in identifying herself with the on-going life of her college and in expanding her maternal instincts, now that her own children are grown, to encompass the new generations of students which inhabit its campus." [25]

She could also take a part-time job, he said, but she shouldn't take work away from men who must feed their families, and, in fact, she won't have the skills or experience for a very "exciting" job.

. . . there is great demand for experienced and reliable women who can relieve younger women of family responsibilities on regular days or afternoons, so that they may either develop community interests or hold part-time jobs of their own. . . . There is no reason why women of culture and breeding, who in any case for years have probably done most of their own housework, should recoil from such arrangements.[26]

If the feminine mystique has not destroyed her sense of humor, a woman might laugh at such a candid description of the life her expensive sex-directed education fits her for: an occasional alumnae reunion and someone else's housework. The sad fact is, in the era of Freud and functionalism and the feminine mystique, few educators escaped such a sex-distortion of their own values. Max Lerner,[27] even Riesman in *The Lonely Crowd*, suggested that women need not seek their own autonomy through productive contribution to society—they might better help their husbands hold on to theirs, through play. And so sex-directed education segregated recent generations of able American women as surely as separate-but-equal education segregated able American Negroes from the opportunity to realize their full abilities in the mainstream of American life.

It does not explain anything to say that in this era of conformity colleges did not really educate anybody. The Jacob report,[28] which leveled this indictment against American colleges generally, and even the more sophisticated indictment by Sanford and his group, does not recognize that the colleges' failure to educate women for an identity beyond their sexual role was undoubtedly a crucial factor in perpetuating, if not creating, that conformity which educators now so fashionably rail against. For it is impossible to educate women to devote themselves so early and completely to their sexual role—women who, as Freud said, can be very active indeed in achieving a passive end—without pulling men into the same comfortable trap. In effect, sex-directed education led to a lack of identity in women most easily solved by early marriage. And a premature commitment to any role—marriage or vocation—closes off the experiences, the testing, the failures and successes in various spheres of activity that are necessary for a person to achieve full maturity, individual identity.

The danger of stunting of boys' growth by early domesticity was recognized by the sex-directed educators. As Margaret Mead put it recently:

Early domesticity has always been characteristic of most savages, of most peasants and of the urban poor. . . . If there are babies, it means, you know, the father's term paper gets all mixed up with the babies' bottle. . . . Early student marriage is domesticating boys so early they don't have a chance for full intellectual development. They don't have a chance to give their entire time, not necessarily to study in the sense of staying in the library—but in the sense that the married students don't have time to experience, to think, to sit up all night in bull sessions, to develop as individuals. This is not only important for the intellectuals, but also the boys who are going to be the future statesmen of the country and lawyers and doctors and all sorts of professional men.[29]

But what of the girls who will never even write the term papers because of the baby's bottle? Because of the feminine mystique, few have seen it as a tragedy that they thereby trap themselves in that one passion, one occupation, one role for life. Advanced educators in the early 1960's have their own cheerful fantasies about postponing women's education until after they have had their babies; they thereby acknowledge that they have resigned themselves almost unanimously to the early marriages, which continue unabated.

But by choosing femininity over the painful growth to full identity, by never achieving the hard core of self that comes not from fantasy but from mastering reality, these girls are doomed to suffer ultimately that bored, diffuse feeling of purposelessness, non-existence, non-involvement with the world that can be called *anomie*, or lack of identity, or merely felt as the problem that has no name.

Still, it is too easy to make education the scapegoat. Whatever the mistakes of the sex-directed educators, other educators have fought a futile, frustrating rear-guard battle trying to make able women "envision new goals and grow by reaching for them." In the last analysis, millions of able women in this free land chose, themselves, not to use the door education could have opened for them. The choice—and the responsibility—for the race back home was finally their own.

8 The Mistaken Choice

A mystique does not compel its own acceptance. For the feminine mystique to have "brainwashed" American women of nonsexual human purposes for more than fifteen years, it must have filled real needs in those who seized on it for others and those who accepted it for themselves. Those needs may not have been the same in all the women or in all the purveyors of the mystique. But there were many needs, at this particular time in America, that made us pushovers for the mystique; needs so compelling that we suspended critical thought, as one does in the face of an intuitive truth. The trouble is, when need is strong enough, intuition can also lie.

There was, just before the feminine mystique took hold in America, a war, which followed a depression and ended with the explosion of an atom bomb. After the loneliness of war and the unspeakableness of the bomb, against the frightening uncertainty, the cold immensity of the changing world, women as well as men sought the comforting reality of home and children. In the foxholes, the GI's had pinned up pictures of Betty Grable, but the songs they asked to hear were lullabies. And when they got out of the army they were too old to go home to their mothers. The needs of sex and love are undeniably real in men and women, boys and girls, but why at this time did they seem to so many the *only* needs?

We were all vulnerable, homesick, lonely, frightened. A pent-up

182

hunger for marriage, home, and children was felt simultaneously by several different generations; a hunger which, in the prosperity of postwar America, everyone could suddenly satisfy. The young GI, made older than his years by the war, could meet his lonely need for love and mother by re-creating his childhood home. Instead of dating many girls until college and profession were achieved, he could marry on the GI bill, and give his own babies the tender mother love he was no longer baby enough to seek for himself. Then there were the slightly older men: men of twenty-five whose marriages had been postponed by the war and who now felt they must make up for lost time; men in their thirties, kept first by depression and then by war from marrying, or if married, from enjoying the comforts of home.

For the girls, these lonely years added an extra urgency to their search for love. Those who married in the thirties saw their husbands off to war; those who grew up in the forties were afraid, with reason, that they might never have the love, the homes and children which few women would willingly miss. When the men came back, there was a headlong rush into marriage. The lonely years when husbands or husbands-to-be were away at war—or could be sent away at a bomb's fall—made women particularly vulnerable to the feminine mystique. They were told that the cold dimension of loneliness which the war had added to their lives was the necessary price they had to pay for a career, for any interest outside the home. The mystique spelled out a choice—love, home, children, or other goals and purposes in life. Given such a choice, was it any wonder that so many American women chose love as their whole purpose?

The baby boom of the immediate postwar years took place in every country. But it was not permeated, in most other countries, with the mystique of feminine fulfillment. It did not in other countries lead to the even greater baby boom of the fifties, with the rise in teenage marriages and pregnancies, and the increase in family size. The number of American women with three or more children doubled in twenty years. And educated women, after the war, led all the others in the race to have more babies.[1] (The generation before mine, the women born between 1910 and

1919, showed the change most sharply. During their twenties, their low pregnancy rate led to warnings that education was going to wipe out the human race; in their thirties, they suddenly showed a sharp *increase* in pregnancies, despite the lowered biological capacity that makes the pregnancy rate decline with age.)

More babies are always born after wars. But today the American population explosion comes in large part from teenage marriages. The number of children born to teenagers rose 165 per cent between 1940 and 1957, according to Metropolitan Life Insurance figures. The girls who would normally go to college but leave or forgo it to marry (eighteen and nineteen are the most frequent ages of marriage of American girls today; half of all American women are married by twenty) are products of the mystique. They give up education without a qualm, truly believing that they will find "fulfillment" as wives and mothers. I suppose a girl today, who knows from statistics or merely from observation that if she waits to marry until she finishes college, or trains for a profession, most of the men will be married to someone else, has as much reason to fear she may miss feminine fulfillment as the war gave the girls in the forties. But this does not explain why they drop out of college to support their husbands, while the boys continue with their education.

It has not happened in other countries. Even in countries where, during the war, many more men were killed and more women were forced forever to miss the fulfillment of marriage, women did not run home again in panic. And in the other countries today, girls are as hungry as boys for the education that is the road to the future.

War made women particularly vulnerable to the mystique, but the war, with all its frustrations, was not the only reason they went home again. Nor can it be explained by "the servant problem," which is an excuse the educated woman often gives to herself. During the war, when the cooks and maids went to work in the war plants, the servant problem was even more severe than in recent years. But at that time, women of spirit often worked out unconventional domestic arrangements to keep their professional commitments. (I knew two young wartime mothers who pooled forces while their husbands were overseas. One, an actress, took both babies in the morning, while the other did graduate work; the second took over in the afternoon, when the other had a rehearsal or matinee. I also knew a woman who switched her baby's night-and-day so he would sleep at a neighbor's house during the hours she was at medical school.) And in the cities, then, the need for nurseries and day-care centers for the children of working mothers was seen, and met.

But in the years of postwar femininity, even women who could afford, and find, a full-time nurse or housekeeper chose to take care of house and children themselves. And in the cities, during the fifties, the nursery and day-care centers for the children of working mothers all but disappeared; the very suggestion of their need brought hysterical outcries from educated housewives as well as the purveyors of the mystique.[2]

When the war ended, of course, GI's came back to take the jobs and fill the seats in colleges and universities that for a while had been occupied largely by girls. For a short time, competition was keen and the resurgence of the old anti-feminine prejudices in business and the professions made it difficult for a girl to keep or advance in a job. This undoubtedly sent many women scurrying for the cover of marriage and home. Subtle discrimination against women, to say nothing of the sex wage differential, is still an unwritten law today, and its effects are almost as devastating and as hard to fight as the flagrant opposition faced by the feminists. A woman researcher on *Time* magazine, for instance, cannot, no matter what her ability, aspire to be a writer; the unwritten law makes the men writers and editors, the women researchers. She doesn't get mad; she likes her job, she likes her boss. She is not a crusader for women's rights; it isn't a case for the Newspaper Guild. But it is discouraging nevertheless. If she is never going to get anywhere, why keep on?

Women were often driven embittered from their chosen fields when, ready and able to handle a better job, they were passed over for a man. In some jobs a woman had to be content to do the work while the man got the credit. Or if she got the better job, she had to face the bitterness and hostility of the man. Because the race to get ahead, in the big organization, in every profession in America, is so terribly competitive for men, competition from women is somehow the last straw—and much easier to fight by simply evoking that unwritten law. During the war, women's abilities, and the inevitable competition, were welcome; after the war they were confronted with that polite but inpenetrable curtain of hostility. It was easier for a woman to love and be loved, and have an excuse not to compete with men.

Still, during the depression, able, spirited girls sacrificed, fought prejudice, and braved competition in order to pursue their careers, even though there were fewer places to compete for. Nor did many see any conflict between career and love. In the prosperous postwar years, there were plenty of jobs, plenty of places in all the professions; there was no real need to give up everything for love and marriage. The less-educated girls, after all, did not leave the factories and go back to being maids. The proportion of women in industry has steadily increased since the war—but not of women in careers or professions requiring training, effort, personal commitment.[3] "I live through my husband and children," a frank member of my own generation told me. "It's easier that way. In this world now, it's easier to be a woman, if you take advantage of it."

In this sense, what happened to women is part of what happened to all of us in the years after the war. We found excuses for not facing the problems we once had the courage to face. The American spirit fell into a strange sleep; men as well as women, scared liberals, disillusioned radicals, conservatives bewildered and frustrated by change—the whole nation stopped growing up. All of us went back into the warm brightness of home, the way it was when we were children and slept peacefully upstairs while our parents read, or played bridge in the living room, or rocked on the front porch in the summer evening in our home towns.

Women went home again just as men shrugged off the bomb, forgot the concentration camps, condoned corruption, and fell into helpless conformity; just as the thinkers avoided the complex larger problems of the postwar world. It was easier, safer, to think about love and sex than about communism, McCarthy, and the uncontrolled bomb. It was easier to look for Freudian sexual roots in man's behavior, his ideas, and his wars than to look critically at his society and act constructively to right its wrongs. There was a kind of personal retreat, even on the part of the most far-sighted, the most spirited; we lowered our eyes from the horizon, and steadily contemplated our own navels.

We can see all this now, in retrospect. Then, it was easier to build the need for love and sex into the end-all purpose of life, avoiding personal commitment to truth in a catch-all commitment to "home" and "family." For the social worker, the psychologist and the numerous "family" counselors, analytically oriented therapy for private patients on personal problems of sex, personality, and interpersonal relations was safer and more lucrative than probing too deeply for the common causes of man's suffering. If you no longer wanted to think about the whole of mankind, at least you could "help" individuals without getting into trouble. Irwin Shaw, who once goaded the American conscience on the great issues of war and peace and racial prejudice now wrote about sex and adultery; Norman Mailer and the young beatnik writers confined their revolutionary spirit to sex and kicks and drugs and advertising themselves in four-letter words. It was easier and more fashionable for writers to think about psychology than politics, about private motives than public purposes. Painters retreated into an abstract expressionism that flaunted discipline and glorified the evasion of meaning. Dramatists reduced human purpose to bitter, pretentious nonsense: "the theater of the absurd." Freudian thought gave this whole process of escape its dimension of endless, tantalizing, intellectual mystery: process within process, meaning hidden within meaning, until meaning itself disappeared and the hopeless, dull outside world hardly existed at all. As a drama critic said, in a rare note of revulsion at the stage world of Tennessee Williams, it was as if no reality remained for man except his sexual perversions, and the fact that he loved and hated his mother.

The Freudian mania in the American culture, apart from the practice of psychotherapy itself, also filled a real need in the forties and fifties: the need for an ideology, a national purpose, an application of the mind to the problems of people. Analysts themselves have recently suggested that the lack of an ideology or national purpose may be partially responsible for the personal emptiness which sends many men and women into psychotherapy; they are actually looking for an identity which therapy alone can never give. The religious revival in America coincided with the rush to psychoanalysis, and perhaps came about for the same reason—behind the search for identity, or for shelter, a vacuum of larger purpose. It is significant that many ministers now spend much of their time in giving psychotherapy—pastoral counseling —to members of their congregations. Do they thereby also evade the larger questions, the real search?

When I was interviewing on college campuses in the late fifties, chaplains and sociologists alike testified to the younger generation's "privatism." A major reason for the early marriage movement, they felt, was that the young saw no other true value in contemporary society. It's easy for the professional social critic to blame the younger generation for cynical preoccupation with private pleasure and material security—or for the empty negativism of beatnikery. But if their parents, teachers, preachers, have abdicated purposes larger than personal emotional adjustment, material success, security, what larger purpose can the young learn?

The five babies, the movement to suburbia, do-it-yourself and even beatnikery filled homely needs; they also took the place of those larger needs and purposes with which the most spirited in this nation were once concerned. "I'm bored with politics . . . there's nothing you can do about it anyhow." When a dollar was too cheap, and too expensive, to live a life for, and your whole society seemed concerned with little else, the family and its loves and problems—this, at least, was good and true. And the literal swallowing of Freud gave the illusion that it was more important than it really was for the whole of suffering society, as the literal parroting of Freudian phrases deluded suffering individuals into believing that they were cured, when underneath they had not yet even faced their real troubles.

Under the Freudian microscope, however, a very different concept of family began to emerge. Oedipus conflict and sibling rivalry became household words. Frustration was as great a peril to childhood as scarlet fever. And singled out for special attention was the "mother." It was suddenly discovered that the mother could be blamed for almost everything. In every case history of troubled child; alcoholic, suicidal, schizophrenic, psychopathic, neurotic adult; impotent, homosexual male; frigid, promiscuous female; ulcerous, asthmatic, and otherwise disturbed American, could be found a mother. A frustrated, repressed, disturbed, martyred, never satisfied, unhappy woman. A demanding, nagging, shrewish wife. A rejecting, overprotecting, dominating mother. World War II revealed that millions of American men were psychologically incapable of facing the shock of war, of facing life away from their "moms." Clearly something was "wrong" with American women.

By unfortunate coincidence, this attack against mothers came about at the same time that American women were beginning to use the rights of their emancipation, to go in increasing numbers to college and professional schools, to rise in industry and the professions in inevitable competition with men. Women were just beginning to play a part in American society that depended not on their sex, but on their individual abilities. It was apparent to the naked eye, obvious to the returning GI, that these American women were indeed more independent, strong-minded, assertive of will and opinion, less passive and feminine than, for instance, the German and Japanese girls who, the GI's boasted, "even washed our backs for us." It was less apparent, however, that these girls were different from their mothers. Perhaps that is why, by some strange distortion of logic, all the neuroses of children past and present were blamed on the independence and individuality of this new generation of American girls—independence and individuality which the housewife-mothers of the previous generation had never had.

The evidence seemed inescapable: the figures on the psychiatric discharges in the war and the mothers in their case histories; the early Kinsey figures on the incapacity of American women to

enjoy sexual orgasm, especially educated women; the fact that so
many women *were* frustrated, and took it out on their husbands
and children. More and more men in America did feel inadequate,
impotent. Many of those first generations of career women did
miss love and children, resented and were resented by the men
they competed with. More and more American men, women,
children were going to mental hospitals, clinics, psychiatrists. All
this was laid at the doorstep of the frustrated American mother,
"masculinized" by her education, prevented by her insistence on
equality and independence from finding sexual fulfillment as a
woman.

It all fitted so neatly with the Freudian rationale that no one
stopped to investigate what these pre-war mothers were really
like. They were indeed frustrated. But the mothers of the maladjusted soldiers, the insecure and impotent postwar males, were not
independent educated career women, but self-sacrificing, dependent, martyred-housewife "moms."

In 1940, less than a fourth of American women worked outside
the home; those who did were for the most part unmarried. A
minuscule 2.5 per cent of mothers were "career women." The
mothers of the GI's who were 18–30 in 1940 were born in the
nineteenth century, or the early 1900's, and were grown up before
American women won the right to vote, or enjoyed the independence, the sexual freedom, the educational or the career opportunities of the twenties. By and large, these "moms" were
neither feminists, nor products of feminism, but American women
leading the traditional feminine life of housewife and mother. Was
it really education, career dreams, independence, which made the
"moms" frustrated, and take it out on their children? Even a book
that helped build the new mystique—Edward Strecker's *Their
Mothers' Sons*—confirms the fact that the "moms" were neither
career women, nor feminists, nor used their education, if they had
it; they lived for their children, they had no interests beyond
home, children, family, or their own beauty. In fact, they fit the
very image of the feminine mystique.

Here is the "mom" whom Dr. Strecker, as consultant to the
Surgeon General of the Army and Navy, found guilty in the case

histories of the vast majority of the 1,825,000 men rejected for
military service because of psychiatric disorders, the 600,000 dis-
charged from the Army for neuropsychiatric reasons, and the
500,000 more who tried to evade the draft—almost 3,000,000 men,
out of 15,000,000 in the service, who retreated into psychoneurosis, often only a few days after induction, because they lacked
maturity, "the ability to face life, live with others, think for
themselves and stand on their own two feet."

A mom is a woman whose maternal behavior is motivated by the
seeking of emotional recompense for the buffets which life has dealt
her own ego. In her relationship with her children, every deed and
almost every breath are designed unconsciously but exclusively to
abscrb her children emotionally and to bind them to her securely. In
order to achieve this purpose, she must stamp a pattern of immature
behavior on her children. . . . The mothers of men and women
capable of facing life maturely are not apt to be the traditional mom
type. More likely mom is sweet, doting, self-sacrificing. . . . takes
no end of trouble and spares herself no pains in selecting clothes for
her grown-up children. She supervises the curl of their hair, the
selection of their friends and companions, their sports, and their social
attitudes and opinions. By and large she does all their thinking for
them. . . . [This domination] is sometimes hard and arbitrary, more
often soft, persuasive and somewhat devious. . . . Most frequent is the
method of indirection in which in some way the child is made to feel
that mom's hurt and trying ever so hard to conceal that hurt. The
soft method is infinitely more successful in blocking manifestations of
youthful thought and action. . . .

The "self-sacrificing" mom when hard-pressed may admit hesitat-
ingly that perhaps she does look "played out" and is actually a bit
tired, but she chirps brightly "What of it?" . . . The implication is
that she does not care how she looks or feels, for in her heart there is
the unselfish joy of service. From dawn until late at night she finds her
happiness in doing for her children. The house belongs to them. It
must be "just so"; the meals on the minute, hot and tempting. Food is
available at all hours. . . . No buttons missing from garments in this
orderly house. Everything is in its proper place. Mom knows where it
is. Uncomplainingly, gladly, she puts things where they belong after
the children have strewn them about, here, there, and everywhere.
. . . Anything the children need or want, mom will cheerfully get for

them. It is the perfect home. . . . Failing to find a comparable peaceful haven in the outside world, it is quite likely that one or more of the brood will remain in or return to the happy home, forever enwombed.[4]

The "mom" may also be "the pretty addlepate" with her cult of beauty, clothing, cosmetics, perfumes, hairdos, diet and exercise, or "the pseudo-intellectual who is forever taking courses and attending lectures, not seriously studying one subject and informing herself thoroughly about it, but one month mental hygiene, the next economics, Greek architecture, nursery schools." These were the "moms" of the sons who could not be men at the front or at home, in bed or out, because they really wanted to be babies. All these moms had one thing in common:

. . . the emotional satisfaction, almost repletion, she derives from keeping her children paddling about in a kind of psychological amniotic fluid rather than letting them swim away with the bold and decisive strokes of maturity from the emotional maternal womb. . . . Being immature herself, she breeds immaturity in her children and, by and large, they are doomed to lives of personal and social insufficiency and unhappiness . . .[5]

I quote Dr. Strecker at length because he was, oddly enough, one of the psychiatric authorities most frequently cited in the spate of postwar articles and speeches condemning American women for their lost femininity—and bidding them rush back home again and devote their lives to their children. Actually, the moral of Strecker's cases was just the opposite; those immature sons had mothers who devoted *too* much of their lives to their children, mothers who had to keep their children babies or they themselves would have no lives at all, mothers who never themselves reached or were encouraged to reach maturity: "the state or quality of being mature; ripeness, full development . . . independence of thought and action"—the quality of being fully human. Which is not quite the same as femininity.

Facts are swallowed by a mystique in much the same way, I guess, as the strange phenomenon by which hamburger eaten by a dog becomes dog, and hamburger eaten by a human becomes human. The facts of the GI's neurosis became, in the 1940's, "proof" that American women had been seduced from feminine fulfillment by an education geared to career, independence, equality with men, "self-realization at any cost"—even though most of these frustrated women were simply housewives. By some fascinating paradox, the massive evidence of psychological damage done to boys and girls by frustrated mothers who devoted all their days to filling children's needs was twisted by the feminine mystique to a summons to the new generation of girls to go back home and devote *their* days to filling children's needs.

Nothing made that hamburger more palatable than the early Kinsey figures which showed that sexual frustration in women was related to their education. Chewed and rechewed was the horrendous fact that between 50 and 85 per cent of the college women polled had never experienced sexual orgasm, while less than one-fifth of high-school educated women reported the same problem. *As Modern Woman: The Lost Sex* interpreted these early Kinsey returns:

Among women with a grade school education or less, complete failure to achieve orgasm diminished toward the vanishing point. Dr. Kinsey and his colleagues reported that practically 100% full orgastic reaction had been found among uneducated Negro women. . . . The psychosexual rule that begins to take form, then, is this: the more educated the woman is, the greater chance there is of sexual disorder, more or less severe . . .[6]

Nearly a decade went by before publication of the full Kinsey report on women, which completely contradicted those earlier findings. How many women realize, even now, that Kinsey's 5,940 case histories of American women showed that the number of females reaching orgasm in marriage, and the number of females reaching orgasm nearly 100 per cent of the time, *was* related to education, but the more educated the woman, the greater chance of sexual fulfillment. The woman with only a grade-school education was more likely never to experience orgasm, while the woman who finished college, and who went on to graduate or professional school, was far more likely to achieve full orgasm nearly 100 per cent of the time. In Kinsey's words:

We found that the number of females reaching orgasm within any five-year period was rather distinctly higher among those with upper educational backgrounds. . . . In every period of marriage, from the first until at least the fifteenth year, a larger number of the females in the sample who had more limited educational backgrounds had completely failed to respond to orgasm in their marital coitus, and a small number of the better educated females had so completely failed. . . .

These data are not in accord with a preliminary, unpublished calculation which we made some years ago. On the basis of a smaller sample, and on the basis of a less adequate method of calculation, we seemed to find a larger number of the females of the lower educational levels responding to orgasm in the marital coitus. These data now need correction . . .[7]

But the mystique nourished by the early incorrect figures was not so easily corrected.

And then there were the frightening figures and case histories of children abandoned and rejected because their mothers worked. How many women realize, even now, that the babies in those publicized cases, who withered away from lack of maternal affection, were not the the children of educated, middle-class mothers who left them in others' care certain hours of the day to practice a profession or write a poem, or fight a political battle—but truly abandoned children: foundlings often deserted at birth by unwed mothers and drunken fathers, children who never had a home or tender loving care. Headlines were made by any study which implied that working mothers were responsible for juvenile delinquency, school difficulties or emotional disturbance in their children. Recently a psychologist, Dr. Lois Meek Stolz, of Stanford University, analyzed all the evidence from such studies. She discovered that at the present time, one can say *anything*—good or bad—about children of employed mothers and support the statement by *some* research findings. But there is no definitive evidence that children are less happy, healthy, adjusted, *because* their mothers work.[8]

The studies that show working women to be happier, better, more mature mothers do not get much publicity. Since juvenile delinquency is increasing, and more women work or "are educated for some kind of intellectual work," there is surely a direct cause-and-effect relationship, one says. Except that evidence indicates there is not. Several years ago, much publicity was given to a study comparing matched groups of delinquent and non-delinquent boys. It was found, among other things, that there was no more delinquency, or school truancy, when the mothers worked regularly than when they were housewives. But, spectacular headlines warned, significantly more delinquents had mothers who worked irregularly. This finding brought guilt and gloom to the educated mothers who had given up full-fledged careers, but managed to keep on in their fields by working part-time, by free-lancing, or by taking temporary jobs with periods at home in between. "Here for years I've been purposely taking temporary jobs and part-time jobs, trying to arrange my working life in the boys' best interests," one such mother was quoted by the *New York Times*, "and now it looks as though I've been doing the worst possible thing!" [9]

Actually, this mother, a woman with professional training who lived in a comfortable middle-class neighborhood, was equating herself with mothers in that study who, it turned out, not only lived in poor socio-economic circumstances, but had in many cases been juvenile delinquents themselves. And they often had husbands who were emotionally disturbed.

The researchers who did that study suggested that the sons of these women had emotional conflicts because the mother was motivated to her sporadic work "not so much to supplement family income as to escape household and maternal responsibilities." But another specialist, analyzing the same findings, thought the basic cause both of the mother's sporadic employment and the son's delinquency was the emotional instability of both parents. Whatever the reason, the situation was in no way comparable to that of most educated women who read themselves into it. In fact, as Dr. Stolz shows, many studies misinterpreted as "proof" that women cannot combine careers and motherhood actually indicate that, where other conditions are equal, the children of mothers who work because they want to are less likely to be disturbed, have problems in school, or to "lack a sense of personal worth" than housewives' children.

The early studies of children of working mothers were done in an era when few married women worked, at day nurseries which served working mothers who were without husbands due to death, divorce or desertion. These studies were done by social workers and economists in order to press for such reforms as mothers' pensions. The disturbances and higher death rate in such children were not found in studies done in this recent decade, when of the millions of married women working, only 1 out of 8 was not living with her husband.

In one such recent study, based on 2,000 mothers, the only significant differences were that more housewife-mothers stated "the children make me nervous" than working mothers; and the housewives seemed to have "more children." A famous study in Chicago which had seemed to show more mothers of delinquents were working outside the home, turned out to show only that more delinquents come from broken homes. Another study of 400 seriously disturbed children (of a school population of 16,000) showed that where no broken home was involved, three times as many of the disturbed children's mothers were housewives as working mothers.

Other studies showed that children of working mothers were less likely to be either extremely aggressive or extremely inhibited, less likely to do poorly in school, or to "lack a sense of personal worth" than children of housewives, and that mothers who worked were more likely to be "delighted" at becoming pregnant, and less likely to suffer conflict over the "role of mother" than housewives.

There also seemed to be a closer and more positive relationship to children among working mothers who liked their work, than among housewife-mothers or mothers who did not like their work. And a study during the thirties of college-educated mothers, who are more able to choose work they like, showed no adverse effect of their employment on their marital and emotional adjustment, or on number or seriousness of children's problems. In general, women who work shared only two attributes; they were more likely to have higher education and to live in cities.[10]

In our own era, however, as droves of educated women have become suburban housewives, who among them did not worry that their child's bedwetting, thumbsucking, overeating, refusal to eat, withdrawal, lack of friends, inability to be alone, aggressiveness, timidity, slow reading, too much reading, lack of discipline, rigidity, inhibition, exhibitionism, sexual precociousness, or sexual lack of interest was a sign of incipient neurosis. If not actual abnormality or actual delinquency, they must be at least signs of parental failure, portents of future neurosis. Sometimes they were. Parenthood, and especially motherhood, under the Freudian spotlight, had to become a full-time job and career if not a religious cult. One false step could mean disaster. Without careers, without any commitment other than their homes, mothers could devote every moment to their children; their full attention could be given to finding signs of incipient neurosis—and perhaps to producing it.

In every case history, of course, you can always find significant facts about the mother, especially if you are looking for facts, or memories, of those supposedly crucial first five years. In America, after all, the mother is always there; she is *supposed* to be there. Is the fact that they are always there, and there only as mothers, somehow linked to the neuroses of their children? Many cultures pass on their conflicts to children through the mothers, but in the modern cultures of the civilized world, not many educate their strongest, ablest women to make a career of their own children.

Not long ago Dr. Spock confessed, a bit uneasily, that Russian children, whose mothers usually have some purpose in their lives besides motherhood—they work in medicine, science, education, industry, government, art—seemed somehow more stable, adjusted, mature, than American children, whose full-time mothers do nothing but worry about them. Could it be that Russian women are somehow better mothers because they have a serious purpose in their own lives? At least, said the good Dr. Spock, these mothers are more sure of themselves as mothers. They are not, like American mothers, dependent on the latest word from the experts, the newest child-care fad.[11] It is clearly a terrible burden on Dr. Spock to have 13,500,000 mothers so unsure of themselves that they bring up their children literally according to his book—and call piteously to him for help when the book does not work.

No headlines marked the growing concern of psychiatrists with the problem of "dependence" in American children and grownup children. The psychiatrist David Levy, in a very famous study of "maternal overprotection," studied in exhaustive detail twenty mothers who had damaged their children to a pathological extent by "maternal infantilization, indulgence and overprotection." [12] A typical case was a twelve-year-old boy who had "infantile temper tantrums in his eleventh year when his mother refused to butter his bread for him. He still demanded her help in dressing. . . . He summed up his requirements in life very neatly by saying that his mother would butter his bread for him until he married, after which his wife would do so . . ."

All these mothers—according to physiological indexes such as menstrual flow, breast milk, and early indications of a "maternal type of behavior"—were unusually strong in their feminine or maternal instinctual base, if it can be described that way. All but two of the twenty, as Dr. Levy himself described it, were responsible, stable and aggressive: "the active or aggressive feature of the responsible behavior was regarded as a distinctly maternal type of behavior; it characterized the lives of 18 of the 20 overprotecting mothers since childhood." In none was there any tinge of unconscious rejection of the child or of motherhood.

What made these twenty strongly maternal women (evidently strength, even aggression, is not masculine when a psychiatrist considers it part of the maternal instinct) produce such pathologically infantile sons? For one thing, the "child was utilized as a means of satisfying an abnormal craving for love." These mothers freshened up, put lipstick on when the son was due home from school, as a wife for a husband or a girl for her date, because they had no other life besides the child. Most, Levy said, had thwarted career ambitions. The "maternal overprotection" was actually caused by these mothers' strength, by their basic feminine energy—responsible, stable, active and aggressive—producing pathology in the child when the mother was blocked from "other channels of expression."

Most of these mothers also had dominating mothers and submissive fathers of their own, and their husbands had also been obedient sons of dominating mothers; in Freudian terms, the castrativeness all around was rather extreme. The sons and mothers were given intensive psychoanalytical therapy for years, which, it was hoped, would break the pathological cycle. But when, some years after the original study, research workers checked on these women and the children they had pathologically over-protected, the results were not quite what was expected. In most cases psychotherapy had not been effective. Yet some of the children, miraculously, did not become pathological adults; not because of therapy, but because by circumstance the mother had acquired an interest or activity in her own life and had simply stopped living the child's life for him. In a few other cases, the child survived because, through his own ability, he had staked out an area of independence of which his mother was not a part.

Other clues to the real problem of the mother-child relationship in America have been seen by social scientists without ever penetrating the mystique. A sociologist named Arnold Green almost by accident discovered another dimension to the relationship between nurturing mother love, or its lack, and neurosis.

It seems that in the Massachusetts industrial town where Green grew up an entire generation was raised under psychological conditions which should have been traumatic: conditions of irrational, vengeful, even brutal parental authority, and a complete lack of "love" between parent and child. The parents, Polish immigrants, tried to enforce rigid old-world rules which their American children did not respect. The children's ridicule, anger, contempt made the bewildered parents resort to a "vengeful, personal, irrational authority which no longer finds support in the future hopes and ambitions of the children."

In exasperation and fear of losing all control over their Americanized youngsters, parents apply the fist and whip rather indiscriminately. The sound of blows, screams, howls, vexations, wails of torment and hatred are so commonplace along the rows of dilapidated millhouses that the passersby pay them scant attention.[18]

Surely, here were the seeds of future neuroses, as all good post-Freudian parents in America understand them. But to Green's

amazement, when he went back and checked as a sociologist on
the neuroses which according to the book must surely be flourish-
ing, he found no known case of Army rejection because of
psychoneurosis in the local Polish community, and in the overt
behavior of an entire generation in the village "no expression of
anxiety, guilty feelings, rigidity of response, repressed hostility—
the various symptoms described as characteristic of the basic
neurotic character." Green wondered. Why didn't those children
become neurotic, why weren't they destroyed by that brutal,
irrational parental authority?

They had none of that constant and watchful nurturing love
that is urged on middle-class mothers by the child psychologizers;
their mothers, like their fathers, worked all day in the factory;
they had been left in the care of older sisters or brothers, had
run free in fields and woods, had avoided their parents wherever
possible. In these families, stress was placed upon work, rather
than personal sentiment: "respect, not love is the tie that binds."
Demonstrations of affection were not altogether lacking, Green
said, "but they had little in common with the definitions of parent-
child love found in the middle-class women's magazines."

It occurred to the sociologist that perhaps the very absence of
this omnipresent nurturing mother love might explain why these
children did not suffer the neurotic symptoms so commonly
found in the sons of middle-class parents. The Polish parents'
authority, however brutal and irrational, was "external to the
core of the self," as Green put it. The Polish parents did not have
the technique or opportunity to "absorb the personality of the
child." Perhaps, Green suggested, "lack of love" and "irrational
authority" do not in themselves cause neurosis, but only within
a certain context of "personality absorption"—the physical and
emotional blanketing of the child which brings about that slavish
dependence upon the parents found among children of the native
white American urban college-educated middle class.

Is "lack of love" the cause of neurosis, or the middle-class
parental nurturing which "absorbs" the child's independent self,
and creates in him an excessive need for love? Psychoanalysts had
always concentrated on the seeds of neuroses; Green wanted to

"find out what there is to being a modern middle-class parent that fertilizes the soil of the child's neurosis, however the individual seed is planted."

As usual, the arrow pointed unerringly to the mother. But Green was not concerned with helping the modern American mother adjust to her role; on the contrary, he found that she lacked any real "role" as a woman in modern society.

She enters marriage and perhaps bears a child with no definite role and series of functions, as formerly. . . . She feels inferior to man because comparatively she has been and is more restricted. The extent of the actual emancipation of women has been commonly exaggerated. . . .

Through a "good" marriage the middle–class girl attains far more status than is possible through a career of her own. But the period of phantom dalliance with a career, or an embarkation upon one, leave her ill-fitted for the drudgery of housecleaning, diapers, and the preparation of meals. . . . The mother has little to do, in or out of the home; she is her single child's sole companion. Modern "scientific child care" enforces a constant supervision and diffused worrying over the child's health, eating spinach, and ego development; this is complicated by the fact that much energy is spent forcing early walking, toilet-training, talking, because in an intensively competitive milieu middle-class parents from the day of birth are constantly comparing their own child's development with that of the neighbors' children.

Perhaps, Green speculates, middle-class mothers

. . . have made "love" of supreme importance in their relation to the child, theirs for him and his for them, partly because of the love-complex of our time, which is particularly ramified within the middle class, and partly as a compensation for the many sacrifices they have made for the child. The child's need for love is experienced precisely because he has been conditioned to need it . . . conditioned to a slavish emotional dependence. . . . Not the need for parental love, but the constant threat of its withdrawal after the child has been conditioned to the need, lies at the root of the most characteristic modern neuroses; Mamma won't like you if you don't eat your spinach, or stop dribbling your milk, or get down from that davenport. To the extent that a child's personality has been absorbed, he will be thrown into a panic by this sort of treatment. . . . In such a child, a disap-

proving glance may produce more terror—than a twenty-minute lash-
ing in little Stanislaus Wojcik.

Green was only concerned with mothers in terms of their
effect on their sons. But it occurred to him that "personality absorption" alone cannot, after all, explain neurosis. Because otherwise, he says, middle-class women of the previous generation
would all have suffered such neuroses—and nobody recorded
such suffering in those women. Certainly the personality of the
middle-class girl of the late nineteenth century was "absorbed"
by her parents, by the demands of "love" and unquestioning
obedience. However, "the rate of neurosis under those conditions
was probably not too high," the sociologist concludes, because
even though the woman's own personality was "absorbed," it was
consistently absorbed "within a role which changed relatively
slightly from childhood into adolescence, courtship, and finally
into marriage"; she never could be her own person.

The modern middle-class boy, on the other hand, is forced to
compete with others, to achieve—which demands a certain degree
of independence, firmness of purpose, aggressiveness, self-assertion. Thus, in the boy, the mother-nourished need for everyone
to love him, the inability to erect his own values and purposes
is neurotic, but not in the girl.

It is provocative, this speculation made by a sociologist in 1946,
but it never penetrated far beyond the inner circles of social
theory, never permeated the bulwarks of the feminine mystique,
despite increasing national awareness that something was wrong
with American mothers. Even this sociologist, who managed to
get behind the mystique and see children in terms other than
their need for more mother love, was concerned only with the
problem of the sons. But was not the real implication that the
role of the middle-class American housewife forces many a
mother to smother, absorb, the personality of both her sons and
daughters? Many saw the tragic waste of American sons who
were made incapable of achievement, individual values, independent action; but they did not see as tragic the waste of the daughters, or of the mothers to whom it happened generations earlier.
If a culture does not expect human maturity from its women, it

does not see its lack as a waste, or as a possible cause of neurosis or conflict. The insult, the real reflection on our culture's definition of the role of women, is that as a nation we only noticed that something was wrong with women when we saw its effects on their sons.

Is it surprising that we misunderstood what was really wrong? How could we understand it, in the static terms of functionalism and adjustment? Educators and sociologists applauded when the personality of the middle-class girl was "consistently" absorbed from childhood through adulthood by her "role as woman." Long live the role, if adjustment is served. The waste of a human self was not considered a phenomenon to be studied in women—only the frustration caused by "cultural inconsistencies in role-conditioning," as the great social scientist Ruth Benedict described the plight of American women. Even women themselves, who felt the misery, the helplessness of their lack of self, did not understand the feeling; it became the problem that has no name. And in their shame and guilt they turned again to their children to escape the problem. So the circle completes itself, from mother to sons and daughters, generation after generation.

The unremitting attack on women which has become an American preoccupation in recent years might also stem from the same escapist motives that sent men and women back to the security of the home. Mother love is said to be sacred in America, but with all the reverence and lip service she is paid, mom is a pretty safe target, no matter how correctly or incorrectly her failures are interpreted. No one has ever been blacklisted or fired for an attack on "the American woman." Apart from the psychological pressures from mothers or wives, there have been plenty of nonsexual pressures in the America of the last decade—the compromising, never-ceasing competition, the anonymous and often purposeless work in the big organization—that also kept a man from feeling like a man. Safer to take it out on his wife and his mother than to recognize a failure in himself or in the sacred American way of life. The men were not always kidding when they said their wives were lucky to be able to stay home all day. It was also soothing to rationalize the rat race by telling themselves that they were in it "for the wife and kids." And so men re-created their own childhood in suburbia, and made mothers of their wives. Men fell for the mystique without a murmur of dissent. It promised them mothers for the rest of their lives, both as a reason for their being and as an excuse for their failures. Is it so strange that boys who grow up with too much mother love become men who can never get enough?

But why did women sit still for this barrage of blame? When a culture has erected barrier after barrier against women as separate selves; when a culture has erected legal, political, social, economic and educational barriers to women's own acceptance of maturity—even after most of those barriers are down it is still easier for a woman to seek the sanctuary of the home. It is easier to live through her husband and children than to make a road of her own in the world. For she is the daughter of that same mom who made it so hard for girl as well as boy to grow up. And freedom is a frightening thing. It is frightening to grow up finally and be free of passive dependence. Why should a woman bother to be anything more than a wife and mother if all the forces of her culture tell her she doesn't have to, will be better off not to, grow up?

And so the American woman made her mistaken choice. She ran back home again to live by sex alone, trading in her individuality for security. Her husband was drawn in after her, and the door was shut against the outside world. They began to live the pretty lie of the feminine mystique, but could either of them really believe it? She was, after all, an American woman, an irreversible product of a culture that stops just short of giving her a separate identity. He was, after all, an American man whose respect for individuality and freedom of choice are his nation's pride. They went to school together; he knows who she is. Does his meek willingness to wax the floor and wash the dishes when he comes home tired on the 6:55 hide from both their guilty awareness of the reality behind the pretty lie? What keeps them believing it, in spite of the warning signs that have cropped up all over the suburban lot? What keeps the women home? What force in our culture is strong enough to write "Occupation: housewife" so large that all the other possibilities for women have been almost obscured?

Powerful forces in this nation must be served by those pretty domestic pictures that stare at us everywhere, forbidding a woman to use her own abilities in the world. The preservation of the feminine mystique in this sense could have implications that are not sexual at all. When one begins to think about it, America depends rather heavily on women's passive dependence, their femininity. Femininity, if one still wants to call it that, makes American women a target and a victim of the sexual sell.

9 The Sexual Sell

Some months ago, as I began to fit together the puzzle of women's retreat to home, I had the feeling I was missing something. I could trace the routes by which sophisticated thought circled back on itself to perpetuate an obsolete image of femininity; I could see how that image meshed with prejudice and misinterpreted frustrations to hide the emptiness of "Occupation: housewife" from women themselves.

But what powers it all? If, despite the nameless desperation of so many American housewives, despite the opportunities open to all women now, so few have any purpose in life other than to be a wife and mother, somebody, something pretty powerful must be at work. The energy behind the feminist movement was too dynamic merely to have trickled dry; it must have been turned off, diverted, by something more powerful than that underestimated power of women.

There are certain facts of life so obvious and mundane that one never talks about them. Only the child blurts out: "Why do people in books never go to the toilet?" Why is it never said that the really crucial function, the really important role that women serve as housewives is *to buy more things for the house*. In all the talk of femininity and woman's role, one forgets that the real business of America is business. But the perpetuation of housewifery, the growth of the feminine mystique, makes sense (and dollars) when one realizes that women are the chief customers of American business. Somehow, somewhere, someone must have figured out that women will buy more things if they are kept in the underused, nameless-yearning, energy-to-get-rid-of state of being housewives.

I have no idea how it happened. Decision-making in industry is not as simple, as rational, as those who believe the conspiratorial theories of history would have it. I am sure the heads of General Foods, and General Electric, and General Motors, and Macy's and Gimbel's and the assorted directors of all the companies that make detergents and electric mixers, and red stoves with rounded corners, and synthetic furs, and waxes, and hair coloring, and patterns for home sewing and home carpentry, and lotions for detergent hands, and bleaches to keep the towels pure white, never sat down around a mahogany conference table in a board room on Madison Avenue or Wall Street and voted on a motion: "Gentlemen, I move, in the interests of all, that we begin a concerted fifty-billion dollar campaign to stop this dangerous movement of American women out of the home. We've got to keep them housewives, and let's not forget it."

A thinking vice-president says: "Too many women getting educated. Don't want to stay home. Unhealthy. If they all get to be scientists and such, they won't have time to shop. But how can we keep them home? They want careers now."

"We'll liberate them to have careers at home," the new executive with horn-rimmed glasses and the Ph.D. in psychology suggests. "We'll make home-making creative."

Of course, it didn't happen quite like that. It was not an economic conspiracy directed against women. It was a byproduct of our general confusion lately of means with ends; just something that happened to women when the business of producing and selling and investing in business for profit—which is merely the way our economy is organized to serve man's needs efficiently —began to be confused with the purpose of our nation, the end of life itself. No more surprising, the subversion of women's lives in America to the ends of business, than the subversion of the sciences of human behavior to the business of deluding women

about their real needs. It would take a clever economist to figure
out what would keep our affluent economy going if the housewife market began to fall off, just as an economist would have
to figure out what to do if there were no threat of war.

It is easy to see why it happened. I learned *how* it happened
when I went to see a man who is paid approximately a million
dollars a year for his professional services in manipulating the
emotions of American women to serve the needs of business.
This particular man got in on the ground floor of the hidden-
persuasion business in 1945, and kept going. The headquarters of
his institute for motivational manipulation is a baronial mansion
in upper Westchester. The walls of a ballroom two-stories high
are filled with steel shelves holding a thousand-odd studies for
business and industry, 300,000 individual "depth interviews,"
mostly with American housewives.[1]

He let me see what I wanted, said I could use anything that
was not confidential to a specific company. Nothing there for
anyone to hide, to feel guilty about—only, in page after page
of those depth studies, a shrewd cheerful awareness of the empty,
purposeless, uncreative, even sexually joyless lives that most Amer-
can housewives lead. In his own unabashed terms, this most helpful of hidden persuaders showed me the function served by keeping American women housewives—the reservoir that their lack
of identity, lack of purpose, creates, to be manipulated into dollars at the point of purchase.

Properly manipulated ("if you are not afraid of that word,"
he said), American housewives can be given the sense of identity,
purpose, creativity, the self-realization, even the sexual joy they
lack—by the buying of things. I suddenly realized the significance of the boast that women wield seventy-five per cent of
the purchasing power in America. I suddenly saw American
women as *victims* of that ghastly gift, that power at the point
of purchase. The insights he shared with me so liberally revealed.
many things. . . .

The dilemma of business was spelled out in a survey made in
1945 for the publisher of a leading women's magazine on the

attitudes of women toward electrical appliances. The message was considered of interest to all the companies that, with the war about to end, were going to have to make consumer sales take the place of war contracts. It was a study of "the psychology of housekeeping"; "a woman's attitude toward housekeeping appliances cannot be separated from her attitude toward homemaking in general," it warned.

On the basis of a national sample of 4,500 wives (middle-class, high-school or college-educated), American women were divided into three categories: "The True Housewife Type," "The Career Woman," and "The Balanced Homemaker." While 51 per cent of the women then fitted "The True Housewife Type" ("From the psychological point of view, housekeeping is this woman's dominating interest. She takes the utmost pride and satisfaction in maintaining a comfortable and well-run home for her family. Consciously or subconsciously, she feels that she is indispensable and that no one else can take over her job. She has little, if any, desire for a position outside the home, and if she has one it is through force or circumstances or necessity"), it was apparent that this group was diminishing, and probably would continue to do so as new fields, interests, education were now open to women.

The largest market for appliances, however, was this "True Housewife"—though she had a certain "reluctance" to accept new devices that had to be recognized and overcome. ("She may even fear that they [appliances] will render unnecessary the old-fashioned way of doing things that has always suited her.") After all, housework was the justification for her whole existence. ("I don't think there is any way to make housework easier for myself," one True Housewife said, "because I don't believe that a machine can take the place of hard work.")

The second type—The Career Woman or Would-Be Career Woman—was a minority, but an extremely "unhealthy" one from the sellers' standpoint; advertisers were warned that it would be to their advantage not to let this group get any larger. For such women, though not necessarily job-holders, "do not believe that a woman's place is primarily in the home." ("Many in this group have never actually worked, but their attitude is: 'I think housekeeping is a horrible waste of time. If my youngsters were old enough and I were free to leave the house, I would use my time to better advantage. If my family's meals and laundry could be taken care of, I would be delighted to go out and get a job.' ") The point to bear in mind regarding career women, the study said, is that, while they buy modern appliances, they are not the ideal type of customer. *They are too critical.*

The third type—"The Balanced Homemaker"—is "from the market standpoint, the ideal type." She has some outside interests, or has held a job before turning exclusively to homemaking; she "readily accepts" the help mechanical appliances can give—but "does not expect them to do the impossible" because she needs to use her own executive ability "in managing a well-run household."

The moral of the study was explicit: "Since the Balanced Homemaker represents the market with the greatest future potential, it would be to the advantage of the appliance manufacturer to make more and more women aware of the desirability of belonging to this group. Educate them through advertising that it is possible to have outside interests and become alert to wider intellectual influences (without becoming a Career Woman). The art of good homemaking should be the goal of every normal woman."

The problem—which, if recognized at that time by one hidden persuader for the home-appliance industry, was surely recognized by others with products for the home—was that "a whole new generation of women is being educated to do work outside the home. Furthermore, an increased desire for emancipation is evident." The solution, quite simply, was to encourage them to be "modern" housewives. The Career or Would-Be Career Woman who frankly dislikes cleaning, dusting, ironing, washing clothes, is less interested in a new wax, a new soap powder. Unlike "The True Housewife" and the "Balanced Homemaker" who prefer to have sufficient appliances and do the housework themselves, the Career Woman would "prefer servants—housework takes too much time and energy." She buys appliances, however, whether or not she has servants, but she is "more likely to complain about the service they give," and to be "harder to sell."

It was too late—impossible—to turn these modern could-or-would-be career women back into True Housewives, but the study pointed out, in 1945, the potential for Balanced House-wifery—the home career. Let them "want to have their cake and eat it too . . . save time, have more comfort, avoid dirt and disorder, have mechanized supervision, yet not want to give up the feeling of personal achievement and pride in a well-run house-hold, which comes from 'doing it yourself.' As one young house-wife said: 'It's nice to be modern—it's like running a factory in which you have all the latest machinery.' "

But it was not an easy job, either for business or advertisers. New gadgets that were able to do almost all the housework crowded the market; increased ingenuity was needed to give American women that "feeling of achievement," and yet keep housework their main purpose in life. Education, independence, growing individuality, everything that made them ready for other purposes had constantly to be countered, channeled back to the home.

The manipulator's services became increasingly valuable. In later surveys, he no longer interviewed professional women; they were not at home during the day. The women in his samples were deliberately True or Balanced Housewives, the new sub-urban housewives. Household and consumer products are, after all, geared to women; seventy-five per cent of all consumer ad-vertising budgets is spent to appeal to women; that is, to house-wives, the women who are available during the day to be inter-viewed, the women with the time for shopping. Naturally, his depth interviews, projective tests, "living laboratories," were designed to impress his clients, but more often than not they contained the shrewd insights of a skilled social scientist, insights that could be used with profit.

His clients were told they had to do something about this

growing need of American women to do creative work—"the major unfulfilled need of the modern housewife." He wrote in one report, for example:

Every effort must be made to sell X Mix, as a base upon which the woman's creative effort is used.

The appeal should emphasize the fact that X Mix aids the woman in expressing her creativity because it takes the drudgery away. At the same time, stress should be laid upon the cooking manipulations, the fun that goes with them, permitting you to feel that X Mix baking is real baking.

But the dilemma again: how to make her spend money on the mix that takes some of the drudgery out of baking by telling her "she can utilize her energy where it really counts"—and yet keep her from being "too busy to bake"? ("I don't use the mix because I don't do any baking at all. It's too much trouble. I live in a sprawled-out apartment and what with keeping it clean and looking after my child and my part-time job, I don't have time for baking.") What to do about their "feeling of disappointment" when the biscuits come out of the oven, and they're really only bread and there is no feeling of creative achievement? ("Why should I bake my own biscuits when there are so many good things on the market that just need to be heated up? It just doesn't make any sense at all to go through all the trouble of mixing your own and then greasing the tin and baking them.") What to do when the woman doesn't get the feeling her mother got, when the cake *had* to be made from scratch? ("The way my mother made them, you had to sift the flour yourself and add the eggs and the butter and you knew you'd really made something you could be proud of.")

The problem can be handled, the report assured:

By using X Mix the woman can prove herself as a wife and mother, not only by baking, but by spending more time with her family. . . . Of course, it must also be made clear that home-baked foods are in every way preferable to bakery-shop foods . . .

Above all, give X Mix "a therapeutic value" by downplaying the easy recipes, emphasizing instead "the stimulating effort of baking." From an advertising viewpoint, this means stressing that "with X Mix in the home, you will be a different woman . . . a happier woman."

Further, the client was told that a phrase in his ad "and you make that cake the easiest, laziest way there is" evoked a "negative response" in American housewives—it hit too close to their "underlying guilt." ("Since they never feel that they are really exerting sufficient effort, it is certainly wrong to tell them that baking with X Mix is the lazy way.") Supposing, he suggested, that this devoted wife and mother behind the kitchen stove, anxiously preparing a cake or pie for her husband or children "is simply indulging her own hunger for sweets." The very fact that baking is work for the housewife helps her dispel any doubts that she might have about her real motivations.

But there are even ways to manipulate the housewives' guilt, the report said:

It might be possible to suggest through advertising that not to take advantage of all 12 uses of X Mix is to limit your efforts to give pleasure to your family. A transfer of guilt might be achieved. Rather than feeling guilty about using X Mix for dessert food, the woman would be made to feel guilty if she doesn't take advantage of this opportunity to give her family 12 different and delicious treats. "Don't waste your skill; don't limit yourself."

By the mid-fifties, the surveys reported with pleasure that the Career Woman ("the woman who clamored for equality—almost for identity in every sphere of life, the woman who reacted to 'domestic slavery' with indignation and vehemence") was gone, replaced by the "less worldly, less sophisticated" woman whose activity in PTA gives her "broad contacts with the world outside her home," but who "finds in housework a medium of expression for her femininity and individuality." She's not like the old-fashioned self-sacrificing housewife; she considers herself the equal of man. But she still feels "lazy, neglectful, haunted by guilt feelings" because she doesn't have enough work to do. The advertiser must manipulate her need for a "feeling of creativeness" into the buying of his product.

After an initial resistance, she now tends to accept instant coffee, frozen foods, precooked foods, and labor-saving items as part of her routine. But she needs a justification and she finds it in the thought that "by using frozen foods I'm freeing myself to accomplish other important tasks as a modern mother and wife."

Creativeness is the modern woman's dialectical answer to the problem of her changed position in the household. Thesis: I'm a housewife. Antithesis: I hate drudgery. Synthesis: I'm creative!

This means essentially that even though the housewife may buy canned food, for instance, and thus save time and effort, she doesn't let it go at that. She has a great need for "doctoring up" the can and thus prove her personal participation and her concern with giving satisfaction to her family.

The feeling of creativeness also serves another purpose: it is an outlet for the liberated talents, the better taste, the freer imagination, the greater initiative of the modern woman. It permits her to use at home *all the faculties that she would display in an outside career.*

The yearning for creative opportunities and moments is a major aspect of buying motivations.

The only trouble, the surveys warned, is that she "tries to use her own mind and her own judgment. She is fast getting away from judging by collective or majority standards. She is developing independent standards." ("Never mind the neighbors. I don't want to 'live up' to them or compare myself to them at every turn.") She can't always be reached now with "keep up with the Joneses"—the advertiser must appeal to her *own* need to live.

Appeal to this thirst. . . . Tell her that you are adding more zest, more enjoyment to her life, that it is within her reach now to taste new experiences and that she is entitled to taste these experiences. Even more positively, you should convey that you are giving her "lessons in living."

"House cleaning should be fun," the manufacturer of a certain cleaning device was advised. Even though his product was, perhaps, less efficient than the vacuum cleaner, it let the housewife use more of her own energy in the work. Further, it let the housewife have the illusion that she has become "a professional, an expert in determining which cleaning tools to use for specific jobs."

This professionalization is a psychological defense of the housewife against being a general "cleaner-upper" and menial servant for her family in a day and age of general work emancipation.

The role of expert serves a two-fold emotional function: (1) it helps the housewife achieve status, and (2) she moves beyond the orbit of her home, into the world of modern science in her search for new and better ways of doing things.

As a result, there has never been a more favorable psychological climate for household appliances and products. The modern housewife . . . is actually aggressive in her efforts to find those household products which, in her expert opinion, really meet her need. This trend accounts for the popularity of different waxes and polishes for different materials in the home, for the growing use of floor polishers, and for the variety of mops and cleaning implements for floors and walls.

The difficulty is to give her the "sense of achievement" of "ego enhancement" she has been persuaded to seek in the housewife "profession," when, in actuality, "her time-consuming task, housekeeping, is not only endless, it is a task for which society hires the lowliest, least-trained, most trod-upon individuals and groups. . . . Anyone with a strong enough back (and a small enough brain) can do these menial chores." But even this difficulty can be manipulated to sell her more things:

One of the ways that the housewife raises her own prestige as a cleaner of her home is through the use of specialized products for specialized tasks. . . .

When she uses one product for washing clothes, a second for dishes, a third for walls, a fourth for floors, a fifth for venetian blinds, etc., rather than an all-purpose cleaner, she feels less like an unskilled laborer, more like an engineer, an expert.

A second way of raising her own stature is to "do things my way" —to establish an expert's role for herself by creating her own "tricks of the trade." For example, she may "always put a bit of bleach in all my washing—even colored, to make them *really* clean!"

Help her to "justify her menial task by building up her role as the protector of her family—the killer of millions of microbes and germs," this report advised. "Emphasize her kingpin role in the family . . . help her be an expert rather than a menial worker . . . make housework a matter of knowledge and skill, rather than a matter of brawn and dull, unremitting effort." An effective way of doing this is to bring out a *new* product. For, it seems, there's a growing wave of housewives "who look forward to new products which not only decrease their daily work load, but actually engage their emotional and intellectual interest in the world of scientific development outside the home."

One gasps in admiration at the ingenuity of it all—the housewife can participate in science itself just by buying something new—or something old that has been given a brand new personality.

Besides increasing her professional status, a *new* cleaning appliance or product increases a woman's feeling of economic security and luxury, just as a new automobile does for a man. This was reported by 28 per cent of the respondents, who agreed with this particular sentiment: "I like to try out new things. I've just started to use a new liquid detergent—and somehow it makes me feel like a queen."

The question of letting the woman use her mind and even participate in science through housework is, however, not without its drawbacks. Science should not relieve housewives of too much drudgery; it must concentrate instead on creating the *illusion* of that sense of achievement that housewives seem to need.

To prove this point, 250 housewives were given a depth test: they were asked to choose among four imaginary methods of cleaning. The first was a completely automatic dust- and dirt-removal system which operated continuously like a home-heating system. The second, the housewife had to press a button to start. The third was portable; she had to carry it around and point it at an area to remove the dirt. The fourth was a brand new, modern object with which she could sweep the dirt away herself. The housewives spoke up in favor of this last appliance. If it "appears new, modern" she would rather have the one that lets her work herself, this report said. "One compelling reason is her desire to be a participant, not just a button-pusher." As one housewife remarked, "As for some magical push-button cleaning system, well, what would happen to my exercise, my feeling of accomplishment, and what would I do with my mornings?"

This fascinating study incidentally revealed that a certain electronic cleaning appliance—long considered one of our great laborsavers—actually made "housekeeping more difficult than it need be." From the response of eighty per cent of those housewives, it seemed that once a woman got this appliance going, she "felt compelled to do cleaning that wasn't really necessary." The electronic appliance actually dictated the extent and type of cleaning to be done.

Should the housewife then be encouraged to go back to that simple cheap sweeper that let her clean only as much as she felt necessary? No, said the report, of course not. Simply give that old-fashioned sweeper the "status" of the electronic appliance as a "labor-saving necessity" for the modern housewife "and then indicate that the modern homemaker would, naturally, own both."

No one, not even the depth researchers, denied that housework was endless, and its boring repetition just did not give that much satisfaction, did not require that much vaunted expert knowledge. But the endlessness of it all was an advantage from the seller's point of view. The problem was to keep at bay the underlying realization which was lurking dangerously in "thousands of depth interviews which we have conducted for dozens of different kinds of house-cleaning products"—the realization that, as one housewife said, "It stinks! I have to do it, so I do it. It's a necessary evil, that's all." What to do? For one thing, put out more and more products, make the directions more complicated, make it really necessary for the housewife to "be an expert." (Washing clothes, the report advised, must become more than a matter of throwing clothes into a machine and pouring in soap. Garments must be carefully sorted, one load given treatment A, a second load treatment B, some washed by hand. The housewife can then "take great pride in knowing just which of the arsenal of products to use on each occasion.")

Capitalize, the report continued, on housewives' "guilt over the hidden dirt" so she will rip her house to shreds in a "deep

cleaning" operation, which will give her a "sense of completeness" for a few weeks. ("The times of thorough cleaning are the
points at which she is most willing to try new products and 'deep
clean' advertising holds out the promise of completion.")

The seller must also stress the joys of completing each separate
task, remembering that "nearly all housekeepers, even those who
thoroughly detest their job, paradoxically find escape from their
endless fate by accepting it—by 'throwing myself into it,' as she
says."

Losing herself in her work—surrounded by all the implements,
creams, powders, soaps, she forgets for a time how soon she will have
to redo the task. In other words, a housewife permits herself to forget
for a moment how rapidly the sink will again fill with dishes, how
quickly the floor will again be dirty, and she seizes the moment of
completion of a task as a moment of pleasure as pure as if she had just
finished a masterpiece of art which would stand as a monument to her
credit forever.

This is the kind of creative experience the seller of things can
give the housewife. In one housewife's own words:

I don't like housework at all. I'm a lousy houseworker. But once in
a while I get pepped up and I'll really go to town . . . When I have
some new kind of cleaning material—like when Glass Wax first came
out or those silicone furniture polishes—I got a real kick out of it,
and I went through the house shining everything. I like to see the
things shine. I feel so good when I see the bathroom just glistening.

And so the manipulator advised:

Identify your product with the physical and spiritual rewards she
derives from the almost religious feeling of basic security provided
by her home. Talk about her "light, happy, peaceful feelings"; her
"deep sense of achievement." . . . But remember she doesn't really
want praise for the sake of praise . . . also remember that her mood
is not simply "gay." She is tired and a bit solemn. Superficially cheerful
adjectives or colors will not reflect her feelings. She will react much
more favorably to simple, warm and sincere messages.

In the fifties came the revolutionary discovery of the teenage
market. Teenagers and young marrieds began to figure promi-

nently in the surveys. It was discovered that young wives, who had only been to high school and had never worked, were more "insecure," less independent, easier to sell. These young people could be told that, by buying the right things, they could achieve middle-class status, without work or study. The keep-up-with-the-Joneses sell would work again; the individuality and independence which American women had been getting from education and work outside the home was not such a problem with the teenage brides. In fact, the surveys said, if the pattern of "happiness through things" could be established when these women were young enough, they could be safely encouraged to go out and get a part-time job to help their husbands pay for all the things they buy. The main point now was to convince the teenagers that "happiness through things" is no longer the prerogative of the rich or the talented; it can be enjoyed by all, if they learn "the right way," the way the others do it, if they learn the embarrassment of being different.

In the words of one of these reports:

49 per cent of the new brides were teenagers, and more girls marry at the age of 18 than at any other age. This early family formation yields a larger number of young people who are on the threshold of their own responsibilities and decision-making in purchases . . .

But the most important fact is of a psychological nature: Marriage today is not only the culmination of a romantic attachment; more consciously and more clear-headedly than in the past, it is also a decision to create a partnership in establishing a comfortable home, equipped with a great number of desirable products.

In talking to scores of young couples and brides-to-be, we found that, as a rule, their conversations and dreams centered to a very large degree around their future homes and their furnishings, around shopping "to get an idea," around discussing the advantages and disadvantages of various products. . . .

The modern bride is deeply convinced of the unique value of married love, of the possibilities of finding real happiness in marriage and of fulfilling her personal destiny in it and through it.

But the engagement period today is a romantic, dreamy and heady period only to a limited extent. It is probably safe to say that the period of engagement tends to be a rehearsal of the material duties and responsibilities of marriage. While waiting for the nuptials, couples work hard, put aside money for definite purchases, or even begin buying on an installment plan.

What is the deeper meaning of this new combination of an almost religious belief in the importance and beauty of married life on the one hand, and the product-centered outlook, on the other? . . .

The modern bride seeks as a conscious goal that which in many cases her grandmother saw as a blind fate and her mother as slavery: to belong to a man, to have a home and children of her own, to choose among all possible careers the career of wife-mother-homemaker.

The fact that the young bride now seeks in her marriage complete "fulfillment," that she now expects to "prove her own worth" and find all the "fundamental meanings" of life in her home, and to participate through her home in "the interesting ideas of the modern era, the future," has enormous "practical applications," advertisers were told. For all these meanings she seeks in her marriage, even her fear that she will be "left behind," can be channeled into the purchase of products. For example, a manufacturer of sterling silver, a product that is very difficult to sell, was told:

Reassure her that only with sterling can she be fully secure in her new role . . . it symbolizes her success as a modern woman. Above all, dramatize the fun and pride that derive from the job of cleaning silver. Stimulate the pride of achievement. "How much pride you get from the brief task that's so much fun . . ."

Concentrate on the very young teenage girls, this report further advised. The young ones will want what "the others" want, even if their mothers don't. ("As one of our teenagers said: 'All the gang has started their own sets of sterling. We're real keen about it—compare patterns and go through the ads together. My own family never had any sterling and they think I'm showing off when I spend my money on it—they think plated's just as good. But the kids think they're way off base.'") Get them in schools, churches, sororities, social clubs; get them through home-economics teachers, group leaders, teenage TV programs and teenage advertising. "This is the big market of the future and word-of-mouth advertising, along with group pressure, is not only the most potent influence but in the absence of tradition, a most necessary one."

As for the more independent older wife, that unfortunate tendency to use materials that require little care—stainless steel, plastic dishes, paper napkins—can be met by making her feel guilty about the effects on the children. ("As one young wife told us: 'I'm out of the house all day long, so I can't prepare and serve meals the way I want to. I don't like it that way—my husband and the children deserve a better break. Sometimes I think it'd be better if we tried to get along on one salary and have a real home life but there are always so many things we need.'") Such guilt, the report maintained, can be used to make her see the product, silver, as a means of holding the family together; it gives "added psychological value." What's more, the product can even fill the housewife's need for identity: "Suggest that it becomes truly a part of *you*, reflecting *you*. Do not be afraid to suggest mystically that sterling will adapt itself to any house and any person."

The fur industry is in trouble, another survey reported, because young high school and college girls equate fur coats with "uselessness" and "a kept woman." Again the advice was to get to the very young before these unfortunate connotations have formed. ("By introducing youngsters to positive fur experiences, the probabilities of easing their way into garment purchasing in their teens is enhanced.") Point out that "the wearing of a fur garment actually establishes femininity and sexuality for a woman." ("It's the kind of thing a girl looks forward to. It means something. It's feminine." "I'm bringing my daughter up right. She always wants to put on 'mommy's coat.' She'll want them. She's a real girl.") But keep in mind that "mink has contributed a negative feminine symbolism to the whole fur market." Unfortunately, two out of three women felt mink-wearers were "predatory . . . exploitative . . . dependent . . . socially nonproductive . . ."

Femininity today cannot be so explicitly predatory, exploitative, the report said; nor can it have the old high-fashion "connotations of stand-out-from-the-crowd, self-centeredness." And so fur's "ego-orientation" must be reduced and replaced with the new femininity of the housewife, for whom ego-orientation must be translated into togetherness, family-orientation.

Begin to create the feeling that fur is a necessity—a delightful necessity . . . thus providing the consumer with moral permission to purchase something she now feels is ego-oriented. . . . Give fur femininity a broader character, developing some of the following status and prestige symbols . . . an emotionally happy woman . . . wife and mother who wins the affection and respect of her husband and her children because of the kind of person she is, and the kind of role she performs. . . .

Place furs in a family setting; show the pleasure and admiration of a fur garment derived by family members, husband and children; their pride in their mother's appearance, in her ownership of a fur garment. Develop fur garments as "family" gifts—enable the whole family to enjoy that garment at Christmas, etc., thus reducing its ego-orientation for the owner and eliminating her guilt over her alleged self-indulgence.

Thus, the only way that the young housewife was supposed to express herself, and not feel guilty about it, was in buying products for the home-and-family. Any creative urges she may have should also be home-and-family oriented, as still another survey reported to the home sewing industry.

Such activities as sewing achieve a new meaning and a new status. Sewing is no longer associated with absolute need. . . . Moreover, with the moral elevation of home-oriented activities, sewing, along with cooking, gardening, and home decorating—is recognized as a means of expressing creativity and individuality and also as a means of achieving the "quality" which a new taste level dictates.

The women who sew, this survey discovered, are the active, energetic, intelligent modern housewives, the new home-oriented modern American women, who have a great unfulfilled need to create, and achieve, and realize their own individuality—which must be filled by some home activity. The big problem for the home-sewing industry was that the "image" of sewing was too "dull"; somehow it didn't achieve the feeling of creating something important. In selling their products, the industry must emphasize the "lasting creativeness" of sewing.

But even sewing can't be too creative, too individual, according to the advice offered to one pattern manufacturer. His patterns required some intelligence to follow, left quite a lot of room for individual expression, and the manufacturer was in trouble for that very reason; his patterns implied that a woman "would know what she likes and would probably have definite ideas." He was advised to widen this "far too limited fashion personality" and get one with "fashion conformity"—appeal to the "fashion-insecure woman," "the conformist element in fashion," who feels "it is not smart to be dressed too differently." For, of course, the manufacturer's problem was not to satisfy woman's need for individuality, for expression or creativity, but to sell more patterns—which is better done by building conformity.

Time and time again, the surveys shrewdly analyzed the needs, and even the secret frustrations of the American housewife; and each time if these needs were properly manipulated, she could be induced to buy more "things." In 1957, a survey told the department stores that their role in this new world was not only to "sell" the housewife but to satisfy her need for "education"— to satisfy the yearning she has, alone in her house, to feel herself a part of the changing world. The store will sell her more, the report said, if it will understand that the real need she is trying to fill by shopping is not anything she can buy there.

Most women have not only a material need, but a psychological compulsion to visit department stores. They live in comparative isolation. Their vista and experiences are limited. They know that there is a vaster life beyond their horizon and they fear that life will pass them by.

Department stores break down that isolation. The woman entering a department store suddenly has the feeling she knows what is going on in the world. Department stores, more than magazines, TV, or any other medium of mass communication, are most women's main source of information about the various aspects of life . . .

There are many needs that the department store must fill, this report continued. For one, the housewife's "need to learn and to advance in life."

We symbolize our social position by the objects with which we surround ourselves. A woman whose husband was making $6,000 a few years ago and is making $10,000 now needs to learn a whole new set of symbols. Department stores are her best teachers of this subject.

For another, there is the need for achievement, which for the new modern housewife, is primarily filled by a "bargain."

We have found that in our economy of abundance, preoccupation with prices is not so much a financial as a psychological need for the majority of women. . . . Increasingly a "bargain" means not that "I can now buy something which I could not afford at a higher price"; it mainly means "I'm doing a good job as a housewife; I'm contributing to the welfare of the family just as my husband does when he works and brings home the paycheck."

The price itself hardly matters, the report said:

Since buying is only the climax of a complicated relationship, based to a large extent on the woman's yearning to know how to be a more attractive woman, a better housewife, a superior mother, etc., use this motivation in all your promotion and advertising. Take every opportunity to explain how your store will help her fulfill her most cherished roles in life . . .

If the stores are women's school of life, ads are the textbooks. They have an inexhaustible avidity for these ads which give them the illusion that they are in contact with what is going on in the world of inanimate objects, objects through which they express so much of so many of their drives . . .

Again, in 1957, a survey very correctly reported that despite the "many positive aspects" of the "new home-centered era," unfortunately too many needs were now centered on the home— that home was not able to fill. A cause for alarm? No indeed; even these needs are grist for manipulation.

The family is not always the psychological pot of gold at the end of the rainbow of promise of modern life as it has sometimes been represented. In fact, psychological demands are being made upon the family today which it cannot fulfill. . . .

Fortunately for the producers and advertisers of America (and also for the family and the psychological well-being of our citizens) much of this gap may be filled, and is being filled, by the acquisition of consumer goods.

Hundreds of products fulfill a whole set of psychological functions that producers and advertisers should know of and use in the development of more effective sales approaches. Just as producing once served as an outlet for social tension, now consumption serves the same purpose.

The buying of things drains away those needs which cannot really be satisfied by home and family—the housewives' need for "something beyond themselves with which to identify," "a sense of movement with others toward aims that give meaning and purpose to life," "an unquestioned social aim to which each individual can devote his efforts."

Deeply set in human nature is the need to have a meaningful place in a group that strives for meaningful social goals. Whenever this is lacking, the individual becomes restless. Which explains why, as we talk to people across the nation, over and over again, we hear questions like these: "What does it all mean?" "Where am I going?" "Why don't things seem more worth while and when we all work so hard and have so darn many things to play with?"

The question is: Can your product fill this gap?

"The frustrated need for privacy in the family life," in this era of "togetherness" was another secret wish uncovered in a depth survey. This need, however, might be used to sell a second car. . . .

In addition to the car the whole family enjoys together, the car for the husband and wife separately—"Alone in the car, one may get the breathing spell one needs so badly and may come to consider the car as one's castle, or the instrument of one's reconquered privacy." Or "individual" "personal" toothpaste, soap, shampoo.

Another survey reported that there was a puzzling "desexualization of married life" despite the great emphasis on marriage and family and sex. The problem: what can supply what the report diagnosed as a "missing sexual spark?" The solution: the report advised sellers to "put the libido back into advertising." Despite the feeling that our manufacturers are trying to sell

everything through sex, sex as found on TV commercials and
ads in national magazines is too tame, the report said, too narrow.
"Consumerism," is desexing the American libido because it "has
failed to reflect the powerful life forces in every individual which
range far beyond the relationship between the sexes." The sellers,
it seemed, have sexed the sex out of sex.

Most modern advertising reflects and grossly exaggerates our present
national tendency to downgrade, simplify and water down the passionate turbulent and electrifying aspects of the life urges of mankind.
. . . No one suggests that advertising can or should become obscene or
salacious. The trouble lies with the fact that through its timidity and
lack of imagination, it faces the danger of becoming libido-poor and
consequently unreal, inhuman and tedious.

How to put the libido back, restore the lost spontaneity, drive,
love of life, the individuality, that sex in America seems to lack?
In an absent-minded moment, the report concludes that "love of
life, as of the other sex, should remain unsoiled by exterior
motives . . . let the wife be more than a housewife . . . a
woman . . ."

One day, having immersed myself in the varied insights these
reports have been giving American advertisers for the last fifteen
years, I was invited to have lunch with the man who runs this
motivational research operation. He had been so helpful in showing me the commercial forces behind the feminine mystique,
perhaps I could be helpful to him. Naively I asked why, since
he found it so difficult to give women a true feeling of creativeness and achievement in housework, and tried to assuage their
guilt and disillusion and frustrations by getting them to buy more
"things"—why didn't he encourage them to buy things for all
they were worth, so they would have time to get out of the home
and pursue truly creative goals in the outside world.

"But we have helped her rediscover the home as the expression
of her creativeness," he said. "We help her think of the modern
home as the artist's studio, the scientist's laboratory. Besides," he
shrugged, "most of the manufacturers we deal with are producing

things which have to do with homemaking."

"In a free enterprise economy," he went on, "we have to develop the need for new products. And to do that we have to liberate women to desire these new products. We help them rediscover that homemaking is more creative than to compete with men. This can be manipulated. We sell them what they ought to want, speed up the unconscious, move it along. The big problem is to liberate the woman not to be afraid of what is going to happen to her, if she doesn't have to spend so much time cooking, cleaning."

"That's what I mean," I said. "Why doesn't the pie-mix ad tell the woman she could use the time saved to be an astronomer?"

"It wouldn't be too difficult," he replied. "A few images—the astronomer gets her man, the astronomer as the heroine, make it glamorous for a woman to be an astronomer . . . but no," he shrugged again. "The client would be too frightened. He wants to sell pie mix. The woman has to want to stay in the kitchen. The manufacturer wants to intrigue her back into the kitchen—and we show him how to do it the right way. If he tells her that all she can be is a wife and mother, she will spit in his face. But we show him how to tell her that it's creative to be in the kitchen. We liberate her need to be creative in the kitchen. If we tell her to be an astronomer, she might go too far from the kitchen. Besides," he added, "if you wanted to have a campaign to liberate women to be astronomers, you'd have to find somebody like the National Education Association to pay for it."

The motivational researchers must be given credit for their insights into the reality of the housewife's life and needs—a reality that often escaped their colleagues in academic sociology and therapeutic psychology, who saw women through the Freudian-functional veil. To their own profit, and that of their clients, the manipulators discovered that millions of supposedly happy American housewives have complex needs which home-and-family, love-and-children, cannot fill. But by a morality that goes beyond the dollar, the manipulators are guilty of using their insights to sell women things which, no matter how ingenious, will never satisfy those increasingly desperate needs. They are guilty of persuading housewives to stay at home, mesmerized in front of a television set, their nonsexual human needs unnamed, unsatisfied, drained by the sexual sell into the buying of things.

The manipulators and their clients in American business can hardly be accused of creating the feminine mystique. But they are the most powerful of its perpetuators; it is their millions which blanket the land with persuasive images, flattering the American housewife, diverting her guilt and disguising her growing sense of emptiness. They have done this so successfully, employing the techniques and concepts of modern social science, and transposing them into those deceptively simple, clever, outrageous ads and commercials, that an observer of the American scene today accepts as fact that the great majority of American women have no ambition other than to be housewives. If they are not solely responsible for sending women home, they are surely responsible for keeping them there. Their unremitting harangue is hard to escape in this day of mass communications; they have seared the feminine mystique deep into every woman's mind, and into the minds of her husband, her children, her neighbors. They have made it part of the fabric of her everyday life, taunting her because she is not a better housewife, does not love her family enough, is growing old.

Can a woman ever feel right cooking on a dirty range? Until today, no range could ever be kept really clean. Now new RCA Whirlpool ranges have oven doors that lift off, broiler drawers that can be cleaned at the sink, drip pans that slide out easily. . . . The first range that any woman can keep completely clean easily . . . and make everything cooked taste better.

Love is said in many ways. It's giving and accepting. It's protecting and selecting . . . knowing what's safest for those you love. Their bathroom tissue is Scott tissue always. . . . Now in four colors and white.

How skillfully they divert her need for achievement into sexual phantasies which promise her eternal youth, dulling her sense of passing time. They even tell her that she can make time stand still:

Does she. . . or doesn't she? She's as full of fun as her kids—and just as fresh looking! Her naturalness, the way her hair sparkles and catches the light—as though she's found the secret of making time stand still. And in a way she has . . .

With increasing skill, the ads glorify her "role" as an American housewife—knowing that her very lack of identity in that role will make her fall for whatever they are selling.

Who is she? She gets as excited as her six-year-old about the opening of school. She reckons her days in trains met, lunches packed, fingers bandaged, and 1,001 details. She could be you, needing a special kind of clothes for your busy, rewarding life.

Are you this woman? Giving your kids the fun and advantages you want for them? Taking them places and helping them do things? Taking the part that's expected of you in church and community affairs . . . developing your talents so you'll be more interesting? You can be the woman you yearn to be with a Plymouth all your own. . . . Go where you want, when you want in a beautiful Plymouth that's yours and nobody else's . . .

But a new stove or a softer toilet paper do not make a woman a better wife or mother, even if she thinks that's what she needs to be. Dyeing her hair cannot stop time; buying a Plymouth will not give her a new identity; smoking a Marlboro will not get her an invitation to bed, even if that's what she thinks she wants. But those unfulfilled promises can keep her endlessly hungry for things, keep her from ever knowing what she really needs or wants.

A full-page ad in the *New York Times*, June 10, 1962, was "Dedicated to the woman who spends a lifetime living up to her potential!" Under the picture of a beautiful woman, adorned by evening dress and jewels and two handsome children, it said: "The only totally integrated program of nutrient make-up and skin care—designed to lift a woman's good looks to their absolute peak. The woman who uses 'Ultima' feels a deep sense of fulfillment. A new kind of pride. For this luxurious Cosmetic Collection is the *ultimate* . . . beyond it there is nothing."

It all seems so ludicrous when you understand what they are up to. Perhaps the housewife has no one but herself to blame if she lets the manipulators flatter or threaten her into buying things that neither fill her family's needs nor her own. But if the ads and commercials are a clear case of caveat emptor, the same sexual sell disguised in the editorial content of a magazine or a television program is both less ridiculous and more insidious. Here the housewife is often an unaware victim. I have written for some of the magazines in which the sexual sell is inextricably linked with the editorial content. Consciously or unconsciously, the editors know what the advertiser wants.

The heart of X magazine is service—complete service to the whole woman who is the American homemaker; service in all the areas of greatest interest to advertisers, who are also business men. It delivers to the advertiser a strong concentration of serious, conscientious, dedicated homemakers. Women more interested in the home and products for the home. Women more willing and able to pay . . .

A memo need never be written, a sentence need never be spoken at an editorial conference; the men and women who make the editorial decisions often compromise their own very high standards in the interests of the advertising dollar. Often, as a former editor of *McCall's* recently revealed,[2] the advertiser's influence is less than subtle. The kind of home pictured in the "service" pages is dictated in no uncertain terms by the boys over in advertising.

And yet, a company has to make a profit on its products; a magazine, a network needs advertising to survive. But even if profit is the only motive, and the only standard of success, I wonder if the media are not making a mistake when they give the client what they think he wants. I wonder if the challenge and the opportunities for the American economy and for business itself might not in the long run lie in letting women grow up, instead of blanketing them with the youth-serum that keeps them mindless and thing-hungry.

The real crime, no matter how profitable for the American economy, is the callous and growing acceptance of the manipulator's advice "to get them young"—the television commercials that children sing or recite even before they learn to read, the big beautiful ads almost as easy as "Look, Sally, Look," the magazines deliberately designed to turn teenage girls into housewife buyers of things before they grow up to be women:

She reads X Magazine from beginning to end . . . She learns how to market, to cook and to sew and everything else a young woman should know. She plans her wardrobe 'round X Magazine's clothes, heeds X Magazine's counsel on beauty and beaus . . . consults X Magazine for the latest teen fads . . . and oh, how she buys from those X Magazine ads! Buying habits start in X Magazine. It's easier to START a habit than to STOP one! (Learn how X Magazine's unique publication, X Magazine-at-school, carries your advertising into high school home economics classrooms.)

Like a primitive culture which sacrificed little girls to its tribal gods, we sacrifice our girls to the feminine mystique, grooming them ever more efficiently through the sexual sell to become consumers of the things to whose profitable sale our nation is dedicated. Two ads recently appeared in a national news magazine, geared not to teenage girls but to executives who produce and sell things. One of them showed the picture of a boy:

I am *so* going to the moon . . . and you can't go, 'cause you're a girl! Children are growing faster today, their interests can cover such a wide range—from roller skates to rockets. X company too has grown, with a broad spectrum of electronic products for worldwide governmental, industrial and space application.

The other showed the face of a girl:

Should a gifted child grow up to be a housewife? Educational experts estimate that the gift of high intelligence is bestowed upon only one out of every 50 children in our nation. When that gifted child is a girl, one question is inevitably asked: "Will this rare gift be wasted if she becomes a housewife?" Let these gifted girls answer that question themselves. Over 90 per cent of them marry, and the majority find the job of being a housewife challenging and rewarding enough to make full use of all their intelligence, time and energy. . . . In her daily roles of nurse, educator, economist and just plain housewife, she is constantly seeking ways to improve her family's life. . . . Millions of women—shopping for half the families in America—do so by saving X Stamps.

If that gifted girl-child grows up to be a housewife, can even the manipulator make supermarket stamps use all of her human intelligence, her human energy, in the century she may live while that boy goes to the moon?

Never underestimate the power of a woman, says another ad. But that power was and is underestimated in America. Or rather, it is only estimated in terms that can be manipulated at the point of purchase. Woman's human intelligence and energy do not really figure in. And yet, they exist, to be used for some higher purpose than housework and thing-buying—or wasted. Perhaps it is only a sick society, unwilling to face its own problems and unable to conceive of goals and purposes equal to the ability and knowledge of its members, that chooses to ignore the strength of women. Perhaps it is only a sick or immature society that chooses to make women "housewives," not people. Perhaps it is only sick or immature men and women, unwilling to face the great challenges of society, who can retreat for long, without unbearable distress, into that thing-ridden house and make it the end of life itself.

10 Housewifery Expands to Fill the Time Available

With a vision of the happy modern housewife as she is described by the magazines and television, by the functional sociologists, the sex-directed educators, and the manipulators dancing before my eyes, I went in search of one of those mystical creatures. Like Diogenes with his lamp, I went as a reporter from suburb to suburb, searching for a woman of ability and education who was fulfilled as a housewife. I went first to the suburban mental health centers and guidance clinics, to reputable local analysts, to knowledgeable local residents, and, stating my purpose, asked them to steer me not to the neurotic, frustrated housewives, but to the able, intelligent, educated women who were adjusted full-time housewives and mothers.

"I know many such housewives who have found fulfillment as women," one psychoanalyst said. I asked him to name four, and went to see them.

One, after five years of therapy, was no longer a driven woman, but neither was she a full-time housewife; she had become a computer programmer. The second was a gloriously exuberant woman, with a fine successful husband and three able, exuberant children. Throughout her married life she had been a professional psychoanalyst. The third, between pregnancies, continued seriously her career as a dancer. And the fourth, after psychotherapy, was moving with an increasingly serious commitment into politics.

I reported back to my guide and said that while all four seemed "fulfilled" women, none were full-time housewives and one, after all, was a member of his own profession. "That's a coincidence with those four," he said. But I wondered if it *was* a coincidence.

In another community, I was directed to a woman who, my informant said, was truly fulfilled as a housewife ("she even bakes her own bread"). I discovered that during the years when her four children were under six and she wrote on the census blank "Occupation: housewife," she had learned a new language (with certification to teach) and had used her previous training in music first as volunteer church organist and then as a paid professional. Shortly after I interviewed her, she took a teaching position.

In many instances, however, the women I interviewed truly fitted the new image of feminine fulfillment—four, five, or six children, baked their own bread, helped build the house with their own hands, sewed all their children's clothes. These women had had no dreams of career, no visions of a world larger than the home; all energy was centered on their lives as housewives and mothers; their only ambition, their only dream already realized. But were they fulfilled women?

In one upper-income development where I interviewed, there were twenty-eight wives. Some were college graduates in their thirties or early forties; the younger wives had usually quit college to marry. Their husbands were, to a rather high degree, engrossed in challenging professional work. Only one of these wives worked professionally; most had made a career of motherhood with a dash of community activity. Nineteen out of the twenty-eight had had natural childbirth (at dinner parties there, a few years ago, wives and husbands often got down on the floor to practice the proper relaxing exercises together). Twenty of the twenty-eight breastfed their babies. At or near forty, many of these women were pregnant. The mystique of feminine fulfillment was so literally followed in this community that if a little girl said: "When I grow up, I'm going to be a doctor," her mother would correct her: "No, dear, you're a girl. You're going to be a wife and mother, like mummy."

But what was mummy really like? Sixteen out of the twenty-eight were in analysis or analytical psychotherapy. Eighteen were taking tranquilizers; several had tried suicide; and some had been hospitalized for varying periods, for depression or vaguely diagnosed psychotic states. ("You'd be surprised at the number of these happy suburban wives who simply go berserk one night, and run shrieking through the street without any clothes on," said the local doctor, not a psychiatrist, who had been called in, in such emergencies.) Of the women who breastfed their babies, one had continued, desperately, until the child was so undernourished that her doctor intervened by force. Twelve were engaged in extramarital affairs in fact or in fantasy.

These were fine, intelligent American women, to be envied for their homes, husbands, children, and for their personal gifts of mind and spirit. Why were so many of them driven women? Later, when I saw this same pattern repeated over and over again in similar suburbs, I knew it could hardly be coincidence. These women were alike mainly in one regard: they had uncommon gifts of intelligence and ability nourished by at least the beginnings of higher education—and the life they were leading as suburban housewives denied them the full use of their gifts.

It was in these women that I first began to notice the tell-tale signs of the problem that has no name; their voices were dull and flat, or nervous and jittery; they were listless and bored, or frantically "busy" around the house or community. They talked about "fulfillment" in the wife-and-mother terms of the mystique, but they were desperately eager to talk about this other "problem," with which they seemed very familiar indeed.

One woman had pioneered the search for good teachers in her community's backward school system; she had served her term on the school board. When her children had all started school, she had thought seriously at thirty-nine about her own future: should she go back to college, get an M.A., and become a professional teacher herself? But then, suddenly, she had decided not to go on—she had a late baby instead, her fifth. I heard that flat tone in her voice when she told me she had now retired from community leadership to "major again in the home."

I heard the same sad, flat tone in an older woman's voice as she told me:

I'm looking for something to satisfy me. I think it would be the most wonderful thing in the world to work, to be useful. But I don't know how to do anything. My husband doesn't believe in wives working. I'd cut off both my arms if I could have my children little, and at home again. My husband says, find something to occupy yourself that you'll enjoy, why should you work? So now I play golf, nearly every day, just myself. When you walk three, four hours a day, at least you can sleep at night.

I interviewed another woman in the huge kitchen of a house she had helped build herself. She was busily kneading the dough for her famous homemade bread; a dress she was making for a daughter was half-finished on the sewing machine; a handloom stood in one corner. Children's art materials and toys were strewn all over the floor of the house, from front door to stove: in this expensive modern house, like many of the open-plan houses in this era, there was no door at all between kitchen and living room. Nor did this mother have any dream or wish or thought or frustration of her own to separate her from her children. She was pregnant now with her seventh; her happiness was complete, she said, spending her days with her children. Perhaps here was a happy housewife.

But just before I left, I said, as an afterthought, that I guessed she was joking when she mentioned that she envied her neighbor, who was a professional designer as well as the mother of three children. "No, I wasn't joking," she said; and this serene housewife, kneading the dough for the bread she always made herself, started to cry. "I envy her terribly," she said. "She knows what she wants to do. I don't know. I never have. When I'm pregnant and the babies are little, I'm *somebody*, finally, a mother. But then, they get older. I can't just keep on having babies."

While I never found a woman who actually fitted that "happy housewife" image, I noticed something else about these able women who were leading their lives in the protective shade of the feminine mystique. They were so *busy*—busy shopping, chauffeuring, using their dishwashers and dryers and electric mixers, busy gardening, waxing, polishing, helping with the children's homework, collecting for mental health, and doing thousands of little chores. In the course of my interviews with these women, I began to see that there was something peculiar about the *time* housework takes today.

On one suburban road there were two colonial houses, each with a big, comfortable living room, a small library, a formal dining room, a big cheerful kitchen, four bedrooms, an acre of garden and lawn, and, in each family, one commuting husband and three school-age children. Both houses were well-kept, with a cleaning woman two days a week; but the cooking and the other housework was done by the wife, who in each case was in her late thirties, intelligent, healthy, attractive, and well-educated.

In the first house, Mrs. W., a full-time housewife, was busy most of every day with cooking, cleaning, shopping, chauffeuring, taking care of the children. Next door Mrs. D., a microbiologist, got most of these chores done before she left for her laboratory at nine, or after she got home at five-thirty. In neither family were the children neglected, though Mrs. D.'s were slightly more self-reliant. Both women entertained a fair amount. Mrs. W., the housewife, did a lot of routine community work, but she did not "have time" to take a policy-making office—which she was often offered as an intelligent capable woman. At most, she headed a committee to run a dance, or a PTA fair. Mrs. D., the scientist, did no routine community work, but, in addition to her job and home, played in a dedicated string quintet (music was her main interest outside of science), and held a policy-making post in the world-affairs organization which had been an interest since college.

How could the same size house and the same size family, under almost identical conditions of income, outside help, style of life, take so much more of Mrs. W.'s time than of Mrs. D.'s? And Mrs. W. was never idle, really. She never had time in the evening to "just read," as Mrs. D. often did.

In a large, modern apartment building in a big eastern city, there were two six-room apartments, both a little untidy, except when the cleaning woman had just left, or before a party. Both the G.'s and the R.'s had three children under ten, one still a baby. Both husbands were in their early thirties, and both were in demanding professional work. But Mr. G., whose wife is a full-time housewife, was expected to do, and did, much more housework when he got home at night or on Saturday than Mr. R., whose wife was a free-lance illustrator and evidently had to get the same amount of housework done in between the hours she spent at her drawing table. Mrs. G. somehow couldn't get her housework done before her husband came home at night and was so tired then that he had to do it. Why did Mrs. R., who did not count the housework as her main job, get it done in so much less time?

I noticed this pattern again and again, as I interviewed women who defined themselves as "housewives," and compared them to the few who pursued professions, part or full time. The same pattern held even where both housewife and professional had full-time domestic help, though more often the "housewives" chose to do their own housework, full time, even when they could well afford two servants. But I also discovered that many frantically busy full-time housewives were amazed to find that they could polish off in one hour the housework that used to take them six—or was still undone at dinnertime—as soon as they started studying, or working, or had some other serious interest outside the home.

Toying with the question, how can one hour of housework expand to fill six hours (same house, same work, same wife), I came back again to the basic paradox of the feminine mystique: that it emerged to glorify woman's role as housewife at the very moment when the barriers to her full participation in society were lowered, at the very moment when science and education and her own ingenuity made it possible for a woman to be both wife and mother and to take an active part in the world outside the home. The glorification of "woman's role," then, seems to be in proportion to society's reluctance to treat women as complete human beings; for the less real function that role has, the more it is decorated with meaningless details to conceal its emptiness. This phenomenon has been noted, in general terms, in the annals of social science and in history—the chivalry of the Middle Ages, for example, and the artificial pedestal of the Victorian woman—but it may come as somewhat of a shock to the emancipated American woman to discover that it applies in a concrete and extreme degree to the housewife's situation in America today.

Did the new mystique of separate-but-equal femininity arise because the growth of women in America could no longer be repressed by the old mystique of feminine inferiority? Could women be prevented from realizing their full capabilities by making their role in the home *equal* to man's role in society? "Woman's place is in the home" could no longer be said in tones of contempt. Housework, washing dishes, diaper-changing had to be dressed up by the new mystique to become equal to splitting atoms, penetrating outer space, creating art that illuminates human destiny, pioneering on the frontiers of society. It had to become the very end of life itself to conceal the obvious fact that it is barely the beginning.

When you look at it this way, the double deception of the feminine mystique becomes quite apparent:

1. The more a woman is deprived of function in society at the level of her own ability, the more her housework, motherwork, wife-work, will expand—and the more she will resist finishing her housework or mother-work, and being without any function at all. (Evidently human nature also abhors a vacuum, even in women.)

2. The time required to do the housework for any given woman varies inversely with the challenge of the other work to which she is committed. Without any outside interests, a woman is virtually forced to devote her every moment to the trivia of keeping house.

The simple principle that "Work Expands to Fill the Time Available" was first formulated by the Englishman C. Northcote Parkinson on the basis of his experience with administrative bureaucracy in World War II. Parkinson's Law can easily be reformulated for the American housewife: Housewifery Expands to Fill the Time Available, or Motherhood Expands to Fill the Time Available, or even Sex Expands to Fill the Time Available. This is, without question, the true explanation for the fact that even with all the new labor-saving appliances, the modern American housewife probably spends more time on housework than her grandmother. It is also part of the explanation for our national preoccupation with sex and love, and for the continued baby boom.

Tabling for the moment the sexual implications, which are vast, let's consider some of the dynamics of the law itself, as an explanation for the disposal of feminine energy in America. To go back several generations: I have suggested that the real cause both of feminism and of women's frustration was the emptiness of the housewife's role. The major work and decisions of society were taking place outside the home, and women felt the need, or fought for the right, to participate in this work. If women had gone on to use their newly-won education and find new identity in this work outside the home, the mechanics of housewifery would have taken the same subsidiary place in their lives as car and garden and workbench in man's life. Motherhood, wifehood, sexual love, family responsibility, would merely have acquired a new emotional importance, as they have for men. (Many observers have noticed the new joy American men have been taking in their children—as their own work week is shortened—without that edge of anger women whose children *are* their work seem to feel.)

But when the mystique of feminine fulfillment sent women back home again, housewifery had to expand into a full-time career. Sexual love and motherhood had to become all of life, had to use up, to dispose of women's creative energies. The very nature of family responsibility had to expand to take the place of responsibility to society. As this began to happen, each labor-saving appliance brought a labor-demanding elaboration of housework. Each scientific advance that might have freed women from the drudgery of cooking, cleaning, and washing, thereby giving her more time for other purposes, instead imposed new drudgery, until housework not only expanded to fill the time available, but could hardly be done in the available time.

The automatic clothes dryer does not save a woman the four or five hours a week she used to spend at the clothesline, if, for instance, she runs her washing machine and dryer every day. After all, she still has to load and unload the machine herself, sort the clothes and put them away. As a young mother said, "Clean sheets twice a week are now possible. Last week, when my dryer broke down, the sheets didn't get changed for eight days. Everyone complained. We all felt dirty. I felt guilty. Isn't that silly?" [1]

The modern American housewife spends far more time washing, drying, and ironing than her mother. If she has an electric freezer or mixer, she spends more time cooking than a woman who does not have these labor-saving appliances. The home freezer, simply by existing, takes up time: beans, raised in the garden, must be prepared for freezing. If you have an electric mixer, you have to use it: those elaborate recipes with the puréed chestnuts, watercress, and almonds take longer than broiling lamb chops.

According to a Bryn Mawr survey made just after the war, in a typical United States farm family, housework took 60.55 hours a week; 78.35 hours in cities under 100,000; 80.57 in cities of over 100,000.[2] With all their appliances, the suburban and city housewives spend more time on housework than the busy farmer's wife. That farmer's wife, of course, has quite a lot of other work to do.

In the 1950's, sociologists and home economists reported puzzlement, and baffling inconsistencies, as to the amount of time American women were still spending on housework. Study after study revealed that American housewives were spending almost as many, or even more, hours a day on housekeeping as women thirty years earlier, despite the smaller, easier-to-care-for homes, and despite the fact that they had seven times as much capital equipment in housekeeping appliances. There were, however, some exceptions. Women who worked many hours a week outside the home—either in paid jobs or community work—did the housekeeping, on which the full-time housewife still spent sixty hours a week, in half the time. They still seemed to do all the home-making activities of the housewife—meals, shopping, cleaning, the children—but even with a thirty-five-hour work week on the job, their work week was only an hour and a half a day longer than the housewife's. That this strange phenomenon caused so little comment was due to the relative scarcity of such women. For the even stranger phenomenon, the real significance of which the mystique hid, was the fact that, despite the growth of the American population and the movement of that population from farm to city with the parallel growth of American industry and professions, in the first fifty years of the twentieth century the proportion of American women working outside the home in-creased very little indeed, while the proportion of American women in the professions actually declined.[3] From nearly half the nation's professional force in 1930, women had dropped to only 35 per cent in 1960, despite the fact that the number of women college graduates had nearly tripled. The phenomenon was the great increase in the numbers of educated women choos-ing to be just housewives.

And yet, for the suburban and city housewife, the fact re-mains that more and more of the jobs that used to be performed in the home have been taken away: canning, baking bread, weav-ing cloth and making clothes, educating the young, nursing the sick, taking care of the aged. It is possible for women to reverse history—or kid themselves that they can reverse it—by baking their own bread, but the law does not permit them to teach their own children at home, and few housewives would match their so-called generalist's skill with the professional expertise of doctor and hospital to nurse a child through tonsillitis or pneu-monia at home.

There is a real basis, then, for the complaint that so many housewives have: "I feel so empty somehow, useless, as if I don't exist." "At times I feel as though the world is going past my door while I just sit and watch." This very sense of emptiness, this uneasy denial of the world outside the home, often drives the housewife to even more effort, more frantic housework to keep the future out of sight. And the choices the housewife makes to fill that emptiness—though she seems to make them for logical and necessary reasons—trap her further in trivial domestic routine.

The woman with two children, for example, bored and restive in her city apartment, is driven by her sense of futility and emptiness to move, "for the children's sake," to a spacious house in the suburbs. The house takes longer to clean, the shopping and gardening and chauffeuring and do-it-yourself routines are so time-consuming that, for a while, the emptiness seems solved. But when the house is furnished, and the children are in school and the family's place in the community has jelled, there is "nothing to look forward to," as one woman I interviewed put it. The empty feeling returns, and so she must redecorate the living room, or wax the kitchen floor more often than necessary—or have another baby. Diapering that baby, along with all the other housework, may keep her running so fast that she will indeed need her husband's help in the kitchen at night. Yet none of it is quite as real, quite as necessary, as it seems.

One of the great changes in America, since World War II, has been the explosive movement to the suburbs, those ugly and endless sprawls which are becoming a national problem. Sociologists point out that a distinguishing feature of these suburbs is the fact that the women who live there are better educated than city women, and that the great majority are full-time housewives.[4]

At first glance, one might suspect that the very growth and existence of the suburbs causes educated modern American women to become and remain full-time housewives. Or did the postwar suburban explosion come, at least in part, as a result of the coincidental choice of millions of American women to "seek fulfillment in the home?" Among the women I interviewed, the decision to move to the suburbs "for the children's sake" followed the decision to give up job or profession and become a full-time housewife, usually after the birth of the first baby, or the second, depending on the age of the woman when the mystique hit. With the youngest wives, of course, the mystique hit so early that the choice of marriage and motherhood as a full-time career ruled out education for any profession, and the move to the suburbs came with marriage or as soon as the wife no longer had to work to support her husband through college or law school.

Families where the wife intends to pursue a definite professional goal are less likely to move to the suburbs. In the city, of course, there are more and better jobs for educated women; more universities, sometimes free, with evening courses, geared to men who work during the day, and often more convenient than the conventional daytime program for a young mother who wants to finish college or work toward a graduate degree. There is also a better supply of full or part-time nurses and cleaning help, nursery schools, day-care centers, after-school play programs. But these considerations are only important to the woman who has commitments outside the home.

There is also less room for housewifery to expand to fill the time available, in the city. That sense of restless "marking time" comes early to the educated, able city housewife, even though, when her babies are little, the time is more than filled with busyness—wheeling the carriage back and forth in the park, sitting on the playground bench because the children can't play outside alone. Still, there's no room in the city apartment for a home freezer, no garden to grow beans in. And all the organizations in the city are so big; the libraries are already built; professionals run the nursery schools and recreation programs.

It is not surprising, then, that many young wives vote for a move to the suburbs as soon as possible. Like the empty plains of Kansas that tempted the restless immigrant, the suburbs in their very newness and lack of structured service, offered, at least at first, a limitless challenge to the energy of educated American women. The women who were strong enough, independent enough, seized the opportunity and were leaders and innovators in these new communities. But, in most cases, these were women educated before the era of feminine fulfillment. The ability of suburban life to fulfill, or truly use the potential of the able, educated American woman seems to depend on her own previous autonomy or self-realization—that is, on her strength to resist the pressures to conform, resist the time-filling busywork of suburban house and community, and find, or make, the same kind of serious commitment outside the home that she would have made in the city. Such a commitment in the suburbs, in the beginning at least, was likely to be on a volunteer basis, but it was challenging, and necessary.

When the mystique took over, however, a new breed of women came to the suburbs. They were looking for sanctuary; they were perfectly willing to accept the suburban community as they found it (their only problem was "how to fit in"); they were perfectly willing to fill their days with the trivia of housewifery. Women of this kind, and most of those that I interviewed were of the post-1950 college generation, refuse to take policy-making positions in community organizations; they will only collect for Red Cross or March of Dimes or Scouts or be den mothers or take the lesser PTA jobs. Their resistance to serious community responsibility is usually explained by "I can't take the time from my family." But much of their time is spent in meaningless busywork. The kind of community work they choose does not challenge their intelligence—or even, sometimes, fill a real function. Nor do they derive much personal satisfaction from it—but it does fill time.

So, increasingly, in the new bedroom suburbs, the really interesting volunteer jobs—the leadership of the cooperative nurseries, the free libraries, the school board posts, the selectmenships and, in some suburbs, even the PTA presidencies—are filled by men.[5] The housewife who doesn't "have time" to take serious responsibility in the community, like the woman who doesn't "have time" to pursue a professional career, evades a serious commitment through which she might finally realize herself; she evades it by stepping up her domestic routine until she is truly trapped.

The dimensions of the trap seem physically unalterable, as the busyness that fills the housewife's day seems inescapably necessary. But is that domestic trap an illusion, despite its all-too-solid reality, an illusion created by the feminine mystique? Take, for instance, the open plan of the contemporary "ranch" or split-

level house, $14,990 to $54,990, which has been built in the millions from Roslyn Heights to the Pacific Palisades. They give the
illusion of more space for less money. But the women to whom
they are sold almost *have* to live the feminine mystique. There
are no true walls or doors; the woman in the beautiful electronic
kitchen is never separated from her children. She need never
feel alone for a minute, need never be by herself. She can forget
her own identity in those noisy open-plan houses. The open
plan also helps expand the housework to fill the time available.
In what is basically one free-flowing room, instead of many
rooms separated by walls and stairs, continual messes continually
need picking up. A man, of course, leaves the house for most of
the day. But the feminine mystique forbids the woman this.

A friend of mine, an able writer turned full-time housewife,
had her suburban dream house designed by an architect to her
own specifications, during the period when she defined herself
as housewife and no longer wrote. The house, which cost approximately $50,000, was almost literally one big kitchen. There
was a separate studio for her husband, who was a photographer,
and cubbyholes for sleeping, but there wasn't any place where
she could get out of the kitchen, away from her children, during
the working hours. The gorgeous mahogany and stainless steel
of her custom-built kitchen cabinets and electric appliances were
indeed a dream, but when I saw that house, I wondered where,
if she ever wanted to write again, she would put her typewriter.

It's strange how few places there are in those spacious houses
and those sprawling suburbs where you can go to be alone. A
sociologist's study of upper-income suburban wives who married
young and woke, after fifteen years of child-living, PTA, do-it-
yourself, garden-and-barbecue, to the realization that they
wanted to do some real work themselves, found that the ones
who did something about this often moved back to the city.[6] But
among the women I talked to, this moment of personal truth
was more likely to be marked by adding a room with a door to
their open-plan house, or simply by putting a door on one room
in the house, "so I can have someplace to myself, just a door
to shut between me and the children when I want to think"—or

work, study, be alone.

Most American housewives, however, do not shut that door. Perhaps they are afraid, finally, to be alone in that room. As another social scientist said, the American housewife's dilemma is that she does not have the privacy to follow real interests of her own, but even if she had more time and space to herself, she would not know what to do with it.[7] If she makes a career of marriage and motherhood, as the mystique tells her, if she becomes the executive of the house—and has enough children to give her quite a business to run—if she exerts the human strength, which she is forbidden by the mystique to exert elsewhere, on running a perfect house and supervising her children and sharing her husband's career in such omnipresent detail that she has only a few minutes to spare for community work, and no time for serious larger interests, who is to say that this is not as important, as good a way to spend a life, as mastering the secrets of the atoms or the stars, composing symphonies, pioneering a new concept in government or society?

For the very able woman, who has the ability to create culturally as well as biologically, the only possible rationalization is to convince herself—as the new mystique tries so hard to convince her—that the minute physical details of child care are indeed mystically creative; that her children will be tragically deprived if she is not there every minute; that the dinner she gives the boss's wife is as crucial to her husband's career as the case he fights in court or the problem he solves in the laboratory. And because husband and children are soon out of the house most of the day, she must keep on having new babies, or somehow make the minutiae of housework itself important enough, necessary enough, hard enough, creative enough to justify her very existence.

If a woman's whole existence is to be justified in this way, if the housewife's work is really so important, so necessary, why should anyone raise an eyebrow because a latter-day Einstein's wife expects her husband to put aside that lifeless theory of relativity and help her with the work that is supposed to be the essence of life itself: diaper the baby and don't forget to rinse the soiled diaper in the toilet before putting it in the diaper pail, and then wax the kitchen floor.

The most glaring proof that, no matter how elaborate, "Occupation: housewife" is not an adequate substitute for truly challenging work, important enough to society to be paid for in its coin, arose from the comedy of "togetherness." The women acting in this little morality play were told that they had the starring roles, that their parts were just as important, perhaps even more important than the parts their husbands played in the world outside the home. Was it unnatural that, since they were doing such a vital job, women insisted that their husbands share in the housework? Surely it was an unspoken guilt, an unspoken realization of their wives' entrapment, that made so many men comply, with varying degrees of grace, to their wives' demands. But having their husbands share the housework didn't really compensate women for being shut out of the larger world. If anything, by removing still more of their functions, it increased their sense of individual emptiness. They needed to share vicariously more and more of their children's and husbands' lives. Togetherness was a poor substitute for equality; the glorification of women's role was a poor substitute for free participation in the world as an individual.

The true emptiness beneath the American housewife's routine has been revealed in many ways. In Minneapolis recently a schoolteacher named Maurice K. Enghausen read a story in the local newspaper about the long work week of today's housewife. Declaring in a letter to the editor that "any woman who puts in that many hours is awfully slow, a poor budgeter of time, or just plain inefficient," this thirty-six-year-old bachelor offered to take over any household and show how it could be done.

Scores of irate housewives dared him to prove it. He took over the household of Mr. and Mrs. Robert Dalton, with four children, aged two to seven, for three days. In a single day, he cleaned the first floor, washed three loads of clothes and hung them out to dry, ironed all the laundry including underwear and sheets, fixed a soup-and-sandwich lunch and a big backyard supper, baked two cakes, prepared two salads for the next day, dressed, undressed, and bathed the children, washed wood-work and scrubbed the kitchen floor. Mrs. Dalton said he was even a better cook than she was. "As for cleaning," she said, "I am more thorough, but perhaps that is unnecessary."

Pointing out that he had kept house for himself for seven years and had earned money at college by housework, Enghausen said, "I still wish that teaching 115 students were as easy as handling four children and a house . . . I still maintain that housework is not the interminable chore that women claim it is." [8]

This claim, periodically expressed by men privately and publicly, has been borne out by a recent time-motion study. Recording and analyzing every movement made by a group of house-wives, this study concluded that most of the energy expended in housework is superfluous. A series of intensive studies sponsored by the Michigan Heart Association at Wayne University disclosed that "women were working more than twice as hard as they should," squandering energy through habit and tradition in wasted motion and unneeded steps.

The puzzling question of "housewife's fatigue" sheds additional light. Doctors in many recent medical conventions report failure to cure it or get to its cause. At a meeting of the American College of Obstetricians and Gynecologists, a Cleveland doctor stated that mothers, who cannot get over "that tired feeling" and complain that their doctors are no help, are neither sick nor maladjusted, but actually tired. "No psychoanalysis or deep probing is necessary," said Dr. Leonard Lovshin, of the Cleveland Clinic. "She has a work day of sixteen hours, a work week of seven days. . . . Being conscientious, she gets involved in Cubs, Brownies, PTA's, heart drives, church work, hauling children to music and dancing." But strangely enough, he remarked, neither the housewife's workload nor her fatigue seemed affected by how many children she had. Most of these patients had only one or two. "A woman with one child just worries four times as much about the one as the woman with four children, and it all comes out even," Dr. Lovshin said.

Some doctors, finding nothing organically wrong with these

chronically tired mothers, told them, "It's all in your mind"; others gave them pills, vitamins, or injections for anemia, low blood pressure, low metabolism, or put them on diets (the average housewife is twelve to fifteen pounds overweight), deprived them of drinking (there are approximately a million known alcoholic housewives in America), or gave them tranquilizers. All such treatments were futile, Dr. Lovshin said, because these mothers were truly tired.[9]

Other doctors, finding that such mothers get as much or more sleep than they need, claimed the basic cause was not fatigue but boredom. This problem became so severe that the women's magazines treated it fulsomely—in the Pollyanna terms of the feminine mystique. In a spate of articles that appeared in the late 1950's, the "cures" suggested were usually of the more-praise-and-appreciation-from-husband variety, even though the doctors interviewed in these articles indicated clearly enough that the cause was in the "housewife-mother" role. But the magazines drew their usual conclusion: that is, and always will be woman's lot, and she just has to make the best of it. Thus, *Redbook* ("Why Young Mothers Are Always Tired," September, 1959) reports the findings of the Baruch study of chronic-fatigue patients:

. . . Fatigue of any kind is a signal that something is wrong. Physical fatigue protects the organism from injury through too great activity of any part of the body. Nervous fatigue, on the other hand, is usually a warning of danger to the personality. This comes out very clearly in the woman patient who complains bitterly that she is "just a housewife," that she is wasting her talents and education on household drudgery and losing her attractiveness, her intelligence, and indeed her very identity as a person, explains Dr. Harley C. Sands, one of the co-heads of the Baruch project. In industry the most fatiguing jobs are those which only partially occupy the worker's attention, but at the same time prevent him from concentrating on anything else. Many young wives say that this mental gray-out is what bothers them most in caring for home and children. "After a while your mind becomes a blank," they say. "You can't concentrate on anything. It's like sleep-walking."

The magazine also quotes a Johns Hopkins psychiatrist to the effect that the major factor which produces chronic fatigue in patients was "monotony unpunctuated by any major triumph or disaster," noting that this "sums up the predicament of many a young mother." It even cites the results of the University of Michigan study in which of 524 women asked "what are some of the things which make you feel 'useful and important,' " almost none answered "housework"; among the women who had jobs, "the overwhelming majority, married and single, felt that the job was more satisfying than the housework." At this point the magazine interjects editorially: "This, of course, does not mean that a career is the alternative to fatigue for a young mother. If anything, the working mother may have more troubles than the housebound young matron." The magazine's happy conclusion: "Since the demands of housework and child-rearing are not very flexible, there is no complete solution to chronic-fatigue problems. Many women, however, can cut down fatigue if they stop asking too much of themselves. By trying to understand realistically what she can—and, more important, what she cannot—do, a woman may, in the long run, be a better wife and mother, albeit a tired one."

Another such article ("Is Boredom Bad for You?" *McCall's*, April, 1957) asked, "Is the housewife's chronic fatigue really boredom?" and answers: "Yes. The chronic fatigue of many housewives is brought on by the repetition of their jobs, the monotony of the setting, the isolation and the lack of stimulation. The heavy household chores, it's been found, aren't enough to explain the fatigue. . . . The more your intelligence exceeds your job requirements, the greater your boredom. This is so to such an extent that experienced employers never hire above-average brains for routine jobs. . . . It is this boredom plus, of course, the day-to-day frustrations which makes the average housewife's job more emotionally fatiguing than her husband's." The cure: "honest enjoyment in some part of the job such as cooking or an incentive such as a party in the offing and, above all, male praise are good antidotes for domestic boredom."

For the women I interviewed, the problem seemed to be not that too much was asked of them, but too little. "A kind of torpor comes over me when I get home from the errands," one woman told me. "It's as if there's nothing I really have to do, though there's plenty to do around the house. So I keep a bottle of martinis in the refrigerator, and I pour myself some so I'll feel more like doing something. Or just to get through till Don comes home."

Other women eat, as they stretch out the housework, just to fill the time available. Obesity and alcoholism, as neuroses, have often been related to personality patterns that stem from childhood. But does this explain why so many American housewives around forty have the same dull and lifeless look; does it explain their lack of vitality, the deadly sameness of their lives, the furtive between-meal snacks, drinks, tranquilizers, sleeping pills? Even given the various personalities of these women, there must be something in the nature of their work, of the lives they lead, that drives them to these escapes.

This is no less true of the American housewife's work than it is of the work of most American men, on the assembly lines or in corporation offices: work that does not fully use a man's capacities leaves in him a vacant, empty need for escape—television, tranquilizers, alcohol, sex. But the husbands of the women I interviewed were often engaged in work that demanded ability, responsibility, and decision. I noticed that when these men were saddled with a domestic chore, they polished it off in much less time than it seemed to take their wives. But, of course, for them this was never the work that justified their lives. Whether they put more energy into it for this reason, just to get it over with, or whether housework did not have to take so much of their energy, they did it more quickly and sometimes even seemed to enjoy it more.

Social critics, during the togetherness era, often complained that men's careers suffered because of all this housework. But most husbands of the women I interviewed didn't seem to let housework interfere with their careers. When husbands did that bit of housework evenings and weekends because their wives had careers, or because their wives had made such a career of housework they could not get it done themselves, or because their wives were too passive, dependent, helpless to get it done, or even because the wives left housework for their husbands, for revenge—it did not expand.

But I noticed that housework did tend to expand to fill the time available with a few husbands who seemed to be using domestic chores as an excuse for not meeting the challenge of their own careers. "I wish he wouldn't insist on vacuuming the whole house on Tuesday evenings. It doesn't need it and he could be working on his book," the wife of a college professor told me. A capable social worker herself, she had managed all her professional life to work out ways of caring for her house and children without hiring servants. With her daughter's help, she did her own thorough housecleaning on Saturday; it didn't need vacuuming on Tuesday.

To do the work that you are capable of doing is the mark of maturity. It is not the demands of housework and children, or the absence of servants, that keep most American women from growing up to do the work of which they are capable. In an earlier era when servants were plentiful, most of the middle-class women who hired them did not use their freedom to take a more active part in society; they were confined by "woman's role" to leisure. In countries like Israel and Russia, where women are expected to be more than just housewives, servants scarcely exist, and yet home and children and love are evidently not neglected.

It is the mystique of feminine fulfillment, and the immaturity it breeds, that prevents women from doing the work of which they are capable. It is not strange that women who have lived for ten or twenty years within the mystique, or who adjusted to it so young that they have never experienced being on their own, should be afraid to face the test of real work in the world and cling to their identity as housewives—even if, thereby, they doom themselves to feeling "empty, useless, as if I do not exist." That housewifery can, must, expand to fill the time available when there is no other purpose in life seems fairly evident. After all, with no other purpose in her life, if the housework were done in an hour, and the children off to school, the bright, energetic housewife would find the emptiness of her days unbearable.

So a Scarsdale woman fired her maid, and even doing her own housework and the usual community work, could not use up all her energy. "We solved the problem," she said, speaking of herself and a friend who had tried to commit suicide. "We go bowling three mornings a week. Otherwise, we'd go out of our minds. At least, now we can sleep at night." "There's always some way you can get rid of it," I heard one woman saying to another over lunch at Schrafft's, debating somewhat listlessly what to do with the "afternoon off" from housewifery that their doctors had ordered. Diet foods and exercise salons have become a lucrative business in that futile battle to take off the fat that cannot be turned into human energy by the American housewife. It is slightly shocking to think that intelligent, educated American women are forced to "get rid of" their creative human energy by eating a chalky powder and wrestling with a machine. But no one is shocked to realize that getting rid of women's creative energy, rather than using it for some larger purpose in society, is the very essence of being a housewife.

To live according to the feminine mystique depends on a reversal of history, a devaluation of human progress. To get women back into the home again, not like the Nazis, by ordering them there, but by "propaganda with a view to restoring woman's sense of prestige and self-esteem as women, actual or potential mothers . . . women who live as women," meant that women had to resist their own "technological unemployment." The canning plants and bakeries did not close down, but even the mystique makers felt the need to defend themselves against the question, "are we, in suggesting that women might, of their own volition, recapture some of their functions around the home, such as cooking, preserving and decorating, trying to turn back the clock of progress?" [10]

Progress is not progress, they argued; in theory, the freeing of women from household drudgery liberates them for the cultivation of higher aims, but "as such aims are understood, many are called and few are chosen, among men no less than among women." Therefore, let all women recapture that work in the home which all women can do easily—and let society stage-manage it so that prestige for women "be shifted emphatically to those women recognized as serving society most fully as women."

For fifteen years and longer, there has been a propaganda campaign, as unanimous in this democratic nation as in the most efficient of dictatorships, to give women "prestige" as house-wives. But can the sense of self in woman, which once rested on necessary work and achievement in the home, be recreated by housework that is no longer really necessary or really uses much ability—in a country and at a time when women can be free, finally, to move on to something more. It is wrong for a woman, for whatever reason, to spend her days in work that is not moving as the world around her is moving, in work that does not truly use her creative energy. Women themselves are discovering that though there is always "some way you can get rid of it," they can have no peace until they begin to *use* their abilities.

Surely there are many women in America who are happy at the moment as housewives, and some whose abilities are fully used in the housewife role. But happiness is not the same thing as the aliveness of being fully used. Nor is human intelligence, human ability, a static thing. Housework, no matter how it is expanded to fill the time available, can hardly use the abilities of a woman of average or normal human intelligence, much less the fifty per cent of the female population whose intelligence, in childhood, was above average.

Some decades ago, certain institutions concerned with the mentally retarded discovered that housework was peculiarly suited to the capacities of feeble-minded girls. In many towns, in-mates of institutions for the mentally retarded were in great demand as houseworkers, and housework was much more difficult then than it is now.

Basic decisions as to the upbringing of children, interior decora-tion, menu-planning, budget, education, and recreation do involve intelligence, of course. But as it was put by one of the few home-and-family experts who saw the real absurdity of the feminine mystique, most housework, the part that still takes the most time, "can be capably handled by an eight-year-old child."

The role of the housewife is, therefore, analogous to that of the president of a corporation who would not only determine policies and make over-all plans but also spend the major part of his time and energy in such activities as sweeping the plant and oiling machines. Industry, of course, is too thrifty of the capacities of its personnel to waste them in such fashion.

The true satisfaction of "creating a home," the personal relationship with husband and children, the atmosphere of hospitality, serenity, culture, warmth, or security a woman gives to the home comes by way of her personality, not her broom, stove, or dishpan. For a woman to get a rewarding sense of total creation by way of the multiple monotonous chores that are her daily lot would be as irrational as for an assembly line worker to rejoice that he had created an automobile because he tightened a bolt. It is difficult to see how clearing up after meals three times a day and making out marketing lists (3 lemons, 2 packages of soap powder, a can of soup), getting at the fuzz in the radiators with the hard rubber appliance of the vacuum cleaner, emptying wastebaskets and washing bathroom floors day after day, week after week, year after year, add up to a sum total of anything except minutiae that laid end to end reach nowhere.[11]

A number of the more disagreeable sexual phenomena of this era can be seen now as the inevitable result of that ludicrous consignment of millions of women to spend their days at work an eight-year-old could do. For no matter how much the "home-and-family career" is rationalized to justify such appalling waste of able womanpower; no matter how ingeniously the manipulators coin new scientific sounding words, "lubrilator" and the like, to give the illusion that dumping the clothes in the washing machines is an act akin to deciphering the genetic code; no matter how much housework is expanded to fill the time available, it still presents little challenge to the adult mind. Into this mental vacuum have flooded an endless line of books on gourmet cooking, scientific treatises on child care, and above all, advice on the techniques of "married love," sexual intercourse. These, too, offer little challenge to the adult mind. The results could almost have been predicted. To the great dismay of men, their wives suddenly became "experts," know-it-alls, whose unshakable superiority at home, a domain they both occupied, was impossible to compete with, and very hard to live with. As Russell Lynes put it, wives began to treat their husbands as part-time servants— or the latest new appliance.[12] With a snap course in home economics or marriage and family under her belt and copies of Dr. Spock and Dr. Van de Velde side by side on the shelf; with all that time, energy and intelligence directed on husband, children, and house, the young American wife—easily, inevitably, disastrously—began to dominate the family even more completely than her "mom."

11 The Sex-Seekers

I did not do a Kinsey study. But when I was on the trail of the problem that has no name, the suburban housewives I interviewed would often give me an explicitly sexual answer to a question that was not sexual at all. I would ask about their personal interests, ambitions, what they did, or would like to do, not necessarily as wives or mothers, but when they were not occupied with their husbands or their children or their housework. The question might even be what they were doing with their education. But some of these women simply assumed that I was asking about sex. Was the problem that has no name a sexual problem, after all? I might have thought so, except that when these women spoke of sex, there was a false note, a strange unreal quality about their words. They made mysterious allusions or broad hints; they were eager to be asked about sex; even if I did not ask, they often took pride in recounting the explicit details of some sexual adventure. They were not making them up; these adventures were real enough. But what made them sound unsexual, so unreal?

A thirty-eight-year-old mother of four told me sex was the only thing that made her "feel alive." But something had gone wrong; her husband did not give her that feeling anymore. They went through the motions, but he was not really interested. She was beginning to feel contemptuous of him in bed. "I need sex to feel alive, but I never really feel him," she said.

In a flat, matter-of-fact tone that added to the unreality, a thirty-year-old mother of five, calmly knitting a sweater, said she was thinking of going away, to Mexico perhaps, to live with a man with whom she was having an affair. She did not love him, but she thought if she gave herself to him "completely" she might find the feeling that she knew now was "the only important thing in life." What about the children? Vaguely, she guessed she would take them along—he wouldn't mind. What was the feeling she was looking for? She had found it at first with her husband, she supposed. At least she remembered that when she married him—she was eighteen—she had "felt so happy I wanted to die." But he did not "give himself completely" to her; he gave so much of himself to his work. So she found that feeling for a while, she thought, with her children. Shortly after she weaned her fifth baby from the breast, at three, she had her first affair. She discovered "it gave me that wonderful feeling again, to give my whole self to someone else." But that affair could not last; he had too many children, so did she. He said when they broke up, "You've given me such a feeling of identity." And she wondered, "what about my own identity?" So she went off by herself for a month that summer, leaving the children with her husband. "I was looking for something, I'm not sure what, but the only way I get that feeling is when I'm in love with someone." She had another affair, but that time the feeling did not appear. So with this new one, she wanted to go away completely. "Now that I know how to get that feeling," she said, knitting calmly, "I will simply keep trying until I find it again."

She did take off for Mexico with that shadowy, faceless man, taking her five children with her; but six months later, she was back, children and all. Evidently she did not find her phantom "feeling." And whatever happened, it was not real enough to affect her marriage, which went on as before. Just what was the feeling she expected to get from sex? And why was it, somehow, always out of reach? Does sex become unreal, a phantasy, when a person needs it to feel "alive," to feel "my own identity"?

In another suburb, I spoke to an attractive woman in her late thirties who had "cultural" interests, though they were rather

vague and unfocused. She started paintings which she did not
finish, raised money for concerts she did not listen to, said she had
not "found her medium yet." I discovered that she engaged in a
sort of sexual status-seeking which had the same vague, unfocused
pretentions as her cultural dabblings, and in fact, was part of it.
She boasted of the intellectual prowess, the professional distinction, of the man who, she hinted, wanted to sleep with her. "It
makes you feel proud, like an achievement. You don't want to
hide it. You want everyone to know, when it's a man of his
stature," she told me. How much she really wanted to sleep with
this man, professional stature or no, was another question. I later
learned from her neighbors that she was a community joke.
Everyone did indeed "know," but her sexual offerings were so
impersonal and predictable that only a newcomer husband would
take them seriously enough to respond.

But the evidently insatiable sexual need of a slightly younger
mother of four in that same suburb was hardly a joke. Her sex-
seeking, somehow never satisfied despite affair after affair, mixed
with much indiscriminate "extramarital petting," as Kinsey would
have put it, had real and disastrous consequences on at least two
other marriages. These women and others like them, the suburban
sex-seekers, lived literally within the narrow boundaries of the
feminine mystique. They were intelligent, but strangely "incomplete." They had given up attempts to make housework or
community work expand to fill the time available; they turned
instead to sex. But still they were unfulfilled. Their husbands did
not satisfy them, they said; extramarital affairs were no better.
In terms of the feminine mystique, if a woman feels a sense of
personal "emptiness," if she is unfulfilled, the cause must be sexual.
But why, then, doesn't sex ever satisfy her?

Just as college girls used the sexual phantasy of married life
to protect them from the conflicts and growing pains and work
of a personal commitment to science, or art, or society, are these
married women putting into their insatiable sexual search the
aggressive energies which the feminine mystique forbids them to
use for larger human purposes? Are they using sex or sexual
phantasy to fill needs that are not sexual? Is that why their sex,

even when it is real, seems like phantasy? Is that why, even when they experience orgasm, they feel "unfulfilled"? Are they driven to this never-satisfied sexual seeking because, in their marriages, they have not found the sexual fulfillment which the feminine mystique promises? Or is that feeling of personal identity, of fulfillment, they seek in sex something that sex alone cannot give?

Sex is the only frontier open to women who have always lived within the confines of the feminine mystique. In the past fifteen years, the sexual frontier has been forced to expand perhaps beyond the limits of possibility, to fill the time available, to fill the vacuum created by denial of larger goals and purposes for American women. The mounting sex-hunger of American women has been documented ad nauseam—by Kinsey, by the sociologists and novelists of suburbia, by the mass media, ads, television, movies, and women's magazines that pander to the voracious female appetite for sex phantasy. It is not an exaggeration to say that several generations of able American women have been successfully reduced to sex creatures, sex-seekers. But something has evidently gone wrong.

Instead of fulfilling the promise of infinite orgastic bliss, sex in the America of the feminine mystique is becoming a strangely joyless national compulsion, if not a contemptuous mockery. The sex-glutted novels become increasingly explicit and increasingly dull; the sex kick of the women's magazines has a sickly sadness; the endless flow of manuals describing new sex techniques hint at an endless lack of excitement. This sexual boredom is betrayed by the ever-growing size of the Hollywood starlet's breasts, by the sudden emergence of the male phallus as an advertising "gimmick." Sex has become depersonalized, seen in terms of these exaggerated symbols. But of all the strange sexual phenomena that have appeared in the era of the feminine mystique, the most ironic are these—the frustrated sexual hunger of American women has increased, and their conflicts over femininity have intensified, as they have reverted from independent activity to search for their sole fulfillment through their sexual role in the home. And as American women have turned their attention to the exclusive, explicit, and aggressive pursuit of sexual fulfillment, or the acting-out of sexual phantasy, the sexual disinterest of American men, and their hostility toward women, have also increased.

I found evidence of these phenomena everywhere. There is, as I have said, an air of exaggerated unreality about sex today, whether it is pictured in the frankly lascivious pages of a popular novel or in the curious, almost asexual bodies of the women who pose for fashion photographs. According to Kinsey, there has been no increase in sexual "outlet" in recent decades. But in the past decade there has been an enormous increase in the American preoccupation with sex and sexual phantasy.[1]

In January, 1950, and again in January, 1960, a psychologist studied every reference to sex in American newspapers, magazines, television and radio programs, plays, popular songs, best-selling novels and nonfiction books. He found an enormous increase in explicit references to sexual desires and expressions (including "nudity, sex organs, scatology, 'obscenity,' lasciviousness and sexual intercourse"). These constituted over fifty per cent of the observed references to human sexuality, with "extra-marital coitus" (including "fornication, adultery, sexual promiscuity, prostitution and venereal disease") in second place. In American media there were more than 2½ times as many references to sex in 1960 as in 1950, an increase from 509 to 1,341 "permissive" sex references in the 200 media studied. The so-called "men's magazines" not only reached new excesses in their preoccupation with specific female sex organs, but a rash of magazines blossomed frankly geared to homosexuality. The most striking new sexual phenomenon, however, was the increased and evidently "insatiable" lasciviousness of best-selling novels and periodical fiction, whose audience is primarily women.

Despite his professional approval of the "permissive" attitude to sex compared to its previous hypocritical denial, the psychologist was moved to speculate:

Descriptions of sex organs . . . are so frequent in modern novels that one wonders whether they have become requisite for sending a work of fiction into the best-selling lists. Since the old, mild depictions of intercourse have seemingly lost their ability to excite, and even sex deviations have now become commonplace in modern fiction, the current logical step seems to be detailed descriptions of the sex organs themselves. It is difficult to imagine what the next step in salaciousness will be.[2]

From 1950 to 1960 the interest of men in the details of intercourse paled before the avidity of women—both as depicted in these media, and as its audience. Already by 1950 the salacious details of the sex act to be found in men's magazines were outnumbered by those in fiction best-sellers sold mainly to women.

During this same period, the women's magazines displayed an increased preoccupation with sex in a rather sickly disguise.[3] Such "health" features as "Making Marriage Work," "Can This Marriage Be Saved," "Tell Me, Doctor," described the most intimate sexual details in moralistic guise as "problems," and women read about them in much the same spirit as they had read the case histories in their psychology texts. Movies and the theater betrayed a growing preoccupation with diseased or perverted sex, each new film and each new play a little more sensational than the last in its attempt to shock or titillate.

At the same time one could see, almost in parallel step, human sexuality reduced to its narrowest physiological limits in the numberless sociological studies of sex in the suburbs and in the Kinsey investigations. The two Kinsey reports, in 1948 and 1953, treated human sexuality as a status-seeking game in which the goal was the greatest number of "outlets," orgasms achieved equally by masturbation, nocturnal emissions during dreams, intercourse with animals, and in various postures with the other sex, pre- extra- or post-marital. What the Kinsey investigators reported and the way they reported it, no less than the sex-glutted novels, magazines, plays and novels, were all symptoms of the increasing depersonalization, immaturity, joylessness and spurious senselessness of our sexual overpreoccupation.

That this spiral of sexual "lust, luridness and lasciviousness" was not exactly a sign of healthy affirmation of human intercourse became apparent as the image of males lusting after women gave way to the new image of women lusting after males. Exaggerated, perverted extremes of the sex situations seemed to be necessary to excite hero and audience alike. Perhaps the best example of this perverse reversal was the Italian movie *La Dolce Vita*, which, with all its artistic and symbolic pretentions, was a hit in America because of its much-advertised sexual titillation. Though a comment on Italian sex and society, this particular movie was in the chief characteristics of its sexual preoccupation devastatingly pertinent to the American scene.

As is increasingly the case in American novels, plays and movies, the sex-seekers were mainly the women, who were shown as mindless over- or under-dressed sex creatures (the Hollywood star) and hysterical parasites (the journalist's girl friend). In addition, there was the promiscuous rich girl who needed the perverse stimulation of the borrowed prostitute's bed, the aggressively sex-hungry women in the candlelit "hide and seek" castle orgy, and finally the divorcée who performed her writhing strip tease to a lonely, bored and indifferent audience.

All the men, in fact, were too bored or too busy to be bothered. The indifferent, passive hero drifted from one sex-seeking woman to another—a Don Juan, an implied homosexual, drawn in phantasy to the asexual little girl, just out of reach across the water. The exaggerated extremes of the sex situations end finally in a depersonalization that creates a bloated boredom—in hero and audience alike. (The very tedium of depersonalized sex may also explain the declining audience of Broadway theaters, Hollywood movies and the American novel.) Long before the final scenes of *La Dolce Vita*—when they all go out to stare at that huge bloated dead fish—the message of the movie was made quite clear: "the sweet life" is dull.

The image of the aggressive female sex-seeker also comes across in novels like *Peyton Place* and *The Chapman Report*—which consciously cater to the female hunger for sexual phantasy. Whether or not this fictional picture of the over-lusting female means that American women have become avid sex-seekers in real life, at least they have an insatiable appetite for books dealing with the sexual act—an appetite that, in fiction and real life, does not always seem to be shared by the men. This discrepancy between the sexual preoccupation of American men and women—in fiction or reality—may have a simple explanation. Suburban housewives, in particular, are more often sex-seekers than sex-finders, not only because of the problems posed by children coming home from school, cars parked overtime in driveways, and gossiping servants, but because, quite simply, men are not all that available. Men in general spend most of their hours in pursuits and passions that are not sexual, and have less need to make sex expand to fill the time available. So, from teen age to late middle age, American women are doomed to spend most of their lives in sexual phantasy. Even when the sexual affair—or the "extramarital petting" which Kinsey found on the increase—is real, it never is as real as the mystique has led the woman to believe.

As the male author of *The Exurbanites* puts it:

While her partner may be, and probably is, engaged in something quite casual to him, accompanied, of course, by verbal blandishments designed to persuade her of just the opposite, she is often quite genuinely caught up in what she conceives to be the real love of her life. Dismayed by the inadequacies of her marriage, confused and unhappy, angry and often humiliated by the behavior of her husband, she is psychologically prepared for the man who will skillfully and judiciously apply charm, wit and seductive behavior. . . . So, at the beach parties, at the Saturday night parties, on the long car rides from place to place—on all of which occasions the couples naturally split up—the first words can be spoken, the ground first prepared, the first fantasies conjured up, the first meaningful glance exchanged, the first desperate kiss snatched. And often, later, when the woman realizes that what was important to her was casual to him, she can cry and then she can dry her tears and look around again.[4]

But what happens when a woman bases her whole identity on her sexual role; when sex is necessary to make her "feel alive"? To state it quite simply, she puts impossible demands on her own body, her "femaleness," as well as on her husband and his "maleness." A marriage counselor told me that many of the young suburban wives he dealt with make "such heavy demands on love and marriage, but there is no excitement, no mystery, sometimes almost literally nothing happens."

It's something she has been trained and educated for, all this sexual information and preoccupation, this clearly laid out pattern that she must devote herself to becoming a wife and mother. There is no wor der of two strangers, man and woman, separate beings, finding each other. It's all laid out ahead of time, a script that's being followed without the struggle, the beauty, the mysterious awe of life. And so she says to him, do something, make me feel something, but there is no power within herself to evoke this.

A psychiatrist states that he has often seen sex "die a slow, withering death" when women, or men, use the family "to make up in closeness and affection for failure to achieve goals and satisfactions in the wider community." [5] Sometimes, he told me, "there is so little real life that finally even the sex deteriorates, and gradually dies, and months go by without any desire, though they are young people." The sexual act "tends to become mechanized and depersonalized, a physical release that leaves the partners even lonelier after the act than before. The expression of tender sentiment shrivels. Sex becomes the arena for the struggle for dominance and control. Or it becomes a drab, hollow routine, carried out on schedule."

Even though they find no satisfaction in sex, these women continue their endless search. For the woman who lives according to the feminine mystique, there is no road to achievement, or status, or identity, except the sexual one: the achievement of sexual conquest, status as a desirable sex object, identity as a sexually successful wife and mother. And yet because sex does not really satisfy these needs, she seeks to buttress her nothingness with things, until often even sex itself, and the husband and the children on whom the sexual identity rests, become possessions, things. A woman who is herself only a sexual object, lives finally in a world of objects, unable to touch in others the individual identity she lacks herself.

Is it the need for some kind of identity or achievement that drives suburban housewives to offer themselves so eagerly to strangers and neighbors—and that makes husbands "furniture" in their own homes? In a recent novel about suburban adultery, the male author says through a butcher who takes advantage of the lonely housewives in the neighborhood:

"Do you know what America is? It's a big, soapy dishpan of boredom . . . and no husband can understand that soapy dishpan. And a woman can't explain it to another woman because they've all got their hands in that same soapy boredom. So all a man has to be is understanding. Yes, baby, I know, I know, you've got a miserable life, here're some flowers, here's some perfume, here's 'I love you,' take off your pants. . . . You, me, we're furniture in our own homes. But if we go next door, ahh! Next door, we're heroes! They're all looking for romance because they've learned it from books and movies. And what can be more romantic than a man who's willing to risk your husband's shotgun to have you. . . . And the only exciting thing about this guy is that he is a stranger . . . she doesn't own him. She tells herself she's in love, and she's willing to risk her home, her happiness, her pride, everything, just to be with this stranger who fills her once a week. . . . Anyplace you've got a housewife, you've also got a potential mistress for a stranger." [6]

Kinsey, from his interviews of 5,940 women, found that American wives, especially of the middle class, after ten or fifteen years of marriage, reported greater sexual desire than their husbands seemed to satisfy. One out of four, by the age of forty, had engaged in some extramarital activity—usually quite sporadic. Some seemed insatiably capable of "multiple orgasms." A growing number engaged in the "extramarital petting" more characteristic of adolescence. Kinsey also found that the sexual desire of American husbands, especially in the middle-class educated groups, seemed to wane as their wives' increased.[7]

But even more disturbing than the signs of increased sexual hunger, unfulfilled, among American housewives in this era of the feminine mystique are the signs of increased conflict over their own femaleness. There is evidence that the signs of feminine sexual conflict, often referred to by the euphemism of "female troubles," occur earlier than ever, and in intensified form, in this era when women have sought to fulfill themselves so early and exclusively in sexual terms.

The chief of the gynecological service of a famous hospital told me that he sees with increasing frequency in young mothers the same impairment of the ovarian cycle—vaginal discharge, delayed periods, irregularities in menstrual flow and duration of flow, sleeplessness, fatigue syndrome, physical disability—that he used to see only in women during menopause. He said:

The question is whether these young mothers will be pathologically blown apart when they lose their reproductive function. I see plenty of women with these menopausal difficulties which are activated, I'm sure, by the emptiness of their lives. And by simply having spent the last 28 years hanging on to the last child until there's nothing left to hang on to. In contrast, women who've had children, sexual relations, but who somehow have much more whole-hearted personalities, without continually having to rationalize themselves as female by having one more baby and holding on to it, have very few hot flashes, insomnia, nervousness, jitteriness.

The ones with female troubles are the ones who have denied their femininity, or are pathologically female. But we see these symptoms now in more and more young wives, in their 20's, young women who are fatally invested in their children, who have not developed resources other than their children—coming in with the same impairments of the ovarian cycle, menstrual difficulties, characteristic of the menopause. A woman 22 years old, who's had three children, with symptoms more frequently seen with menopause . . . I say to her, "the only trouble with you is that you've had too many babies too fast" and reserve to myself the opinion "your personality has not developed far enough."

At this same hospital, studies have been made of women recovering from hysterectomy, women with menstrual complaints, and women with difficult pregnancies. The ones who suffered the most pain, nausea, vomiting, physical and emotional distress, depression, apathy, anxiety, were women "whose lives revolved almost exclusively around the reproductive function and its gratification in motherhood. A prototype of this attitude was expressed by one woman who said, 'In order to be a woman, I have to be able to have children.' " [8] The ones who suffered least had "well-integrated egos," had resources of the intellect and were directed outward in their interests, even in the hospital, rather than preoccupied with themselves and their sufferings.

Obstetricians have seen this too. One told me:

It's a funny thing. The women who have the backaches, the bleeding, the difficult pregnancy and delivery, are the ones who think their whole purpose in life is to have babies. Women who have other interests than just being reproductive machines have less trouble having babies. Don't ask me to explain it. I'm no psychiatrist. But we've all noticed it.

Another gynecologist spoke of many patients in this era of "femaleness-fulfilled" to whom neither having babies nor sexual intercourse brought "fulfillment." They were, in his words:

Women who feel very unsure about their sex and need to have children again and again to prove that they are feminine; women who have the fourth or fifth child because they can't think of anything else to do; women who are dominant and this is something else to dominate; and then I have hundreds of patients who are college girls who don't know what to do with themselves, their mothers bring them in for diaphragms. Because they are immature, going to bed means nothing— it is like taking medicine, no orgasm, nothing. For them getting married is an evasion.

The high incidence of cramps with menstruation, nausea and vomiting during pregnancy, depression with childbirth, and severe physiological and psychological distress at menopause have come to be accepted as a "normal" part of feminine biology.[9] Are these stigmata that mark the stages of the female sexual cycle—menstruation, pregnancy, menopause—part of the fixed and eternal nature of women as they are popularly assumed to be, or are they somehow related to that unnecessary choice between "femininity" and human growth, sex and self? When a woman is a "sex creature," does she see unconsciously in each step of her feminine sexual cycle a giving up, a kind of death, of her very reason for existence? These women who crowd the clinics are personifications of the feminine mystique. The lack of orgasm, the increasing "female troubles," the promiscuous and insatiable sex-seeking, the depression at the moment of becoming a mother, the strange eagerness of women to have their female sex organs removed by hysterectomies without medical cause—all these betray the big lie of the mystique. Like the self-fulfilling prophecy of death in Samarra, the feminine mystique, with its outcry against loss of femininity, is making it increasingly difficult for women to affirm their femininity, and for men to be truly masculine, and for either to enjoy human sexual love.

The air of unreality that hovered over my interviews with suburban housewife sex-seekers, the unreality that pervades the sex-preoccupied novels, plays, and movies—as it pervades the ritualistic sex talk at suburban parties—I suddenly saw for what it was, on an island ostensibly far removed from suburbia, where sex-seeking is omnipresent, in pure phantasy. During the week, this island is an exaggeration of a suburb, for it is utterly removed from outside stimuli, from the world of work and politics; the men do not even come home at night. The women who were spending the summer there were extremely attractive young housewives. They had married early; they lived through their husbands and children; they had no interest in the world outside the home. Here on this island, unlike the suburb, these women had no way to make committees or housework expand to fill the time available. But they found a new diversion that killed two birds with one stone, a diversion that gave them a spurious sense of sexual status, but relieved them of the frightening necessity to prove it. On this island, there was a colony of "boys" right out of the world of Tennessee Williams. During the week when their husbands were working in the city, the young housewives had "wild" orgies, all-night parties, with these sexless boys. In a sort of humorous puzzlement, a husband who took the boat over unexpectedly one midweek to console his bored and lonely wife, speculated: "Why do they do it? Maybe it has something to do with this place being a matriarchy."

Perhaps, too, it had something to do with boredom—there just was not anything else to do. But it looked like sex; that's what made it so exciting, even though there was, of course, no sexual contact. Perhaps, these housewives and their boyfriends recognized themselves in each other. For like the call girl in Truman Capote's *Breakfast at Tiffany's* who spends the sexless night with the passive homosexual, they were equally childlike in their retreat from life. And in each other, they sought the same nonsexual reassurance.

But in the suburbs where most hours of the day there are virtually no men at all—to give even the appearance of sex— women who have no identity other than sex creatures must ultimately seek their reassurance through the possession of "things." One suddenly sees why manipulators cater to sexual hunger in their attempt to sell products which are not even remotely sexual. As long as woman's needs for achievement and identity can be channeled into this search for sexual status, she is easy prey for any product which presumably promises her that status—a status that cannot be achieved by effort or achievement of her own. And since that endless search for status as a desirable sexual object is seldom satisfied in reality for most American housewives (who at best can only try to *look* like Elizabeth Taylor), it is very easily translated into a search for status through the possession of objects.

Thus women are aggressors in suburban status-seeking and their search has the same falseness and unreality as their sex-seeking. Status, after all, is what men seek and acquire through their work in society. A woman's work—housework—cannot give her status; it has the lowliest status of almost any work in society. A woman must acquire her status vicariously through her husband's work. The husband himself, and even the children, become symbols of status, for when a woman defines herself as a housewife, the house and the things in it are, in a sense, her identity; she needs these external trappings to buttress her emptiness of self, to make her feel like somebody. She becomes a parasite, not only because the things she needs for status come ultimately from her husband's work, but because she must dominate, own him, for the lack of an identity of her own. If her husband is unable to provide the things she needs for status, he becomes an object of contempt, just as she is contemptuous of him if he cannot fill her sexual needs. Her very dissatisfaction with herself she feels as dissatisfaction with her husband and their sexual relations. As a psychiatrist put it: "She demands too much satisfaction from her marital relations. Her husband resents it and becomes unable to function sexually with her at all."

Could this be the reason for the rising tide of resentment among the new young husbands at the girls whose only ambition was to be their wives? The old hostility against domineering "moms" and aggressive career girls may, in the long run, pale before the new male hostility for the girls whose active pursuit of the "home career" has resulted in a new kind of domination and aggression. To be the tool, the sex-instrument, the "man around the house," is evidently no dream-come-true for a man.

In March, 1962, a reporter noted in *Redbook* a new phenomenon on the suburban scene: that "young fathers feel trapped":

Many husbands feel that their wives, firmly quoting authorities on home management, child rearing and married love, have set up a tightly scheduled, narrowly conceived scheme of family living that leaves little room for a husband's authority or point of view. (A husband said "Since I've been married, I feel I've lost all my guts. I don't feel like a man anymore. I'm still young, yet I don't get much out of life. I don't want advice, but I sometimes feel like something is bursting loose inside.") The husbands named their wives as their chief source of frustration, superseding children, employers, finances, relatives, community and friends. . . . The young father is no longer free to make his own mistakes or to swing his own weight in a family crisis. His wife, having just read Chapter VII, knows exactly what should be done.

The article goes on to quote a social worker:

The modern wife's insistence on achieving sexual satisfaction for herself may pose a major problem for her husband. A husband can be teased, flattered and cajoled into performing as an expert lover. But if his wife scorns and upbraids him as though he had proved unable to carry a trunk up the attic stairs, she is in for trouble. . . . It's alarming to note that five years after marriage, a sizable number of American husbands have committed adultery and a much larger proportion are seriously tempted to do so. Often, infidelity is less a search for pleasure than a means of self-assertion.

Four years ago, I interviewed a number of wives on a certain pseudo-rural road in a fashionable suburb. They had everything they wanted: lovely houses, a number of children, attentive husbands. Today, on that same road, there are a growing spate of dream-houses in which, for various and sometimes unaccountable reasons, the wives now live alone with the children, while the husbands—doctors, lawyers, account chiefs—have moved to the city. Divorce, in America, according to the sociologists, is in almost every instance sought by the husband, even if the wife ostensibly gets it.[10] There are, of course, many reasons for divorce, but chief among them seems to be the growing aversion and hostility that men have for the feminine millstones hanging around their necks, a hostility that is not always directed at their wives, but at their mothers, the women they work with—in fact, women in general.

According to Kinsey, the majority of the American middle-class males' sexual outlets are not in relations with their wives after the fifteenth year of marriage; at fifty-five, one out of two American men is engaging in extramarital sex.[11] This male sex-seeking—the office romance, the casual or intense affair, even the depersonalized sex-for-sex's-sake satirized in the recent movie *The Apartment*—is, as often as not, motivated simply by the need to escape from the devouring wife. Sometimes the man seeks the human relationship that got lost when he became merely an appendage to his wife's aggressive "home career." Sometimes his aversion to his wife finally makes him seek in sex an object totally divorced from any human relationship. Sometimes, in phantasy more often than in fact, he seeks a girl-child, a Lolita, as sexual object—to escape that grownup woman who is devoting all her aggressive energies, as well as her sexual energies, to living through him. There is no doubt that male outrage against women—and inevitably, against sex—has increased enormously in the era of the feminine mystique.[12] As a man wrote in a letter to the *Village Voice*, New York's Greenwich Village newspaper, in February, 1962: "It isn't a problem anymore of whether White is too good to marry Black, or vice versa, but whether women are good enough to marry men, since women are on the way out."

The public symbol of this male hostility is the retreat of American playwrights and novelists from the problems of the world to an obsession with images of the predatory female, the passive martyred male hero (in homo- or heterosexual clothes), the promiscuous childlike heroine, and the physical details of arrested sexual development. It is a special world, but not so special that millions of men and women, boys and girls cannot identify with it. Tennessee Williams' "Suddenly Last Summer" is a flagrant example of this world.

The aging homosexual hero from an old Southern family, haunted by the monstrous birds that devour baby sea turtles, has wasted his life in pursuit of his lost golden youth. He himself has been "eaten" by his seductively feminine mother, just as, in the end, he is literally eaten by a band of young boys. It is significant that the hero of this play never appears; he is without a face, without a body. The only undeniably "real" character is the man-eating mother. She appears again and again in Williams' plays and in the plays and novels of his contemporaries, along with the homosexual sons, the nymphomaniacal daughters, and the revengeful male Don Juans. All of these plays are an agonized shout of obsessed love-hate against women. Significantly, a great many of these plays are written by Southern writers, where the "femininity" which the mystique enshrines remains most intact.

This male outrage is the result, surely, of an implacable hatred for the parasitic women who keep their husbands and sons from growing up, who keep them immersed at that sickly level of sexual phantasy. For the fact is that men, too, are now being drawn away from the large world of reality into the stunted world of sexual phantasy in which their daughters, wives, mothers have been forced to look for "fulfillment." And, for men too, sex itself is taking on the unreal character of phantasy—depersonalized, dissatisfying, and finally inhuman.

Is there, after all, a link between what is happening to the women in America and increasingly overt male homosexuality? According to the feminine mystique, the "masculinization" of American women which was caused by emancipation, education, equal rights, careers, is producing a breed of increasingly "feminine" men. But is this the real explanation? As a matter of fact, the Kinsey figures showed no increase in homosexuality in the generations which saw the emancipation of women. The Kinsey report revealed in 1948 that 37 per cent of American men had had at least some homosexual experience, that 13 per cent were predominantly homosexual (for at least three years between 16 and 55), and 4 per cent exclusively homosexual—some 2,000,-

ooo men. But there was "no evidence that the homosexual group involved more males or fewer males today than it did among older generations." [13]

Whether or not there has been an increase in homosexuality in America, there has certainly been in recent years an increase in its overt manifestations.[14] I do not think that this is unrelated to the national embrace of the feminine mystique. For the feminine mystique has glorified and perpetuated in the name of femininity a passive, childlike immaturity which is passed on from mothers to sons, as well as to daughters. Male homosexuals—and the male Don Juans, whose compulsion to test their potency is often caused by unconscious homosexuality—are, no less than the female sex-seekers, Peter Pans, forever childlike, afraid of age, grasping at youth in their continual search for reassurance in some sexual magic.

The role of the mother in homosexuality was pinpointed by Freud and the psychoanalysts. But the mother whose son becomes homosexual is usually not the "emancipated" woman who competes with men in the world, but the very paradigm of the feminine mystique—a woman who lives through her son, whose femininity is used in virtual seduction of her son, who attaches her son to her with such dependence that he can never mature to love a woman, nor can he, often, cope as an adult with life on his own. The love of men masks his forbidden excessive love for his mother; his hatred and revulsion for all women is a reaction to the one woman who kept him from becoming a man. The conditions of this excessive mother-son love are complex. Freud wrote:

In all the cases examined we have ascertained that the later inverts go through in their childhood a phase of very intense but short-lived fixation on the woman (usually the mother) and after overcoming it, they identify themselves with the woman and take themselves as the sexual object; that is, proceeding on a narcissistic basis, they look for young men resembling themselves in persons whom they wish to love as their mother loved them.[15]

Extrapolating from Freud's insights, one could say that such an excess of love-hate is almost implicit in the relationship of mother and son—when her exclusive role as wife and mother, her relegation to the home, force her to live through her son. Male homosexuality was and is far more common than female homosexuality. The father is not as often tempted or forced by society to live through or seduce his daughter. Not many men become overt homosexuals, but a great many have suppressed enough of this love-hate to feel not only a deep repugnance for homosexuality, but a general and sublimated revulsion for women.

Today, when not only career, but any serious commitment outside the home, are out of bounds for truly "feminine" house-wife-mothers, the kind of mother-son devotion which can produce latent or overt homosexuality has plenty of room to expand to fill the time available. The boy smothered by such parasitical mother-love is kept from growing up, not only sexually, but in all ways. Homosexuals often lack the maturity to finish school and make sustained professional commitments. (Kinsey found homosexuality most common among men who do not go beyond high school, and least common among college graduates.) [16] The shallow unreality, immaturity, promiscuity, lack of lasting human satisfaction that characterize the homosexual's sex life usually characterize all his life and interests. This lack of personal commitment in work, in education, in life outside of sex, is hauntingly "feminine." Like the daughters of the feminine mystique, the sons spend most of their lives in sexual phantasy; the sad "gay" homosexuals may well feel an affinity with the young housewife sex-seekers.

But the homosexuality that is spreading like a murky smog over the American scene is no less ominous than the restless, immature sex-seeking of the young women who are the aggressors in the early marriages that have become the rule rather than the exception. Nor is it any less frightening than the passivity of the young males who acquiesce to early marriage rather than face the world alone. These victims of the feminine mystique start their search for the solace of sex at an earlier and earlier age. In recent years, I have interviewed a number of sexually promiscuous girls from comfortable suburban families, including a number —and this number is growing [17]—of girls who marry in their early teens because they are pregnant. Talking to these girls, and to the professional workers who are trying to help them, one quickly sees that sex, for them, is not sex at all. They have not even begun to experience a sexual response, much less "fulfillment." They use sex—pseudo-sex—to erase their lack of identity; it seldom matters who the boy is; the girl almost literally does not "see" him when she has as yet no sense of herself. Nor will she ever have a sense of herself if she uses the easy rationalizations of the feminine mystique to evade in sex-seeking the efforts that lead to identity.

Early sex, early marriage, has always been a characteristic of underdeveloped civilizations and, in America, of rural and city slums. One of the most striking of Kinsey's findings, however, was that a delay in sexual activity was less a characteristic of socio-economic origin than of the ultimate destination—as measured, for instance, by education. A boy from a slum background, who put himself through college and became a scientist or judge, showed the same postponement of sexual activity in adolescence as others who later became scientists or judges, not as others from the same slum background. Boys from the right side of the tracks, however, who did not finish college or become scientists or judges showed more of that earlier sexual activity that was characteristic of the slum.[18] Whatever this indicates about the relationship between sex and the intellect, a certain postponement of sexual activity seemed to accompany the growth in mental activity required and resulting from higher education, and the achievement of the professions of highest value to society.

Among the girls in the Kinsey survey, there even seemed to be a relationship between the ultimate level of mental or intellectual growth as measured by education, and sexual satisfaction. Girls who married in their teens—who, in Kinsey's cases, usually stopped education with high school—started having sexual intercourse five or six years earlier than girls who continued their education through college or into professional training. This earlier sexual activity did not, however, usually lead to orgasm; these girls were still experiencing less sexual fulfillment, in terms of orgasm, five, ten and fifteen years after marriage than those who had continued their education.[19] As with the promiscuous girls in the suburbs, early sexual preoccupation seemed to indicate a weak core of self which even marriage did not strengthen.

Is this the real reason for the kind of compulsive sex-seeking seen today in promiscuity, early and late, heterosexual or homosexual? Is it a coincidence that the many phenomena of depersonalized sex—sex without self, sex for lack of self—are becoming so rampant in the era when American women are told to live by sex alone? Is it a coincidence that their sons and daughters have selves so weak that they resort at an increasingly early age to a dehumanized, faceless sex-seeking? Psychiatrists have explained that the key problem in promiscuity is usually "low self-esteem," which often seems to stem from an excessive mother-child attachment; the type of sex-seeking is relatively irrelevant. As Clara Thompson, speaking of homosexuality, says:

Overt homosexuality may express fear of the opposite sex, fear of adult responsibility . . . it may represent a flight from reality into absorption in bodily stimulation very similar to the auto-erotic activities of the schizophrenic, or it may be a symptom of destructiveness of oneself or others. . . . People who have a low self-esteem . . . have a tendency to cling to their own sex because it is less frightening. . . . However, the above considerations do not invariably produce homosexuality, for the fear of disapproval from the culture and the need to conform often drive these very people into marriage. The fact that one is married by no means proves that one is a mature person. . . . The mother-child attachment is sometimes found to be the important part of the picture. . . . Promiscuity is possibly more frequent among homosexuals than heterosexuals, but its significance in the personality structure is very similar in the two. In both, the chief interest is in genitals and body stimulation. The person chosen to share the experience is not important. The sexual activity is compulsive and is the sole interest.[20]

Compulsive sexual activity, homosexual or heterosexual, usually veils a lack of potency in other spheres of life. Contrary to the feminine mystique, sexual satisfaction is not necessarily a mark of fulfillment, in woman or man. According to Erich Fromm:

Often psychoanalysts see patients whose ability to love and so be close to others is damaged and yet who function very well sexually and indeed make sexual satisfaction a substitute for love because their sexual potency is their only power in which they have confidence. Their inability to be productive in all other spheres of life and the resulting unhappiness is counterbalanced and veiled by their sexual activities.[21]

There is a similar undertone to the sex-seeking in colleges, even though the potential ability to be "productive in all other spheres of life" is high. A psychiatrist consultant for Harvard-Radcliffe students recently pointed out that college girls often seek "security" in these intense sexual relationships because of their own feelings of inadequacy, when, probably for the first time in their lives, they have to work hard, face real competition, think actively instead of passively—which is "not only a strange experience, but almost akin to physical pain."

The significant facts are the lowered self-esteem and the diminution in zest, energy, and capacity to function in a creative way. The depression seems to be a kind of declaration of dependence, of helplessness, and a muted cry for help as well. And it occurs at some time and in varying intensity in practically every girl during her career at college.[22]

All this may simply represent "the first response of a sensitive, naive adolescent to a new, frighteningly complicated and sophisticated environment," the psychiatrist said. But if the adolescent is a girl, she evidently should not, like the boy, be expected to face the challenge, master the painful work, meet the competition. The psychiatrist considers it "normal" that the girl seeks her "security" in "love," even though the boy himself may be "strikingly immature, adolescent, and dependent"—"a slender reed, at least from the point of view of the girl's needs." The feminine mystique hides the fact that this early sex-seeking, harmless enough for the boy or girl who looks for no more than it offers, cannot give these young women that "clearer image of themselves"—the self-esteem they need and "the vigor to lead satisfying and creative lives." But the mystique does not always hide from the boy the fact that the girl's dependence on him is not really sexual, and that it may stifle his growth. Hence the boy's hostility—even as he helplessly succumbs to the sexual invitation.

A Radcliffe student recently wrote a sensitive account of a boy's growing bitterness at the girl who cannot study without him—a bitterness not even stilled by the sex with which they nightly evade study together.

She was bending down the corner of a page and he wanted to tell her to stop; the little mechanical action irritated him out of all proportion, and he wondered if he was so tense because they hadn't made love for four days . . . I bet she needs it now, he thought, that's why she's so quivery, close to tears, and maybe that's why I loused up the exam. But he knew it was not an excuse; he felt his resentment heating as he wondered why he had not really reviewed. . . . The clock would never let him forget the amount of time he was wasting . . . he slammed his books closed and began to stack them together. Eleanor looked up and he saw the terror in her eyes . . .

"Look, I'm going to walk you back now," he said . . . "I've got to get something done tonight" . . . He remembered that he had a long walk back, but as he bent hurriedly to kiss her she slipped her arms around him and he had to pull back hard in order to get away. She let go at last, and no longer smiling, she whispered: "Hal, don't go." He hesitated. "Please, don't go, please . . ." She strained up to kiss him and when she opened her mouth he felt tricked, for if he put his tongue between her lips, he would not be able to leave. He kissed her, beginning half-consciously to forget that he should go . . . he pulled her against him, hearing her moan with pain and excitation. Then he drew back and said, his voice already labored: "Isn't there anywhere we can go?" . . . She was looking around eagerly and hopefully and he wondered again, how much of her desire was passion and how much grasping: girls used sex to get a hold on you, he knew—it was so easy for them to pretend to be excited.[23]

These are, of course, the first of the children who grew up under the feminine mystique, these youngsters who use sex as such a suspiciously easy solace when they face the first hard hurdles in the race. Why is it so difficult for these youngsters to endure discomfort, to make an effort, to postpone present pleasure for future long-term goals? Sex and early marriage are the easiest way out; playing house at nineteen evades the responsibility of growing up alone. And even if a father tried to get his son to be "masculine," to be independent, active, strong, both mother and father encouraged their daughter in that passive, weak, grasping dependence known as "femininity," expecting her, of course, to find "security" in a boy, never expecting her to live her own life.

And so the circle tightens. Sex without self, enshrined by the feminine mystique, casts an ever-darkening shadow over man's image of woman and woman's image of herself. It becomes harder for both son and daughter to escape, to find themselves in the world, to love another in human intercourse. The million married before the age of nineteen, in earlier and earlier travesty of sex-seeking, betray an increased immaturity, emotional dependence, and passivity on the part of the newest victims of the feminine mystique. The shadow of sex without self may be dispelled momentarily in a sunny suburban dream house. But what will these childlike mothers and immature fathers do to their children, in that phantasy paradise where the pursuit of pleasure and things hides the loosening links to complex modern reality? What kind of sons and daughters are raised by girls who became mothers before they have ever faced that reality, or sever their links to it by becoming mothers?

There are frightening implications for the future of our nation in the parasitical softening that is being passed on to the new generation of children as a result of our stubborn embrace of the feminine mystique. The tragedy of children acting out the sexual phantasies of their housewife-mothers is only one sign of the progressive dehumanization that is taking place. And in this "acting out" by the children, the feminine mystique can finally be seen in all its sick and dangerous obsolescence.

12 Progressive Dehumanization: The Comfortable Concentration Camp

 The voices now deploring American women's retreat to home reassure us that the pendulum has begun to swing in the opposite direction. But has it? There are already signs that the daughters of the able and energetic women who went back home to live in the housewife image find it more difficult than their mothers to move forward in the world. Over the past fifteen years a subtle and devastating change seems to have taken place in the character of American children. Evidence of something similar to the housewife's problem that has no name in a more pathological form has been seen in her sons and daughters by many clinicians, analysts, and social scientists. They have noted, with increasing concern, a new and frightening passivity, softness, boredom in American children. The danger sign is not the competitiveness engendered by the Little League or the race to get into college, but a kind of infantilism that makes the children of the housewife-mothers incapable of the effort, the endurance of pain and frustration, the discipline needed to compete on the baseball field, or get into college. There is also a new vacant sleepwalking, playing-a-part quality of youngsters who do what they are supposed to do, what the other kids do, but do not seem to feel alive or real in doing it.

In an eastern suburb in 1960, I heard a high-school sophomore

282

stop a psychiatrist who had just given an assembly talk and ask him for "the name of that pill that you can take to hypnotize yourself so you'll wake up knowing everything you need for the test without studying." That same winter two college girls on a train to New York during the middle of midyear exam week told me they were going to some parties to "clear their minds" instead of studying for the exams. "Psychology has proved that when you're really motivated, you learn instantly," one explained. "If the professor can't make it interesting enough so that you know it without working, that's his fault, not yours." A bright boy who had dropped out of college told me it was a waste of his time; "intuition" was what counted, and they didn't teach that at college. He worked a few weeks at a gas station, a month at a bookstore. Then he stopped work and spent his time literally doing nothing—getting up, eating, going to bed, not even reading.

I saw this same vacant sleepwalking quality in a thirteen-year-old girl I interviewed in a Westchester suburb in an investigation of teenage sexual promiscuity. She was barely passing in her school work even though she was intelligent; she "couldn't apply herself," as the guidance counselor put it. She seemed always bored, not interested, off in a daze. She also seemed not quite awake, like a puppet with someone else pulling the strings, when every afternoon she got into a car with a group of older boys who had all "dropped out" of school in their search for "kicks."

The sense that these new kids are, for some reason, not growing up "real" has been seen by many observers. A Texas educator, who was troubled because college boys were not really interested in the courses they were taking as an automatic passport to the right job, discovered they also were not really interested in anything they did outside of school either. Mostly, they just "killed time." A questionnaire revealed that there was literally nothing these kids felt strongly enough about to die for, as there was nothing they actually did in which they felt really alive. Ideas, the conceptual thought which is uniquely human, were completely absent from their minds or lives.[1]

A social critic, one or two perceptive psychoanalysts, tried to pinpoint this change in the younger generation as a basic change in the American character. Whether for better or worse, whether it was a question of sickness or health, they saw that the human personality, recognizable by a strong and stable core of self, was being replaced by a vague, amorphous "other-directed personality." [2] In the 1950's, David Riesman found no boy or girl with that emerging sense of his own self which used to mark human adolescence, "though I searched for autonomous youngsters in several public schools and several private schools." [3]

At Sarah Lawrence College, where students had taken a large responsibility for their own education and for the organization of their own affairs, it was discovered that the new generation of students was helpless, apathetic, incapable of handling such freedom. If left to organize their own activities, no activities were organized; a curriculum geared to the students' own interests no longer worked because the students did not have strong interests of their own. Harold Taylor, then president of Sarah Lawrence, described the change as follows:

Whereas in earlier years it had been possible to count on the strong motivation and initiative of students to conduct their own affairs, to form new organizations, to invent new projects either in social welfare, or in intellectual fields, it now became clear that for many students the responsibility for self-government was often a burden to bear rather than a right to be maintained. . . . Students who were given complete freedom to manage their own lives and to make their own decisions often did not wish to do so. . . . Students in college seem to find it increasingly difficult to entertain themselves, having become accustomed to depend upon arranged entertainment in which their role is simply to participate in the arrangements already made. . . . The students were unable to plan anything for themselves which they found interesting enough to engage in.[4]

The educators, at first, blamed this on the caution and conservatism of the McCarthy era, the helplessness engendered by the atom bomb; later, in the face of Soviet advances in the space race, the politicians and public opinion blamed the general "softness" of the educators. But, whatever their own weaknesses, the best of the educators knew only too well that they were dealing with a passivity which the children brought with them to school, a frightening "basic passivity which . . . makes heroic demands on those who must daily cope with them in or out of school." [5] The physical passivity of the younger generation showed itself in a muscular deterioration, finally alarming the White House. Their emotional passivity was visible in bearded, undisciplined beat-nikery—a singularly passionless and purposeless form of adolescent rebellion. Juvenile delinquency ratios just as high as those in the city slums began to show up in the pleasant bedroom suburbs among the children of successful, educated, respected and self-respecting members of society, middle-class children who had all the "advantages," all the "opportunities." A movie called "I Was a Teenage Frankenstein" may not have seemed funny to parents in Westchester and Connecticut who were visited by the vice squad in 1960 because their kids were taking drugs at parties in each others' pine-paneled playrooms. Or the Bergen County parents whose kids were arrested in 1962 for mass violation of the graves in a suburban cemetery; or the parents in a Long Island suburb whose daughters at thirteen were operating a virtual "call girl" service. Behind the senseless vandalism, the riots in Florida at spring vacation, the promiscuity, the rise in teenage venereal disease and illegitimate pregnancies, the alarming dropouts from high school and college, was this new passivity. For these bored, lazy, "gimme" kids, "kicks" was the only way to kill the monotony of vacant time.

That this passivity was more than a question of boredom—that it signaled a deterioration of the human character—was felt by those who studied the behavior of the American GI's who were prisoners of war in Korea in the 1950's. An Army doctor, Major Clarence Anderson, who was allowed to move freely among the prison camps to treat the prisoners, observed:

On the march, in the temporary camps, and in the permanent ones, the strong regularly took food from the weak. There was no discipline to prevent it. Many men were sick, and these men, instead of being helped and nursed by the others, were ignored, or worse. Dysentery was common, and it made some men too weak to walk. On winter nights, helpless men with dysentery were rolled outside the huts by their comrades and left to die in the cold.[6]

Some thirty-eight per cent of the prisoners died, a higher prisoner death rate than in any previous American war, including the Revolution. Most prisoners became inert, inactive, withdrawing into little shells they had erected against reality. They did nothing to get food, firewood, keep themselves clean, or communicate with each other. The Major was struck by the fact that these new American GI's almost universally "lacked the old Yankee resourcefulness," an ability to cope with a new and primitive situation. He concluded: "This was partly—but only partly, I believe—the result of the psychic shock of being captured. It was also, I think, the result of some new failure in the childhood and adolescent training of our young men—a new softness." Discounting the Army's propaganda point, an educational psychologist commented: "There was certainly something terribly wrong with these young men; not softness, but hardness, slickness, and brittleness. I would call it ego-failure—a collapse of identity. . . . Adolescent growth can and should lead to a completely human adulthood, defined as the development of a stable sense of self . . ." ⁷

The Korean prisoners, in this sense, were models of a new kind of American, evidently nurtured in ways "inimical to clarity and growth" at the hands of individuals themselves "insufficiently characterized" to develop "the kind of character and mind that conceives itself too clearly to consent to its own betrayal."

The shocked recognition that this passive non-identity was "something new in history" came, and only came, when it began to show up in the boys. But the apathetic, dependent, infantile, purposeless being, who seems so shockingly nonhuman when remarked as the emerging character of the new American man, is strangely reminiscent of the familiar "feminine" personality as defined by the mystique. Aren't the chief characteristics of femininity—which Freud mistakenly related to sexual biology—passivity; a weak ego or sense of self; a weak superego or human conscience; renunciation of active aims, ambitions, interests of one's own to live through others; incapacity for abstract thought; retreat from activity directed outward to the world, in favor of activity directed inward or phantasy?

What does it mean, this emergence now in American boys as

well as girls, of a personality arrested at the level of infantile phantasy and passivity? The boys and girls in whom I saw it were children of mothers who lived within the limits of the feminine mystique. They were fulfilling their roles as women in the accepted, normal way. Some had more than normal ability, and some had more than normal education, but they were alike in the intensity of their preoccupation with their children, who seemed to be their main and only interest.

One mother, who was terribly disturbed that her son could not learn to read, told me that when he came home with his first report card from kindergarten, she was as "excited as a kid myself, waiting for someone to ask me out on a date Saturday night." She was convinced that the teachers were wrong when they said he wandered around the room in a dream, could not pay attention long enough to do the reading-readiness test. Another mother said that she could not bear it when her sons suffered any trouble or distress at all. It was as if they were herself. She told me:

I used to let them turn over all the furniture and build houses in the living room that would stay up for days, so there was no place for me even to sit and read. I couldn't bear to make them do what they didn't want to do, even take medicine when they were sick. I couldn't bear for them to be unhappy, or fight, or be angry at me. I couldn't separate them from myself somehow. I was always understanding, patient. I felt guilty leaving them even for an afternoon. I worried over every page of their homework; I was always concentrating on being a good mother. I was proud that Steve didn't get in fights with other kids in the neighborhood. I didn't even realize anything was wrong until he started doing so badly in school, and having nightmares about death, and didn't want to go to school because he was afraid of the other boys.

Another woman said:

I thought I had to be there every afternoon when they got home from school. I read all the books they were assigned so I could help them with their schoolwork. I haven't been as happy and excited for years as the weeks I was helping Mary get her clothes ready for college. But I was so upset when she wouldn't take art. That had been my dream, before I got married, of course. Maybe it's better to live your own dreams.

I do not think it is a coincidence that the increasing passivity —and dreamlike unreality—of today's children has become so widespread in the same years that the feminine mystique encouraged the great majority of American women—including the most able, and the growing numbers of the educated—to give up their own dreams, and even their own education, to live through their children. The "absorption" of the child's personality by the middle-class mother—already apparent to a perceptive sociologist in the 1940's—has inevitably increased during these years. Without serious interests outside the home, and with housework routinized by appliances, women could devote themselves almost exclusively to the cult of the child from cradle to kindergarten. Even when the children went off to school their mothers could share their lives, vicariously and sometimes literally. To many, their relationship with their children became a love affair, or a kind of symbiosis.

"Symbiosis" is a biological term; it refers to the process by which, to put it simply, two organisms live as one. With human beings, when the fetus is in the womb, the mother's blood supports its life; the food she eats makes it grow, its oxygen comes from the air she breathes, and she discharges its wastes. There is a biological oneness in the beginning between mother and child, a wonderful and intricate process. But this relationship ends with the severing of the umbilical cord and the birth of the baby into the world as a separate human being.

At this point, child psychologists construe a psychological or emotional "symbiosis" between mother and child in which mother love takes the place of the amniotic fluid which perpetually bathed and fed the fetus in the womb. This emotional symbiosis feeds the psyche of the child until he is ready to be psychologically born, as it were. Thus the psychological writers—like the literary and religious eulogists of mother-love before the psychological era—depict a state in which mother and baby still retain a mystical oneness; they are not really separate beings. "Symbiosis," in the hands of the psychological popularizers, strongly implied that the constant loving care of the mother was absolutely necessary for the child's growth, for an indeterminate number of years.

But in recent years the "symbiosis" concept has crept with increasing frequency into the case histories of disturbed children. More and more of the new child pathologies seem to stem from that very symbiotic relationship with the mother, which has somehow kept children from becoming separate selves. These disturbed children seem to be "acting out" the mother's unconscious wishes or conflicts—infantile dreams she had not outgrown or given up, but was still trying to gratify for herself in the person of her child.

The term "acting out" is used in psychotherapy to describe the behavior of a patient which is not in accord with the reality of a given situation, but is the expression of unconscious infantile wishes or phantasy. It sounds mystical to say that the unconscious infantile wishes the disturbed child is "acting out" are not his own but his mother's. But therapists can trace the actual steps whereby the mother, who is using the child to gratify her own infantile dreams, unconsciously pushes him into the behavior which is destructive to his growth. The Westchester executive's wife who had pushed her daughter at thirteen into sexual promiscuity had not only been grooming her in the development of her sexual charms—in a way that completely ignored the child's own personality—but, even before her breasts began to develop, had implanted, by warnings and by a certain intensity of questioning, her expectation that the child would act out in real life her mother's phantasies of prostitution.

It has never been considered pathological for mothers or fathers to act out their dreams through their children, except when the dream ignores and distorts the reality of the child. Novels, as well as case histories, have been written about the boy who became a bad businessman because that was his father's dream for him, when he might have been a good violinist; or the boy who ends up in the mental hospital to frustrate his mother's dream of him as a great violinist. If in recent years the process has begun to seem pathological, it is because the mothers' dreams which the children are acting out have become increasingly infantile. These mothers have themselves become more infantile, and because they are forced to seek more and more gratification through the child, they are incapable of finally separating themselves from the child. Thus, it would seem, it is the child who supports life in the mother in that "symbiotic" relationship, and the child is virtually destroyed in the process.

This destructive symbiosis is literally built into the feminine mystique. And the process is progressive. It begins in one generation, and continues into the next, roughly as follows:

1. By permitting girls to evade tests of reality, and real commitments, in school and the world, by the promise of magical fulfillment through marriage, the feminine mystique arrests their development at an infantile level, short of personal identity, with an inevitably weak core of self.

2. The greater her own infantilism, and the weaker her core of self, the earlier the girl will seek "fulfillment" as a wife and mother and the more exclusively will she live through her husband and children. Thus, her links to the world of reality, and her own sense of herself, will become progressively weaker.

3. Since the human organism has an intrinsic urge to grow, a woman who evades her own growth by clinging to the childlike protection of the housewife role will—insofar as that role does not permit her own growth—suffer increasingly severe pathology, both physiological and emotional. Her motherhood will be increasingly pathological, both for her and for her children. The greater the infantilization of the mother, the less likely the child will be able to achieve human selfhood in the real world. Mothers with infantile selves will have even more infantile children, who will retreat even earlier into phantasy from the tests of reality.

4. The signs of this pathological retreat will be more apparent in boys, since even in childhood boys are expected to commit themselves to tests of reality which the feminine mystique permits the girls to evade in sexual phantasy. But these very expectations ultimately make the boys grow further toward a strong self and make the girls the worst victims, as well as the "typhoid Marys" of the progressive dehumanization of their own children.

From psychiatrists and suburban clinicians, I learned how this process works. One psychiatrist, Andras Angyal, describes it, not necessarily in relation to women, as "neurotic evasion of growth." There are two key methods of evading growth. One is "noncommitment": a man lives his life—school, job, marriage—"going through the motions without ever being wholeheartedly committed to any actions." He vaguely experiences himself as "playing a role." On the surface, he may appear to be moving normally through life, but what he is actually doing is "going through the motions."

The other method of evading growth Angyal called the method of "vicarious living." It consists in a systematic denial and repression of one's own personality, and an attempt to substitute some other personality, an "idealized conception, a standard of absolute goodness by which one tries to live, suppressing all those genuine impulses that are incompatible with the exaggerated and unrealistic standard," or simply taking the personality that is "the popular cliché of the time."

The most frequent manifestation of vicarious living is a particularly structured dependence on another person, which is often mistaken for love. Such extremely intense and tenacious attachments, however, lack all the essentials of genuine love—devotion, intuitive understanding, and delight in the being of the other person in his own right and in his own way. On the contrary, these attachments are extremely possessive and tend to deprive the partner of a "life of his own." . . . The other person is needed not as someone to relate oneself to; he is needed for filling out one's inner emptiness, one's nothingness. This nothingness originally was only a phantasy, but with the persistent self-repression it approaches the state of being actual.

All these attempts at gaining a substitute personality by vicarious living fail to free the person from a vague feeling of emptiness. The repression of genuine, spontaneous impulses leaves the person with a painful emotional vacuousness, almost with a sense of nonexistence . . .[8]

"Noncommitment" and "vicarious living," Angyal concludes, "can be understood as attempted solutions of the conflict between the impulse to grow and the fear of facing new situations"—but, though they may temporarily lessen the pressure, they do not actually resolve the problem; "their result, even if not their intent, is always an evasion of personal growth."

Noncommitment and vicarious living are, however, at the very heart of our conventional definition of femininity. This is the way the feminine mystique teaches girls to seek "fulfillment as women"; this is the way most American women live today. But if the human organism has an innate urge to grow, to expand and become all it can be, it is not surprising that the bodies and the minds of healthy women begin to rebel as they try to adjust to a role that does not permit this growth. Their symptoms which so puzzle the doctors and the analysts are a warning sign that they cannot forfeit their own existence, evade their own growth, without a battle.

I have seen this battle being fought by women I interviewed and by women of my own community, and unfortunately, it is often a losing battle. One young girl, first in high school and later in college, gave up all her serious interests and ambitions in order to be "popular." Married early, she played the role of the conventional housewife, in much the same way as she played the part of a popular college girl. I don't know at what point she lost track of what was real and what was façade, but when she became a mother, she would sometimes lie down on the floor and kick her feet in the kind of tantrum she was not able to handle in her three-year-old daughter. At the age of thirty-eight, she slashed her wrists in attempted suicide.

Another extremely intelligent woman, who gave up a challenging career as a cancer researcher to become a housewife, suffered a severe depression just before her baby was born. After she recovered she was so "close" to him that she had to stay with him at nursery school every morning for four months, or else he went into a violent frenzy of tears and tantrums. In first grade, he often vomited in the morning when he had to leave her. His violence on the playground approached danger to himself and others. When a neighbor took away from him a baseball bat with which he was about to hit a child on the head, his mother objected violently to the "frustration" of her child. She found it extremely difficult to discipline him herself.

Over a ten-year period, as she went correctly through all the motions of motherhood in suburbia, except for this inability to deal firmly with her children, she seemed visibly less and less alive, less and less sure of her own worth. The day before she hung herself in the basement of her spotless split-level house, she took her three children for a checkup by the pediatrician, and made arrangements for her daughter's birthday party.

Few suburban housewives resort to suicide, and yet there is other evidence that women pay a high emotional and physical price for evading their own growth. They are not, as we now know, the biologically weaker of the species. In every age group, fewer women die than men. But in America, from the time when women assume their feminine sexual role as housewives, they no longer live with the zest, the enjoyment, the sense of purpose that is characteristic of true human health.

During the 1950's, psychiatrists, analysts, and doctors in all fields noted that the housewife's syndrome seemed to become increasingly pathological. The mild undiagnosable symptoms—bleeding blisters, malaise, nervousness, and fatigue of young housewives—became heart attacks, bleeding ulcers, hypertension, bronchopneumonia; the nameless emotional distress became a psychotic breakdown. Among the new housewife-mothers, in certain sunlit suburbs, this single decade saw a fantastic increase in "maternal psychoses," mild-to-suicidal depressions or hallucinations over childbirth. According to medical records compiled by Dr. Richard Gordon and his wife Katherine (psychiatrist and social psychologist, respectively) in the suburbs of Bergen County, N.J., during the 1950's, approximately one out of three young mothers suffered depression or psychotic breakdown over childbirth. This compared to previous medical estimates of psychotic breakdown in one out of 400 pregnancies, and less severe depressions in one out of 80.

In Bergen County during 1953–57 one out of 10 of the 746 adult psychiatric patients were young wives who broke down over childbirth. In fact, young housewives (18 to 44) suffering not only childbirth depression, but all psychiatric and psychosomatic disorders with increasing severity, became during the fifties by far the predominant group of adult psychiatric patients. The number of disturbed young wives was more than half again as big as the number of young husbands, and three times as big as any other group. (Other surveys of both private and public patients in the suburbs have turned up similar findings.) From the beginning to the end of the fifties, the young housewives also increasingly displaced men as the main sufferers of coronary attack, ulcers, hypertension and bronchial pneumonia. In the hospital serving this suburban county, women now make up 40 per cent of the ulcer patients.[9]

I went to see the Gordons, who had attributed the increased pathologies of these new young housewives—not found among women in comparable rural areas, or older suburbs and cities— to the "mobility" of the new suburban population. But the "mobile" husbands were not breaking down as were their wives and their children. Previous studies of childbirth depression had indicated that successful professional or career women sometimes suffered "role-conflict" when they became housewife-mothers. But these new victims, whose rate of childbirth depression or breakdown was so much greater than all previous estimates, had never wanted to be anything more than housewife-mothers; that was all that was expected of them. The Gordons pointed out that their findings do not indicate that the young housewives are necessarily subjected to more stress than their husbands; for some reason, the women simply show an increased tendency to succumb to stress. Could that mean that the role of housewife-mother was too much for them; or could it mean that it was not enough?

These women did not share the same childhood seeds of neurosis; some, in fact, showed none. But a striking similarity that emerged in their case histories was the fact that they had abandoned their education below the level of their ability. The sufferers were the ones who quit high school or college; more often than comparable women their age, they had started college—and left, usually after a year.[10] Many also had come from "the more restrictive ethnic groups" (Italian or Jewish) or from small towns in the South where "women were protected and kept dependent." Most had not pursued either education or job, nor moved in the world on their own in any capacity. A few who broke down had held relatively unskilled jobs, or had the beginnings of interests which they gave up when they became suburban housewife-mothers. But most had had no ambition other than that of marrying an up-and-coming man; many were fulfilling not only their own dreams but also the frustrated status dreams of their mothers, in marrying ambitious, capable men. As Dr. Gordon described them to me: "They were not capable women. They had never done anything. They couldn't even organize the committees which needed to be organized in these places. They had never been required to apply themselves, learn how to do a job and then do it. Many of them quit school. It's easier to have a baby than get an A. They never learned to take stresses, pain, hard work. As soon as the going was tough, they broke down."

Perhaps because these girls were more passive, more dependent than other women, walled up in the suburbs, they sometimes seemed to become as infantile as their children. And their children showed a passivity and infantilism that seemed pathological—very early in the sons. One finds in the suburban mental-health clinics today, the overwhelming majority of the child patients are boys, in dramatic and otherwise inexplicable reversal of the fact that most of the adult patients in all clinics and doctors' offices today are women—that is, housewives. Putting aside the theoretical terms of his profession a Boston analyst who has many women patients told me:

It is true, there are too many more women patients than men. Their complaints are varied, but if you look underneath, you find this underlying feeling of emptiness. It is not inferiority. It is almost like nothingness. The situation is that they are not pursuing any goals of their own.

Another doctor, in a suburban mental-health clinic, told me of the young mother of a sixteen-year-old girl who, since their move to the suburb seven years ago, has been completely preoccupied with her children except for a little "do good" work in the community. Despite this mother's constant anxiety about her daughter ("I think about her all day—she doesn't have any friends and will she get into college?"), she *forgot* the day her daughter was to take her college entrance exams.

Her anxiousness about her daughter and what she was doing was her own anxiety about herself, and what she wasn't doing. When these women suffer with the preoccupation of what they aren't doing with themselves, the children actually get very little real contact with them. I think of another child, 2 years old, with very severe symptoms because he has almost no actual contact with his mother. She is very much in the home, all day, every day. I have to teach her to have even physical contact with the child. But it won't be solved until the mother faces her own need for self-fulfillment. Being available to one's children has nothing to do with the amount of time—being able to be there for each child in terms of what he needs can happen in a split second. And a mother can be there all day, and not be there for the child, because of her preoccupation with herself. So he holds his breath in temper tantrums; he fights in anger; he refuses to let her leave him at nursery school; even at 9 a boy still requires his mother to go to the bathroom with him, lie down with him or he can't go to sleep. Or he becomes withdrawn to the point of schizophrenia. And she is frantically trying to answer the child's needs and demands. But if she was really able to fulfill herself, she would be able to be there for her child. She has to be complete herself, and there herself, to help the child to grow, and learn to handle reality, even to know what his own real feelings are.

In another clinic, a therapist spoke of a mother who was panicky because her child could not learn to read at school, though his intelligence tested high. The mother had left college, thrown herself into the role of housewife, and had lived for the time when her son would go to school, and she would fulfill herself in his achievement. Until therapy made the mother "separate" herself from the child, he had no sense of himself as a separate being at all. He could, would, do nothing, even in play, unless someone told him to. He could not even learn to read, which took a self of his own.

The strange thing was, the therapist said, like so many other women of this era of the "feminine role," in her endeavor to be a "real woman," a good wife and mother, "she was really playing a very masculine role. . . . She was really pushing everyone around— dominating the children's lives, ruling the house with an iron hand, managing the carpentry, nagging her husband to do odd jobs he never finished, managing the finances, supervising the recreation and the education—and her husband was just the man who paid the bills."

In a Westchester community whose school system is world famous, it was recently discovered that graduates with excellent high-school records did very poorly in college and did not make much of themselves afterwards. An investigation revealed a simple psychological cause. All during high school, the mothers literally had been doing their children's homework and term papers. They had been cheating their sons and daughters out of their own mental growth.

Another analyst illuminates how juvenile delinquency is caused by the child's acting out of the mother's needs, when the mother's growth has been stunted.

> Regularly the more important parent—usually the mother, although the father is always in some way involved—has been seen unconsciously to encourage the amoral or antisocial behavior of the child. The neurotic needs of the parent . . . are vicariously gratified by the behavior of the child. Such neurotic needs of the parent exist either because of some current inability to satisfy them in the world of adults, or because of the stunting experiences in the parent's own childhood— or more commonly, because of a combination of both of these factors.[11]

Those who have observed and tried to help young delinquents have seen this progressive dehumanization process in action, and have discovered that love is not enough to counteract it. The symbiotic love or permissiveness which has been the translation of mother love during the years of the feminine mystique is not enough to create a social conscience and strength of character in a child. For this it takes a mature mother with a firm core of self, whose own sexual, instinctual needs are integrated with social conscience. "Firmness bespeaks a parent who has learned . . . how all of his major goals may be reached in some creative course of action . . ."[12]

A therapist reported the case of a nine-year-old girl who stole. She will outgrow it, said her protective mother—with a "permissiveness born of her own need for vicarious satisfaction." At one point, the nine-year-old asked the therapist, "When is my mother going to do her own stealing?"

At its most extreme, this pattern of progressive dehumanization can be seen in the cases of schizophrenic children: "autistic" or "atypical" children, as they are sometimes called. I visited a famous clinic which has been studying these children for almost twenty years. During this period, cases of these children, arrested at a very primitive, sub-infantile level, have seemed to some to be on the increase. The authorities differ as to the cause of this strange condition, and whether it is actually on the increase or only seems to be because it is now more often diagnosed. Until quite recently, most of these children were thought to be mentally retarded. But the condition is being seen more frequently now, in hospitals and clinics, by doctors and psychiatrists. And it is not the same as the irreversible, organic types of mental retardation. It can be treated, and sometimes cured.

These children often identify themselves with things, inanimate objects—cars, radios, etc., or with animals—pigs, dogs, cats. The crux of the problem seems to be that these children have not organized or developed strong enough selves to cope even with the child's reality; they cannot distinguish themselves as separate from the outside world; they live on the level of things or of instinctual biological impulse that has not been organized into a human framework at all. As for the causes, the authorities felt they "must examine the personality of the mother, who is the medium through which the primitive infant transforms himself into a socialized human being." [13]

At the clinic I visited (The James Jackson Putnam Children's Center in Boston) the workers were cautious about drawing conclusions about these profoundly disturbed children. But one of the doctors said, a bit impatiently, about the increasing stream of "missing egos, fragile egos, poorly developed selves" that he has encountered—"It's just the thing we've always known, if the parent has a fragile ego, the child will."

Most of the mothers of the children who never developed a core of human self were "extremely immature individuals" themselves, though on the surface they "give the impression of being well-adjusted." They were very dependent on their own mothers, fled this dependency into early marriage, and "have struggled heroically to build and maintain the image they have created of a fine woman, wife and mother."

The need to be a mother, the hope and expectation that through this experience she may become a real person, capable of true emotions, is so desperate that of itself it may create anxiety, ambivalence, fear of failure. Because she is so barren of spontaneous manifestations of maternal feelings, she studies vigilantly all the new methods of upbringing and reads treatises about physical and mental hygiene.[14]

Her omnipresent care of her child is based not on spontaneity but on following the "picture of what a good mother should be," in the hope that "through identification with the child, her own flesh and blood, she may experience vicariously the joys of real living, of genuine feeling."

And thus, the child is reduced from "passive inertia" to "screaming in the night" to non-humanness. "The passive child is less of a threat because he does not make exaggerated demands on the mother, who feels constantly in danger of revealing that emotionally she has little or nothing to offer, that she is a fraud." When she discovers that she cannot really find her own fulfillment through the child:

. . . she fights desperately for control, no longer of herself perhaps, but of the child. The struggles over toilet training and weaning are generally battles in which she tries to redeem herself. The child becomes the real victim—victim of the mother's helplessness which, in turn, creates an aggression in her that mounts to destruction. The only way for the child to survive is to retreat, to withdraw, not only from the dangerous mother, but from the whole world as well." [15]

And so he becomes a "thing," or an animal, or "a restless wanderer in search of no one and no place, weaving about the room, swaying back and forth, circling the walls as if they were bars he would break through."

In this clinic, the doctors were often able to trace a similar pattern back several generations. The dehumanization was indeed progressive.

In view of these clinical observations, we may assume that the conflict we have discovered in two generations may well have existed for generations before and will continue in those to come, unless the pattern is interrupted by therapeutic intervention or the child rescued by a masculine father-figure, a hope which our experience would not lead us to expect.[16]

But neither therapy nor love was enough to help these children, if the mother continued to live vicariously through the child. I noticed this same pattern in many of the women I interviewed, women who dominated their daughters, or bred them into passive dependence and conformity or unconsciously pushed them into sexual activities. One of the most tragic women I interviewed was the mother of that "sleepwalking" thirteen-year-old girl. A wealthy executive's wife whose life was filled with all the trappings, she lived the very image of suburban "togetherness," except that it was only a shell. Her husband's real life was centered in his business; a life that he could not, or would not, share with his wife. She had sought to recapture her sense of life by unconsciously pushing her thirteen-year-old daughter into promiscuity. She lived in her daughter's pseudo-sex life, which for the girl was so devoid of actual feeling that she became in it merely a "thing."

Quite a few therapists and counselors were trying to "help" the mother and the father, on the premise, I suppose, that if the mother's sexual-emotional needs were filled in her marriage by her husband, she would not need to solve them through her daughter—and her daughter could grow out of the "thingness" to womanhood herself. It was because the husband had so many problems of his own and the prospects of the mother ever getting enough love from him looked dim, that the counselors were trying to get the mother to develop some real interests in her own life.

But with other women I have encountered who have evaded their own growth in vicarious living and lack of personal purposes, not even the most loving of husbands have managed to stop the progressive damage to their own lives and the lives of their children. I have seen what happens when women unconsciously push their daughters into too early sexuality, because the sexual adventure was the only real adventure—or means of achieving status or identity—in their own lives. Today these daughters, who acted out their mothers' dreams or frustrated ambitions in the "normal" feminine way and hitched their wagons to the rising stars of ambitious, able men, are, in too many cases, as frustrated and unfulfilled as their mothers. They do not all rush barefoot to the police station for fear they will murder the husband and baby who, they think, trap them in that house. All their sons do not become violent menaces in the neighborhood and at school; all their daughters do not act out their mothers' sexual phantasies and become pregnant at fourteen. Nor do all such housewives begin drinking at 11 A.M. to hide the clunking whir of the dishwasher, the washing machine, the dryer, that are finally the only sounds of life in that empty house, as the children, one by one, go off to school.

But in suburbs like Bergen County, the rate of "separations" increased a wild 100% during the 1950's, as the able, ambitious men kept on growing in the city while their wives evaded growth in vicarious living or noncommitment, fulfilling their feminine role at home. As long as the children were home, as long as the husband was there, the wives suffered increasingly severe illnesses, but recovered. But in Bergen County, during this decade, there was a drastic increase in suicides of women over forty-five, and of hospitalized women psychiatric patients whose children had grown up and left home.[17] The housewives who had to be hospitalized and who did not recover quickly were, above all, those who had never developed their own abilities in work outside the home.[18]

The massive breakdown that may take place as more and more of these new young housewife-mothers who are the products of the feminine mystique reach their forties is still a matter of speculation. But the progressive infantilization of their sons and daughters, as it is mirrored in the rash of early marriages, has become an alarming fact. In March, 1962, at the national conference of the Child Study Association, the new early marriages and parenthood, which had formerly been considered an indication of "improved emotional maturity" in the younger generation, were at last recognized as a sign of increasing "infantilization." The millions of American youngsters who, in the 1960's, were marrying before they were twenty, betrayed an immaturity and emotional dependence which seeks marriage as a magic short-cut to adult status, a magic solution to problems they cannot face themselves, professionals in the child-and-family field agreed. These infantile brides and grooms were diagnosed as the victims of this generation's "sick, sad love affair with their own children."

Many girls will admit that they want to get married because they do not want to work any longer. They harbor dreams of being taken care of for the rest of their lives without worry, with just enough furnishing, to do little housework, interesting downtown shopping trips, happy children, and nice neighbors. The dream of a husband seems somehow less important but in the fantasies of girls about marriage, it usually concerns a man who has the strength of an indestructible, reliable, powerful father, and the gentleness, givingness, and self-sacrificing love of a good mother. Young men give as their reason for wanting to marry very often the desire to have a motherly woman in the house, and regular sex just for the asking without trouble and bother. . . . In fact, what is supposed to secure maturity and independence is in reality a concealed hope to secure dependency, to prolong the child-parent relationship with the privileges of being a child, and with as little as possible of its limitations.[19]

And there were other ominous signs across the nation of mounting uncontrollable violence among young parents and their children trapped in that passive dependence. A psychiatrist reported that such wives were reacting to hostility from their husbands by becoming even more dependent and passive, until they sometimes became literally unable to move, to take a step, by themselves. This did not make their husbands treat them with more love, but more rage. And what was happening to the rage the wives did not dare to use against their husbands? Consider this recent news item (*Time*, July 20, 1962) about the "Battered-Child Syndrome."

To many doctors, the incident is becoming distressingly familiar. A child, usually under three, is brought to the office with multiple fractures—often including a fractured skull. The parents express appropriate concern, report that the child fell out of bed, or tumbled down the stairs, or was injured by a playmate. But x-rays and experience lead the doctor to a different conclusion: the child has been beaten by his parents.

Gathering documentation from 71 hospitals, a University of Colorado team found 302 battered-child cases in a single year; 33 died, 85 suffered permanent brain damage. The parents, who were driven "to kick and punch their children, twist their arms, beat them with hammers or the buckle end of belts, burn them with cigarettes or electric irons," were as likely to live in those suburban split-levels as in tenements. The A.M.A. predicted that when statistics on the battered-child syndrome are complete, "it is likely that it will be found to be a more frequent cause of death than such well-recognized and thoroughly studied diseases as leukemia, cystic fibrosis and muscular dystrophy."

The "parent" with most opportunity to beat that battered child was, of course, the mother. As one young mother of four said to the doctor, as she confessed to the wish to kill herself:

There doesn't seem any reason for me to go on living. I don't have anything to look forward to. Jim and I don't even talk to each other any more except about the bills and things that need to be fixed in the house. I know he resents being so old and tied down when he's still young, and he blames it on me because it was I that wanted us to get married then. But the worst thing is, I feel so envious of my own children. I almost hate them, because they have their lives ahead, and mine is over.

It may or may not be a symbolic coincidence but the same week the child-and-family profession recognized the real significance of the early marriages, the *New York Times Book Review* (Sunday, March 18, 1962) recorded a new and unprecedented popularity among American adults of books about "love" affairs between human beings and animals. In half a century, there have not been as many books about animals on the American best-seller lists as in the last three years (1959–62). While animals have always dominated the literature for small children, with maturity human beings become more interested in other human beings. (It is only a symbol, but in the Rorschach test, a preponderance of animal over human images is a sign of infantilism). And so progressive dehumanization has carried the American mind in the last fifteen years from youth worship to that "sick love affair" with our own children; from preoccupation with the physical details of sex, divorced from a human framework, to a love affair between man and animal. Where will it end?

I think it will not end, as long as the feminine mystique masks the emptiness of the housewife role, encouraging girls to evade their own growth by vicarious living, by non-commitment. We have gone on too long blaming or pitying the mothers who devour their children, who sow the seeds of progressive dehumanization, because they have never grown to full humanity themselves. If the mother is at fault, why isn't it time to break the pattern by urging all these Sleeping Beauties to grow up and live their own lives? There never will be enough Prince Charmings, or enough therapists to break that pattern now. It is society's job, and finally that of each woman alone. For it is not the strength of the mothers that is at fault but their weakness, their passive childlike dependency and immaturity that is mistaken for "femininity." Our society forces boys, insofar as it can, to grow up, to endure the pains of growth, to educate themselves to work, to move on. Why aren't girls forced to grow up—to achieve somehow the core of self that will end the unnecessary dilemma, the mistaken choice between femaleness and humanness that is implied in the feminine mystique?

It is time to stop exhorting mothers to "love" their children more, and face the paradox between the mystique's demand that women devote themselves completely to their home and their children, and the fact that most of the problems now being treated in child-guidance clinics are solved only when the mothers are helped to develop autonomous interests of their own, and no longer need to fill their emotional needs through their children. It is time to stop exhorting women to be more "feminine" when it breeds a passivity and dependence that depersonalizes sex and imposes an impossible burden on their husbands, a growing passivity in their sons.

It is not an exaggeration to call the stagnating state of millions of American housewives a sickness, a disease in the shape of a progressively weaker core of human self that is being handed down to their sons and daughters at a time when the dehumanizing aspects of modern mass culture make it necessary for men and women to have a strong core of self, strong enough to retain human individuality through the frightening, unpredictable pressures of our changing environment. The strength of women is not the cause, but the cure for this sickness. Only when women are permitted to use their full strength, to grow to their full capacities, can the feminine mystique be shattered and the progressive dehumanization of their children be stopped. And most women can no longer use their full strength, grow to their full human capacity, as housewives.

It is urgent to understand how the very condition of being a housewife can create a sense of emptiness, non-existence, nothingness, in women. There are aspects of the housewife role that make it almost impossible for a woman of adult intelligence to retain a sense of human identity, the firm core of self or "I" without which a human being, man or woman, is not truly alive. For women of ability, in America today, I am convinced there is something about the housewife state itself that is dangerous. In a sense that is not as far-fetched as it sounds, the women who "adjust" as housewives, who grow up wanting to be "just a housewife," are in as much danger as the millions who walked to their own death in the concentration camps—and the millions more who refused to believe that the concentration camps existed.

In fact, there is an uncanny, uncomfortable insight into why a woman can so easily lose her sense of self as a housewife in certain psychological observations made of the behavior of prisoners in Nazi concentration camps. In these settings, purposely contrived for the dehumanization of man, the prisoners literally became "walking corpses." Those who "adjusted" to the conditions of the camps surrendered their human identity and went almost indifferently to their deaths. Strangely enough, the conditions which destroyed the human identity of so many prisoners were not the torture and the brutality, but conditions similar to those which destroy the identity of the American housewife.

In the concentration camps the prisoners were forced to adopt childlike behavior, forced to give up their individuality and merge themselves into an amorphous mass. Their capacity for self-determination, their ability to predict the future and to prepare for it, was systematically destroyed. It was a gradual process which occurred in virtually imperceptible stages—but at the end, with the destruction of adult self-respect, of an adult frame of reference, the dehumanizing process was complete. This was the process as observed by Bruno Bettelheim, psychoanalyst and educational psychologist, when he was a prisoner at Dachau and Buchenwald in 1939.[20]

When they entered the concentration camp, prisoners were almost traumatically cut off from their past adult interests. This in itself was a major blow to their identity over and above their physical confinement. A few, though only a few, were able to work privately in some way that had interested them in the past. But to do this alone was difficult; even to talk about these larger adult interests, or to show some initiative in pursuing them, aroused the hostility of other prisoners. New prisoners tried to keep their old interests alive, but "old prisoners seemed mainly concerned with the problem of how to live as well as possible inside the camp."

To old prisoners, the world of the camp was the only reality.[21] They were reduced to childlike preoccupation with food, elimination, the satisfaction of primitive bodily needs; they had no privacy, and no stimulation from the outside world. But, above all, they were forced to spend their days in work which produced great fatigue—not because it was physically killing, but because it was monotonous, endless, required no mental concentration, gave no hope of advancement or recognition, was sometimes senseless and was controlled by the needs of others or the tempo of machines. It was work that did not emanate from the prisoner's own personality; it permitted no real initiative, no expression of the self, not even a real demarcation of time.

And the more the prisoners gave up their adult human identity, the more they were preoccupied with the fear that they were

PROGRESSIVE DEHUMANIZATION

losing their sexual potency, and the more preoccupied they became with the simplest animal needs. It brought them comfort, at
first, to surrender their individuality, and lose themselves in the
anonymity of the mass—to feel that "everyone was in the same
boat." But strangely enough, under these conditions, real friendships did not grow.[22] Even conversation, which was the prisoners'
favorite pastime and did much to make life bearable, soon ceased
to have any real meaning.[23] So rage mounted in them. But the
rage of the millions that could have knocked down the barbed
wire fences and the SS guns was turned instead against themselves, and against the prisoners even weaker than they. Then
they felt even more powerless than they were, and saw the SS
and the fences as even more impregnable than they were.

It was said, finally, that not the SS but the prisoners themselves
became their own worst enemy. Because they could not bear to
see their situation as it really was—because they denied the very
reality of their problem, and finally "adjusted" to the camp itself
as if it were the only reality—they were caught in the prison of
their own minds. The guns of the SS were not powerful enough
to keep all those prisoners subdued. They were manipulated to
trap themselves; they imprisoned themselves by making the concentration camp the whole world, by blinding themselves to the
larger world of the past, their responsibility for the present, and
their possibilities for the future. The ones who survived, who
neither died nor were exterminated, were the ones who retained
in some essential degree the adult values and interests which had
been the essence of their past identity.

All this seems terribly remote from the easy life of the American suburban housewife. But is her house in reality a comfortable
concentration camp? Have not women who live in the image of
the feminine mystique trapped themselves within the narrow walls
of their homes? They have learned to "adjust" to their biological
role. They have become dependent, passive, childlike; they have
given up their adult frame of reference to live at the lower human
level of food and things. The work they do does not require
adult capabilities; it is endless, monotonous, unrewarding. American women are not, of course, being readied for mass extermina-

tion, but they are suffering a slow death of mind and spirit. Just as with the prisoners in the concentration camps, there are American women who have resisted that death, who have managed to retain a core of self, who have not lost touch with the outside world, who use their abilities to some creative purpose. They are women of spirit and intelligence who have refused to "adjust" as housewives.

It has been said time and time again that education has kept American women from "adjusting" to their role as housewives. But if education, which serves human growth, which distills what the human mind has discovered and created in the past, and gives man the ability to create his own future—if education has made more and more American women feel trapped, frustrated, guilty as housewives, surely this should be seen as a clear signal that *women have outgrown the housewife role.*

It is not possible to preserve one's identity by adjusting for any length of time to a frame of reference that is in itself destructive to it. It is very hard indeed for a human being to sustain such an "inner" split—conforming outwardly to one reality, while trying to maintain inwardly the values it denies. The comfortable concentration camp that American women have walked into, or have been talked into by others, is just such a reality, a frame of reference that denies woman's adult human identity. By adjusting to it, a woman stunts her intelligence to become childlike, turns away from individual identity to become an anonymous biological robot in a docile mass. She becomes less than human, preyed upon by outside pressures, and herself preying upon her husband and children. And the longer she conforms, the less she feels as if she really exists. She looks for her security in things, she hides the fear of losing her human potency by testing her sexual potency, she lives a vicarious life through mass daydreams or through her husband and children. She does not want to be reminded of the outside world; she becomes convinced there is nothing she can do about her own life or the world that would make a difference. But no matter how often she tries to tell herself that this giving up of personal identity is a necessary sacrifice for her children and husband, it serves no real purpose. So the aggressive energy she should be using in the world becomes instead the terrible anger that she dare not turn against her husband, is ashamed of turning against her children, and finally turns against herself, until she feels as if she does not exist. And yet in the comfortable concentration camp as in the real one, something very strong in a woman resists the death of herself.

Describing an unforgettable experience in a real concentration camp, Bettelheim tells of a group of naked prisoners—no longer human, merely docile robots—who were lined up to enter the gas chamber. The SS commanding officer, learning that one of the women prisoners had been a dancer, ordered her to dance for him. She did, and as she danced, she approached him, seized his gun and shot him down. She was immediately shot to death, but Bettelheim is moved to ask:

Isn't it probable that despite the grotesque setting in which she danced, dancing made her once again a person. Dancing, she was singled out as an individual, asked to perform in what had once been her chosen vocation. No longer was she a number, a nameless depersonalized prisoner, but the dancer she used to be. Transformed however momentarily, she responded like her old self, destroying the enemy bent on her destruction even if she had to die in the process.

Despite the hundreds of thousands of living dead men who moved quietly to their graves, this one example shows that in an instant, the old personality can be regained, its destruction undone, once we decide on our own that we wish to cease being units in a system. Exercising the lost freedom that not even the concentration camp could take away—to decide how one wishes to think and feel about the conditions of one's life—this dancer threw off her real prison. This she could do because she was willing to risk her life to achieve autonomy once more.[24]

The suburban house is not a German concentration camp, nor are American housewives on their way to the gas chamber. But they are in a trap, and to escape they must, like the dancer, finally exercise their human freedom, and recapture their sense of self. They must refuse to be nameless, depersonalized, manipulated, and live their own lives again according to a self-chosen purpose. They must begin to grow.

13 The Forfeited Self

Scientists of human behavior have become increasingly interested in the basic human need to grow, man's will to be all that is in him to be. Thinkers in many fields—from Bergson to Kurt Goldstein, Heinz Hartmann, Allport, Rogers, Jung, Adler, Rank, Horney, Angyal, Fromm, May, Maslow, Bettelheim, Riesman, Tillich and the existentialists—all postulate some positive growth tendency within the organism, which, from within, drives it to fuller development, to self-realization. This "will to power," "self-assertion," "dominance," or "autonomy," as it is variously called, does not imply aggression or competitive striving in the usual sense; it is the individual affirming his existence and his potentialities as a being in his own right; it is "the courage to be an individual." [1] Moreover, many of these thinkers have advanced a new concept of the psychologically healthy man—and of normality and pathology. Normality is considered to be the "highest excellence of which we are capable." The premise is that man is happy, self-accepting, healthy, without guilt, only when he is fulfilling himself and becoming what he can be.

In this new psychological thinking, which seeks to understand what makes men human, and defines neurosis in terms of that which destroys man's capacity to fulfill his own being, the significant tense is the future. It is not enough for an individual to be loved and accepted by others, to be "adjusted" to his culture.

He must take his existence seriously enough to make his own commitment to life, and to the future; he forfeits his existence by failing to fulfill his entire being.

For years, psychiatrists have tried to "cure" their patients' conflicts by fitting them to the culture. But adjustment to a culture which does not permit the realization of one's entire being is not a cure at all, according to the new psychological thinkers.

Then the patient accepts a confined world without conflict, for now his world is identical with the culture. And since anxiety comes only with freedom, the patient naturally gets over his anxiety: he is relieved from his symptoms because he surrenders the possibilities which caused his anxiety. . . . There is certainly a question how far this gaining of release from conflict by giving up being can proceed without generating in individuals and groups a submerged despair, a resentment which will later burst out in self-destructiveness, for history proclaims again and again that sooner or later man's need to be free will out.[2]

These thinkers may not know how accurately they are describing the kind of adjustment that has been inflicted on American housewives. What they are describing as unseen self-destruction in man, is, I think, no less destructive in women who adjust to the feminine mystique, who expect to live through their husbands and children, who want only to be loved and secure, to be accepted by others, who never make a commitment of their own to society or to the future, who never realize their human potential. The adjusted, or cured ones who live without conflict or anxiety in the confined world of home have forfeited their own being; the others, the miserable, frustrated ones, still have some hope. For the problem that has no name, from which so many women in America suffer today, is caused by adjustment to an image that does not permit them to become what they now can be. It is the growing despair of women who have forfeited their own existence, although by so doing they may also have evaded that lonely, frightened feeling that always comes with freedom.

Anxiety occurs at the point where some emerging potentiality or possibility faces the individual, some possibility of fulfilling his existence; but this very possibility involves the destroying of present security, which thereupon gives rise to the tendency to deny the new potentiality.[3]

The new thinking, which is by no means confined to existentialists, would not analyze "away" a person's guilt over refusing to accept the intellectual and spiritual possibilities of his existence. Not all feelings of human guilt are unfounded; guilt over the murder of another is not to be analyzed away, nor is guilt over the murder of oneself. As was said of a man: "The patient was guilty because he had locked up some essential potentialities in himself." [4]

The failure to realize the full possibilities of their existence has not been studied as a pathology in women. For it is considered normal feminine adjustment, in America and in most countries of the world. But one could apply to millions of women, adjusted to the housewife's role, the insights of neurologists and psychiatrists who have studied male patients with portions of their brain shot away and schizophrenics who have for other reasons forfeited their ability to relate to the real world. Such patients are seen now to have lost the unique mark of the human being: the capacity to transcend the present and to act in the light of the possible, the mysterious capacity to shape the future.[5]

It is precisely this unique human capacity to transcend the present, to live one's life by purposes stretching into the future—to live not at the mercy of the world, but as a builder and designer of that world—that is the distinction between animal and human behavior, or between the human being and the machine. In his study of soldiers who had sustained brain injuries, Dr. Kurt Goldstein found that what they lost was no more nor less than the ability of abstract human thought: to think in terms of "the possible," to order the chaos of concrete detail with an idea, to move according to a purpose. These men were tied to the immediate situation in which they found themselves; their sense of time and space was drastically curtailed; they had lost their human freedom.[6]

A similar dailyness shrinks the world of a depressed schizophrenic, to whom "each day was a separate island with no past and no future." When such a patient has a terrifying delusion that his execution is imminent, it is "the result, not the cause, of his own distorted attitude toward the future."

There was no action or desire which, emanating from the present, reached out to the future, spanning the dull, similar days. As a result, each day kept an unusual independence; failing to be immersed in the perception of any life continuity, each day life began anew, like a solitary island in a gray sea of passing time. . . . There seemed to be no wish to go further; every day was an exasperating monotony of the same words, the same complaints, until one felt that this being had lost all sense of necessary continuity. . . . His attention was short-lived and he seemed unable to go beyond the most banal questions.[7]

Recent experimental work by various psychologists reveals that sheep can bind past and future into the present for a span of about fifteen minutes, and dogs for half an hour. But a human being can bring the past of thousands of years ago into the present as guide to his personal actions, and can project himself in imagination into the future, not only for half an hour, but for weeks and years. This capacity to "transcend the immediate boundaries of time," to act and react, and see one's experience in the dimensions of both past and future, is the unique characteristic of human existence.[8] The brain-injured soldiers thus were doomed to the inhuman hell of eternal "dailyness."

The housewives who suffer the terror of the problem that has no name are victims of this same deadly "dailyness." As one of them told me, "I can take the real problems; it's the endless boring days that make me desperate." Housewives who live according to the feminine mystique do not have a personal purpose stretching into the future. But without such a purpose to evoke their full abilities, they cannot grow to self-realization. Without such a purpose, they lose the sense of who they are, for it is purpose which gives the human pattern to one's days.[9]

American housewives have not had their brains shot away, nor are they schizophrenic in the clinical sense. But if this new thinking is right, and the fundamental human drive is not the urge for pleasure or the satisfaction of biological needs, but the need to grow and to realize one's full potential, their comfortable, empty, purposeless days are indeed cause for a nameless terror. In the name of femininity, they have evaded the choices that would have given them a personal purpose, a sense of their own being. For, as the existentialists say, the values of human life never come about automatically. "The human being can lose his own being by his own choices, as a tree or stone cannot." [10]

It is surely as true of women's whole human potential what earlier psychological theorists have only deemed true of her sexual potential—that if she is barred from realizing her true nature, she will be sick. The frustration not only of needs like sex, but of individual abilities could result in neurosis. Her anxiety can be soothed by therapy, or tranquilized by pills or evaded temporarily by busywork. But her unease, her desperation, is nonetheless a warning that her human existence is in danger, even though she has found fulfillment, according to the tenets of the feminine mystique, as a wife and mother.

Only recently have we come to accept the fact that there is an evolutionary scale or hierarchy of needs in man (and thus in woman), ranging from the needs usually called instincts because they are shared with animals, to needs that come later in human development. These later needs, the needs for knowledge, for self-realization, are as instinctive, in a human sense, as the needs shared with other animals of food, sex, survival. The clear emergence of the later needs seems to rest upon prior satisfaction of the physiological needs. The man who is extremely and dangerously hungry has no other interest but food. Capacities not useful for the satisfying of hunger are pushed into the background. "But what happens to man's desires when there is plenty of food and his belly is chronically filled? At once, other (and higher) needs emerge and these, rather than the physiological hungers, dominate the organism." [11]

In a sense, this evolving hierarchy of needs moves further and further away from the physiological level which depends on the material environment, and tends toward a level relatively independent of the environment, more and more self-determined. But a man can be fixated on a lower need level; higher needs can be confused or channeled into the old avenues and may never emerge.

The progress leading finally to the highest human level is easily blocked—blocked by deprivation of a lower need, as the need for food or sex; blocked also by channeling all existence into these lower needs and refusing to recognize that higher needs exist.

In our culture, the development of women has been blocked at the physiological level with, in many cases, no need recognized higher than the need for love or sexual satisfaction. Even the need for self-respect, for self-esteem and for the esteem of others— "the desire for strength, for achievement, for adequacy, for mastery and competence, for confidence in the face of the world, and for independence and freedom"—is not clearly recognized for women. But certainly the thwarting of the need for self-esteem, which produces feelings of inferiority, of weakness, and of helplessness in man, can have the same effect on woman. Self-esteem in woman, as well as in man, can only be based on real capacity, competence, and achievement; on deserved respect from others rather than unwarranted adulation. Despite the glorification of "Occupation: housewife," if that occupation does not demand, or permit, realization of woman's full abilities, it cannot provide adequate self-esteem, much less pave the way to a higher level of self-realization.

We are living through a period in which a great many of the higher human needs are reduced to, or are seen as, symbolic workings-out of the sexual need. A number of advanced thinkers now seriously question such "explanations by reduction." While every kind of sexual symbolism and emotional pathology can be found by those who explore, with this aim, the works and early life of a Shakespeare, a da Vinci, a Lincoln, an Einstein, a Freud, or a Tolstoi, these "reductions" do not explain the work that lived beyond the man, the unique creation that was his, and not that of a man suffering a similar pathology. But the sexual symbol is easier to see than sex itself as a symbol. If women's needs for identity, for self-esteem, for achievement, and finally for expression of her unique human individuality are not recognized by herself or others in our culture, she is forced to seek identity and self-esteem in the only channels open to her: the pursuit of sexual fulfillment, motherhood, and the possession of material things. And, chained to these pursuits, she is stunted at a lower level of living, blocked from the realization of her higher human needs.

Of course, little is known about the pathology or the dynamics of these higher human needs—the desire to know and understand, the search for knowledge, truth, and wisdom, the urge to solve the cosmic mysteries—because they are not important in the clinic in the medical tradition of curing disease. Compared to the symptoms of the classical neuroses, such as the ones Freud saw as emanating from the repression of the sexual need, this kind of psychopathology would be pale, subtle, and easily overlooked— or defined as normal.

But it is a fact, documented by history, if not in the clinic or laboratory, that man has always searched for knowledge and truth, even in the face of the greatest danger. Further, recent studies of psychologically healthy people have shown that this search, this concern with great questions, is one of the defining characteristics of human health. There is something less than fully human in those who have never known a commitment to an idea, who have never risked an exploration of the unknown, who have never attempted the kind of creativity of which men and women are potentially capable. As A. H. Maslow puts it:

Capacities clamor to be used, and cease their clamor only when they are well used. That is, capacities are also needs. Not only is it fun to use our capacities, but it is also necessary. The unused capacity or organ can become a disease center or else atrophy, thus diminishing the person.[12]

But women in America are not encouraged, or expected, to use their full capacities. In the name of femininity, they are encouraged to evade human growth.

Growth has not only rewards and pleasure, but also many intrinsic pains and always will have. Each step forward is a step into the un-familiar and is thought of as possibly dangerous. It also frequently means giving up something familiar and good and satisfying. It fre-quently means a parting and a separation with consequent nostalgia, loneliness and mourning. It also often means giving up a simpler and easier and less effortful life in exchange for a more demanding, more difficult life. Growth forward is in spite of these losses and therefore requires courage, strength in the individual, as well as protection, permission and encouragement from the environment, especially for the child.[13]

What happens if the environment frowns on that courage and strength—sometimes virtually forbids, and seldom actually encourages that growth in the child who is a girl? What happens if human growth is considered antagonistic to femininity, to fulfillment as a woman, to woman's sexuality? The feminine mystique implies a choice between "being a woman" or risking the pains of human growth. Thousands of women, reduced to biological living by their environment, lulled into a false sense of anonymous security in their comfortable concentration camps, have made a wrong choice. The irony of their mistaken choice is this: the mystique holds out "feminine fulfillment" as the prize for being only a wife and mother. But it is no accident that thousands of suburban housewives have not found that prize. The simple truth would seem to be that women will never know sexual fulfillment and the peak experience of human love until they are allowed and encouraged to grow to their full strength as human beings. For according to the new psychological theorists, self-realization, far from preventing the highest sexual fulfillment, is inextricably linked to it. And there is more than theoretical reason to believe that this is as true for women as for men.

In the late thirties, Professor Maslow began to study the relationship between sexuality and what he called "dominance feeling" or "self-esteem" or "ego level" in women—130 women, of college education or of comparable intelligence, between twenty and twenty-eight, most of whom were married, of Protestant middle-class city background.[14] He found, contrary to what one might expect from the psychoanalytical theories and the conventional images of femininity, that the more "dominant" the woman, the greater her enjoyment of sexuality—and the greater her ability to "submit" in a psychological sense, to give herself freely in love, to have orgasm. It was not that these women higher in "dominance" were more "highly sexed," but they were, above all, more completely themselves, more free to be themselves—and this seemed inextricably linked with a greater freedom to give themselves in love. These women were not, in the usual sense, "feminine," but they enjoyed sexual fulfillment to a much higher degree than the conventionally feminine women in the same study.

I have never seen the implications of this research discussed in popular psychological literature about femininity or women's sexuality. It was, perhaps, not noticed at the time, even by the theorists, as a major landmark. But its findings are thought-provoking for American women today, who lead their lives according to the dictates of the feminine mystique. Remember that this study was done in the late 1930's, before the mystique became all-powerful. For these strong, spirited, educated women, evidently there was no conflict between the driving force to be themselves and to love. Here is the way Professor Maslow contrasted these women with their more "feminine" sisters—in terms of themselves, and in terms of their sexuality:

High dominance feeling involves good self-confidence, self-assurance, high evaluation of the self, feelings of general capability or superiority, and lack of shyness, timidity, self-consciousness or embarrassment. Low dominance feeling involves lack of self-confidence, self-assurance and self-esteem; instead there are extensive feelings of general and specific inferiority, shyness, timidity, fearfulness, self-consciousness. . . . The person who describes herself as completely lacking in what she may call "self-confidence in general" will describe herself as self confident in her home, cooking, sewing or being a mother . . . but almost always underestimates to a greater or lesser degree her specific abilities and endowments; the high dominance person usually gauges her abilities accurately and realistically.[15]

These high-dominance women were not "feminine" in the conventional sense, partly because they felt free to choose rather than be bound by convention, and partly because they were stronger as individuals than most women.

Such women prefer to be treated "Like a person, not like a woman." They prefer to be independent, stand on their own two feet, and generally do not care for concessions that imply they are inferior, weak or that they need special attention and cannot take care of themselves. This is not to imply that they cannot behave conventionally. They do when it is necessary or desirable for any reason, but they do not take the ordinary conventions seriously. A common phrase is "I can be nice and sweet and clinging-vine as anyone else, but my tongue is in my cheek." . . . Rules per se generally mean nothing to these women. It is only when they approve of the rules and can see and approve of the purpose behind them that they will obey them. . . . they are strong, purposeful and do live by rules, but these rules are autonomous and personally arrived at. . . .

Low dominance women are very different. They . . . usually do not dare to break rules, even when they (rarely) disapprove of them. . . . Their morality and ethics are usually entirely conventional. That is, they do what they have been taught to do by their parents, their teachers, or their religion. The dictum of authority is usually not questioned openly, and they are more apt to approve of the status quo in every field of life, religious, economic, educational and political.[16]

Professor Maslow found that the higher the dominance, or strength of self in a woman, the less she was self-centered and the more her concern was directed outward to other people and to problems of the world. On the other hand, the main preoccupation of the more conventionally feminine low-dominance women was themselves and their own inferiorities. From a psychological point of view, a high-dominance woman was more like a high-dominance man than she was like a low-dominance woman. Thus Professor Maslow suggested that either you have to describe as "masculine" both high-dominance men and women or drop the terms "masculine" and "feminine" altogether because they are so "misleading."

Our high dominance women feel more akin to men than to women in tastes, attitudes, prejudices, aptitudes, philosophy, and inner personality in general. . . . Many of the qualities that are considered in our culture to be "manly" are seen in them in high degree, e.g., leadership, strength of character, strong social purpose, emancipation from trivialities, lack of fear, shyness, etc. They do not ordinarily care to be housewives or cooks alone, but wish to combine marriage with a career. . . . Their salary may come to no more than the salary of a housekeeper, but they feel other work to be more important than sewing, cooking, etc.[17]

Above all, the high-dominance woman was more psychologically free—more autonomous. The low-dominance woman was not free to be herself, she was other-directed. The more her self-depreciation, self-distrust, the more likely she was to feel another's opinion more valid than her own, and to wish she were more like someone else. Such women "usually admire and respect others more than they do themselves"; and along with this "tremendous respect for authority," with idolization and imitation of others, with the complete "voluntary subordination to others" and the great respect for others, went "hatred, and resentment, envy, jealousy, suspicion, distrust."

Where the high-dominance women were freely angry, the low-dominance women did not "have 'nerve' enough to say what they think and courage enough to show anger when it is necessary." Thus, their "feminine" quietness was a concomitant of "shyness, inferiority feelings, and a general feeling that anything they could say would be stupid and would be laughed at." Such a woman "does not want to be a leader except in her fantasies, for she is afraid of being in the forefront, she is afraid of responsibility, and she feels that she would be incompetent."

And again Professor Maslow found an evident link between strength of self and sexuality, the freedom to be oneself and the freedom to "submit." He found that the women who were "timid, shy, modest, neat, tactful, quiet, introverted, retiring, more feminine, more conventional," were not capable of enjoying the kind of sexual fulfillment which was freely enjoyed by women high in dominance and self-esteem.

It would seem as if every sexual impulse or desire that has ever been spoken of may emerge freely and without inhibition in these women. . . . Generally the sexual act is apt to be taken not as a serious rite with fearful aspects, and differing in fundamental quality from all other acts, but as a game, as fun, as a highly pleasurable animal act.[18]

Moreover, Maslow found that, even in dreams and fantasies, women of above-average dominance enjoyed sexuality, while in low-dominance women the sexual dreams are always "of the romantic sort, or else are anxious, distorted, symbolized and concealed."

Did the makers of the mystique overlook such strong and sexually joyous women when they defined passivity and renunciation of personal achievement and activity in the world as the price of feminine sexual fulfillment? Perhaps Freud and his followers did not see such women in their clinics when they created that image of passive femininity. Perhaps the strength of self which Maslow found in the cases he studied was a new phenomenon in women.

The mystique kept even the behavioral scientists from exploring the relationship between sex and self in women in the ensuing era. But, quite aside from questions of women, in recent years behavioral scientists have become increasingly uneasy about basing their image of human nature on a study of its diseased or stunted specimens—patients in the clinic. In this context, Professor Maslow later set about to study people, dead and alive, who showed no evidence of neurosis, psychosis, or psychopathic personality; people who, in his view, showed positive evidence of self-realization, or "self-actualization," which he defined as "the full use and exploitation of talents, capacities, potentialities. Such people seem to be fulfilling themselves and to be doing the best that they are capable of doing. . . . They are people who have developed or are developing to the full stature of which they are capable." [19]

There are many things that emerged from this study which bear directly on the problem of women in America today. For one thing, among the public figures included in his study, Professor Maslow was able to find only two women who had actually fulfilled themselves—Eleanor Roosevelt and Jane Addams. (The men included Lincoln, Jefferson, Einstein, Freud, G. W. Carver, Debs, Schweitzer, Kreisler, Goethe, Thoreau, William James, Spinoza, Whitman, Franklin Roosevelt, Beethoven.) Apart from public and historical figures, he studied at close range a small number of unnamed subjects who met his criteria—all in their 50's and 60's—and he screened 3,000 college students, finding only twenty who seemed to be developing in the direction of self-actualization; here also, there were very few women.. As a matter of fact, his findings implied that self-actualization, or the full realization of human potential, was hardly possible at all for women in our society.

Professor Maslow found in his study that self-actualizing people invariably have a commitment, a sense of mission in life that, makes them live in a very large human world, a frame of reference beyond privatism and preoccupation with the petty details of daily life.

These individuals customarily have some mission in life, some task to fulfill, some problem outside themselves which enlists much of their energies. . . . In general, these tasks are nonpersonal or unselfish, concerned rather with the good of mankind in general, or of a nation in general. . . . Ordinarily concerned with basic issues and eternal questions, such people live customarily in the widest possible frame of reference. . . . They work within a framework of values that are broad and not petty, universal and not local, and in terms of a century rather than a moment. . . .[20]

Further, Professor Maslow saw that self-actualizing people, who live in a larger world, somehow thereby never stale in their enjoyment of the day-to-day living, the trivialities which can become unbearably chafing to those for whom they are the only world. They ". . . have the wonderful capacity to appreciate again and again, freshly and naively, the basic goods of life with awe, pleasure, wonder, and even ecstasy, however stale these experiences may have become to others." [21]

He also reported "the very strong impression that the sexual pleasures are found in their most intense and ecstatic perfection in self-actualizing people." It seemed as if fulfillment of personal capacity in this larger world opened new vistas of sexual ecstasy. And yet sex, or even love, was not the driving purpose in their lives.

In self-actualizing people, the orgasm is simultaneously more important and less important than in average people. It is often a profound and almost mystical experience, and yet the absence of sexuality is more easily tolerated by these people. . . . Loving at a higher need level makes the lower needs and their frustrations and satisfactions less important, less central, more easily neglected. But it also makes them more wholeheartedly enjoyed when gratified. . . . Food is simultaneously enjoyed and yet regarded as relatively unimportant in the total scheme of life. . . . Sex can be wholeheartedly enjoyed, enjoyed far beyond the possibility of the average person, even at the same time that it does not play a central role in the philosophy of life. It is something to be enjoyed, something to be taken for granted, something to build upon, something that is very basically important like water or food, and that can be enjoyed as much as these; but gratification should be taken for granted.[22]

With such people, the sexual orgasm is not always a "mystical experience"; it may also be taken rather lightly, bringing "fun, merriment, elation, feeling of well-being, gaiety. . . . It is cheerful, humorous, and playful—and not primarily a striving, it is basically an enjoyment and a delight." He also found, in contradiction both to the conventional view and to esoteric theorists of sex, that in self-actualizing people the quality of both love and sexual satisfaction improves with the age of the relationship. ("It is a very common report from these individuals that sex is better than it used to be and seems to be improving all the time.") For, as such a person, with the years, becomes more and more himself, and truer to himself, he seems also to have deeper and more profound relations with others, to be capable of more fusion, greater love, more perfect identification with others, more transcendence of the boundaries of the self, without ever giving up his own individuality.

What we see is a fusion of great ability to love and at the same time great respect for the other and great respect for oneself. . . . Throughout the most intense and ecstatic love affairs, these people remain themselves and remain ultimately masters of themselves as well, living by their own standards, even though enjoying each other intensely.[23]

In our society, love has customarily been defined, at least for women, as a complete merging of egos and a loss of separateness —"togetherness," a giving up of individuality rather than a strengthening of it. But in the love of self-actualizing people, Maslow found that the individuality is strengthened, that "the ego is in one sense merged with another, but yet in another sense remains separate and strong as always. The two tendencies, to transcend individuality and to sharpen and strengthen it, must be seen as partners and not as contradictory."

He also found in the love of self-actualizing people the tendency to more and more complete spontaneity, the dropping of defenses, growing intimacy, honesty, and self-expression. These people found it possible to be themselves, to feel natural; they could be psychologically (as well as physically) naked and still feel loved and wanted and secure; they could let their faults, weaknesses, physical and psychological shortcomings be freely seen. They did not always have to put their best foot forward, to hide false teeth, gray hairs, signs of age; they did not have to "work" continually at their relationships; there was much less mystery and glamour, much less reserve and concealment and secrecy. In such people, there did not seem to be hostility between the sexes. In fact, he found that such people "made no really sharp differentiation between the roles and personalities of the two sexes."

That is, they did not assume that the female was passive and the male active, whether in sex or love or anything else. These people were all so certain of their maleness or femaleness that they did not mind taking on some of the cultural aspects of the opposite sex role. It was especially noteworthy that they could be both active and passive lovers, and this was the clearest in the sexual act and in physical lovemaking. Kissing and being kissed, being above or below in the sexual act, taking the initiative, being quiet and receiving love, teasing and being teased—these were all found in both sexes.[24]

And thus, while in the conventional and even in the sophisticated view, masculine and feminine love, active and passive, seem to be at opposite poles, in self-actualizing people "the dichotomies are resolved and the individual becomes both active and passive, both selfish and unselfish, both masculine and feminine, both self-interested and self-effacing."

Love for self-actualizing people differed from the conventional definition of love in yet another way; it was not motivated by need, to make up a deficiency in the self; it was more purely "gift" love, a kind of "spontaneous admiration." [25]

Such disinterested admiration and love used to be considered a superhuman ability, not a natural human one. But as Maslow says, "human beings at their best, fully grown, show many characteristics one thought, in an earlier era, to be supernatural prerogatives."

And there, in the words "fully grown," is the clue to the mystery of the problem that has no name. The transcendence of self, in sexual orgasm, as in creative experience, can only be attained by one who is himself, or herself, complete, by one who has realized his or her own identity. The theorists know this is true for man, though they have never thought through the implications for women. The suburban doctors, gynecologists, obstetricians, child-guidance clinicians, pediatricians, marriage counselors, and ministers who treat women's problems have all seen it, without putting a name to it, or even reporting it as a phenomenon. What they have seen confirms that for woman, as for man, the need for self-fulfillment—autonomy, self-realization, independence, individuality, self-actualization—is as important as the sexual need, with as serious consequences when it is thwarted. Woman's sexual problems are, in this sense, by-products of the suppression of her basic need to grow and fulfill her potentialities as a human being, potentialities which the mystique of feminine fulfillment ignores.

Psychoanalysts have long suspected that woman's intelligence does not fully flower when she denies her sexual nature; but by the same token can her sexual nature fully flower when she must deny her intelligence, her highest human potential? All the words that have been written criticizing American women for castrating their husbands and sons, for dominating their children, for their material greediness, for their sexual frigidity or denial of femininity may simply mask this one underlying fact: that woman, no more than man, can live by sex alone; that her struggle for identity, autonomy—that "personally productive orientation based on the human need for active participation in a creative task"—is inextricably linked with her sexual fulfillment, as a condition of her maturity. In the attempt to live by sex alone, in the image of the feminine mystique, ultimately she must "castrate" the husband and sons who can never give her enough satisfaction to make up for lack of a self, and pass on to her daughters her own unspoken disappointment, self-denigration, and discontent.

Professor Maslow told me that he thought self-actualization is only possible for women today in America if one person can grow through another—that is, if the woman can realize her own potential through her husband and children. "We do not know if this is possible or not," he said.

The new theorists of the self, who are men, have usually evaded the question of self-realization for a woman. Bemused themselves by the feminine mystique, they assume that there must be some strange "difference" which permits a woman to find self-realization by living through her husband and children, while men must grow to theirs. It is still very difficult, even for the most advanced psychological theorist, to see woman as a separate self, a human being who, in that respect, is no different in her need to grow than is a man. Most of the conventional theories about women, as well as the feminine mystique, are based on this "difference." But the actual basis for this "difference" is the fact that the possibility for true self-realization has not existed for women until now.

Many psychologists, including Freud, have made the mistake of assuming from observations of women who did not have the education and the freedom to play their full part in the world, that it was woman's essential nature to be passive, conformist, dependent, fearful, childlike—just as Aristotle, basing his picture of human nature on his own culture and particular period of time, made the mistake of assuming that just because a man was a slave, this was his essential nature and therefore "it was good for him to be a slave."

Now that education, freedom, the right to work on the great human frontiers—all the roads by which men have realized themselves—are open to women, only the shadow of the past enshrined in the mystique of feminine fulfillment keeps women from finding their road. The mystique promises women sexual fulfillment through abdication of self. But there is massive statistical evidence that the very opening to American women of those roads to their own identity in society brought a real and dramatic increase in woman's capacity for sexual fulfillment: the orgasm. In the years between the "emancipation" of women won by the feminists and the sexual counterrevolution of the feminine mystique, American women enjoyed a decade-by-decade increase in sexual orgasm. And the women who enjoyed this the most fully were, above all, the women who went furthest on the road to self-realization, women who were educated for active participation in the world outside the home.

This evidence is found in two famous studies, generally not cited for this purpose. The first of these, the Kinsey report, was based on interviews with 5,940 women who grew up in the various decades of the twentieth century during which the emancipation of women was won, and before the era of the feminine mystique. Even according to Kinsey's measure of sexual fulfillment, the orgasm (which many psychologists, sociologists, and analysts have criticized for its narrow, mechanistic, over-physiological emphasis, and its disregard of basic psychological nuances), his study shows a dramatic increase in sexual fulfillment during these decades. The increase began with the generation born between 1900 and 1909, who were maturing and marrying in the 1920's—the era of feminism, the winning of the vote and the great emphasis on women's rights, independence, careers, and equality with men, including the right to sexual fulfillment. The increase in wives reaching orgasm and the decrease in frigid women continued in each succeeding generation down to the youngest generation in the Kinsey sample which was marrying in the 1940's.[26]

And the most "emancipated" women, women educated beyond college for professional careers, showed a far greater capacity for complete sexual enjoyment, full orgasm, than the rest. Contrary to the feminine mystique, the Kinsey figures showed that the more educated the woman, the more likely she was to enjoy full sexual orgasm more often, and the less likely to be frigid. The greater sexual enjoyment of women who had completed college, compared to those who had not gone beyond grade school or high school, and the even greater sexual enjoyment of women who had gone beyond college into higher professional training showed

up from the first year of marriage, and continued to show up in
the fifth, tenth, and fifteenth years of marriage. While Kinsey
found only one American woman in ten who had never experienced sexual orgasm, the majority of women he interviewed did
not experience it completely, all or almost all of the time—except
for those women who were educated beyond college. The Kinsey figures also showed that women who married before twenty
were least likely to experience sexual orgasm, and were likely
to enjoy it less frequently in or out of marriage, though they
started sexual intercourse five or six years earlier than women
who finished college or graduate school.

While the Kinsey data showed that over the years "a distinctly
higher proportion of the better educated females, in contrast to
the grade school and high school females, had actually reached
orgasm in a higher percentage of their marital coitus," the increased enjoyment of sex did not, for the most part, mean an
increased incidence of it, in the woman's life. On the whole,
there was a slight trend in the opposite direction. And that increase in extramarital sex was less marked with professionally
trained women.[27]

Perhaps something about the supposedly "unfeminine" strength,
or self-realization achieved by women educated for professional
careers enabled them to enjoy greater sexual fulfillment in their
marriages than other women—as measured by the orgasm—
and thus less likely to seek it outside of marriage. Or perhaps they
simply had less need to seek status, achievement, or identity in
sex. The relationship between woman's sexual fulfillment and
self-realization indicated by Kinsey's findings is underlined by
the fact that, as many critics have pointed out, Kinsey's sample
was over-representative of professional women, college graduates, women with unusually high "dominance" or strength of
self. Kinsey's sample underrepresented the "typical" American
housewife who devotes her life to husband, home and children;
it underrepresented women with little education; because of its
use of volunteers, it underrepresented the kind of passive, submissive, conformist women whom Maslow found to be incapable
of sexual enjoyment.[28] The increase in sexual fulfillment and

decrease in frigidity which Kinsey found during the decades after women's emancipation may not have been felt by the "average" American housewife as much as by this minority of women who directly experienced emancipation through education and participation in the professions. Nevertheless, the decrease in frigidity was so dramatic in that large, if unrepresentative, sample of nearly 6,000 women, that even Kinsey's critics found it significant.

It was hardly an accident that this increase in woman's sexual fulfillment accompanied her progress to equal participation in the rights, education, work, and decisions of American society. The coincidental sexual emancipation of American men—the lifting of the veil of contempt and degradation from sexual intercourse—was surely related to the American male's new regard for the American woman as an equal, a person like himself, and not just a sexual object. Evidently, the further women progressed from that state, the more sex became an act of human intercourse rather than a dirty joke to men; and the more women were able to love men, rather than submit, in passive distaste, to their sexual desire. In fact, the feminine mystique itself—with its acknowledgement of woman as subject and not just object of the sexual act, and its assumption that her active, willing participation was essential to man's pleasure—could not have come without the emancipation of women to human equality. As the early feminists foresaw, women's rights did indeed promote greater sexual fulfillment, for men and women.

Other studies also showed that education and independence increased the American woman's ability to enjoy a sexual relationship with a man, and thus to affirm more fully her own sexual nature as a woman. Repeated reports, before and after Kinsey, showed college-educated women to have a much lower than average divorce rate. More specifically, a massive and famous sociological study by Ernest W. Burgess and Leonard S. Cottrell indicated that women's chances of happiness in marriage increased as their career preparation increased—with teachers, professional nurses, women doctors, and lawyers showing fewer unhappy marriages than any other group of women. These women were more likely to enjoy happiness in marriage than women who held skilled office positions, who in turn, had happier marriages than women who had not worked before marriage, or who had no vocational ambition, or who worked at a job that was not in accordance with their own ambitions, or whose only work training or experience was domestic or unskilled. In fact, the higher the woman's income at the time of her marriage, the more probable her married happiness. As the sociologists put it:

Apparently in the case of wives, the traits that make for success in the business world as measured by monthly income are the traits that make for success in marriage. The point, of course, may be made that income indirectly measures education since the amount of educational training influences income.[29]

Among 526 couples, less than ten per cent showed "low" marital adjustment where the wife had been employed seven or more years, had completed college or professional training, and had not married before twenty-two. Where wives had been educated *beyond college*, less than 5 per cent of marriages scored "low" in happiness. The following table shows the relationship between the marriage and the educational achievement of the wife.

Marriage Adjustment Scores at Different Educational Levels

Wife's Educational Level	Marital Adjustment Score			
	Very low	*Low*	*High*	*Very high*
Graduate work	0.0	4.6	38.7	56.5
College	9.2	18.9	22.9	48.9
High School	14.4	16.3	32.2	37.1
Grades Only	33.3	25.9	25.9	14.8

One might have predicted from such evidence a relatively poor chance of married happiness, or of sexual fulfillment, or even of orgasm, for the women whom the mystique encouraged to marry before twenty, to forgo higher education, careers, independence, and equality with men in favor of femininity. And, as

a matter of fact, the youngest group of wives studied by Kinsey
—the generation born between 1920 and 1929 who met the
feminine mystique head-on in the 1940's when the race back
home began—showed, by the fifth year of marriage, a sharp
reversal of that trend toward increased sexual fulfillment in
marriage which had been manifest in every decade since women's
emancipation in the 1920's.

The percentage of women enjoying orgasm in all or nearly all of
their married sex life in the fifth year of marriage had risen from 37%
of women in the generation born before 1900 to 42% in the generations
born in the next two decades. The youngest group, whose fifth year
of marriage was in the late 1940's, enjoyed full orgasm in even less
cases (36%) than women born before 1900.[30]

Would a new Kinsey study find the young wives who are
products of the feminine mystique enjoying even less sexual
fulfillment than their more emancipated, more independent, more
educated, more grownup-when-married forebears? Only fourteen per cent of Kinsey's women had married by twenty; a bare
majority—fifty-three per cent—had married by twenty-five,
though most did marry. This is quite a difference from the
America of the 1960's, when fifty per cent of women marry in
their teens.

Recently, Helene Deutsch, the eminent psychoanalyst who went
even further than Freud in equating femininity with masochistic
passivity and, in warning women that "outward-directed activity"
and "masculinizing" intellectuality might interfere with a fully
feminine orgasm, threw a psychoanalytic conference into an
uproar by suggesting that perhaps too much emphasis had been
put on "the orgasm" for women. In the 1960's, she was suddenly
not so sure that women had to have, or could have, a real orgasm.
Perhaps a more "diffuse" fulfillment was all that could be expected. After all, she had women patients who were absolutely
psychotic who seemed to have orgasms; but most women she
saw now did not seem to have them at all.

What did it mean? Could women, then, not experience orgasm?
Or had something happened, during this time when so much

emphasis has been placed on sexual fulfillment, to keep women from experiencing orgasm? The experts did not all agree. But in other contexts, not concerned with women, analysts reported that passive people who "psychologically feel empty"—who fail to "develop adequate egos," have "little sense of their own identity"—cannot submit to the experience of sexual orgasm for fear of their own non-existence.[31] Fanned into an all-consuming sexual search by the popularizers of Freudian "femininity," many women had, in effect, renounced everything for the orgasm that was supposed to be at the end of the rainbow. To say the least, they directed quite a lot of their emotional energies and needs toward the sexual act. As somebody said about a truly beautiful woman in America, her image has been so overexposed in the ads, television, movies, that when you see the real thing, you're disappointed. Without even delving into the murky depths of the unconscious, one might assume it was asking a lot of the beautiful orgasm, not only to live up to its overadvertised claims, but to constitute the equivalent of an A in sex, a salary raise, a good review on opening night, promotion to senior editor or associate professor, much less the basic "experience of oneself," the sense of identity.[32] As one psychotherapist reported:

One of the major reasons, ironically, why so many women are not achieving full-flowering sexuality today is because they are so over determined to achieve it. They are so ashamed if they do not reach the heights of expressive sensuality that they tragically sabotage their own desires. That is to say, instead of focusing clearly on the real problem at hand, these women are focusing on quite a different problem, namely, "Oh, what an idiot and an incompetent person I am for not being able to achieve satisfaction without difficulty." Today's women are often obsessed with the notion of *how*, rather than *what*, they are doing when they are having marital relations. That is fatal.

If sex itself, as another psychoanalyst put it, is beginning to have a "depressive" quality in America, it is perhaps because too many Americans—especially the women sex-seekers—are putting into the sexual search all their frustrated needs for self-realization. American women are suffering, quite simply, a massive sickness of sex without self. No one has warned them that sex can never be a substitute for personal identity; that sex itself cannot give identity to a woman, any more than to a man; that there may be no sexual fulfillment at all for the woman who seeks her self in sex.

The question of how a person can most fully realize his own capacities and thus achieve identity has become an important concern of the philosophers and the social and psychological thinkers of our time—and for good reason. Thinkers of other times put forth the idea that people were, to a great extent, defined by the work they did. The work that a man had to do to eat, to stay alive, to meet the physical necessities of his environment, dictated his identity. And in this sense, when work is seen merely as a means of survival, human identity was dictated by biology.

But today the problem of human identity has changed. For the work that defined man's place in society and his sense of himself has also changed man's world. Work, and the advance of knowledge, has lessened man's dependence on his environment; his biology and the work he must do for biological survival are no longer sufficient to define his identity. This can be most clearly seen in our own abundant society; men no longer need to work all day to eat. They have an unprecedented freedom to choose the kind of work they will do; they also have an unprecedented amount of time apart from the hours and days that must actually be spent in making a living. And suddenly one realizes the significance of today's identity crisis—for women, and increasingly, for men. One sees the human significance of work—not merely as the means of biological survival, but as the giver of self and the transcender of self, as the creator of human identity and human evolution.

For "self-realization" or "self-fulfillment" or "identity" does not come from looking into a mirror in rapt contemplation of one's own image. Those who have most fully realized themselves, in a sense that can be recognized by the human mind even though it cannot be clearly defined, have done so in the service of a human purpose larger than themselves. Men from varying disciplines have used different words for this mysterious process from which comes the sense of self. The religious mystics, the philosophers, Marx, Freud—all had different names for it: man finds himself by losing himself; man is defined by his relation to the means of production; the ego, the self, grows through understanding and mastering reality—through work and love.

The identity crisis, which has been noted by Erik Erikson and others in recent years in the American man, seems to occur for lack of, and be cured by finding, the work, or cause, or purpose that evokes his own creativity.[33] Some never find it, for it does not come from busy-work or punching a time clock. It does not come from just making a living, working by formula, finding a secure spot as an organization man. The very argument, by Riesman and others, that man no longer finds identity in the work defined as a paycheck job, assumes that identity for man comes through creative work of his own that contributes to the human community: the core of the self becomes aware, becomes real, and grows through work that carries forward human society.

Work, the shopworn staple of the economists, has become the new frontier of psychology. Psychiatrists have long used "occupational therapy" with patients in mental hospitals; they have recently discovered that to be of real psychological value, it must be not just "therapy," but real work, serving a real purpose in the community. And work can now be seen as the key to the problem that has no name. The identity crisis of American women began a century ago, as more and more of the work important to the world, more and more of the work that used their human abilities and through which they were able to find self-realization, was taken from them.

Until, and even into, the last century, strong, capable women were needed to pioneer our new land; with their husbands, they ran the farms and plantations and Western homesteads. These women were respected and self-respecting members of a society whose pioneering purpose centered in the home. Strength and independence, responsibility and self-confidence, self-discipline and courage, freedom and equality were part of the American character for both men and women, in all the first generations.

The women who came by steerage from Ireland, Italy, Russia, and Poland worked beside their husbands in the sweatshops and the laundries, learned the new language, and saved to send their sons and daughters to college. Women were never quite as "feminine," or held in as much contempt, in America as they were in Europe. American women seemed to European travelers, long before our time, less passive, childlike, and feminine than their own wives in France or Germany or England. By an accident of history, American women shared in the work of society longer, and grew with the men. Grade- and high-school education for boys and girls alike was almost always the rule; and in the West, where women shared the pioneering work the longest, even the universities were coeducational from the beginning.

The identity crisis for women did not begin in America until the fire and strength and ability of the pioneer women were no longer needed, no longer used, in the middle-class homes of the Eastern and Midwestern cities, when the pioneering was done and men began to build the new society in industries and professions outside the home. But the daughters of the pioneer women had grown too used to freedom and work to be content with leisure and passive femininity.[34]

It was not an American, but a South African woman, Mrs. Olive Schreiner, who warned at the turn of the century that the quality and quantity of women's functions in the social universe were decreasing as fast as civilization was advancing; that if women did not win back their right to a full share of honored and useful work, woman's mind and muscle would weaken in a parasitic state; her offspring, male and female, would weaken progressively, and civilization itself would deteriorate.[35]

The feminists saw clearly that education and the right to participate in the more advanced work of society were women's greatest needs. They fought for and won the rights to new, fully human identity for women. But how very few of their daughters and granddaughters have chosen to use their education and their abilities for any large creative purpose, for responsible work in society? How many of them have been deceived, or have deceived themselves, into clinging to the outgrown, childlike femininity of "Occupation: housewife"?

It was not a minor matter, their mistaken choice. We now know that the same range of potential ability exists for women as for men. Women, as well as men, can only find their identity in work that uses their full capacities. A woman cannot find her identity through others—her husband, her children. She cannot find it in the dull routine of housework. As thinkers of every age have said, it is only when a human being faces squarely the fact that he can forfeit his own life, that he becomes truly aware of himself, and begins to take his existence seriously. Sometimes this awareness comes only at the moment of death. Sometimes it comes from a more subtle facing of death: the death of self in passive conformity, in meaningless work. The feminine mystique prescribes just such a living death for women. Faced with the slow death of self, the American woman must begin to take her life seriously.

"We measure ourselves by many standards," said the great American psychologist William James, nearly a century ago. "Our strength and our intelligence, our wealth and even our good luck, are things which warm our heart and make us feel ourselves a match for life. But deeper than all such things, and able to suffice unto itself without them, is the sense of the amount of effort which we can put forth." [36]

If women do not put forth, finally, that effort to become all that they have it in them to become, they will forfeit their own humanity. A woman today who has no goal, no purpose, no ambition patterning her days into the future, making her stretch and grow beyond that small score of years in which her body can fill its biological function, is committing a kind of suicide. For that future half a century after the child-bearing years are over is a fact that an American woman cannot deny. Nor can she deny that as a housewife, the world is indeed rushing past her door while she just sits and watches. The terror she feels is real, if she has no place in that world.

The feminine mystique has succeeded in burying millions of American women alive. There is no way for these women to break out of their comfortable concentration camps except by finally putting forth an effort—that human effort which reaches beyond biology, beyond the narrow walls of home, to help shape the future. Only by such a personal commitment to the future can American women break out of the housewife trap and truly find fulfillment as wives and mothers—by fulfilling their own unique possibilities as separate human beings.

14 A New Life Plan for Women

 "Easy enough to say," the woman inside the housewife's trap remarks, "but what can I do, alone in the house, with the children yelling and the laundry to sort and no grandmother to babysit?" It is easier to live through someone else than to become complete yourself. The freedom to lead and plan your own life is frightening if you have never faced it before. It is frightening when a woman finally realizes that there is no answer to the question "who am I" except the voice inside herself. She may spend years on the analyst's couch, working out her "adjustment to the feminine role," her blocks to "fulfillment as a wife and mother." And still the voice inside her may say, "That's not it." Even the best psychoanalyst can only give her the courage to listen to her own voice. When society asks so little of women, every woman has to listen to her own inner voice to find her identity in this changing world. She must create, out of her own needs and abilities, a new life plan, fitting in the love and children and home that have defined femininity in the past with the work toward a greater purpose that shapes the future.

To face the problem is not to solve it. But once a woman faces it, as women are doing today all over America without much help from the experts, once she asks herself "What do I want to do?" she begins to find her own answers. Once she begins to see through the delusions of the feminine mystique—and realizes

338

that neither her husband nor her children, nor the things in her house, nor sex, nor being like all the other women, can give her a self—she often finds the solution much easier than she anticipated.

Of the many women I talked to in the suburbs and cities, some were just beginning to face the problem, others were well on their way to solving it, and for still others it was no longer a problem. In the stillness of an April afternoon with all her children in school, a woman told me:

I put all my energies into the children, carting them around, worrying about them, teaching them things. Suddenly, there was this terrible feeling of emptiness. All that volunteer work I'd taken on— Scouts, PTA, the League, just didn't seem worth doing all of a sudden. As a girl, I wanted to be an actress. It was too late to go back to that. I stayed in the house all day, cleaning things I hadn't cleaned in years. I spent a lot of time just crying. My husband and I talked about its being an American woman's problem, how you give up a career for the children, and then you reach a point where you can't go back. I felt so envious of the few women I know who had a definite skill and kept working at it. My dream of being an actress wasn't real—I didn't work at it. Did I have to throw my whole self into the children? I've spent my whole life just immersed in other people, and never even knew what kind of a person I was myself. Now I think even having another baby wouldn't solve that emptiness long. You can't go back— you have to go on. There must be some real way I can go on myself.

This woman was just beginning her search for identity. Another woman had made it to the other side, and could look back now and see the problem clearly. Her home was colorful, casual, but technically she was no longer "just a housewife." She was paid for her work as a professional painter. She told me that when she stopped conforming to the conventional picture of femininity she finally began to *enjoy* being a woman. She said:

I used to work so hard to maintain this beautiful picture of myself as a wife and mother. I had all of my children by natural childbirth. I breastfed them all. I got mad once at an older woman at a party when I said childbirth is the most important thing in life, the basic animal, and she said, "Don't you want to be more than an animal?"

You do want something more, only you don't know what it is. So you put even more into housekeeping. It's not challenging enough, just ironing dresses for your little girls, so you go in for ruffly dresses that need more ironing, and bake your own bread, and refuse to get a dishwasher. You think if you make a big enough challenge out of it, then somehow it will be satisfying. And still it wasn't.

I almost had an affair. I used to feel so discontented with my husband. I used to feel outraged if he didn't help with the housework. I insisted that he do dishes, scrub floors, everything. We wouldn't quarrel, but you can't deceive yourself sometimes in the middle of the night.

I couldn't seem to control this feeling that I wanted something more from life. So I went to a psychiatrist. He kept trying to make me enjoy being feminine, but it didn't help. And then I went to one who seemed to make me find out who I was, and forget about this beautiful feminine picture. I realized I was furious at myself, furious at my husband, because I'd left school.

I used to put the kids in the car and just drive because I couldn't bear to be alone in the house. I kept wanting to do something, but I was afraid to try. One day on a back road I saw an artist painting, and it was like a voice I couldn't control saying "Do you give lessons?"

I'd take care of the house and kids all day, and after I finished the dishes at night, I'd paint. Then I took the bedroom we were going to use for another baby—five children was part of my beautiful picture —and used it for a studio for myself. I remember one night working and working and suddenly it was 2 A.M. and I was finished. I looked at the picture, and it was like finding myself.

I can't think what I was trying to do with my life before, trying to fit some picture of an oldtime woman pioneer. I don't have to prove I'm a woman by sewing my own clothes. I am a woman, and I am myself, and I buy clothes and love them. I'm not such a darned patient, loving, perfect mother anymore. I don't change the kids' clothes top to bottom every day, and no more ruffles. But I seem to have more time to enjoy them. I don't spend much time on housework now, but it's done before my husband gets home. We bought a dishwasher.

The longer it takes to wash dishes, the less time you have for anything else. It's not creative, doing the same thing over and over. Why should a woman feel guilty at getting rid of this repetitive work. There's no virtue in dishwashing, scrubbing floors. Dacron, dishwashers, drip dry—this is fine, this is the direction physical life should take. This is our time, our only time on earth. We can't keep throwing it away. My time is all I've got, and this is what I want to do with it.

I don't need to make such a production of my marriage now because it's real. Somehow, once I began to have the sense of myself, I became aware of my husband. Before, it was like he was part of me, not a separate human being. I guess it wasn't till I stopped trying to be feminine that I began to enjoy being a woman.

And then, there were others, teetering back and forth, aware of the problem but not yet quite sure what to do about it. The chairman of a suburban fund-raising committee said:

I envy Jean who stays at home and does the work she wants to do. I haven't opened my easel in two months. I keep getting so involved in committees I don't care about. It's the thing to do to get in with the crowd here. But it doesn't make me feel quiet inside, the way I feel when I paint. An artist in the city told me, "You should take yourself more seriously. You can be an artist and a housewife and a mother—all three." I guess the only thing that stops me is that it's hard work.

A young Ohio woman told me:

Lately, I've felt this need. I felt we simply had to have a bigger house, put on an addition, or move to a better neighborhood. I went on a frantic round of entertaining but that was like living for the interruptions of your life.

My husband thinks that being a good mother is the most important career there is. I think it's even more important than a career. But I don't think most women are all mother. I enjoy my kids, but I don't like spending all my time with them. I'm just not their age. I could make housework take up more of my time. But the floors don't need vacuuming more than twice a week. My mother swept them every day.

I always wanted to play the violin. When I went to college, girls who took music seriously were peculiar. Suddenly, it was as if some voice inside me said, now is the time, you'll never get another chance. I felt embarrassed, practicing at forty. It exhausts me and hurts my shoulder, but it makes me feel at one with something larger than myself. The universe suddenly becomes real, and you're part of it. You feel as if you really exist.

It would be quite wrong for me to offer any woman easy how-to answers to this problem. There are no easy answers, in America today; it is difficult, painful, and takes perhaps a long time for each woman to find her own answer. First, she must unequivocally say "no" to the housewife image. This does not mean, of course, that she must divorce her husband, abandon her children, give up her home. She does not have to choose between marriage and career; that was the mistaken choice of the feminine mystique. In actual fact, it is not as difficult as the feminine mystique implies, to combine marriage and motherhood and even the kind of lifelong personal purpose that once was called "career." It merely takes a new life plan—in terms of one's whole life as a woman.

The first step in that plan is to see housework for what it is— not a career, but something that must be done as quickly and efficiently as possible. Once a woman stops trying to make cooking, cleaning, washing, ironing, "something more," she can say "no, I don't want a stove with rounded corners, I don't want four different kinds of soap." She can say "no" to those mass daydreams of the women's magazines and television, "no" to the depth researchers and manipulators who are trying to run her life. Then, she can use the vacuum cleaner and the dishwasher and all the automatic appliances, and even the instant mashed potatoes for what they are truly worth—to save time that can be used in more creative ways.

The second step, and perhaps the most difficult for the products of sex-directed education, is to see marriage as it really is, brushing aside the veil of over-glorification imposed by the feminine mystique. Many women I talked to felt strangely discontented with their husbands, continually irritated with their children, when they saw marriage and motherhood as the final fulfillment of their lives. But when they began to use their various abilities with a purpose of their own in society, they not only spoke of a new feeling of "aliveness" or "completeness" in themselves, but of a new, though hard to define, difference in the way they felt about their husbands and children. Many echoed this woman's words:

The funny thing is, I enjoy my children more now that I've made room for myself. Before, when I was putting my whole self into the children, it was as if I was always looking for something through them. I couldn't just enjoy them as I do now, as though they were a sunset, something outside me, separate. Before, I felt so tied down by them, I'd try to get away in my mind. Maybe a woman has to be *by herself* to be really *with* her children.

A New England lawyer's wife told me:

I thought I had finished. I had come to the end of childhood, had married, had a baby, and I was happy with my marriage. But somehow I was disconsolate, because I assumed this was the end. I would take up upholstery one week, Sunday painting the next. My house was spotless. I devoted entirely too much time to entertaining my child. He didn't need all that adult companionship. A grown woman playing with a child all day, disintegrating herself in a hundred directions to fill the time, cooking fancy food when no one needs it, and then furious if they don't eat it—you lose your adult common sense, your whole sense of yourself as a human being.

Now I'm studying history, one course a year. It's work, but I haven't missed a night in 2½ years. Soon I'll be teaching. I love being a wife and mother, but I know now that when marriage is the end of your life, because you have no other mission, it becomes a miserable, tawdry thing. Who said women have to be happy, to be amused, to be entertained? You have to work. You don't have to have a job. But you have to tackle something yourself, and see it through, to feel alive.

An hour a day, a weekend, or even a week off from motherhood is not the answer to the problem that has no name. That "mother's hour off," [1] as advised by child-and-family experts or puzzled doctors as the antidote for the housewife's fatigue or trapped feeling, assumes automatically that a woman is "just a housewife," now and forever a mother. A person fully used by his work can enjoy "time off." But the mothers I talked to did not find any magical relief in an "hour off"; in fact, they often gave it up on the slightest pretext, either from guilt or from boredom. A woman who has no purpose of her own in society, a woman who cannot let herself think about the future because she is doing nothing to give herself a real identity in it, will continue to feel a desperation in the present—no matter how many "hours off" she takes. Even a very young woman today must think of herself as a human being first, not as a mother with time on her hands, and make a life plan in terms of her own abilities, a commitment of her own to society, with which her commitments as wife and mother can be integrated.

A woman I interviewed, a mental-health educator who was for many years "just a housewife" in her suburban community, sums it up: "I remember my own feeling that life wasn't full enough for me. I wasn't using myself in terms of my capacities. It wasn't enough making a home. You can't put the genie back in the bottle. You can't just deny your intelligent mind; you need to be part of the social scheme."

And looking over the trees of her garden to the quiet, empty suburban street, she said:

If you knock on any of these doors, how many women would you find whose abilities are being used? You'd find them drinking, or sitting around talking to other women and watching children play because they can't bear to be alone, or watching TV or reading a book. Society hasn't caught up with women yet, hasn't found a way yet to use the skills and energies of women except to bear children. Over the last fifteen years, I think women have been running away from themselves. The reason the young ones have swallowed this feminine business is because they think if they go back and look for all their satisfaction in the home, it will be easier. But it won't be. Somewhere along the line a woman, if she is going to come to terms with herself, has to find herself as a person.

The only way for a woman, as for a man, to find herself, to know herself as a person, is by creative work of her own. There is no other way. But a job, any job, is not the answer—in fact, it can be part of the trap. Women who do not look for jobs equal to their actual capacity, who do not let themselves develop the lifetime interests and goals which require serious education and training, who take a job at twenty or forty to "help out at home" or just to kill extra time, are walking, almost as surely as the ones who stay inside the housewife trap, to a nonexistent future.

If a job is to be the way out of the trap for a woman, it must be a job that she can take seriously as part of a life plan, work in which she can grow as part of society. Suburban communities, particularly the new communities where social, cultural, educational, political, and recreational patterns are not as yet firmly established, offer numerous opportunities for the able, intelligent woman. But such work is not necessarily a "job." In Westchester, on Long Island, in the Philadelphia suburbs, women have started mental-health clinics, art centers, day camps. In big cities and small towns, women all the way from New England to California have pioneered new movements in politics and education. Even if this work was not thought of as "job" or "career," it was often so important to the various communities that professionals are now being paid for doing it.

In some suburbs and communities there is now little work left for the nonprofessional that requires intelligence—except for the few positions of leadership which most women, these days, lack the independence, the strength, the self-confidence to take. If the community has a high proportion of educated women, there simply are not enough such posts to go around. As a result, community work often expands in a kind of self-serving structure of committees and red tape, in the purest sense of Parkinson's law, until its real purpose seems to be just to keep women busy. Such busywork is not satisfying to mature women, nor does it help the immature to grow. This is not to say that being a den mother, or serving on a PTA committee, or organizing a covered-dish supper is not useful work; for a woman of intelligence and ability, it is simply not enough.

One woman I interviewed had involved herself in an endless whirl of worthwhile community activities. But they led in no direction for her own future, nor did they truly utilize her exceptional intelligence. Indeed, her intelligence seemed to deteriorate; she suffered the problem that has no name with increasing severity until she took the first step toward a serious commitment. Today she is a "master teacher," a serene wife and mother.

At first, I took on the hospital fund-raising committee, the clerical volunteers committee for the clinic. I was class mother for the children's field trips. I was taking piano lessons to the tune of $30 a week, paying baby sitters so I could play for my own amusement. I did the Dewey decimal system for the library we started, and the usual den mother and PTA. The financial outlay for all these things which were only needed to fill up my life was taking a good slice out of my husband's income. And it still didn't fill up my life. I was cranky and moody. I would burst into tears for no reason. I couldn't even concentrate to finish a detective story.

I was so busy, running from morning till night, and yet I never had any real feeling of satisfaction. You raise your kids, sure, but how can that justify your life? You have to have some ultimate objective, some long-term goal to keep you going. Community activities are short-term goals; you do a project; it's done; then you have to hunt for another one. In community work, they say you mustn't bother the young mothers with little children. This is the job of the middle-aged ones whose kids are grown. But it's just the ones who are tied down with the kids who need to do this. When you're not tied down by kids, drop that stuff—you need real work.

Because of the feminine mystique (and perhaps because of the simple human fear of failure, when one does compete, without sexual privilege or excuse), it is the jump from amateur to professional that is often hardest for a woman on her way out of the trap. But even if a woman does not have to work to eat, she can find identity only in work that is of real value to society [2]—work for which, usually, our society pays. Being paid is, of course, more than a reward—it implies a definite commitment. For fear of that commitment, hundreds of able, educated suburban housewives today fool themselves about the writer or actress they might have been, or dabble at art or music in the dilettante's limbo of "self-enrichment," or apply for jobs as receptionists or saleswomen, jobs well below their actual abilities. These are also ways of evading growth.

The growing boredom of American women with volunteer work, and their preference for paid jobs, no matter how low-level, has been attributed to the fact that professionals have taken over most of the posts in the community requiring intelligence. But the fact that women did not become professionals themselves, the reluctance of women in the last twenty years to commit themselves to work, paid or unpaid, requiring initiative, leadership and responsibility is due to the feminine mystique. This attitude of noncommitment among young housewives was confirmed by a recent study done in Westchester County.[3] In an upper-income suburb, more than 50% of a group of housewives between 25 and 35, with husbands in the over-$25,000-a-year income group, wanted to go to work: 13% immediately, the rest in 5 to 15 years. Of those who planned to go to work, 3 out of 4 felt inadequately prepared. (All of these women had some college education but only one a graduate degree; a third had married at twenty or before.) These women were not driven to go to work by economic need but by what the anthropologist who made the survey called "the psychological need to be economically productive." Evidently, volunteer work did not meet this need; though 62% of these women were doing volunteer work, it was of the "one-day and under" variety. And though they wanted jobs and felt inadequately prepared, of the 45% taking courses, very few were working toward a degree. The element of phantasy in their work plans was witnessed by "the small businesses that open and close with sad regularity." When an alumnae association sponsored a two-session forum in the suburb on "How Women in the Middle Years Can Return to Work," twenty-five women attended. As a beginning step, each woman was asked to come to the second meeting with a résumé. The résumé took some thought, and, as the researcher put it, "sincerity of purpose." Only one woman was serious enough to write the résumé.

In another suburb, there is a guidance center which in the early years of the mental-health movement gave real scope to the intelligence of college-educated women of the community. They never did therapy, of course, but in the early years they administered the center and led the educational parent-discussion groups. Now that "education for family living" has become professionalized, the center is administered and the discussion groups led by professionals, often brought in from the city, who have M.A.'s or doctorates in the field. In only a very few cases did the women who "found themselves" in the work of the guidance center go on in the new profession, and get their own M.A.'s and Ph.D.'s. Most backed off when to continue would have meant breaking away from the housewife role, and becoming seriously committed to a profession.

Ironically, the only kind of work which permits an able woman to realize her abilities fully, to achieve identity in society in a life plan that can encompass marriage and motherhood, is the kind that was forbidden by the feminine mystique; the lifelong commitment to an art or science, to politics or profession. Such a commitment is not tied to a specific job or locality. It permits year-to-year variation—a full-time paid job in one community, part-time in another, exercise of the professional skill in serious volunteer work or a period of study during pregnancy or early motherhood when a full-time job is not feasible. It is a continuous thread, kept alive by work and study and contacts in the field, in any part of the country.

The women I found who had made and kept alive such long-term commitments did not suffer the problem that has no name. Nor did they live in the housewife image. But music or art or politics offered no magic solution for the women who did not, or could not, commit themselves seriously. The "arts" seem, at first glance, to be the ideal answer for a woman. They can, after all, be practiced in the home. They do not necessarily imply that dreaded professionalism, they are suitably feminine, and seem to offer endless room for personal growth and identity, with no need to compete in society for pay. But I have noticed that when women do not take up painting or ceramics seriously enough to become professionals—to be paid for their work, or for teaching it to others, and to be recognized as a peer by other professionals—sooner or later, they cease dabbling; the Sunday painting, the idle ceramics do not bring that needed sense of self when they are of no value to anyone else. The amateur or dilettante whose own work is not good enough for anyone to want to pay to hear or see or read does not gain real status by it in society, or real personal identity. These are reserved for those who have made the effort, acquired the knowledge and expertise to become professionals.

There are, of course, a number of practical problems involved in making a serious professional commitment. But somehow those problems only seem insurmountable when a woman is still half-submerged in the false dilemmas and guilts of the feminine mystique—or when her desire for "something more" is only phantasy, and she is unwilling to make the necessary effort. Over and over, women told me that the crucial step for them was simply to take the first trip to the alumnae employment agency, or to send for the application for teacher certification, or to make appointments with former job contacts in the city. It is amazing how many obstacles and rationalizations the feminine mystique can throw up to keep a woman from making that trip or writing that letter.

One suburban housewife I knew had once been a newspaper woman, but she was sure she could never get that kind of job again; she had been away too long. And, of course, she couldn't really leave her children (who, by then, were all in school during the day). As it turned out, when she finally decided to do something about it, she found an excellent job in her old field after only two trips into the city. Another woman, a psychiatric social worker, said that she could not take a regular agency job, only volunteer jobs without deadlines that she could put down when she felt like it, because she could not count on a cleaning woman. Actually, if she had hired a cleaning woman, which many of her neighbors were doing for much less reason, she would have had to commit herself to the kind of assignments that would have been a real test of her ability. Obviously she was afraid of such a test.

A great many suburban housewives today step back from, or give up, volunteer activity, art, or job at the very point when all that is needed is a more serious commitment. The PTA leader won't run for the school board. The League of Women Voters' leader is afraid to move on into the rough mainstream of her political party. "Women can't get a policy-making role," she says. "I'm not going to lick stamps." Of course, it would require more effort for her to win a policy-making role in her party against the prejudices and the competition of the men.

Some women take the jobs but do not make the necessary new life plan. I interviewed two women of ability, both of whom were bored as housewives and both of whom got jobs in the same research institute. They loved the increasingly challenging work, and were quickly promoted. But, in their thirties, after ten years as housewives, they earned very little money. The first woman, clearly recognizing the future this work held for her, spent virtually her entire salary on a three-day-a-week cleaning woman. The second woman, who felt her work was justified only if it "helped out with family expenses," would not spend any money for cleaning help. Nor did she consider asking her husband and children to help out with household chores, or save time by ordering groceries by phone and sending the laundry out. She quit her job after a year from sheer exhaustion. The first woman, who made the necessary household changes and sacrifices, today, at thirty-eight, has one of the leading jobs at the institute and makes a substantial contribution to her family's income, over and above what she pays for her part-time household help. The second, after two weeks of "rest," began to suffer the old desperation. But she persuaded herself that she will "cheat" her husband and children less by finding work she can do at home.

The picture of the happy housewife doing creative work at home—painting, sculpting, writing—is one of the semi–delusions of the feminine mystique. There are men and women who can do it; but when a man works at home, his wife keeps the children strictly out of the way, or else. It is not so easy for a woman; if she is serious about her work she often must find some place away from home to do it, or risk becoming an ogre to her children in her impatient demands for privacy. Her attention is divided and her concentration interrupted, on the job and as a mother. A no-nonsense nine-to-five job, with a clear division between professional work and housework, requires much less discipline and is usually less lonely. Some of the stimulation and the new friendships that come from being part of the professional world can be lost by the woman who tries to fit her career into the physical confines of her housewife life.

A woman must say "no" to the feminine mystique very clearly indeed to sustain the discipline and effort that any professional commitment requires. For the mystique is no mere intellectual construct. A great many people have, or think they have, a vested interest in "Occupation: housewife." However long it may take for women's magazines, sociologists, educators, and psychoanalysts to correct the mistakes that perpetuate the feminine mystique, a woman must deal with them now, in the prejudices, mistaken fears, and unnecessary dilemmas voiced by her husband; her friends and neighbors; perhaps her minister, priest, or rabbi; or her child's kindergarten teacher; or the well-meaning social worker at the guidance clinic; or her own innocent little children. But resistance, from whatever source, is better seen for what it is.

Even the traditional resistance of religious orthodoxy is masked today with the manipulative techniques of psychotherapy. Women of orthodox Catholic or Jewish origin do not easily break through the housewife image; it is enshrined in the canons of their religion, in the assumptions of their own and their husbands' childhoods, and in their church's dogmatic definitions of marriage and motherhood. The ease with which dogma can be dressed in the psychological tenets of the mystique can be seen in this "Suggested Outline for Married Couples' Discussions" from the Family Life Bureau of the Archdiocese of New York. A panel of three or four married couples, after rehearsal by a "priest-moderator," are instructed to raise the question: "Can a working wife be a challenge to the authority of the husband?"

Most of the engaged couples are convinced that there is nothing unusual or wrong in the wife working. . . . Don't antagonize. Be suggestive, rather than dogmatic. . . . The panel couples should point out that the bride who is happy at a 9-to-5 o'clock job has this to think about:
a. She may be subtly undermining her husband's sense of vocation as the bread-winner and head of the house. The competitive business world can inculcate in the working bride attitudes and habits which may make it difficult for her to adjust to her husband's leadership. . . .

c. At the end of a working day, she presents her husband with a tired mind and body at a time when he looks forward to the cheerful encouragement and fresh enthusiasm of his spouse. . . .

d. For some brides, the tension of doubling as business woman and part-time housewife may be one of several factors contributing to sterility . . .

One Catholic woman I interviewed withdrew from the state board of the League of Woman Voters, when, in addition to the displeasure of the priest and her own husband, the school psychologist claimed that her daughter's difficulties at school were due to her political activity. "It is more difficult for a Catholic woman to stay emancipated," she told me. "I have retired. It will be better for everyone concerned if I am just a housewife." At this point the telephone rang, and I eavesdropped with interest on a half-hour of high political strategy, evidently not of the League but of the local Democratic Party. The "retired" politician came back into the kitchen to finish preparing dinner, and confessed that she now hid her political activity at home "like an alcoholic or a drug addict, but I don't seem to be able to give it up."

Another woman, of Jewish tradition, gave up her profession as a doctor when she became a doctor's wife, devoting herself to bringing up their four children. Her husband was not overjoyed when she began brushing up to retake her medical exams after her youngest reached school age. An unassertive, quiet woman, she exerted almost unbelievable effort to obtain her license after fifteen years of inactivity. She told me apologetically: "You just can't stop being interested. I tried to make myself, but I couldn't." And she confessed that when she gets a night call, she sneaks out as guiltily as if she were meeting a lover.

Even to a woman of less orthodox tradition, the most powerful weapon of the feminine mystique is the argument that she rejects her husband and her children by working outside the home. If, for any reason, her child becomes ill or her husband has troubles of his own, the feminine mystique, insidious voices in the community, and even the woman's own inner voice will blame her "rejection" of the housewife role. It is then that many a woman's commitment to herself and society dies aborning or takes a serious detour.

One woman told me that she gave up her job in television to become "just a housewife" because her husband suddenly decided his troubles in his own profession were caused by her failure to "play the feminine role"; she was trying to "compete" with him; she wanted "to wear the pants." She, like most women today, was vulnerable to such charges—one psychiatrist calls it the "career woman's guilt syndrome." And so she began to devote all the energies she had once put into her work to running her family—and to a nagging critical interest in her husband's career.

In her spare time in the suburbs, however, she rather absentmindedly achieved flamboyant local success as the director of a little-theater group. This, on top of her critical attention to her husband's career, was far more destructive to his ego and a much more constant irritation to him and to her children than her professional work in which she had competed impersonally with other professionals in a world far away from home. One day, when she was directing a little-theater rehearsal, her son was hit by an automobile. She blamed herself for the accident, and so she gave up the little-theater group, resolving this time, cross her heart, that she would be "just a housewife."

She suffered, almost immediately, a severe case of the problem that has no name; her depression and dependence made her husband's life hell. She sought analytic help, and in a departure from the nondirective approach of orthodox analysts, her therapist virtually ordered her to get back to work. She started writing a serious novel with finally the kind of commitment she had evaded, even when she had a job. In her absorption, she stopped worrying about her husband's career; imperceptibly, she stopped phantasying another accident every time her son was out of her sight. And still, though she was too far along to retreat, she sometimes wondered if she were putting her marriage on the chopping block.

Contrary to the mystique, her husband—reacting either to the contagious example of her commitment, or to the breathing space afforded by the cessation of her hysterical dependence, or for independent reasons of his own—buckled down to the equivalent of that novel in his own career. There were still problems, of course, but not the old ones; when they broke out of their own traps, somehow their relationship with each other began growing again.

Still, with every kind of growth, there are risks. I encountered one woman in my interviews whose husband divorced her shortly after she went to work. Their marriage had become extremely destructive. The sense of identity that the woman achieved from her work may have made her less willing to accept the destructiveness, and perhaps precipitated the divorce; but it also made her more able to survive it.

In other instances, however, women told me that the violent objections of their husbands disappeared when they finally made up their own minds and went to work. Had they magnified their husband's objections to evade decision themselves? Husbands I have interviewed in this same context were sometimes surprised to find it "a relief" to be no longer the only sun and moon in their wives' world; they were the object of less nagging and fewer insatiable demands and they no longer had to feel guilt over their wives' discontent. As one man put it: "Not only is the financial burden lighter—and frankly, that is a relief—but the whole burden of living seems easier since Margaret went to work."

There are husbands, however, whose resistance is not so easily dispelled. The husband who is unable to bear his wife's saying "no" to the feminine mystique often has been seduced himself by the infantile phantasy of having an ever-present mother, or is trying to relive that phantasy through his children. It is difficult for a woman to tell such a husband that she is not his mother and that their children will be better off without her constant attention. Perhaps if she becomes more truly herself and refuses to act out his phantasy any longer, he will suddenly wake up and see *her* again. And then again, perhaps he will look for another mother.

Another hazard a woman faces on her way out of the housewife trap is the hostility of other housewives. Just as the man evading growth in his own work resents his wife's growth, so women who are living vicariously through their husbands and children resent the woman who has a life of her own. At dinner parties, the nursery school affair, the PTA open house, a woman who is more than just a housewife can expect a few barbs from her suburban neighbors. She no longer has the time for idle gossip over endless cups of coffee in the breakfast nook; she can no longer share with other wives that cozy "we're all in the same boat" illusion; her very presence rocks that boat. And she can expect her home, her husband, and her children to be scrutinized with more than the usual curiosity for the slightest sign of a "problem." This kind of hostility, however, sometimes masks a secret envy. The most hostile of the "happy housewives" may be the first to ask her neighbor with the new career for advice about moving on herself.

For the woman who moves on, there is always the sense of loss that accompanies change: old friends, familiar and reassuring routines lost, the new ones not yet clear. It is so much easier for a woman to say "yes" to the feminine mystique, and not risk the pains of moving on, that the will to make the effort—"ambition"—is as necessary as ability itself, if she is going to move out of the housewife trap. "Ambition," like "career," has been made a dirty word by the feminine mystique. When Polly Weaver, "College and Careers" editor of *Mademoiselle*, surveyed 400 women in 1956 on the subject of "ambition" and "competition," [4] most of them had "guilty feelings" about being ambitious. They tried, in Miss Weaver's words, to "make it uplifting, not worldly and selfish like eating. We were surprised . . . at the number of women who drive themselves from morning to night for a job or the community or church, for example, but don't want a nickel's worth out of it for themselves. They don't want money, social position, power, influence, recognition. . . . Are these women fooling themselves?"

The mystique would have women renounce ambition for themselves. Marriage and motherhood is the end; after that, women are supposed to be ambitious only for their husbands and their children. Many women who indeed "fool themselves" push husband and children to fulfill that unadmitted ambition of their own. There were, however, many frankly ambitious women among those who responded to the *Mademoiselle* survey—and they did not seem to suffer from it.

The ambitious women who answered our questionnaire had few regrets over sacrifices of sweet old friends, family picnics, and time for reading books no one talks about. They got more than they gave up, they said, and cited new friends, the larger world they move in, the great spurts of growth they had when they worked with the brilliant and talented—and most of all the satisfaction of working at full steam, putt-putting along like a pressure cooker. In fact, some happy ambitious women make the people around them happy—their husbands, children, their colleagues. . . . A very ambitious woman is not happy, either, leaving her prestige entirely to her husband's success. . . . To the active, ambitious woman, ambition is the thread that runs through her life from beginning to end, holding it together and enabling her to think of her life as a work of art instead of a collection of fragments . . .

For the women I interviewed who had suffered and solved the problem that has no name, to fulfill an ambition of their own, long buried or brand new, to work at top capacity, to have a sense of achievement, was like finding a missing piece in the puzzle of their lives. The money they earned often made life easier for the whole family, but none of them pretended this was the only reason they worked, or the main thing they got out of it. That sense of being complete and fully a part of the world— "no longer an island, part of the mainland"—had come back. They knew that it did not come from the work alone, but from the whole—their marriage, homes, children, work, their changing, growing links with the community. They were once again human beings, not "just housewives." Such women are the lucky ones. Some may have been driven to that ambition by childhood rejection, by an ugly-duckling adolescence, by unhappiness in marriage, by divorce or widowhood. It is both an irony and an indictment of the feminine mystique that it often forced the unhappy ones, the ugly ducklings, to find themselves, while girls who fitted the image became adjusted "happy" housewives and have never found out who they are. But to say that "frustration" can be good for a girl would be to miss the point; such frustration should not have to be the price of identity for a woman, nor is it in itself the key. The mystique has kept both pretty girls and ugly ones, who might have written poems like Edith Sitwell, from discovering their own gifts; kept happy wives and unhappy ones who might have found themselves as Ruth Benedict did in anthropology, from even discovering their own field. And suddenly the final piece of the puzzle fits into place.

There was one thing without which even the most frustrated seldom found their way out of the trap. And, regardless of childhood experience, regardless of luck in marriage, there was one thing that produced frustration in all women of this time who tried to adjust to the housewife image. There was one thing shared by all I encountered who finally found their own way.

The key to the trap is, of course, education. The feminine mystique has made higher education for women seem suspect, unnecessary and even dangerous. But I think that education, and only education, has saved, and can continue to save, American women from the greater dangers of the feminine mystique.

In 1957 when I was asked to do an alumnae questionnaire of my own college classmates fifteen years after their graduation from Smith, I seized on the chance, thinking that I could disprove the growing belief that education made women "masculine," hampered their sexual fulfillment, caused unnecessary conflicts and frustrations. I discovered that the critics were half-right; education was dangerous and frustrating—but only when women did not use it.

Of the 200 women who answered that questionnaire in 1957, 89 per cent were housewives. They had lived through all the possible frustrations that education can cause in housewives. But when they were asked, "What difficulties have you found in working out your role as a woman? . . . What are the chief satisfactions and frustrations of your life today? . . . How have

you changed inside? . . . How do you feel about getting older?
. . . What do you wish you had done differently? . . ." it was
discovered that their real problems, as women, were not caused
by their education. In general, they regretted only one thing—
that they had not taken their education seriously enough, that
they had not planned to put it to serious use.

Of the 97 per cent of these women who married—usually
about three years after college—only 3 per cent had been divorced; of 20 per cent who had been interested in another man
since marriage, most "did nothing about it." As mothers, 86
per cent planned their children's births and enjoyed their pregnancies; 70 per cent breastfed their babies from one to nine
months. They had more children than their mothers (average:
2.94), but only 10 per cent had ever felt "martyred" as mothers.
Though 99 per cent reported that sex was only "one factor
among many" in their lives, they neither felt over and done with
sexually, nor were they just beginning to feel the sexual satisfaction of being a woman. Some 85 per cent reported that sex "gets
better with the years," but they also found it "less important than
it used to be." They shared life with their husbands "as fully as
one can with another human being," but 75 per cent admitted
readily that they could not share all of it.

Most of them (60 per cent) could not honestly say, in reporting their main occupation as homemaker, that they found it
"totally fulfilling." They only spent an average of four hours
a day on housework and they did not "enjoy" it. It was perhaps
true that their education made them frustrated in their role as
housewives. Educated before the era of the feminine mystique,
many of them had faced a sharp break from their emerging
identity in that housewife role. And yet most of these women
continued to grow within the framework of suburban housewifery—perhaps because of the autonomy, the sense of purpose,
the commitment to larger values which their education had given
them.

Some 79 per cent had found some way to pursue the goals that
education had given them, for the most part within the physical
confines of their communities. The old Helen Hokinson carica-

tures notwithstanding, their assumption of community responsibility was, in general, an act of maturity, a commitment that used and renewed strength of self. For these women, community activity almost always had the stamp of innovation and individuality, rather than the stamp of conformity, status-seeking, or escape. They set up cooperative nursery schools in suburbs where none existed; they started teen-age canteens and libraries in schools where Johnny wasn't reading because, quite simply, there were no good books. They innovated new educational programs that finally became a part of the curriculum. One was personally instrumental in getting 13,000 signatures for a popular referendum to get politics out of the school system. One publicly spoke out for desegregation of schools in the South. One got white children to attend a *de facto* segregated school in the North. One pushed an appropriation for mental-health clinics through a Western state legislature. One set up museum art programs for school children in each of three cities she had lived in since marriage. Others started or led suburban choral groups, civic theaters, foreign-policy study groups. Thirty per cent were active in local party politics, from the committee level to the state assembly. Over 90 per cent reported that they read the newspaper thoroughly every day and voted regularly. They evidently never watched a daytime television program and seemed almost never to play bridge, or read women's magazines. Of the fifteen to three hundred books apiece they had read in that one year, half were not best sellers.

Facing forty, most of these women could report quite frankly that their hair was graying, and their "skin looks faded and tired," and yet say, with not much regret for lost youth, "I have a growing sense of self-realization, inner serenity and strength." "I have become more my real self."

"How do you visualize your life after your children are grown?" they were asked on the questionnaire. Most of them (60 per cent) had concrete plans for work or study. They planned to finish their education finally, for many who had no career ambitions in college had them now. A few had reached "the depths of bitterness," "the verge of disillusion and despair."

trying to live just as housewives. A few confessed longingly that "running my house and raising four children does not really use my education or the ability I once seemed to have. If only it were possible to combine motherhood and a career." And the most bitter were those who said: "Never have found out what kind of a person I am. I wasted college trying to find myself in social life. I wish now that I had gone into something deeply enough to have a creative life of my own." But most did know, now, who they were and what they wanted to do; and 80 per cent regretted not having planned, seriously, to *use* their education in professional work. Passive appreciation and even active participation in community affairs would no longer be enough when their children were a little older. Many women reported that they were planning to teach; fortunately for them, the great need for teachers gave them a chance to get back in the stream. Others anticipated years of further study before they would be qualified in their chosen fields.

These 200 Smith graduates have their counterparts in women all over the country, women of intelligence and ability, fighting their way out of the housewife trap, or never really trapped at all because of their education. But these graduates of 1942 were among the last American women educated before the feminine mystique.

In another questionnaire answered by almost 10,000 graduates of Mount Holyoke in 1962—its 125th anniversary year—one sees the effect of the mystique on women educated in the last two decades. The Mount Holyoke alumnae showed a similar high marriage and low divorce rate (2 per cent over-all). But before 1942, most were married at twenty-five or older; after 1942, the marriage age showed a dramatic drop, and the percentage having four or more children showed a dramatic rise. Before 1942, two-thirds or more of the graduates went on to further study; that proportion has steadily declined. Few, in recent classes, have won advanced degrees in the arts, sciences, law, medicine, education, compared to the 40 per cent in 1937. A drastically decreasing number also seem to share the larger vistas of national or international commitment; participation in local political clubs had dropped to 12 per cent by the class of 1952. From 1942 on, few graduates had any professional affiliation. Half of all the Mount Holyoke alumnae had worked at one time but were no longer working, primarily because they had chosen "the role of housewife." Some had returned to work—both to supplement income and because they liked to work. But in the classes from 1942 on, where most of the women were now housewives, nearly half did not intend to return to work.

The declining area of commitment to the world outside the home from 1942 on is a clear indication of the effect of the feminine mystique on educated women. Having seen the desperate emptiness, the "trapped" feeling of many young women who were educated under the mystique to be "just a housewife," I realize the significance of my classmates' experience. Because of their education many of them were able to combine serious commitments of their own with marriage and family. They could participate in community activities that required intelligence and responsibility, and move on, with a few years' preparation, into professional social work or teaching. They could get jobs as substitute teachers or part-time social workers to finance the courses needed for certification. They had often grown to the point where they did not want to return to the fields they had worked in after college, and they could even get into a new field with the core of autonomy that their education had given them.

But what of the young women today who have never had a taste of higher education, who quit college to marry or marked time in their classrooms waiting for the "right man?" What will they be at forty? Housewives in every suburb and city are seeking more education today, as if a course, any course, will give them the identity they are groping toward. But the courses they take, and the courses they are offered, are seldom intended for real use in society. Even more than the education she evaded at eighteen in sexual phantasy, the education a woman can get at forty is permeated, contaminated, diluted by the feminine mystique.

Courses in golf, bridge, rug-hooking, gourmet cooking, sewing are intended, I suppose, for real use, by women who stay in the housewife trap. The so-called intellectual courses offered in the usual adult education centers—art appreciation, ceramics, short-story writing, conversational French, Great Books, astronomy in the Space Age—are intended only as "self-enrichment." The study, the effort, even the homework that imply a long-term commitment are not expected of the housewife.

Actually, many women who take these courses desperately need serious education; but if they have never had a taste of it, they do not know how and where to look for it, nor do they even understand that so many adult education courses are unsatisfactory simply because they are not serious. The dimension of reality essential even to "self-enrichment" is barred, almost by definition, in a course specifically designed for "housewives." This is true, even where the institution giving the course has the highest standards. Recently, Radcliffe announced an "Institute for Executives' Wives" (to be followed presumably by an "Institute for Scientists' Wives," or an "Institute for Artists' Wives," or an "Institute for College Professors' Wives"). The executive's wife or the scientist's wife, at thirty-five or forty, whose children are all at school is hardly going to be helped to the new identity she needs by learning to take a more detailed, vicarious share of her husband's world. What she needs is training for creative work of her own.

Among the women I interviewed, education was the key to the problem that has no name only when it was part of a new life plan, and meant for serious use in society—amateur or professional. They were able to find such education only in the regular colleges and universities. Despite the wishful thinking engendered by the feminine mystique in girls and in their educators, an education evaded at eighteen or twenty-one is insuperably harder to obtain at thirty-one or thirty-eight or forty-one, by a woman who has a husband and three or four children and a home. She faces, in the college or university, the prejudices created by the feminine mystique. No matter how brief her absence from the academic proving ground, she will have to demonstrate her seriousness of purpose over and over again to be readmitted. She must then compete with the teeming hordes of children she and others like her have overproduced in this era. It is not easy for a grown woman to sit through courses geared to teenagers, to be treated as a teenager again, to have to prove that she deserves to be taken as seriously as a teenager. A woman has to exercise great ingenuity, endure many rebuffs and disappointments, to find an education that fits her need, and also make it fit her other commitments as wife and mother.

One woman I interviewed who had never gone to college, decided, after psychotherapy, to take two courses a year at a nearby university which, fortunately, had an evening school. At first, she had no idea where it was leading her, but after two years, she decided to major in history and prepare to teach it in high school. She maintained a good record, even though she was often impatient with the slow pace and the busywork. But, at least, studying with some purpose made her feel better than when she used to read mystery stories or magazines at the playground. Above all, it was leading to something real for the future. But at the rate of two courses a year (which then cost $420, and two evenings a week in class), it would have taken her ten years to get a B.A. The second year, money was scarce, and she could only take one course. She could not apply for a student loan unless she went full time, which she could not do until her youngest was in first grade. In spite of it all, she stuck it out that way for four years—noticing that more and more of the other housewives in her classes dropped out because of money, or because "the whole thing was going to take too long."

Then, with her youngest in first grade, she became a full-time student in the regular college, where the pace was even slower because the students were "less serious." She couldn't endure the thought of all the years ahead to get an M.A. (which she would need to teach high-school history in that state), so she switched to an education major. She certainly would not have continued this expensive, tortuous education if, by now, she had not had a clear life plan to use it, a plan that required it. Committed to elementary teaching, she was able to get a government loan for part of her full-time tuition (now exceeding $1,000 a year), and in another two years she will be finished.

Even against such enormous obstacles, more and more women, with virtually no help from society and with belated and begrudging encouragement from educators themselves, are going back to school to get the education they need. Their determination betrays women's underestimated human strength and their urgent need to use it. But only the strongest, after nearly twenty years of the feminine mystique, can move on by themselves. For this is not just the private problem of each individual woman. There are implications of the feminine mystique that must be faced on a national scale.

The problem that has no name—which is simply the fact that American women are kept from growing to their full human capacities—is taking a far greater toll on the physical and mental health of our country than any known disease. Consider the high incidence of emotional breakdown of women in the "role crises" of their twenties and thirties; the alcoholism and suicides in their forties and fifties; the housewives' monopolization of all doctors' time. Consider the prevalence of teenage marriages, the growing rate of illegitimate pregnancies, and even more seriously, the pathology of mother-child symbiosis. Consider the alarming passivity of American teenagers. If we continue to produce millions of young mothers who stop their growth and education short of identity, without a strong core of human values to pass on to their children, we are committing, quite simply, genocide, starting with the mass burial of American women and ending with the progressive dehumanization of their sons and daughters.

These problems cannot be solved by medicine, or even by psychotherapy. We need a drastic reshaping of the cultural image of femininity that will permit women to reach maturity, identity, completeness of self, without conflict with sexual fulfillment. A massive attempt must be made by educators and parents—and ministers, magazine editors, manipulators, guidance counselors— to stop the early-marriage movement, stop girls from growing up wanting to be "just a housewife," stop it by insisting, with the same attention from childhood on that parents and educators give to boys, that girls develop the resources of self, goals that will permit them to find their own identity.

It is, of course, no easier for an educator to say "no" to the feminine mystique than for an individual girl or woman. Even the most advanced of educators, seriously concerned with the desperate need of housewives with leftover lives on their hands, hesitate to buck the tide of early marriage. They have been brow-beaten by the oracles of popularized psychoanalysis and still tremble with guilt at the thought of interfering with a woman's sexual fulfillment. The rearguard argument offered by the oracles who are, in some cases, right on college campuses themselves, is that since the primary road to identity for a woman is marriage and motherhood, serious educational interests or commitments which may cause conflicts in her role as wife and mother should be postponed until the childbearing years are over. Such a warning was made in 1962 by a psychiatric consultant to Yale University—which had been considering admitting women as undergraduates for the same serious education it gives men.

Many young women—if not the majority—seem to be incapable of dealing with future long-range intellectual interests until they have proceeded through the more basic phases of their own healthy growth as women. . . . To be well done, the mother's job in training children and shaping the life of her family should draw on all a woman's resources, emotional and intellectual, and upon all her skills. The better her training, the better chance she will have to do the job well, provided that emotional road-blocks do not stand in her way: provided, that is, that she has established a good basis for the development of adult femininity, and that during the course of her higher education, she is not subjected to pressures which adversely affect that development. . . . To urge upon her conflicting goals, to stress that a career and a profession in the man's world should be the first consideration in planning her life, can adversely affect the full development of her identity. . . . Of all the social freedoms won by her grandmothers, she prizes first the freedom to be a healthy, fulfilled woman, and she wants to be free of guilt and conflict about it. . . . This means that though jobs are often possible within the framework of marriage, "careers" rarely are . . .[5]

The fact remains that the girl who wastes—as waste she does —her college years without acquiring serious interests, and wastes

her early job years marking time until she finds a man, gambles
with the possibilities for an identity of her own, as well as the
possibilities for sexual fulfillment and wholly affirmed motherhood. The educators who encourage a woman to postpone larger
interests until her children are grown make it virtually impossible
for her ever to acquire them. It is not that easy for a woman
who has defined herself wholly as wife and mother for ten or
fifteen or twenty years to find new identity at thirty-five or forty
or fifty. The ones who are able to do it are, quite frankly, the
ones who made serious commitments to their earlier education, the
ones who wanted and once worked at careers, the ones who bring
to marriage and motherhood a sense of their own identity—not
those who somehow hope to acquire it later on. A recent study
of fifty women college graduates in an eastern suburb and city,
the year after the oldest child had left home, showed that, with
very few exceptions, the only women who had any interests to
pursue—in work, in community activities, or in the arts—had
acquired them in college. The ones who lacked such interests
were not acquiring them now; they slept late, in their "empty
nests," and looked forward only to death.[6]

Educators at every women's college, at every university, junior
college, and community college, must see to it that women make
a lifetime commitment (call it a "life plan," a "vocation," a "life
purpose" if that dirty word *career* has too many celibate connotations) to a field of thought, to work of serious importance
to society. They must expect the girl as well as the boy to take
some field seriously enough to want to pursue it for life. This
does not mean abandoning liberal education for women in favor
of "how to" vocational courses. Liberal education, as it is given
at the best of colleges and universities, not only trains the mind
but provides an ineradicable core of human values. But liberal
education must be planned for serious use, not merely dilettant-
ism or passive appreciation. As boys at Harvard or Yale or Columbia or Chicago go on from the liberal arts core to study architecture, medicine, law, science, girls must be encouraged to go
on, to make a life plan. It has been shown that girls with this kind
of a commitment are less eager to rush into early marriage, less

panicky about finding a man, more responsible for their sexual behavior.[7] Most of them marry, of course, but on a much more mature basis. Their marriages then are not an escape but a commitment shared by two people that becomes part of their commitment to themselves and society. If, in fact, girls are educated to make such commitments, the question of sex and when they marry will lose its overwhelming importance.[8] It is the fact that women have no identity of their own that makes sex, love, marriage, and children seem the only and essential facts of women's life.

In the face of the feminine mystique with its powerful hidden deterrents, educators must realize that they cannot inspire young women to commit themselves seriously to their education without taking some extraordinary measures. The few so far attempted barely come to grips with the problem. Mary Bunting's new Institute for Independent Study at Radcliffe is fine for women who already know what they want to do, who have pursued their studies to the Ph.D. or are already active in the arts, and merely need some respite from motherhood to get back in the mainstream. Even more important, the presence of these women on the campus, women who have babies and husbands and who are still deeply committed to their own work, will undoubtedly help dispel the image of the celibate career woman and fire some of those Radcliffe sophomores out of the "climate of unexpectation" that permits them to meet the nation's highest standard of educational excellence to use it later only in marriage and motherhood. This is what Mary Bunting had in mind. And it can be done elsewhere, in even simpler ways.

It would pay every college and university that wants to encourage women to take education seriously to recruit for their faculties all the women they can find who have combined marriage and motherhood with the life of the mind—even if it means concessions for pregnancies or breaking the old rule about hiring the wife of the male associate professor who has her own perfectly respectable M.A. or Ph.D. As for the unmarried woman scholars, they must no longer be treated like lepers. The simple truth is that they have taken their existence seriously, and have

fulfilled their human potential. They might well be, and often
are, envied by women who live the very image of opulent togetherness, but have forfeited themselves. Women, as well as
men, who are rooted in human work are rooted in life.

It is essential, above all, for educators themselves to say "no"
to the feminine mystique and face the fact that the only point
in educating women is to educate them to the limit of their
ability. Women do not need courses in "marriage and the family"
to marry and raise families; they do not need courses in homemaking to make homes. But they must study science—to discover in science; study the thought of the past—to create new
thought; study society—to pioneer in society. Educators must
also give up these "one thing at a time" compromises. That separate layering of "education," "sex," "marriage," "motherhood,"
"interests for the last third of life," will not solve the role crisis.
Women must be educated to a new integration of roles. The
more they are encouraged to make that new life plan—integrat-
ing a serious, lifelong commitment to society with marriage and
motherhood—the less conflicts and unnecessary frustrations they
will feel as wives and mothers, and the less their daughters will
make mistaken choices for lack of a full image of woman's identity.

I could see this in investigating college girls' rush to early marriage. The few who were not in such a desperate hurry to "get
a man" and who committed themselves to serious long-range interests—evidently not worried that they would thereby lose their
"femininity"—almost all had mothers, or other private images of
women, who were committed to some serious purpose. ("My
mother happens to be a teacher." "My best friend's mother is a
doctor; she always seems so busy and happy.")

Education itself can help provide that new image—and the
spark in girls to create their own—as soon as it stops compromising and temporizing with the old image of "woman's role." For
women as well as men, education is and must be the matrix of
human evolution. If today American women are finally breaking
out of the housewife trap in search of new identity, it is quite
simply because so many women have had a taste of higher edu-

cation—unfinished, unfocused, but still powerful enough to force them on.

For that last and most important battle *can* be fought in the mind and spirit of woman herself. Even without a private image, many girls in America who have been educated simply as people were given a strong enough sense of their human possibility to carry them past the old femininity, past that search for security in man's love, to find a new self. A Swarthmore graduate, entering her internship, told me that at first, as she felt herself getting more and more "independent" in college, she worried a lot about having dates and getting married, wanted to "latch on to a boy." "I tried to beat myself down to be feminine. Then I got interested in what I was doing and stopped worrying," she said.

It's as if you've made some kind of shift. You begin to feel your competence in doing things. Like a baby learning to walk. Your mind begins to expand. You find your own field. And that's a wonderful thing. The love of doing the work and the feeling there's something there and you can trust it. It's worth the unhappiness. They say a man has to suffer to grow, maybe something like that has to happen to women too. You begin not to be afraid to be yourself.

Drastic steps must now be taken to re-educate the women who were deluded or cheated by the feminine mystique. Many of the women I interviewed who felt "trapped" as housewives have in the last few years started to move out of the trap. But there are as many others who are sinking back again, because they did not find out in time what they wanted to do, or because they were not able to find a way to do it. In almost every case, it took too much time, too much money, using existing educational facilities. Few housewives can afford full-time study. Even if colleges admit them on a part-time basis—and many will not—few women can endure the slow-motion pace of usual undergraduate college education stretched over ten or more years. Some institutions are now willing to gamble on housewives, but will they be as willing when the flood of their college-bound offspring reaches its full height? The pilot programs that have been started at Sarah Lawrence and the University of Minnesota begin to show the way, but they do not face the time-money problem which is, for so many women, the insurmountable one.

What is needed now is a national educational program, similar to the GI bill, for women who seriously want to continue or resume their education—and who are willing to commit themselves to its use in a profession. The bill would provide properly qualified women with tuition fees, plus an additional subsidy to defray other expenses—books, travel, even, if necessary, some household help. Such a measure would cost far less than the GI bill. It would permit mothers to use existing educational facilities on a part-time basis and carry on individual study and research projects at home during the years when regular classroom attendance is impossible. The whole concept of women's education would be regeared from four-year college to a life plan under which a woman could continue her education, without conflict with her marriage, her husband and her children.

The GI's, matured by war, needed education to find their identity in society. In no mood for time-wasting, they astonished their teachers and themselves by their scholastic performance. Women who have matured during the housewife moratorium can be counted on for similar performance. Their desperate need for education and the desperate need of this nation for the untapped reserves of women's intelligence in all the professions justify these emergency measures.[9]

For those women who did not go to college, or quit too soon, for those who are no longer interested in their former field, or who never took their education seriously, I would suggest first of all an intensive concentrated re-immersion in, quite simply, the humanities—not abridgments and selections like the usual freshman or sophomore survey, but an intensive study like the educational experiments attempted by the Bell Telephone Company or the Ford Foundation for young executives who had conformed so completely to the role of organization man that they were not capable of the initiative and vision required in top executive ranks. For women, this could be done by a national program, along the lines of the Danish Folk-High-School movement, which would first bring the housewife back into the mainstream of thought with a concentrated six-week summer course, a sort of intellectual "shock therapy." She would be subsidized so that she could leave home and go to a resident college, which is not otherwise used during the summer. Or she could go to a metropolitan center on an equally intensive basis, five days a week for six or eight weeks during the summer, with a day camp provided for the children.

Assume that this educational shock treatment awakens able women to purposes requiring the equivalent of a four-year college program for further professional training. That college program could be completed in four years or less, without full-time classroom attendance, by a combination of these summer institutes, plus prescribed reading, papers, and projects that could be done during the winter at home. Courses taken on television or at local community colleges and universities on an extension basis, could be combined with tutorial conferences at midyear or every month. The courses would be taken for credit, and the customary degrees would be earned. Some system of "equivalents" would have to be worked out, not to give a woman credit for work that does not meet requirements, but to give her credit for truly serious work, even if it is done at times, places, and in ways that violate conventional academic standards.

A number of universities automatically bar housewives by barring part-time undergraduate or graduate work. Perhaps they have been burned by dilettantes. But part-time college work, graduate or undergraduate, geared to a serious plan, is the only kind of education that can prevent a housewife from becoming a dilettante; it is the only way a woman with husband and children can get, or continue, an education. It could also be the most practical arrangement from the university's point of view. With their facilities already overtaxed by population pressures, universities and women alike would benefit from a study program that does not require regular classroom attendance. While it makes a great deal of sense for the University of Minnesota to work out its excellent Plan for Women's Continuing Education [10] in terms of the regular university facilities, such a plan will not help the woman who must begin her education all over again to find out what she wants to do. But existing facilities, in any institution, can be used to fill in the gaps once a woman is under way on her life plan.

Colleges and universities also need a new life plan—to become lifetime institutions for their students; offer them guidance, take care of their records, and keep track of their advanced work or refresher courses, no matter where they are taken. How much greater that allegiance and financial support from their alumnae if, instead of the teaparties to raise funds and a sentimental reunion every fifth June, a woman could look to her college for continuing education and guidance. Barnard alumnae can, and do, come back and take, free, any course at any time, if they meet the qualifications for it. All colleges could conduct summer institutes to keep alumnae abreast of developments in their fields during the years of young motherhood. They could accept parttime students and offer extension courses for the housewife who could not attend classes regularly. They could advise her on reading programs, papers, or projects that could be done at home. They could also work out a system whereby projects done by their alumnae in education, mental health, sociology, political science in their own communities could be counted as equivalent credits toward a degree. Instead of collecting dimes, let women volunteers serve supervised professional apprenticeships and collect the credits that are recognized in lieu of pay for medical internes. Similarly, when a woman has taken courses at a number of different institutions, perhaps due to her husband's geographical itinerary, and has earned her community credits from agency, hospital, library or laboratory, her college of origin, or some national center set up by several colleges, could give her the orals, the comprehensives, and the appropriate examinations for a degree. The concept of "continuing education" is already a reality for men in many fields. Why not for women? Not education for careers instead of motherhood, not education for temporary careers before motherhood, not education to make them "better wives and mothers," but an education they will use as full members of society.

"But how many American women really want to do more

with their lives?" the cynic asks. A fantastic number of New Jersey housewives responded to an offer of intensive retraining in mathematics for former college women willing to commit themselves to becoming mathematics teachers. In January, 1962, a simple news story in the *New York Times* announced that Sarah Lawrence's Esther Raushenbush had obtained a grant to help mature women finish their education or work for graduate degrees on a part-time basis that could be fitted in with their obligations as mothers. The response literally put the small Sarah Lawrence switchboard out of commission. Within twenty-four hours, Mrs. Raushenbush had taken over 100 telephone calls. "It was like bank night," the operator said. "As if they had to get in there right away, or they might miss the chance." Interviewing the women who applied for the program, Mrs. Raushenbush, like Virginia Senders at Minnesota, was convinced of the realit of their need. They were not "neurotically rejecting" their husbands and children; they did not need psychotherapy, but they did need more education—in a hurry—and in a form they could get without neglecting their husbands and families.

Education and re-education of American women for a serious purpose cannot be effected by one or two far-sighted institutions; it must be accomplished on a much wider scale. And no one serves this end who repeats, even for expedience or tact, the clichés of the feminine mystique. It is quite wrong to say, as some of the leading women educators are saying today, that women must of course use their education, but not, heaven forbid, in careers that will compete with men.[11] When women take their education and their abilities seriously and put them to use, ultimately they have to compete with men. It is better for a woman to compete impersonally in society, as men do, than to compete for dominance in her own home with her husband, compete with her neighbors for empty status, and so smother her son that he cannot compete at all. Consider this recent news item about America's latest occupational therapy for the pent-up feminine need to compete:

It is a typical weekday in Dallas. Daddy is at work. Baby is having his morning nap. In an adjoining room, Brother (age 3) is riding a new

rocking horse and Sis (5) is watching TV cartoons. And Mommy?
Mommy is just a few feet away, crouching over the foul line on Lane
53, her hip twisted sharply to the left to steer the blue-white-marbled
ball into the strike pocket between the one and three pins. Mommy
is bowling. Whether in Dallas or Cleveland or Albuquerque or Spo-
kane, energetic housewives have dropped dustcloth and vacuum and
hauled the children off to the new alleys, where fulltime nurses stand
ready to babysit in the fully equipped nurseries.
Said the manager of Albuquerque's Bowl-a-Drome: "Where else
can a woman compete after she gets married? They need competition
just like men do. . . . It sure beats going home to do the dishes!" [12]

It is perhaps beside the point to remark that bowling alleys
and supermarkets have nursery facilities, while schools and colleges and scientific laboratories and government offices do not.
But it is very much to the point to say that if an able American
woman does not use her human energy and ability in some meaningful pursuit (which necessarily means competition, for there
is competition in every serious pursuit of our society), she will
fritter away her energy in neurotic symptoms, or unproductive
exercise, or destructive "love."

It also is time to stop giving lip service to the idea that there
are no battles left to be fought for women in America, that
women's rights have already been won. It is ridiculous to tell
girls to keep quiet when they enter a new field, or an old one,
so the men will not notice they are there. In almost every professional field, in business and in the arts and sciences, women
are still treated as second-class citizens. It would be a great service
to tell girls who plan to work in society to expect this subtle,
uncomfortable discrimination—tell them not to be quiet, and
hope it will go away, but fight it. A girl should not expect special
privileges because of her sex, but neither should she "adjust" to
prejudice and discrimination.

She must learn to compete then, not as a woman, but as a
human being. Not until a great many women move out of the
fringes into the mainstream will society itself provide the arrangements for their new life plan. But every girl who manages to stick
it out through law school or medical school, who finishes her

M.A. or Ph.D. and goes on to use it, helps others move on. Every woman who fights the remaining barriers to full equality which are masked by the feminine mystique makes it easier for the next woman. The very existence of the President's Commission on the Status of Women, under Eleanor Roosevelt's leadership, creates a climate where it is possible to recognize and do something about discrimination against women, in terms not only of pay but of the subtle barriers to opportunity. Even in politics, women must make their contribution not as "housewives" but as citizens. It is, perhaps, a step in the right direction when a woman protests nuclear testing under the banner of "Women Strike for Peace." But why does the professional illustrator who heads the movement say she is "just a housewife," and her followers insist that once the testing stops, they will stay happily at home with their children? Even in the city strongholds of the big political party machines, women can—and are beginning to—change the insidious unwritten rules which let them do the political housework while the men make the decisions.[13]

When enough women make life plans geared to their real abilities, and speak out for maternity leaves or even maternity sabbaticals, professionally run nurseries, and the other changes in the rules that may be necessary, they will not have to sacrifice the right to honorable competition and contribution anymore than they will have to sacrifice marriage and motherhood. It is wrong to keep spelling out unnecessary choices that make women unconsciously resist either commitment or motherhood [14]—and that hold back recognition of the needed social changes. It is not a question of women having their cake and eating it, too. A woman is handicapped by her sex, and handicaps society, either by slavishly copying the pattern of man's advance in the professions, or by refusing to compete with man at all. But with the vision to make a new life plan of her own, she can fulfill a commitment to profession and politics, and to marriage and motherhood with equal seriousness.

Women who have done this, in spite of the dire warnings of the feminine mystique, are in a sense "mutations," the image of what the American woman can be. When they did not or could not work full time for a living, they spent part-time hours on work which truly interested them. Because time was of the essence, they often skipped the time-wasting, self-serving details of both housewifery and professional busywork.

Whether they knew it or not, they were following a life plan. They had their babies before or after internship, between fellowships. If good full-time help was not available in the children's early years, they gave up their jobs and took a part-time post that may not have paid handsomely, but kept them moving ahead in their profession. The teachers innovated in PTA, and substituted; the doctors took clinical or research jobs close to home; the editors and writers started free-lancing. Even if the money they made was not needed for groceries or household help (and usually it was), they earned tangible proof of their ability to contribute. They did not consider themselves "lucky" to be housewives; they competed in society. They knew that marriage and motherhood are an essential part of life, but not the whole of it.

These "mutations" suffered—and surmounted—the "cultural discontinuity in role conditioning," the "role crisis" and the identity crisis. They had problems, of course, tough ones—juggling their pregnancies, finding nurses and housekeepers, having to give up good assignments when their husbands were transferred. They also had to take a lot of hostility from other women—and many had to live with the active resentment of their husbands. And, because of the mystique, many suffered unnecessary pains of guilt. It took, and still takes, extraordinary strength of purpose for women to pursue their own life plans when society does not expect it of them. However, unlike the trapped housewives whose problems multiply with the years, these women solved their problems and moved on. They resisted the mass persuasions and manipulations, and did not give up their own, often painful, values for the comforts of conformity. They did not retreat into privatism, but met the challenges of the real world. And they know quite surely now who they are.

They were doing, perhaps without seeing it clearly, what every man and woman must do now to keep up with the increasingly explosive pace of history, and find or keep individual identity in our mass society. The identity crisis in men and women cannot be solved by one generation for the next; in our rapidly changing society, it must be faced continually, solved only to be faced again in the span of a single lifetime. A life plan must be open to change, as new possibilities open, in society and in oneself. No woman in America today who starts her search for identity can be sure where it will take her. No woman starts that search today without struggle, conflict, and taking her courage in her hands. But the women I met, who were moving on that unknown road, did not regret the pains, the efforts, the risks.

In the light of woman's long battle for emancipation, the recent sexual counterrevolution in America has been perhaps a final crisis, a strange breath-holding interval before the larva breaks out of the shell into maturity—a moratorium during which many millions of women put themselves on ice and stopped growing. They say that one day science will be able to make the human body live longer by freezing its growth. American women lately have been living much longer than men—walking through their leftover lives like living dead women. Perhaps men may live longer in America when women carry more of the burden of the battle with the world, instead of being a burden themselves. I think their wasted energy will continue to be destructive to their husbands, to their children, and to themselves until it is used in their own battle with the world. But when women as well as men emerge from biological living to realize their human selves, those leftover halves of life may become their years of greatest fulfillment.[16]

Then the split in the image will be healed, and daughters will not face that jumping-off point at twenty-one or forty-one. When their mothers' fulfillment makes girls sure they want to be women, they will not have to "beat themselves down" to be feminine; they can stretch and stretch until their own efforts will tell them who they are. They will not need the regard of boy or man to feel alive. And when women do not need to live through their husbands and children, men will not fear the love and strength of women, nor need another's weakness to prove their own masculinity. They can finally see each other as they are. And this may be the next step in human evolution.

Who knows what women can be when they are finally free to become themselves? Who knows what women's intelligence will contribute when it can be nourished without denying love? Who knows of the possibilities of love when men and women share not only children, home, and garden, not only the fulfillment of their biological roles, but the responsibilities and passions of the work that creates the human future and the full human knowledge of who they are? It has barely begun, the search of women for themselves. But the time is at hand when the voices of the feminine mystique can no longer drown out the inner voice that is driving women on to become complete.

Epilogue

When *The Feminine Mystique* was at the printer's, and my last child was in school all day, I decided I would go back to school myself and get my Ph.D. Armed with my publisher's announcement, a copy of my *summa cum laude* undergraduate degree and twenty-years-back graduate record, and the New World Foundation report of the educational project I had dreamed up and run in Rockland County, I went to see the head of the social psychology department at Columbia. He was very tolerant and kind, but surely, at forty-two, after all those undisciplined years as a housewife, I must understand that I wouldn't be able to meet the rigors of full-time graduate study for a Ph.D. and the mastery of statistics that was required. "But I used statistics throughout the book," I pointed out. He looked blank. "Well, my dear," he said, "what do you want to bother your head getting a Ph.D. for, anyhow?"

I began to get letters from other women who now saw through the feminine mystique, who wanted to stop doing their children's homework and start doing their own; they were also being told they really weren't capable of doing anything else now but making homemade strawberry jam or helping their children do fourth-grade arithmetic. It wasn't enough just to take yourself seriously as a person. Society had to change, somehow, for women to make it as people. It wasn't possible to live any longer as "just a housewife." But what other way was there to live?

I remember getting stuck at that point, even when I was writing *The Feminine Mystique*. I had to write a last chapter, giving a solution to "the problem that has no name," suggesting new patterns, a way out of the conflicts, whereby women could use their abilities fully in society and find their own existential human identity, sharing its action, decisions, and challenges without at the same time renouncing home, children, love, their own sexuality. My mind went blank. You do have to say "no" to the old way before you can begin to find the new "yes" you need. Giving a name to the problem that had no name was the necessary first step. But it wasn't enough.

Personally, I couldn't operate as a suburban housewife any longer, even if I had wanted to. For one thing, I became a leper in my own suburb. As long as I only wrote occasional articles most people never read, the fact that I wrote during the hours when the children were in school was no more a stigma than, for instance, solitary morning drinking. But now that I was acting like a real writer and even being interviewed on television, the sin was too public, it could not be condoned. Women in other suburbs were writing me letters as if I were Joan of Arc, but I practically had to flee my own crabgrass-overgrown yard to keep from being burned at the stake. Although we had been fairly popular, my husband and I were suddenly no longer invited to our neighbors' dinner parties. My kids were kicked out of the car pool for art and dancing classes. The other mothers had a fit when I now called a cab when it was my turn, instead of driving the children myself. We had to move back to the city, where the kids could do their own thing without my chauffeuring and where I could be with them at home during some of the hours I now spent commuting. I couldn't stand being a freak alone in the suburbs any longer.

At first, that strange hostility my book—and later the movement—seemed to elicit from some women amazed and puzzled me. Even in the beginning, there wasn't the hostility I had expected from men. Many men bought *The Feminine Mystique* for their wives and urged them to go back to school or to work. I realized soon enough that there were probably millions of women who had felt as I had, like a freak, absolutely alone, as a suburban housewife. But if you were afraid to face your real feelings about the husband and children you were presumably living for, then someone like me opening up the can of worms was a menace.

I didn't blame women for being scared. I was pretty scared myself. It isn't really possible to make a new pattern of life all by yourself. I've always dreaded being alone more than anything else. The anger I had not dared to face in myself during all the years I tried to play the helpless little housewife with my husband —and feeling more helpless the longer I played it—was beginning to erupt now, more and more violently. For fear of being alone, I almost lost my own self-respect trying to hold on to a marriage that was based no longer on love but on dependent hate. It was easier for me to start the women's movement which was needed to change society than to change my own personal life.

It seemed time to start writing that second book, but I couldn't find any new patterns in society beyond the feminine mystique. I could find a few individual women, knocking themselves out to meet *Good Housekeeping* standards, trying to raise Spockian children while working at a full-time job and feeling guilty about it. And conferences were being held about the availability of continuing education for women, because all those aging full-time housewife-mothers, whose babies were now in college, were beginning to be trouble—drinking, taking too many pills, committing suicide. Whole learned journals were devoted to the discussion of "women and their options"—the "stages" of women's lives. Women, we were told, could go to school, work a bit, get married, stay with the children fifteen to twenty years, and then go back to school and work—no problem; no need for role conflicts.

The women who were advancing this theory were among the exceptional few to reach top jobs because they somehow had *not* dropped out for fifteen or twenty years. And these same women were advising the women flocking back to their continuing-education programs that they couldn't really expect to get real jobs or professional training after fifteen years at home;

ceramics, or professional volunteer work—that was the realistic adjustment.

Talk, that's all it was, talk. In 1965, the long awaited report of the President's Commission on the Status of Women detailed the discriminatory wages women were earning (half the average for men), and the declining ratio of women in professional and executive jobs. The Commission recommended that women be counseled to use their abilities in society, and suggested that child-care centers and other services be provided to enable women to combine motherhood and work. But Margaret Mead, in her introduction to the report, said, in effect, If women are all going to want to make big decisions and discoveries, who is going to stay home and bandage the child's knee or listen to the husband's troubles? (No matter that, with her husbands' help and even before her child's knees were in school all day, she herself was making big anthropological discoveries and decisions. Perhaps women who have made it as "exceptional" women don't really identify with other women. For them, there are three classes of people: men, other women, and themselves; their very status as exceptional women depends on keeping other women quiet, and not rocking the boat.)

The President's Commission report was duly buried in bureaucratic file drawers. That summer of 1965, I got a third of the way through the book I wanted to write about going beyond the feminine mystique; by then I knew that there weren't any new patterns, only new problems that women weren't going to be able to solve unless society changed. And all the talk, and the reports, and the Commission, and the continuing-education programs were only examples of tokenism—maybe even an attempt to block a real movement on the part of women themselves to change society.

It seemed to me that something more than talk had to happen. "The only thing that's changed so far is our own consciousness," I wrote, closing that second book, which I never finished, because the next sentence read, "What we need is a political movement, a social movement like that of the blacks." I had to take action. On the plane to Washington, pondering what to do, I saw a student reading a book, *The First Step to Revolution Is Consciousness*, and it was like an omen.

I went to Washington because a law had been passed, Title VII of the Civil Rights Act of 1964, banning sex discrimination in employment along with race discrimination. The sex discrimination part had been tacked on as a joke and a delaying maneuver by a southern congressman, Howard Smith of Virginia. At the first press conferences after the law went into effect, the administrator in charge of enforcing it joked about the ban on sex discrimination. "It will give men equal opportunity to be *Playboy* bunnies," he said.

In Washington I found a seething underground of women in the government, the press, and the labor unions who felt powerless to stop the sabotage of this law that was supposed to break through the sex discrimination that pervaded every industry and profession, every factory, school, and office. Some of these women felt that I, as a now known writer, could get the public's ear.

One day, a cool young woman lawyer, who worked for the agency that was not enforcing the law against sex discrimination, carefully closed the door of her office and said to me with tears in her eyes, "I never meant to be so concerned about women. I like men. But I'm getting an ulcer, the way women are being betrayed. We may never have another chance like this law again. Betty, you have to start an NAACP for women. You are the only one free enough to do it."

I wasn't an organization woman. I never even belonged to the League of Women Voters. However, there was a meeting of state commissioners on the status of women in Washington in June. I thought that, among the women there from the various states, we would get the nucleus of an organization that could at least call a press conference and raise the alarm among women throughout the country.

Pauli Murray, an eminent black lawyer, came to that meeting, and Dorothy Haener and Caroline Davis from the UAW, and Kay Clarenbach, head of the Governor's Commission in Wisconsin, and Katherine Conroy of the Communications Workers of America, and Aileen Hernandez, then a member of the Equal

Employment Opportunities Commission. I asked them to come to my hotel room one night. Most didn't think women needed a movement like the blacks, but everyone was mad at the sabotage of Title VII. The consensus was that the conference could surely take respectable action to insist that the law be enforced.

I went to bed relieved that probably a movement wouldn't have to be organized. At six the next morning, I got a call from one of the top token women in the Johnson administration, urging me not to rock the boat. At eight the phone rang again; this time it was one of the reluctant sisters of the night before, angry now, really angry. "We've been told that this conference doesn't have the power to take any action at all, or even the right to offer a resolution. So we've got a table for us all to eat together at lunch, and we'll start the organization." At the luncheon we each chipped in a dollar. I wrote the word "NOW" on a paper napkin; our group should be called the National Organization *for* Women, I said, "because men should be part of it." Then I wrote down the first sentence of the NOW statement of purpose, committing ourselves to "take *action* to bring women into full participation in the mainstream of American society now, exercising all the privileges and responsibilities thereof, in truly equal partnership with men."

The changes necessary to bring about that equality were, and still are, very revolutionary indeed. They involve a sex-role revolution for men and women which will restructure all our institutions: child rearing, education, marriage, the family, the architecture of the home, the practice of medicine, work, politics, the economy, religion, psychological theory, human sexuality, morality, and the very evolution of the race.

I now see the women's movement for equality as simply the necessary first stage of a much larger sex-role revolution. I never did see it in terms of class or race: women, as an oppressed class, fighting to overthrow or take power away from men as a class, the oppressors. I knew the movement had to include men as equal members, though women would have to take the lead in the first stage.

There is only one way for women to reach full human potential—by participating in the mainstream of society, by exercising their own voice in all the decisions shaping that society. For women to have full identity and freedom, they must have economic independence. Breaking through the barriers that had kept them from the jobs and professions rewarded by society was the first step, but it wasn't sufficient. It would be necessary to change the rules of the game to restructure professions, marriage, the family, the home. The manner in which offices and hospitals are structured, along the rigid, separate, unequal, unbridgeable lines of secretary/executive, nurse/doctor, embodies and perpetuates the feminine mystique. But the economic part would never be complete unless a dollar value was somehow put on the work done by women in the home, at least in terms of social security, pensions, retirement pay. And housework and child rearing would have to be more equally shared by husband, wife, and society.

Equality and human dignity are not possible for women if they are not able to earn. When the young radical kids came into the movement, they said it was "boring" or "reformist" or "capitalist co-option" to place so much emphasis on jobs and education. But very few women can afford to ignore the elementary economic facts of life. Only economic independence can free a woman to marry for love, not for status or financial support, or to leave a loveless, intolerable, humiliating marriage, or to eat, dress, rest, and move if she plans not to marry. But the importance of work for women goes beyond economics. How else can women participate in the action and decisions of an advanced industrial society unless they have the training and opportunity and skills that come from participating in it?

Women also had to confront their sexual nature, not deny or ignore it as earlier feminists had done. Society had to be restructured so that women, who happen to be the people who give birth, could make a human, responsible choice whether or not—and when—to have children, and not be barred thereby from participating in society in their own right. This meant the right to birth control and safe abortion; the right to maternity leave and child-care centers if women did not want to retreat completely from adult society during the childbearing years; and the equivalent of a GI bill for retraining if women chose to stay home with the children. For it seemed to me that most women would still choose to have children, though not so many if child rearing was no longer their only road to status and economic support—a vicarious participation in life.

I couldn't define "liberation" for women in terms that denied the sexual and human reality of our need to love, and even sometimes to depend upon, a man. What had to be changed was the obsolete feminine and masculine sex roles that dehumanized sex, making it almost impossible for women and men to make love, not war. How could we ever really know or love each other as long as we played those roles that kept us from knowing or being ourselves? Weren't men as well as women still locked in lonely isolation, alienation, no matter how many sexual acrobatics they put their bodies through? Weren't men dying too young, suppressing fears and tears and their own tenderness? It seemed to me that men weren't really the enemy—they were fellow victims, suffering from an outmoded masculine mystique that made them feel unnecessarily inadequate when there were no bears to kill.

In these past years of action, I have seen myself and other women becoming both stronger and more gentle, taking ourselves more seriously, yet beginning to really have fun as we stopped playing the old roles. We discovered we could trust each other. I love the women with whom I took the adventurous and joyous actions of these years. No one realized how pitifully few we were in the beginning, how little money we had, how little experience.

What gave us the strength and the nerve to do what we did, in the name of American women, of women of the world? It was, of course, because we were doing it for ourselves. It was not charity for poor others; we, the middle-class women who started this, were all poor, in a sense that goes beyond dollars. It was hard even for housewives whose husbands weren't poor to get money to fly to board meetings of NOW. It was hard for women who worked to get time off from their jobs, or take precious weekend time from their families. I have never worked so hard for money, gone so many hours with so little sleep or

time off to eat or even go to the toilet, as in these first years of
the women's movement.

I was subpoenaed on Christmas Eve, 1966, to testify before a
judge in Foley Square, because the airlines were outraged at our
insistence that they were guilty of sex discrimination by forcing
stewardesses to resign at age thirty or upon their marriage. (Why,
I had wondered, are they going to such lengths? Surely they don't
think men ride the airlines because stewardesses are nubile. And
then I realized how much money the airlines saved by firing
those pretty stewardesses before they had time to accumulate
pay increases, vacation time, and pension rights. And how I love
it now when stewardesses hug me on an airplane and tell me they
are not only married and over thirty, but can even have children
and keep flying!)

I felt a certain urgency of history, that we would be failing
the generation coming up if we evaded the question of abortion
now. I also felt we had to get the Equal Rights Amendment
added to the Constitution despite the claim of union leaders that
it would end "protective" laws for women. We had to take the
torch of equality from the lonely, bitter old women who had
been fighting all alone for the amendment, which had been bot-
tled up in Congress for nearly fifty years since women had
chained themselves to the White House fence to get the vote.

On our first picket line at the White House fence ("Rights
Not Roses") on Mother's Day in 1967, we threw away chains of
aprons, flowers, and mock typewriters. We dumped bundles of
newspapers onto the floor of the Equal Employment Opportunities Commission in protest against its refusal to enforce the Civil
Rights law against sex-segregated "Help Wanted: Male" ads (for
the good jobs) and "Help Wanted: Female" ads (for gal Friday–
type jobs). This was supposed to be just as illegal now as ads
reading "Help Wanted: White" and "Help Wanted: Colored."
We announced we were going to sue the federal government for
not enforcing the law equally on behalf of women (and then
called members of our underground in the Justice Department to
see if one could do that)—and we did.

I gave lectures in southern finishing schools and commence-

ment addresses at out-of-the-way colleges of home economics—
as well as at Yale, UCLA, and Harvard—to pay my way in
organizing NOW chapters (we never did have money for an
organizing staff). Our only real office in those years was my
apartment. It wasn't possible to keep up with the mail. But when
women like Wilma Heide from Pittsburgh, or Karen De Crow
in Syracuse, Eliza Paschall in Atlanta, Jacqui Ceballos—so many
others—were so determined to have NOW chapters that they
called long distance when we didn't answer their letters, the only
thing to do was to have them become local NOW organizers.

I remember so many way stations: Going to lunch at the for-
men-only Oak Room at the Plaza Hotel with fifty NOW women
and demanding to be served . . . Testifying before the Senate
against the nomination to the Supreme Court of a sexist judge
named Carswell who refused to hear a case of a woman who was
fired because she had preschool children . . . Seeing the first
sign of a woman's underground in the student movement, when
I was asked to lead a rap session at the National Student Congress in College Park, Maryland, in 1968 . . . After a resolution
for the liberation of women from the mimeograph machines was
laughed down at the SDS convention, hearing the young radical
women telling me they had to have a separate women's-lib group
—because if they really spoke out at SDS meetings, they might
not get married . . . Helping Sheila Tobias plan the Cornell in-
tersession on women in 1968, which started the first women's-
studies programs (how many universities have them now!) . . .
Persuading the NOW board that we should hold a Congress to
Unite Women with the young radicals despite differences in ideology and style . . . So many way stations.

I admired the flair of the young radicals when they got off the
rhetoric of sex/class warfare and conducted actions like picketing
the Miss America beauty contest in Atlantic City. But the media
began to publicize, in more and more sensational terms, the more
exhibitionist, down-with-men, down-with-marriage, down-with-
childbearing rhetoric and actions. Those who preached the man-
hating sex/class warfare threatened to take over the New York
NOW and the national NOW and drive out the women who

wanted equality but who also wanted to keep on loving their husbands and children. Kate Millett's *Sexual Politics* was hailed as the
ideology of sex/class warfare by those who claimed to be the
radicals of the women's movement. After the man-hating faction
broke up the second Congress to Unite Women with hate talk,
and even violence, I heard a young radical say, "If I were an
agent of the CIA and wanted to disrupt this movement, that's
just what I would do."

By 1970, it was beginning to be clear that the women's movement was more than a temporary fad, it was the fastest-growing
movement for basic social and political change of the decade. The
black movement had been taken over by extremists; the student
movement was immobilized by its fetish for leaderless structure
and by the growing alienation from extremist hate rhetoric.
Someone was trying to take over our movement, too—or to stop
it, immobilize it, splinter it—under the guise of radical rhetoric
and a similar fetish against leadership and structure. "It's fruitless
to speculate whether they are CIA agents, or sick, or on a private
power trip, or just plain stupid," a black leader warned me. "If
they continually disrupt, you simply have to fight them."

It seemed to me the women's movement had to get out of sexual politics. I thought it was a joke at first—those strangely hu-
morless papers about clitoral orgasms that would liberate women
from sexual dependence on a man's penis, and the "consciousness-
raising" talk that women should insist now on being on top in bed
with men. Then I realized, as Simone de Beauvoir once wrote,
that these women were in part acting out sexually their rebellion
and resentment at being "underneath" in society generally, being
dependent on men for their personal definition. But their resentment was being manipulated into an orgy of sex hatred that
would vitiate the power they now had to change the conditions
they resented. I'm not sure what motivates those who viciously
promulgate, or manipulate, man hate in the women's movement.
Some of the disrupters seemed to come from extreme left groups,
some seemed to be using the women's movement to proselytize
lesbianism, others seemed to be honestly articulating the legitimate
and too-long-buried rage of women into a rhetoric of sex/class

warfare, which I consider to be based on a false analogy with obsolete or irrelevant ideologies of class warfare or race separatism. The man-haters were given publicity far out of proportion to their numbers in the movement because of the media's hunger for sensationalism. Many women in the movement go through a temporary period of great hostility to men when they first become conscious of their situation; when they start acting to change their situation, they outgrow what I call pseudo-radical infantilism. But that man-hating rhetoric increasingly disturbs most women in the movement, in addition to keeping many women out of the movement.

On the plane to Chicago, preparing to bow out as president of NOW, feeling powerless to fight the man-haters openly and refusing to front for them, I suddenly knew what had to be done. A woman from Florida had written to remind me that August 26, 1970, was the fiftieth anniversary of the constitutional amendment giving women the vote. We needed to call a national action—a strike of women to call attention to the unfinished business of equality: equal opportunity for jobs and education, the right to abortion and child-care centers, the right to our own share of political power. It would unite women again in serious action—women who had never been near a "women's lib" group. (NOW, the largest such group, and the only one with a national structure, had only 3,000 members in thirty cities in 1970.) I remember that, to transmit this new vision to the NOW convention in Chicago, warning of the dangers of aborting the women's movement, I spoke for nearly two hours and got a standing ovation. The grass-roots strength of NOW went into organizing the August 26 strike. In New York, women filled the temporary headquarters volunteering to do anything and everything; they hardly went home at night.

Mayor Lindsay wouldn't close Fifth Avenue for our march, and I remember starting that march with the hoofs of policemen's horses trying to keep us confined to the sidewalk. I remember looking back, jumping up to see over marchers' heads. I never saw so many women; they stretched back for so many blocks you couldn't see the end. I locked one arm with my beloved Judge

Dorothy Kenyon (who, at eighty-two, insisted on walking with me instead of riding in the car we had provided for her), and the other arm with a young woman on the other side. I said to the others in the front ranks, "Lock arms, sidewalk to sidewalk!" We overflowed till we filled the whole of Fifth Avenue. There were so many of us they couldn't stop us; they didn't even try. It was, as they say, the first great nationwide action of women (hundreds of men also marched with us) since women won the vote itself fifty years before. Reporters who had joked about the "bra-burners" wrote that they had never seen such beautiful women as the proud, joyous marchers who joined together that day. For all women were beautiful on that day.

On August 26, it suddenly became both political and glamorous to be a feminist. At first, politics had seemed to be something altogether separate from what we were doing in the women's movement. The regular politicians—right, left, center; Republican, Democrat, splinter—certainly weren't interested in women. In 1968, I had testified in vain at the conventions of both political parties, trying to get a single word about women in either the Republican or Democratic platform. When Eugene McCarthy, the chief sponsor of the Equal Rights Amendment, announced that he was going to run for president to end the Vietnam war, I began to connect my own politics, at least, to the women's drive for equality. I called Bella Abzug and asked how I could work for McCarthy. But not even the other women working for him thought women's issues were relevant politically, and many NOW members were critical of me for campaigning openly for McCarthy.

At the 1970 NOW convention in Chicago, I said we had a human responsibility as women to end the Vietnam war. Neither men nor women should be drafted to fight an obscene, immoral war like the one in Vietnam, but we had to take equal responsibility for ending it. Two years earlier, in 1968, standing outside the Conrad Hilton Hotel in Chicago at the Democratic National Convention, I had watched helmeted troopers clubbing down the long-haired young, my own son among them. I began to see that these young men, saying they didn't have to napalm all the children in Vietnam and Cambodia to prove they were men, were defying the masculine mystique as we had defied the feminine one. Those young men, and their elders like them, were the other half of what we were doing.

And during that summer of 1970, I started trying to organize a woman's political caucus; later, it stuck together enough to get Bella Abzug elected to Congress. She and Gloria Steinem joined me as conveners of our August 26 Women's Strike for Equality march. So many women who had been afraid before joined our march that day; we, and the world, suddenly realized the possibilities of women's political power. This power was first tested in the summer of 1972 in Miami when, for the first time, women played a major role in the political conventions. Although inexperienced caucus leaders may have been too easily co-opted by Nixon or McGovern, or infiltrated by Watergate agents, they brought change to the political arena. They won commitments from both parties on child-care, preschool, and after-school programs. And Shirley Chisholm stayed in the Democratic race right to the end. By 1976, I predict, even the Republicans will have a woman running seriously for vice-president, if not for president.

And so most of the agenda of Stage 1 of the sex-role revolution—which is how I now see the women's movement for equality—have been accomplished, or are in the process of being resolved. The Equal Rights Amendment was approved by Congress with hardly a murmur in either house after we organized the National Women's Political Caucus. The amendment's main opponent, Emanuel Celler, has been retired from Congress by one of the many new young women who, these days, are running for office instead of looking up Zip Codes. The Supreme Court has ruled that no state can deny a woman her right to choose childbirth or abortion. Over 1,000 lawsuits have been filed forcing universities and corporations to take affirmative action to end sex discrimination and the other conditions that keep women from getting top jobs. The American Telephone and Telegraph Company has been ordered to pay $15 million in reparations to women who didn't even apply for jobs better than telephone operator before because such jobs weren't open to women. Every professional association, newspaper office, television station, church, company, hospital, and school in almost every city has a women's caucus or a group taking action on the concrete conditions that keep women down.

Lately, I've been asked to lead consciousness-raising sessions for the men who plan the training of guidance counselors in New York and Minnesota, priests in Missouri, the Air Force Academy in Colorado, and even investment bankers. (I've also organized the First Women's Bank & Trust Company to help women get control of their own money and use their economic power.) The State Department has said that women can't be fired from the Foreign Service just because they are married and that secretaries can't be told to go for coffee. Women are beginning to change the very practice of medicine by establishing self-help clinics that enable women to take active responsibility for their own bodies. Psychoanalytic conferences ask me, and other movement women, to help them change their definition of feminine and masculine. Women are being ordained as ministers and rabbis and deacons, though the Pope says they still can't say Mass. And the nuns and priests whose ecumenical rebellion is on the front edge of the sex-role revolution are asking, "Is God He?"

The women's movement is no longer just an American possibility. I've been asked to help organize groups in Italy, Brazil, Mexico, Colombia, Sweden, France, Israel, Japan, India, and even in Czechoslovakia and other Socialist countries. I hope that by next year we'll have our first world conference of feminists, perhaps in Sweden.

The United States Census Bureau reports a drastic decline in the birth rate, which I credit as much to women's new aspirations as to The Pill. The women's movement is strong enough now to bring out into the open real differences in ideology: I think my view of the sex-role revolution will emerge as the belief of those in the mainstream, and the man-hating fringe will evaporate, having represented a temporary phase, or even a planned diversion. It would be unrealistic, of course, not to expect forces threatened by the women's movement to try to organize or provoke a backlash—as they are doing now in many states to prevent ratification of the Equal Rights Amendment. For example, women were given a week off by employers in Ohio, bused over the state line, and put up in motels in an attempt to pressure the Kentucky legislature to block the Equal Rights Amendment. But I remember that the liquor companies spent millions of dollars to prevent ratification of women's right to vote in Tennessee fifty years ago. And today who is financing the campaign to stop the final act of the women's movement for equality? Not a conspiracy of men to keep women down; rather, it is a conspiracy of those whose power, or profit, rests on the manipulation of the fears and impotent rage of passive women. Women—the last and largest group of people in this nation to demand control of their own destiny—will change the very nature of political power in this country.

In the decade since the publication of *The Feminine Mystique*, the women's movement has changed my whole life, too, no less powerfully or joyfully than the lives of other women who stop to tell me about themselves. I couldn't keep living my schizophrenic life: leading other women out of the wilderness while holding on to a marriage that destroyed my self-respect. I finally found the courage to get a divorce in May, 1969. I am less alone now than I ever was holding on to the false security of my marriage. I think the next great issue for the women's movement is basic reform of marriage and divorce.

My life still keeps changing, with Emily off to Radcliffe this fall, Daniel getting his Ph.D. at Princeton, and Jonathan exploring new roads of his own. I've finished my first stint as a visiting professor of sociology at Temple University, and I've written my own uncensored column for *McCall's*. I've moved high into an airy, magic New York tower, with open sky and river and bridges to the future all around. I've started a weekend commune of grownups for whom marriage hasn't worked—an extended family of choice, whose members are now moving into new kinds of marriages.

The more I've become myself—and the more strength, support, and love I've somehow managed to take from, and give to, other women in the movement—the more joyous and real I feel loving a man. I've seen great relief in women this year as I've spelled out my personal truth: that the assumption of your own identity, equality, and even political power does not mean you stop needing to love, and be loved by, a man, or that you stop caring for your kids. I would have lost my own feeling for the women's movement if I had not been able, finally, to admit tenderness.

One mystical footnote: I used to be terribly afraid of flying. After I wrote *The Feminine Mystique*, I suddenly stopped being afraid; now I fly on jets across the ocean and on one-engine air taxis in the hills of West Virginia. I guess that, existentially, once you start really living your life, and doing your work, and loving, you are not afraid to die. Sometimes, when I realize how much flying I do, I think there's a possibility that I will die in an airplane crash. But not for quite a while, I hope, because the pieces of my own life as woman with man are coming together in a new pattern of human sex and human politics. I now can write that new book.

I think the energy locked up in those obsolete masculine and feminine roles is the social equivalent of the physical energy locked up in the realm of $E = MC^2$—the force that unleashed the holocaust of Hiroshima. I believe the locked-up sexual energies have helped to fuel, more than anyone realizes, the terrible violence erupting in the nation and the world during these past ten years. If I am right, the sex-role revolution will liberate these energies from the service of death and will make it really possible for men and women to "make love, not war."

Thoughts on Becoming
a Grandmother

 I had been invited to speak at a scientific symposium in Israel on "Mankind, 2000." (He will be eighteen in the year 2000!) Emily had deigned to go with me, on her last spring vacation before finishing medical school. They had been rather cross about that, because the baby was due in three or four weeks, and what if it was born while we were gone? The grandmother's presence was certainly not essential (surely not), but the future aunt, my daughter-the-doctor, was supposed to be on standby, up there at Harvard Medical School, to fly down when labor began and be their personal medical support system at the birthing center. Approaching parenthood with far more confidence than I remember having at that time, Jonathan, my second son, and Helen, the future mother, scorned the sterile, dehumanized, alienating technology of a male-dominated obstetrical-gynecological professional hospital delivery. The future grandmother, ideologically happy at such an expression of second-stage feminism so close to home, and, above all, applauding the zeal and conscientiousness with which the father-to-be shared the birthing preparations, from the first decision about the nurse-midwife to the final breathing exercises, had certain doubts about the absence of sophisticated medical expertise and life-saving equipment if complications arose, but she was not exactly consulted. On the other hand, the future parents seemed to find a certain fortuitous advantage in our making that pilgrimage to Jerusalem, with the birth impending. . . .

On the trip things are a bit tense between Emily and me, with currents of unexpressed mother-daughter love and the need to be no longer dependent on that love, for both of us, for we both know that this is probably the last time she will be my giggly roommate, sister-traveler on such a trip, as she has been, off and on, since she was eleven or twelve. Internship, residency, a serious young man, await her return. She turns away from me, our first day in Jerusalem, as we stand in the rain before the Wailing Wall, and I see her slip a little piece of paper out of her purse and put it in a crevice in the wall. When I ask her later, all she will say is that it is a private matter between her and her brother. She has to fly back for the start of medical-school classes again, before my symposium ends.

On my own last day in Jerusalem, those abstract speculations about women and men in the twenty-first century having been delivered, I wander the holy streets of the Old City, not luxuriating as I usually do in the mystery of its past, but impatient, suddenly, to be back where that birth is due. But I have called them that morning in New York, and Jonathan has reported that the baby is in no hurry to get out, the nurse-midwife says not for another week or two. So with no need for me to stop over, I will fly straight back to Boston, where I am doing research at Harvard. Just before sunset, on impulse, I retrace the route to the Wailing Wall. I am not myself formally religious, though lately as I have become interested in the religion of my ancestors, I sometimes suspect I may have inadvertently lived a religious life. (The women's movement, for me, was at times almost a religious experience.) Standing before that wall in Jerusalem, feeling the power of all those centuries of prayer and belief, I say my own silent prayer for a happy, healthy baby. I find myself murmuring the words of the traditional Hebrew prayer that links the generations of our ancestors to whom this wall was holy to that baby who will also say those words, *Shema Yisrael . . .*

All the way back on the plane, in and out of sleep—for I am

tired after this hectic week—I'm nagged by a kind of unreasoning apprehension about the birth that for some reason I feel may even now be taking place. The words of the Rilke poem come to me:

> We are nearing the land that is life.
> You will recognize it by its seriousness.

When we finally land at Logan Airport and I hear my name on the paging system, I am hardly surprised. *Baby born early this morning, a boy, everyone fine, at Lenox Hill Hospital.* But they weren't supposed to be at a hospital! I get the bags through customs, and take the shuttle back to New York. They all are there, at the hospital, my shaken family. A few hours after labor began, there was untoward bleeding. The conscientious birthing-center midwife sent Helen immediately in an ambulance to the nearest hospital. The baby was seen in the X ray to be positioned wrong, face up. All the preparations for natural childbirth notwithstanding, the doctors now took over. Emily had flown down that night from Boston, as planned, but they wouldn't even let her on the hospital floor. The obstetrician who was on call that night got a flat tire on the way to the hospital, and they had kept Helen strapped up on the operating table, not knowing what was happening. Over her objections, they injected a drug that made her contractions stop. When the doctor finally arrived, he sent Jonathan out and said he had to do a Caesarean because the monitor showed the baby to be "stressed." But Helen felt sure that if only they had let her down, let her squat in the way she had been taught, she could have had the baby naturally. They had had a night of fear and terror, all of them, and I had not been there to help. But *the baby was fine*, Helen was fine (she looked terrible, still in shock, to me). Could I see the baby?

And Jonathan takes me to the nursery corridor. I study the baby through the glass. He looks *familiar*, that baby. He looks like Jonathan, as a baby—no, like Danny, my first-born—no, not quite like either of them. But familiar. Later, from a distance, I see Jonathan, scrubbed up in a hospital gown, shaken still but beaming now, his dimples showing, stiffly, proudly, self-consciously, tenderly carrying that baby, his son. (Even in such an Establishment hospital the new father is now allowed to fetch the baby in to the mother to nurse.)

Banished to the waiting room while the feeding takes place, I meet the baby's grandfather, from whom I have been divorced thirteen years now. He had shared their night of fear, while I had been on that plane. He had tried to get another doctor in. He had relived, obviously, another such night, over thirty years ago, when in similar shock and disbelief and outrage he and I had had to sign an agreement permitting our first-born, Jonathan's older brother, Daniel, to be taken by Caesarean. (To this day, just like Helen, I wonder if it was really necessary. If they had just let me try harder, longer, could I have done it naturally?)

There has been a great distance between us in the last dozen years, but there is healing in that shared memory, in this moment of shared support of our son, in the seriousness of new life going on from that shared beginning. "He seems so emotional," says my former husband of his son. "He was crying so. Do you think he's too emotional?" I don't, of course. Things might have been different if that older father, whom I no longer really know, had not been so afraid of feelings. There is pain for me in the distance, now, from all that happened between us, in knowing that we cannot really share this moment, and yet, there is the healing joy: "Hello, Grandma." "Hello, Grandpa."

In bedside conference, the whole family discusses boys' names. They had a girl's name ready but could not agree on a boy's. They do not decide for a week, until just before the naming, the *bris*. The baby's name is Rafael: "healer," it means. And then his mother's name, Nakdimen, which she has kept, hyphenated in accepted feminist style.

A postfeminist baby, with a traditional Jewish *bris* ceremony of circumcision and naming. My other son, Daniel, flies in from Chicago, where he is a theoretical physicist now, wearing, in lieu of a yarmulke, the beret he bought during his postdoctorate fellowship in Paris. And Jonathan's best friend, Michael, flies in from Lummi Island, off the coast of Washington, where he's still living in that log cabin he and Jonathan shared during their salmon-fisherman years, before Jon came back and finished college. And Steve, the third of those three musketeers, whose wife, Estelle, is now pregnant too—the boys intend to continue their friendship into the next generation! And those two boys' mothers, and my friend Natalie, and her kids, who grew up with mine, and Jon and Helen's new friends. It is moving, the gathering of this tribe linked by years of shared life and love, for this formal celebration of birth, of the glory of generation. We all feel it. "You will recognize it by its seriousness." I am a grandmother!

Since none of my close friends has had the experience of being a grandmother yet—we sometimes wondered if we ever would, given our daughters' preoccupation with their legal, publishing, banking, medical, and other careers, and our sons' seeming disinclination to marital commitment—I have no role model as a modern feminist grandmother. (My own achievement, finally, of this state, is not only envied by my friends but gives them hope!) "How does it feel, being a grandmother?" they keep asking me, curious, and so envious. Envious? An earlier convention assumed that if a woman allowed herself to be honest, she would feel some pain at such a public, undeniable announcement of the loss of her own youth. "Aren't you excited about being a grandfather?" Natalie asked my former husband. "I don't like to talk about it much," he said. "It would make the young women I take out think I was old." A new friend, male, who also recently achieved this state, said, "I don't *have* any feelings about it. I don't feel old enough to be a grandfather." But that's not, for some reason, the way the women I know feel. Not me. Turning another corner is the way I feel. Excited, curious. In my own moving from the battles of the women's movement to a new stage in my pursuit of personal and political truth, I welcome this new grounding in the land that is life. Generation is what I feel, the *goodness* of it.

There is a delight, a comfort, an easing of the burden, somehow, a renewal of joy in my own life, to feel the stream of life of which I am part going on like this. (I get a vaguely similar feeling when the daughters of the women's movement come up to me with their "it changed my whole life" and their new choices and problems, but that joy is less personal, less vivid.) "Face it," said Emily, "now that your children are getting married and having children of our own, we aren't your *children* any more. You can't go on thinking of us that way." True? Yes, and no. . . . As research recently has shown, for women generally now, as for me, the empty nest is not traumatic, as it once was, or was assumed to be, back in the days of the feminine mystique, when woman was defined only as a wife and mother. Yet even now, surely part of our personhood is defined by that powerful experience as mother, which is far more than mystique. It is a sort of heavy joyous-painful shadow, under and over everything else we do during those mother years. For me, as for others, now that that part is nearly finished, there is relief, release, a lightening of shadow, as I see them make their own way into life at last, their own persons—my kids, so intensely, satisfyingly themselves, in work, in love, and now, beginning with kids of their own. As they enter this new cycle of generation, they even seem to come back home again, in a different way.

Jonathan is a lovely father. I like to watch him, tender, competent, responsible, enjoying, so sure, as he slings Rafi over his shoulder, feeds him bits of banana, and straps him into that backpack. I like to watch the flow between him and Helen as they share the concrete, omnipresent, never-finished mundane daily details of the feeding, undressing, wiping, patting, comforting, rocking, cleaning up, soothing, playing, laughing, endless watching, that is parenting. There is an evolution going on here. They share those details of parenting more consciously, and more organically, than we did. But his father and I shared them more than my father and mother did. Still, it is quite clear that Jonathan is not the baby's mother. She is breast-feeding, of course. I defiantly breast-fed all three of mine, for nearly a year each time, though it was not so fashionable then. But I was not nearly so confident a mother as she is.

She amazes and delights me, that young daughter-in-law of

mine, in the clarity of her choices. She had just finished college, having dropped out for a while to go to Israel, and to work, as had my son. He was making up for lost time, doing two years' graduate work in one for his engineering degree. They agonized together over the decision, finally, to take what life was offering them, and have the baby. "I would have hated to feel I had to have the baby," she said. "Knowing that we really chose to have a baby, since I could have had an abortion, makes a big difference."

Watching her, I sense that this consciousness of chosen motherhood today gives, and requires, a sense of autonomy, identity, *self* in a woman that is different from the passive "anatomy is destiny" of past generations and the glorified feminine mystique of mine; beyond the pill and abortion, the consciousness of other choices, other women's career patterns, clarifies the values. This kind of chosen motherhood is a step beyond the ambivalent reactions and superwoman demands of first-stage feminism. There is, for sure, an evolution here.

My mother, who had to quit the newspaper job she loved when she married my father and started to have babies, covered some very conflictful feelings about herself as a woman by being the perfect housewife and perfect mother and shifting her own frustrated ambitions to excessive demands on her husband and children, which we never seemed to satisfy. She "raised" us compulsively by the book. The book, then, was Watson's behaviorism. No matter how much the baby cried, you "conditioned" by picking it (me) up to feed it only when the schedule said—every four hours, by the clock. Since I didn't want to be like my mother—and had no other image of what a woman could be or feel—I had very little confidence in myself as a mother. I had to blindly follow the book. Oh, how Dr. Spock could make me feel guilty! (Even today, the slightest hint from these grown-up children of mine about my lacks as a mother can arouse painful tremors of guilt in tough skin that hardly flinches at political abuse from the vicious likes of Phyllis Schlafly.) And I was fired from my newspaper job, when I was pregnant with Jonathan—I didn't have all that much choice. That firing would be a violation of the law against sex discrimination, today. Then, it wasn't even a grievance the union would take up.

Helen gets some of her strength from her own mother, who was a survivor of the Holocaust. But she has consciously repudiated the traditional passivity, the martyrdom to men, and the fears that she associates with her mother. She is, in her own mind, an independent, self-created woman.

I like to think that the new sense and possibilities of choice, and the new images of woman as person, that the movement opened have helped to give Helen and others of her postfeminist generation a good enough feeling about being a woman so that they can *trust themselves*. I've seen some books about parenting around Jonathan and Helen's apartment, but Helen doesn't consult any baby bible the slavish way I did Dr. Spock. She already feels she knows better than the experts about her own baby, and she probably does. My friends Jackie and Binky, who also had their first babies this year—from very conscious choice indeed, in their midthirties, in the midst of demanding careers—were confident enough to simply take the babies home from the hospital, ahead of schedule, when they seemed not to be doing well under hospital routine.

Given the strong feminist images of the family she married into, the fact that Helen felt no need to apologize for having taken a "hiatus" from any career to concentrate that first year on mothering bespeaks a real sureness of herself as a woman, which I applaud. "Sometimes I feel bored out of my skin," she admitted cheerfully, taking off for her class in karate (not a bad skill for a mother wheeling a baby in a tough city neighborhood, but also a way to vent those irritations of endless mothering which the feminine mystique used to deny). She also started studying graphology, which always fascinated her, and can now analyze handwriting with an accuracy that would probably stand up in court better than a lie detector. "You'd make a good psychotherapist," I tell her. "I'm not sure I want to waste the time getting all those degrees," she says. There's no sense whatsoever that she is martyring herself, or that she ever thought of herself as "just as a housewife." But there is also no sense that she feels the need to be a superwoman. Her present, very part-time job is no "career." But her search is serious. And she certainly takes no nonsense from Jonathan, who has his *macho* tendencies.

This same year, some of my friends having their first babies in their mid-thirties are having other problems. Barnard College, which still has no maternity-leave policy, made one of these women come back to work less than a month after her baby was born. Only 18 percent of women now working have the right to take a maternity leave, and come back to their jobs, to say nothing about men and paternity leave. Yet by the end of the decade, a Ford Foundation projection says, only one mother out of four will be able to stay home full time with a child. Luckily, Jonathan's engineering job pays enough so that they could choose to have Helen stay home for a while—at the price of crowding three people into a studio apartment meant for one.

Watching Jonathan with the baby, seeing his new confidence and sureness, I sense that he gets his own identity as a man at least as much from his new role as husband and father, and from the community he and Helen are building with other couples like themselves in New York's Upper West Side, as from his job as engineer. To his own surprise as a child of the 1960's, he puts on a suit now, and goes every morning to that job, which he even enjoys except for the rigid 9-to-5 schedule. "I'm really into something, and they all go out to lunch. Or I've just about got it licked, and it's five o'clock, time to go." Or the baby has kept them up all night, and the alarm clock still goes off. Would he do his job as well or better, even from his employer's point of view, if he had a more flexible schedule, geared to the needs of parenting?

I have never been forgiven for a certain excessively ambitious fantasy about that second son of mine, playing cowboy with such *command* in the Kennedy years, who could, for sure, grow up to be "the first Jewish president." That's not been my ambition for him for a long time, though he's probably still suspicious. Watch-

ing him come into his own now as a father, seeing his sensitivity
to Rafi's needs, I think he really is a second-stage man, though it
embarrasses him to have me say this.

You get the picture, maybe, that I take a special delight in my
son—in all my kids. They were such special bonuses, such surprising undeserved pluses in my life—gifts. What did I *do* to deserve them? And they were so much *themselves*, from the very
beginning. I can still remember how each one looked in the delivery room—how Jonathan as a flannel-wrapped new-born kicked
with that lusty energy he still has. I remember Jonathan at three,
in the cowboy hat he never took off, getting down from his little
horse-on-wheels to climb into my lap; and all those businesses he
and his friends started at eight and nine that were such a nuisance
to cancel, with the mail-order houses.

I can still remember Danny, my first-born, smiling at me with
recognition for the first time, under a street light as we were
wheeling him home one dark night in his baby carriage after
visiting friends. I can still remember making a game, swinging
hands, he and I down the sidewalk, when he was four, going
along with me to collect unemployment insurance, after I was
fired for getting pregnant with Jonathan. I can still remember my
walks with Emily, each afternoon after she got home from
nursery school, swinging hands and singing our own song with
many verses that we called "Swing High, Swing Low." I can still
remember rocking them on my lap in the middle of the night, to
soothe them back to sleep after a stomach-ache or a bad dream,
the songs I would make up, each a personal running commentary
on each child's life—"I have a little boy and his name is Jonathan"
. . . his dog, his cat, his baby sister, his baseball bat. (The week
after they brought Rafi home from the hospital, Emily took that
red rocker, the only piece of furniture I still have from those days,
from its corner in her old room to Jonathan's place, for them to
nurse Rafi in.)

There is so much I remember still of the vivid intensity of
those days of my own motherhood, which comes back to me as I
watch them with Rafi now—and so much I realize is gone forever, lost even in memory. The omnipresent daily details of those

mother years, which seemed so pressing then, so harassing, and sometimes so clouded with guilts and conflict and that "problem that had no name," in those cramped apartments, those houses so vivid in my memory and theirs, so crowded with life—I only wish now that I'd savored them all more, at the time.

This being a grandmother is not the same kind of experience, not at all. I marvel at this mysterious treasure, this grandbaby, suddenly with us, here, now, himself, a new person carrying on our lifestream; I stare at him, I take him in with my eyes and heart, but I don't have to change his diapers, or get up in the middle of the night with him, or feel responsible for him all the time. I have not exactly been overzealous in offering to baby-sit, though there have been many hints. Of course, I was up in Cambridge. And then I had to go to Rome and Paris and San Francisco to lecture. I called them from the airport, on my way back to Sag Harbor from California in early winter, to see how things were going. "Great," they said. "Where are you? Why don't you come over and baby-sit with your grandson? We could go out." But I had a dinner date that night—I was going out myself.

I wonder at the men of my age and acquaintance who are starting over again with new babies, second and third families of their own—new fathers, with the diapers and all, at fifty, sixty, almost seventy! Does replay parenthood really make them feel younger, as they say? I wonder. I have no wish to go through all that again, myself. Sour grapes maybe, since I don't have that choice. But I've done that already! The one thing I envy them—which I get a whiff of myself as grandmother—is the second chance to enjoy it, without the hangups and the career pressures, or the pressures from career avoidance or abeyance, that got in the way the first time around.

They brought him to Sag Harbor for Thanksgiving. He was just beginning to crawl. It was not exactly over the hill and through the trees to Grandma stuffing the turkey. Not this grandma. The last few years, never knowing where my own kids are going to be and when they are going to decide whether or not they want to come home for Thanksgiving, I've developed a sort of tradition of communal Thanksgiving with my "family of friends." The ones I shared a weekend house with in the first years after my divorce (we called it a commune, to the kids' annoyance—"aging would-be hippies!") have each now, remarried or alone, acquired her or his own house within a ten-mile radius of my own beloved little house on the cove in Sag Harbor. I seem to play the role of den mother or matriarch in that loosely woven communal family, to which we readily welcome each other's friends, new and old, whether recently separated, or feeling stranded with children off at school, or newly on their own, or having such hassles with kids or spouse that they welcome the support of a communal Thanksgiving.

So Cynthia was stuffing the turkey, and Natalie (Gittelson) and the "Gitteldaughters" were baking the pies, and Arthur was bringing the wine, and since Jonathan and Helen are vegetarians, I made a big production with the vegetables. Baby onions and mushrooms from a recipe I got over the phone from Joan Whitman, and garlicked brussels sprouts from Craig Claiborne's recipe in the newspaper, and candied sweet potatoes the way I've always done them without any recipe at all, and two kinds of cranberry sauce from the can (vegetables are better cooked fresh, but cranberry sauce tastes fine from the can; I'd feel pretentious making it from scratch).

In the end, we seemed to have acquired an excess of stranded single men. Men are still more helpless, somehow, at times like Thanksgiving. It was our first Thanksgiving in my new dining room–studio that got built, finally, out of what had been a useless side stoop, back shed, and attic over the kitchen. I hadn't had space before for a dining table big enough for a holiday family dinner; we'd had to set up picnic tables in the living room, and when you wanted seconds you had to go out the front door and around the house to the back door to get into the kitchen.

Between courses, this Thanksgiving, at one point six adoring women were kneeling at Rafi's feet. Natalie, of course, is dying to be a grandmother. "It will all work out," I assure her, in my new smugness. The Gitteldaughters are positively possessive about Rafi. "We've checked out other babies," they report to me;

"there's no comparison." It all reminds me of a prediction Isaac Asimov, my prophetic science-fiction-writer friend, once made— that having a baby was becoming so expensive, problem-laden, oft postponed, and in some parts of our society, rare, that the day would come when a baby would be regarded as a "national treasure."

In the last few months, in Cambridge and other cities, at least six women in their mid-thirties and early forties have asked my advice about having a baby "by myself." They are women who spent their twenties and thirties concentrating on careers, some of them after the disillusionment of too early marriages, followed by divorce. Now, either they are involved with men who've had enough troubles with their own kids and want no more, or they are not in intimate relationship with any man, and do not expect or even want to marry again. A few have become lesbian. But, up against the biological clock now, they seem to feel an overpowering urge to have a baby. "I give myself till I'm thirty-eight," one says. "Then, if I haven't found anyone, I'll go ahead anyhow, and have a kid by myself. The question is, shall I use a sperm bank and artificial insemination, or shall I ask a friend? But then, he might have a claim to the baby, and I wouldn't want that."

I'm not sure how I feel about all this. Remembering the pressures of my own mother years, watching the pressures on Jonathan and Helen, I think the care of a baby is tough enough with two parents. To start with, at least.

Don't get me wrong, I haven't gone back to the feminine mystique. I don't think having a baby is absolutely necessary, or even sufficient, for any and every woman's fulfillment. *Chosen motherhood* is the real liberation. The *choice* to have a child makes the whole experience of motherhood different, and the choice to be generative in other ways can at last be made, and is being made by many women now, without guilt. In those years of the feminine mystique, I saw too many women, who had no choice or had babies for the wrong reasons, cover up their own negative feelings about motherhood with compulsive smothering —or lash out in psychic or physical child abuse—to their own misery and their family's. But don't underestimate the power of that choice to be generative. I don't believe motherhood is a biological instinct in women, not as it is in animals. But it is a very basic human potential, in our genes and our psyches, that does somehow demand to be used.

The mystery and wonder of life renewing itself has been celebrated by all societies through all the ages of human history. An awe behind and beyond mystique forced men to invent elaborate rites to imitate, or compensate for not being able to have, the unique experience of birth. That experience seems intensified by choice, lifted from the realm of simple animal necessity to that of human freedom, as women and men now so clearly choose to take part in the stream of ongoing life when they do not really have to have children—not just because the pill and abortion are available, but because sons and daughters are no longer social security for old age, or needed extra hands to till the fields. And it costs so much, in time, energy, and money itself, to bring kids up now; trade-offs have to be made, in terms of career success, standard of living.

On a personal level, the postfeminist generation seems to me to be learning that one can't have it all perfectly, all at once. There are risks in the way Helen and Jon are doing it, and other risks in waiting till thirty-five to have a baby, or in combining motherhood with a full-time job. Tinka is getting so thin she looks almost anoretic from the pressures of her demanding agency partnership and the new insistence of two-year-old Max that only she can meet his demands. When they entertain clients at home, as they often must, she can no longer keep Max out of their hair with a baby-sitter. J.B. is a sharing father, sure, but Max just doesn't make those same demands on him. What Tinka desperately needs, she tells me, is some women friends who also have two-year-olds and will *understand*; but where, how, is she to make such friends, when she must rush home from the office at six to feed Max his supper, and trek with him to the country each weekend? I've heard the same complaint from my economist friend, Sylvia, the one who was denied maternity leave, so I do some mother-matching. Tinka and Sylvia now have an evening play group for their hyperactive two-year-olds, and that supportive woman friend in each other.

At the surprise party for Jon's thirtieth birthday, for which Helen borrowed my apartment, eight children, from a baby born after Rafi to a seven-year-old, were milling sweetly—at least, were not bawling nuisances—under the feet of some forty celebrating grown-ups at nearly midnight. Have baby-sitters gone out of style? I wondered. "It's not only that they're so expensive," said Ruthie, my niece-the-dentist, finally taking sleepy Mia home. "Because we can't be with Mia when we work, we want her with us the rest of the time. We'd miss too much otherwise."

The ways they are working things out over time, in this postfeminist generation—the how, when, why, and where of having children, or not, of family and work—are not the same for everyone and probably never will be again, as earlier family patterns seemed to be. That diversity seems a plus to me, compared to the single pattern of the perfect family, enshrined in the feminine mystique, that we tried to emulate, only to feel so guilty when we couldn't. But society doesn't provide enough support for the new patterns, or the old ones, when not even grandmothers have time to baby-sit, and not even women's colleges give enough maternity leave, and judges don't count the care of home and kids as equal to a wage contribution in divorce settlements or pension entitlement, and Reagan is cutting even the inadequate child-care programs that now exist. Still, given the great numbers of those sons and daughters of the postwar baby boom now having their own babies—late or soon—and the great numbers of their eager grandmothers, by 1984 some candidate for national or state office, some adviser to a would-be president, is going to realize how politically sexy such issues as maternity-paternity leave, flextime, job sharing, and child care might be.

Finally, I offer to baby-sit, myself. They have come up to Cambridge on my last weekend there, in January, to drive me and all my books and papers back home after my Harvard year. I haven't seen the baby for over a month. He's got hair now; he's lost the Buckminster Fuller look. Have I told you how unusual, how exceptional, how objectively beautiful my grandbaby is? He has these intense blue eyes. He has these distinctive big ears, clones of Jonathan's. He can pull himself up by the coffee table and stands up now, his little behind fitting onto his cocky legs in a way that looks familiar indeed. His daddy's behind (if I remember correctly, his granddaddy's, too). "Hey, gene pool," I say, taking in the amazing energy of that baby, the intent way he grabs a crumb off the floor, studies it, makes a beeline—crawling fast across the room—to his daddy talking on the telephone, stares up at him, his whole face abeam. I get down on all fours myself, to make friends again. He studies me solemnly: *Who's this foolish lady? What is she to me?* He takes his own sweet time about it: *Where have I seen her before?* And finally, that smile, that enchanting smile that makes me melt.

I am a bit nervous about baby-sitting this priceless new being. It's a long time since I've taken care of a baby, after all. "You won't have any trouble," they assure me, studying the movie page. I catch their dubious glances. Am I really competent to leave him with? My brilliant young psychologist friend Ellen Langer calls to invite me for a farewell dinner. A tenured Harvard professor at thirty-five, she was married and divorced very young, and has lived a single life for many years, concentrating on her brilliant career. Two psychotherapist friends, also thirty-ish, unmarried, are visiting for the weekend in her stunning modern triplex town house.

"I have to baby-sit for my grandbaby," I tell her.

"Wonderful," she says, with her usual zeal for novel psychological experiment. "We will help you baby-sit. It will be an interesting experience."

So Rafi, his stroller, a supply of those disposable snap-on diapers, a jar of baby carrots, and grandmother are deposited at Ellen's triplex, and the liberated parents assure me that they will telephone from the restaurant before they go into the movie, just to check. Rafi has fallen asleep in the car. He does not even seem to notice his parents leave. Those three psychological amazons devour him with unscientific attention. Soon, passed from arm to arm, lap to lap, he's wide awake, rising to the challenge of his audience, my gene pool all right. Ellen's gourmet meal is being nibbled in absent-minded bites; nobody even asks what's in the elaborate antipasto; three Ph.D.'s and one L.H.D. (Hon.) are cooing gibberish baby talk. "Why is it," says my experimental-psychologist hostess acidly, "that four otherwise brilliant adults are reduced to submoronic levels of communication by one small baby? If we could free ourselves from our stereotyped ideas of a baby, we would talk to him like a human being, and he would respond accordingly," I do find myself murmuring the most asinine endearments—"Rif Raf," "gush gosh," "sweet-potato pie" —but Rafi does not seem really to invite intellectual dialogue.

He is getting fretful. Whichever lap he's in, he keeps turning his head around, as if he's looking for something. "He's discovered his mother is gone," I say apprehensively. "He's looking for her."

"Don't be silly," says Ellen. "There you go with the stereotypes again. Why should he miss his mother? He's getting plenty of attention from us. He doesn't know the difference. He's probably wet." And before I can stop them, two of the amazons have carried Rafi off to the top floor of the triplex to experiment with diapering.

"Hey, wait a minute," I start to object. "He's my grandbaby."

"Ah, let them," says the other guest. "You've done it already. Let them have the experience." Hearing his little cries, I am about to go to the rescue when they bring him down triumphantly—diapered, dry, stunned into momentary silence. Now he starts looking around again, and begins to cry a little more vociferously. I suddenly realize he may be thirsty. Panic, no milk in the breasts here! Then, I remember they said to give him juice. Apple? Orange? She only has cranberry. I don't remember giving that to my babies, but cranberry juice is very healthy, good for the kidneys. I start to tear open the container. "Could I have a cup or glass?" I ask.

"You drink it from the container with a straw," Ellen says.

"A baby can't drink from a straw," I tell her.

"Oh, there you go again with those stereotypes," says my bril-

liant psychologist friend. "How do you know he couldn't drink
from a straw if you didn't expect him not to? Let's try it." I am
in no mood for such experiments with my grandbaby. I'm not
sure I could stop serious crying. I've just seen *Tootsie*; I'd rather
leave that scene to Dustin Hoffman. I pour the juice into a high-
ball glass, and he clutches it eagerly with both hands and slurps
away. Holding him on my lap, I keep tilting the glass, so he won't
drown. Success!

With Rafi restored to cheer and charm, I notice all that beautiful veal and salad still hardly touched and suggest that he can
now be put down for crawling exercise while we finish eating. I
make a fence of three of Ellen's chrome-and-leather chairs in
front of the fireplace, and upend a fourth to block the stairwell.
"Aren't you being a bit obsessively overprotective?" one of the
visiting psychotherapists protests. Ellen is smiling caustically.
Perhaps she feels disillusioned, seeing her fearless feminist mentor
turn into a baby-talking fuss-budget. Rafi does a quick ex-
ploratory tour of the premises. I *swear* he's looking for someone.
He starts to whimper again. One of the guests has long curly
brown hair like Helen's, and a similar build. From the far end of
the kitchen, he suddenly catches sight of her, smiles that enchanting beam of recognition, and makes a beeline for her lap. She is
dazzled at being thus singled out. But on her lap—which is not his
mother's, after all—he starts whimpering again, more seriously.
All three are now trying to distract him with stimulating, noisy
tricks. I can just see that frantic scene from *Tootsie*, with the
four of us playing Dustin Hoffman.

Inchoate stirrings of knowledge long unused awake in whatever brain cells still carry the imprints left by my own mothering. I stand on grandmotherly personal privilege, and rescue my
grandbaby from that high-powered adoring clique. I carry him
off to be quiet in the space under the spiral staircase where tall
green plants make shadows on the white walls. I walk around
with him among the plants; he stops crying and reaches to touch
the green leaves. I murmur little singsongs, the way I used to do
with them, and he puts his head down on my shoulder, quiet and
mellow. He falls asleep. The stroller I gave them for a baby

present opens out into a slanting little bed. I put him gently down in it, turn its back to the light, and push it back and forth, gently rocking with one hand as we finish dinner.

It seems that Jonathan has called in the middle of all that, but Ellen has said everything is under control and I don't need to talk to him. Later, she drives us home. And that night, in my bedroom in Cambridge, Rafi, to his parents' amazement, for the first time sleeps the night through. I take no credit. It is simply a developmental coincidence. But the next morning, as I frantically pack the dozen boxes of papers and books accumulated during that year in Cambridge—the research for my next book, *The Fountain of Age*—I look up now and then and catch my grandbaby staring at *me* with that smile of recognition. He knows me now! "We're going to be friends, you and I," I venture, now that we've been tested. I wonder how long before I can take him with me on a trip. Maybe, when he's eight? "Venice," I tell him. "What do you say to Venice?" He smiles, mysteriously. . . .

There was no room in the station wagon, on top of my books, papers, and other junk, beside the baby and all his paraphernalia, for my plants. I've never had a green thumb, but there in my otherwise bleak Cambridge apartment on top of that new concrete-block Harvard dormitory, I'd somehow made flourish two tree-bushes in baskets, three jade plants, and a hanging fern. I decided to hand them on to Ellen. When she came to pick them up, she said they'd stayed up half the night, she and her friends, discussing the pros and cons of having babies, with or without husbands. "It would be hard to do it alone," I said. "If you didn't have a husband, you'd need some other kind of support system." Maybe she's brilliant enough to dream up a support system better than a husband, but maybe not. I wonder how she and my son Danny would get along. . . .

Someone has suggested that women are so anxious to become grandmothers because they want revenge on their children—they just can't wait to relish, with vicious glee, the spectacle of those loved-hated children as victims of the martyrdom they suffered as mothers. (Men, by contrast, don't pay that suffering price as fathers, and aren't anxious to be grandfathers, because they don't want to feel old. Of course, I have a hunch from my research for *The Fountain of Age* that the very embrace of changing, evolving life that makes women relish even becoming grandmothers is what helps keep women alive longer than men. But that's another story.)

About that vicious glee. Back now in New York, I have dinner one night in Jonathan and Helen's crowded apartment. They've appropriated the screen I brought back from Haiti—jungle animals on one side, flowers on the other, I was going to use it to hide my messy desk when I entertain in my Sag Harbor studio—to make a semiprivate space around Rafi's crib. But he still won't go to sleep as long as he senses them, us, in the room, talking. He loves life too much, that kid. Finally, as he gets very peevish, his sweet mother and daddy give up on the rocking, the patting, the songs, and simply turn out all the lights, and we sit there grimly around the dining table, not even talking, while our lentil soup gets cold, just letting him cry till he falls asleep. Which he finally does. They light some candles, we eat the zucchini soufflé, which by now has fallen a bit, and Jon grins at me sheepishly. "Well, now you know he isn't always such an angel," he says. *He's also a pain in the ass. What else is new?* I forbear to say. They wanted to show him off, in all his perfection, and he didn't oblige! Oh well, I enjoy watching them *enjoy*, and *suffer*, as parents themselves.

I'm just waiting for the day when that strong-minded Rafi, and his future siblings and cousins, reach the critical age and start giving those irritatingly superior children of mine some of the same flak they gave me, getting under their skin about not being such perfect parents. I never really *suffered* from the diapering, the dirt, the sleepless nights, their inexhaustible energy as children; it was only that superior condescension and those guilt-producing accusations they occasionally turned on me in their adolescence—and their own times of misery, in love or work, which still cause pangs of pain and guilt in me—that made my kids cease to be unalloyed joys. I told myself, of course, that they had to turn on me that way, to deny their dependence and cut their mother-strings, to grow up! But it didn't really help, when Emily, for instance, reminded me of the time she brought me home a May basket she'd made at school, and rang the doorbell and hid, but I was in the middle of a paragraph of *The Feminine Mystique*, and kept yelling at *her* to answer the door, so she never gave me the May basket, and now she never would! Jonathan and his sister and brother may not make the same mistakes as I did, but there's no way they can be such perfect angelic parents—with Rafi, and the others to come—that they will not get some of that guilt flak back from their children some day. I expect it's realizing this already that's made them so much sweeter to their old mother since the baby came.

"What's he going to call you?" the baby's parents keep asking. My kids called their Massachusetts grandmother "Grandma" and the one in California "Granny," but they didn't really know either one. Both my grandmothers were dead when I was five. I want this little Rafi to know me, I want to know this little person, who is carrying my blood and energy and spirit into new life. His being gladdens my heart. I can't wait for him to start talking to me. He can call me any name he wants.

Notes

Chapter 1. THE PROBLEM THAT HAS NO NAME

1. See the Seventy-fifth Anniversary Issue of *Good Housekeeping*, May, 1960, "The Gift of Self," a symposium by Margaret Mead, Jessamyn West, *et al.*
2. Lee Rainwater, Richard P. Coleman, and Gerald Handel, *Workingman's Wife*, New York, 1959.
3. Betty Friedan, "If One Generation Can Ever Tell Another," *Smith Alumnae Quarterly*, Northampton, Mass., Winter, 1961. I first became aware of "the problem that has no name" and its possible relationship to what I finally called "the feminine mystique" in 1957, when I prepared an intensive questionnaire and conducted a survey of my own Smith College classmates fifteen years after graduation. This questionnaire was later used by alumnae classes of Radcliffe and other women's colleges with similar results.
4. Jhan and June Robbins, "Why Young Mothers Feel Trapped," *Redbook*, September, 1960.
5. Marian Freda Poverman, "Alumnae on Parade," *Barnard Alumnae Magazine*, July, 1957.

Chapter 2. THE HAPPY HOUSEWIFE HEROINE

1. Betty Friedan, "Women Are People Too!" *Good Housekeeping*, September, 1960. The letters received from women all over the United States in response to this article were of such emotional intensity that I was convinced that "the problem that has no name" is by no means confined to the graduates of the women's Ivy League colleges.
2. In the 1960's, an occasional heroine who was not a "happy housewife" began to appear in the women's magazines. An editor of *McCall's* explained it: "Sometimes we run an offbeat story for pure entertainment value." One such novelette, which was written to order by Noel Clad for *Good Housekeeping* (January, 1960), is called "Men Against Women." The heroine—a happy career woman —nearly loses child as well as husband.

Chapter 3. THE CRISIS IN WOMAN'S IDENTITY

1. Erik H. Erikson, *Young Man Luther, A Study in Psychoanalysis and History*, New York, 1958, pp. 15 ff. See also Erikson, *Childhood and Society*, New York, 1950, and Erikson, "The Problem of Ego Identity," *Journal of the American Psychoanalytical Association*, Vol. 4, 1956, pp. 56–121.

Chapter 4. THE PASSIONATE JOURNEY

1. See Eleanor Flexner, *Century of Struggle: The Woman's Rights Movement in The United States*, Cambridge, Mass., 1959. This definitive history of the woman's rights movement in the United States, published in 1959 at the height of the era of the feminine mystique, did not receive the attention it deserves, from either the intelligent reader or the scholar. In my opinion, it should be required reading for every girl admitted to a U.S. college. One reason the mystique prevails is that very few women under the age of forty know the facts of the woman's rights movement. I am much indebted to Miss Flexner for many factual clues I might otherwise have missed in my attempt to get at the truth behind the feminine mystique and its monstrous image of the feminists.

2. See Sidney Ditzion, *Marriage, Morals and Sex in America—A History of Ideas*, New York, 1953. This extensive bibliographical essay by the librarian of New York University documents the continuous interrelationship between movements for social and sexual reform in America, and, specifically, between man's movement for greater self-realization and sexual fulfillment and the woman's rights movement. The speeches and tracts assembled reveal that the movement to emancipate women was often seen by the men as well as the women who led it in terms of "creating an equitable balance of power between the sexes" for "a more satisfying expression of sexuality for both sexes."

3. *Ibid.*, p. 107.

4. Yuri Suhl, *Ernestine L. Rose and the Battle for Human Rights*, New York, 1959, p. 158. A vivid account of the battle for a married woman's right to her own property and earnings.

5. Flexner, *op. cit.*, p. 30.

6. Elinor Rice Hays, *Morning Star, A Biography of Lucy Stone*, New York, 1961, p. 83.

7. Flexner, *op. cit.*, p. 64.

8. Hays, *op. cit.*, p. 136.

9. *Ibid.*, p. 285.
10. Flexner, *op. cit.*, p. 46.
11. *Ibid.*, p. 73.
12. Hays, *op. cit.*, p. 221.
13. Flexner, *op. cit.*, p. 117.
14. *Ibid.*, p. 235.
15. *Ibid.*, p. 299.
16. *Ibid.*, p. 173.
17. Ida Alexis Ross Wylie, "The Little Woman," *Harper's* Magazine, November, 1945.

Chapter 5. THE SEXUAL SOLIPSISM OF SIGMUND FREUD

1. Clara Thompson, *Psychoanalysis: Evolution and Development*, New York, 1950, pp. 131 ff:

Freud not only emphasized the biological more than the cultural, but he also developed a cultural theory of his own based on his biological theory. There were two obstacles in the way of understanding the importance of the cultural phenomena he saw and recorded. He was too deeply involved in developing his biological theories to give much thought to other aspects of the data he collected. Thus he was interested chiefly in applying to human society his theory of instincts. Starting with the assumption of a death instinct, for example, he then developed an explanation of the cultural phenomena he observed in terms of the death instinct. Since he did not have the perspective to be gained from knowledge of comparative cultures, he could not evaluate cultural processes as such. . . . Much which Freud believed to be biological has been shown by modern research to be a reaction to a certain type of culture and not characteristic of universal human nature.

2. Richard La Piere, *The Freudian Ethic*, New York, 1959, p. 62.
3. Ernest Jones, *The Life and Work of Sigmund Freud*, New York, 1953, Vol. I, p. 384.
4. *Ibid.*, Vol II (1955), p. 432.
5. *Ibid.*, Vol. I, pp. 7–14, 294; Vol. II, p. 483.
6. Bruno Bettelheim, *Love Is Not Enough: The Treatment of Emotionally Disturbed Children*, Glencoe, Ill., 1950, pp. 7 ff.
7. Ernest L. Freud, *Letters of Sigmund Freud*, New York, 1960, Letter 10, p. 27; Letter 26, p. 71; Letter 65, p. 145.
8. *Ibid.*, Letter 74, p. 60; Letter 76, pp. 161 ff.
9. Jones, *op. cit.*, Vol. I, pp. 176 f.
10. *Ibid.*, Vol. II, p. 422.
11. *Ibid.*, Vol. I, p. 271:

His descriptions of sexual activities are so matter-of-fact that many readers have found them almost dry and totally lacking in warmth. From all I know of him, I should say that he displayed less than the average personal interest in what is often an absorbing topic. There was never any gusto or even savor in mentioning a sexual topic. . . . He always gave the impression of being an unusually chaste person—the word "puritanical" would not be out of place—and all we know of his early development confirms this conception.

12. *Ibid.*, Vol. I, p. 102.
13. *Ibid.*, Vol. I, pp. 110 ff.
14. *Ibid.*, Vol. I, p. 124.
15. *Ibid.*, Vol. I, p. 127.
16. *Ibid.*, Vol. I, p. 138.
17. *Ibid.*, Vol. I, p. 151.
18. Helen Walker Puner, *Freud, His Life and His Mind*, New York, 1947, p. 152.
19. Jones, *op. cit.*, Vol. II, p. 121.
20. *Ibid.*, Vol. I, pp. 301 ff. During the years Freud was germinating his sexual theory, before his own heroic self-analysis freed him from a passionate dependence on a series of men, his emotions were focused on a flamboyant nose-and-throat doctor named Fliess. This is one coincidence of history that was quite fateful for women. For Fliess had proposed, and obtained Freud's lifelong allegiance to, a fantastic "scientific theory" which reduced all phenomena of life and death to "bisexuality," expressed in mathematical terms through a periodic table based on the number 28, the female menstrual cycle. Freud looked forward to meetings with Fliess "as for the satisfying of hunger and thirst." He wrote him: "No one can replace the intercourse with a friend that a particular, perhaps feminine side of me, demands." Even after his own self-analysis, Freud still expected to die on the day predicted by Fliess' periodic table, in which everything could be figured out in terms of the female number 28, or the male 23, which was derived from the end of one female menstrual period to the beginning of the next.
21. *Ibid.*, Vol. I, p. 320.
22. Sigmund Freud, "Degradation in Erotic Life," in *The Collected Papers of Sigmund Freud*, Vol. IV.
23. Thompson, *op. cit.*, p. 133.
24. Sigmund Freud, "The Psychology of Women," in *New Introductory Lectures on Psychoanalysis*, tr. by W. J. H. Sprott, New York, 1933, pp. 170 f.
25. *Ibid.*, p. 182.
26. *Ibid.*, p. 184.
27. Thompson, *op. cit.*, pp. 12 f:

The war of 1914–18 further focussed attention on ego drives. . . . Another idea came into analysis around this period . . . and that was that aggression

as well as sex might be an important repressed impulse. . . . The puzzling
problem was how to include it in the theory of instincts. . . . Eventually
Freud solved this by his second instinct theory. Aggression found its place
as part of the death instinct. It is interesting that normal self-assertion, i.e.,
the impulse to master, control or come to self-fulfilling terms with the environment, was not especially emphasized by Freud.

28. Sigmund Freud, "Anxiety and Instinctual Life," in *New Introduc-
    tory Lectures on Psychoanalysis*, p. 149.
29. Marynia Farnham and Ferdinand Lundberg, *Modern Woman:
    The Lost Sex*, New York and London, 1947, pp. 142 ff.
30. Ernest Jones, *op. cit.*, Vol. II, p. 446.
31. Helene Deutsch, *The Psychology of Women—A Psychoanalytical
    Interpretation*, New York, 1944, Vol. I, pp. 224 ff.
32. *Ibid.*, Vol. I, pp. 251 ff.
33. Sigmund Freud, "The Anatomy of the Mental Personality," in
    New Introductory Lectures on Psychoanalysis, p. 96.

Chapter 6. THE FUNCTIONAL FREEZE, THE
FEMININE PROTEST, AND
MARGARET MEAD

1. Henry A. Bowman, *Marriage for Moderns*, New York, 1942, p. 21.
2. *Ibid.*, pp. 22 ff.
3. *Ibid.*, pp. 62 ff.
4. *Ibid.*, pp. 74–76.
5. *Ibid.*, pp. 66 ff.
6. Talcott Parsons, "Age and Sex in the Social Structure of the United
   States," in *Essays in Sociological Theory*, Glencoe, Ili., 1949, pp.
   223 ff.
7. Talcott Parsons, "An Analytical Approach to the Theory of Social
   Stratification," *op. cit.*, pp. 174 ff.
8. Mirra Komarovsky, *Women in the Modern World, Their Education and Their Dilemmas*, Boston, 1953, pp. 52–61.
9. *Ibid.*, p. 66.
10. *Ibid.*, pp. 72–74.
11. Mirra Komarovsky, "Functional Analysis of Sex Roles," *American
    Sociological Review*, August, 1950. See also "Cultural Contradictions
    and Sex Roles," *American Journal of Sociology*, November, 1946.
12. Kingsley Davis, "The Myth of Functional Analysis as a Special
    Method in Sociology and Anthropology," *American Sociological
    Review*, Vol. 24, No. 6, December, 1959, pp. 757–772. Davis points
    out that functionalism became more or less identical with sociology
    itself. There is provocative evidence that the very study of sociology,
    in recent years, has persuaded college women to limit themselves to

their "functional" traditional sexual role. A report on "The Status of Women in Professional Sociology" (Sylvia Fleis Fava, *American Sociological Review*, Vol. 25, No. 2, April, 1960) shows that while most of the students in sociology undergraduate classes are women, from 1949 to 1958 there was a sharp decline in both the number and proportion of degrees in sociology awarded to women. (4,143 B.A.'s in 1949 down to a low of 3,200 in 1955, 3,606 in 1958). And while one-half to two-thirds of the undergraduate degrees in sociology were awarded to women, women received only 25 to 43 per cent of the masters' degrees, and only 8 to 19 per cent of the Ph.D.'s. While the number of women earning graduate degrees in all fields has declined sharply during the era of the feminine mystique, the field of sociology showed, in comparison to other fields, an unusually high "mortality" rate.

13. Margaret Mead, *Sex and Temperament in Three Primitive Societies*, New York, 1935, pp. 279 f.
14. Margaret Mead, *From the South Seas*, New York, 1939, p. 321.
15. Margaret Mead, *Male and Female*, New York, 1955, pp. 16–18.
16. *Ibid.*, p. 26.
17. *Ibid.*, footnotes, pp. 289 f:

I did not begin to work seriously with the zones of the body until I went to the Arapesh in 1931. While I was generally familiar with Freud's basic work on the subject, I had not seen how it might be applied in the field until I read Geza Roheim's first field report, "Psychoanalysis of Primitive Culture Types" . . . I then sent home for abstracts of K. Abraham's work. After I became acquainted with Erik Homburger Erikson's systematic handling of these ideas, they became an integral part of my theoretical equipment.

18. *Ibid.*, pp. 50 f.
19. *Ibid.*, pp. 72 ff.
20. *Ibid.*, pp. 84 ff.
21. *Ibid.*, p. 85.
22. *Ibid.*, pp. 125 ff.
23. *Ibid.*, pp. 135 ff.
24. *Ibid.*, pp. 274 ff.
25. *Ibid.*, pp. 278 ff.
26. *Ibid.*, pp. 276–285.
27. Margaret Mead, Introduction to *From the South Seas*, New York, 1939, p. xiii. "It was no use permitting children to develop values different from those of their society . . ."
28. Marie Jahoda and Joan Havel, "Psychological Problems of Women in Different Social Roles—A Case History of Problem Formulation in Research," *Educational Record*, Vol. 36, 1955, pp 325–333.

Chapter 7. THE SEX-DIRECTED EDUCATORS

1. Mabel Newcomer, *A Century of Higher Education for Women*, New York, 1959, pp. 45 ff. The proportion of women among college students in the U.S. increased from 21 per cent in 1870 to 47 per cent in 1920; it had declined to 35.2 per cent in 1958. Five women's colleges had closed; 21 had become coeducational; 2 had become junior colleges. In 1956, 3 out of 5 women in the coeducational colleges were taking secretarial, nursing, home economics, or education courses. Less than 1 out of 10 doctorates were granted to women, compared to 1 in 6 in 1920, 13 per cent in 1940. Not since before World War I have the percentages of American women receiving professional degrees been as consistently low as in this period. The extent of the retrogression of American women can also be measured in terms of their failure to develop to their own potential. According to *Womanpower*, of all the young women *capable* of doing college work, only one out of four goes to college, compared to one out of two men; only one out of 300 women capable of earning a Ph.D. actually does so, compared to one out of 30 men. If the present situation continues, American women may soon rank among the most "backward" women in the world. The U.S. is probably the only nation where the proportion of women gaining higher education has decreased in the past 20 years; it has steadily increased in Sweden, Britain, and France, as well as the emerging nations of Asia and the communist countries. By the 1950's, a larger proportion of French women were obtaining higher education than American women; the proportion of French women in the professions had more than doubled in fifty years. The proportion of French women in the medical profession alone is five times that of American women; 70% of the doctors in the Soviet Union are women, compared to 5% in America. See Alva Myrdal and Viola Klein, *Women's Two Roles—Home and Work*, London, 1956, pp. 33–64.

2. Mervin B. Freedman, "The Passage through College," in *Personality Development During the College Years*, ed. by Nevitt Sanford, *Journal of Social Issues*, Vol. XII, No. 4, 1956, pp. 15 f.

3. John Bushnel, "Student Culture at Vassar," in *The American College*, ed. by Nevitt Sanford, New York and London, 1962, pp. 509 f.

4. Lynn White, *Educating our Daughters*, New York, 1950, pp. 18–48.

5. *Ibid.*, p. 76.

6. *Ibid.*, pp. 77 ff.

7. *Ibid.*, p. 79.

8. See Dael Wolfle, *America's Resources of Specialized Talent*, New York, 1954.

9. Cited in an address by Judge Mary H. Donlon in proceedings of "Conference on the Present Status and Prospective Trends of Research on the Education of Women," 1957, American Council on Education, Washington, D.C.

10. See "The Bright Girl: A Major Source of Untapped Talent," *Guidance Newsletter*, Science Research Associates Inc., Chicago, Ill., May, 1959.

11. See Dael Wolfle, *op. cit.*

12. John Summerskill, "Dropouts from College," in *The American College*, p. 631.

13. Joseph M. Jones, "Does Overpopulation Mean Poverty?" Center for International Economic Growth, Washington, 1962. See also *United Nations Demographic Yearbook*, New York, 1960, pp. 580 ff. By 1958, in the United States, more girls were marrying from 15–19 years of age than from any other age group. In all of the other advanced nations, and many of the emerging underdeveloped nations, most girls married from 20–24 or after 25. The U.S. pattern of teenage marriage could only be found in countries like Paraguay, Venezuela, Honduras, Guatemala, Mexico, Egypt, Iraq and the Fiji Islands.

14. Nevitt Sanford, "Higher Education as a Social Problem" in *The American College*, p. 23.

15. Elizabeth Douvan and Carol Kaye, "Motivational Factors in College Entrance," in *The American College*, pp. 202–206.

16. *Ibid.*, pp. 208 f.

17. Esther Lloyd-Jones, "Women Today and Their Education," *Teachers' College Record*, Vol. 57, No. 1, October, 1955; and No. 7, April, 1956. See also Opal David, *The Education of Women—Signs for the Future*, American Council on Education, Washington, D.C., 1957.

18. Mary Ann Guitar, "College Marriage Courses—Fun or Fraud?" *Mademoiselle*, February, 1961.

19. Helene Deutsch, *op. cit.*, Vol. I, p. 290.

20. Mirra Komarovsky, *op. cit.*, p. 70. Research studies indicate that 40 per cent of college girls "play dumb" with men. Since the ones who do not include those not excessively overburdened with intelligence, the great majority of American girls who are gifted with high intelligence evidently learn to hide it.

21. Jean Macfarlane and Lester Sontag, Research reported to the Commission on the Education of Women, Washington, D.C., 1954, (mimeo ms.).

22. Harold Webster, "Some Quantitative Results," in *Personality De-*

velopment During the College Years, ed. by Nevitt Sanford, *Journal of Social Issues*, 1956, Vol. 12, No. 4, p. 36.

23. Nevitt Sanford, *Personality Development During the College Years, Journal of Social Issues*, 1956, Vol. 12, No. 4.

24. Mervin B. Freedman, "Studies of College Alumni," in *The American College*, p. 878.

25. Lynn White, *op. cit.*, p. 117.

26. *Ibid.*, pp. 119 f.

27. Max Lerner, *America As a Civilization*, New York, 1957, pp. 608–611:

The crux of it lies neither in the biological nor economic disabilities of women but in their sense of being caught between a man's world which they have no real will to achieve and a world of their own in which they find it hard to be fulfilled. . . . When Walt Whitman exhorted women "to give up toys and fictions and launch forth, as men do, amid real, independent, stormy life," he was thinking—as were many of his contemporaries—of the wrong kind of equalitarianism. . . . If she is to discover her identity, she must start by basing her belief in herself on her womanliness rather than on the movement for feminism. Margaret Mead has pointed out that the biological life cycle of the woman has certain well-marked phases from menarche through the birth of her children to her menopause; that in these stages of her life cycle, as in her basic bodily rhythms, she can feel secure in her womanhood and does not have to assert her potency as the male does. Similarly, while the multiple roles that she must play in life are bewildering, she can fulfill them without distraction if she knows that her central role is that of a woman. . . . Her central function, however, remains that of creating a life style for herself and for the home in which she is life creator and life sustainer.

28. See Philip E. Jacob, *Changing Values in College*, New York, 1957.

29. Margaret Mead, "New Look at Early Marriages," interview in *U.S. News and World Report*, June 6, 1960.

Chapter 8. THE MISTAKEN CHOICE

1. See the *United Nations Demographic Yearbook*, New York, 1960, pp. 99–118 and pp. 476–490; p. 580. The annual rate of population increase in the U.S. in the years 1955–59 was far higher than that of other Western nations, and higher than that of India, Japan, Burma, and Pakistan. In fact, the increase for North America (1.8) exceeded the world rate (1.7). The rate for Europe was .8; for the USSR 1.7; Asia 1.8; Africa 1.9; and South America 2.3. The increase in the underdeveloped nations was, of course, largely due to medical advances and the drop in death rate; in America it was almost completely due to increased birth rate, earlier marriage, and larger

families. For the birth rate continued to rise in the U.S. from 1950 to 1959, while it was falling in countries like France, Norway, Sweden, the USSR, India and Japan. The U.S. was the only so-called "advanced" nation, and one of the few nations in the world where, in 1958, more girls married at ages 15–19 than at any other age. Even the other countries which showed a rise in the birth rate —Germany, Canada, the United Kingdom, Chile, New Zealand, Peru—did not show this phenomenon of teenage marriage.

2. See "The Woman with Brains (continued)," *New York Times Magazine*, January 17, 1960, for the outraged letters in response to an article by Marya Mannes, "Female Intelligence—Who Wants It?" *New York Times Magazine*, January 3, 1960.

3. See National Manpower Council, *Womanpower*, New York, 1957. In 1940, more than half of all employed women in the U.S. were under 25, and one-fifth were over 45. In the 1950's peak participation in paid employment occurs among young women of 18 and 19— and women over 45, the great majority of whom hold jobs for which little training is required. The new preponderance of older married women in the working force is partly due to the fact that so few women in their twenties and thirties now work, in the U.S. Two out of five of all employed women are now over 45, most of them wives and mothers, working part time at unskilled work. Those reports of millions of American wives working outside the home are misleading in more ways than one: of all employed women, only one-third hold full-time jobs, one-third work full time only part of the year—for instance, extra saleswomen in the department stores at Christmas—and one-third work part time, part of the year. The women in the professions are, for the most part, that dwindling minority of single women; the older untrained wives and mothers, like the untrained 18-year-olds, are concentrated at the lower end of the skill ladder and the pay scales, in factory, service, sales and office work. Considering the growth in the population, and the increasing professionalization of work in America, the startling phenomenon is not the much-advertised, relatively insignificant increase in the numbers of American women who now work outside the home, but the fact that two out of three adult American women do *not* work outside the home, and the increasing millions of young women who are not skilled or educated for work in any profession. See also Theodore Caplow, *The Sociology of Work*, 1954, and Alva Myrdal and Viola Klein, *Women's Two Roles— Home and Work*, London, 1956.

4. Edward Strecker, *Their Mothers' Sons*, Philadelphia and New York, 1946, pp. 52–59.

5. *Ibid.*, pp. 31 ff.

6. Farnham and Lundberg, *Modern Woman, The Lost Sex*, p. 271. See also Lynn White, *Educating Our Daughters*, p. 90.

Preliminary results of the careful study of American sex habits being conducted at the University of Indiana by Dr. A. C. Kinsey indicate that there is an inverse correlation between education and the ability of a woman to achieve habitual orgastic experience in marriage. According to the present evidence, admittedly tentative, nearly 65 per cent of the marital intercourse had by women with college backgrounds is had without orgasm for them, as compared to about 15 per cent for married women who have gone no further than grade school.

7. Alfred C. Kinsey, *et al.*, Staff of the Institute for Sex Research, Indiana University, *Sexual Behavior in the Human Female*, Philadelphia and London, 1953, pp. 378 f.
8. Lois Meek Stolz, "Effects of Maternal Employment on Children: Evidence from Research," *Child Development*, Vol. 31, No. 4, 1960, pp. 749-782.
9. H. F. Southard, "Mothers' Dilemma: To Work or Not?" *New York Times Magazine*, July 17, 1960.
10. Stolz, *op. cit.* See also Myrdal and Klein, *op. cit.*, pp. 125 ff.
11. Benjamin Spock, "Russian Children Don't Whine, Squabble or Break Things—Why?" *Ladies' Home Journal*, October, 1960.
12. David Levy, *Maternal Overprotection*, New York, 1943.
13. Arnold W. Green, "The Middle-Class Male Child and Neurosis," *American Sociological Review*, Vol. II, No. 1, 1946.

Chapter 9. THE SEXUAL SELL

1. The studies upon which this chapter is based were done by the Staff of the Institute for Motivational Research, directed by Dr. Ernest Dichter. They were made available to me through the courtesy of Dr. Dichter and his colleagues, and are on file at the Institute, in Croton-on-Hudson, New York.
2. Harrison Kinney, *Has Anybody Seen My Father?*, New York, 1960.

Chapter 10. HOUSEWIFERY EXPANDS TO FILL THE TIME AVAILABLE

1. Jhan and June Robbins, "Why Young Mothers Feel Trapped," *Redbook*, September, 1960.
2. Carola Woerishoffer Graduate Department of Social Economy and Social Research, "Women During the War and After," Bryn Mawr College, 1945.

3. Theodore Caplow points out in *The Sociology of Work*, p. 234, that with the rapidly expanding economy since 1900, and the extremely rapid urbanization of the United States, the increase in the employment of women from 20.4% in 1900 to 28.5% in 1950 was exceedingly modest. Recent studies of time spent by American housewives on housework, which confirm my description of the Parkinson effect, are summarized by Jean Warren, "Time: Resource or Utility," *Journal of Home Economics*, Vol. 49, January, 1957, pp. 21 ff. Alva Myrdal and Viola Klein in *Women's Two Roles— Home and Work* cite a French study which showed that working mothers reduced time spent on housework by 30 hours a week, compared to a full-time housewife. The work week of a working mother with three children broke down to 35.2 hours on the job, 48.3 hours on housework; the full-time housewife spent 77.7 hours on housework. The mother with a full-time job or profession, as well as the housekeeping and children, worked only one hour a day longer than the full-time housewife.

4. Robert Wood, *Suburbia, Its People and Their Politics*, Boston, 1959.

5. See "Papa's Taking Over the PTA Mama Started," *New York Herald Tribune*, February 10, 1962. At the 1962 national convention of Parent-Teacher Associations, it was revealed that 32% of the 46,457 PTA presidents are now men. In certain states the percentage of male PTA heads is even higher, including New York (33 per cent), Connecticut (45 per cent) and Delaware (80 per cent).

6. Nanette E. Scofield, "Some Changing Roles of Women in Suburbia: A Social Anthropological Case Study," transactions of the New York Academy of Sciences, Vol. 22, No. 6, April, 1960.

7. Mervin B. Freedman, "Studies of College Alumni," in *The American College*, pp. 872 f.

8. Murray T. Pringle, "Women Are Wretched Housekeepers," *Science Digest*, June, 1960.

9. See *Time*, April 20, 1959.

10. Farnham and Lundberg, *Modern Women: The Lost Sex*, p. 369.

11. Edith M. Stern, "Women are Household Slaves," *American Mercury*, January, 1949.

12. Russell Lynes, "The New Servant Class," in *A Surfeit of Honey*, New York, 1957, p. 49–64.

Chapter 11. THE SEX-SEEKERS

1. Several social historians have commented on America's sexual preoccupation from the male point of view. "America has come to stress sex as much as any civilization since the Roman," says Max

Lerner (*America as a Civilization*, p. 678). David Riesman in *The Lonely Crowd* (New Haven, 1950, p. 172 ff.) calls sex "the Last Frontier."

> More than before, as job-mindedness declines, sex permeates the daytime as well as the playtime consciousness. It is viewed as a consumption good not only by the old leisure classes but by the modern leisure masses. . . .
> One reason for the change is that women are no longer objects for the acquisitive consumer but are peer-groupers themselves. . . . Today, millions of women, freed by technology from many household tasks, given by technology many aids to romance, have become pioneers with men on the frontiers of sex. As they become knowing consumers, the anxiety of men lest they fail to satisfy the women also grows . . .

It is mainly the clinicians who have noted that the men are often less eager now than their wives as sexual "consumers." The late Dr. Abraham Stone, whom I interviewed shortly before his death, said that the wives complain more and more of sexually "inadequate" husbands. Dr. Karl Menninger reports that for every wife who complains of her husband's excessive sexuality, a dozen wives complain that their husbands are apathetic or impotent. These "problems" are cited in the mass media as additional evidence that American women are losing their "femininity"—and thus provide new ammunition for the mystique. See John Kord Lagemann, "The Male Sex," *Redbook*, December, 1956.

2. Albert Ellis, *The Folklore of Sex*, New York, 1961, p. 123.

3. See the amusing parody, "The Pious Pornographers," by Ray Russell, in *The Permanent Playboy*, New York, 1959.

4. A. C. Spectorsky, *The Exurbanites*, New York, 1955, p. 223.

5. Nathan Ackerman, *The Psychodynamics of Family Life*, New York, 1958, pp. 112–127.

6. Evan Hunter, *Strangers When We Meet*, New York, 1958, pp. 231–235.

7. Kinsey, *et al.*, *Sexual Behavior in the Human Female*, pp. 353 ff., p. 426.

8. Doris Menzer-Benaron M.D., *et al.*, "Patterns of Emotional Recovery from Hysterectomy," *Psychosomatic Medicine*, XIX, No. 5, September, 1957, pp. 378–388.

9. The fact that 75 per cent to 85 per cent of young mothers in America today feel negative emotions—resentment, grief, disappointment, outright rejection—when they become pregnant for the first time has been established in many studies. In fact, the perpetrators of the feminine mystique report findings to reassure young mothers that they are only "normal" in feeling this strange rejection of pregnancy—and that the only real problem is their "guilt" over feeling it. Thus *Redbook* magazine, in "How Women Really Feel

about Pregnancy" (November, 1958), reports that the Harvard School of Public Health found 80 to 85 per cent of "normal women reject the pregnancy when they become pregnant"; Long Island College Clinic found that less than a fourth of women are "happy" about their pregnancy; a New Haven study finds only 17 of 100 women "pleased" about having a baby. Comments the voice of editorial authority:

> The real danger that arises when a pregnancy is unwelcome and filled with troubled feelings is that a woman may become guilty and panic-stricken because she believes her reactions are unnatural or abnormal. Both marital and mother-child relations can be damaged as a result. . . . Sometimes a mental-health specialist is needed to allay guilt feelings. . . . Nor is there any time when a normal woman does not have feelings of depression and doubt when she learns that she is pregnant.

Such articles never mention the various studies which indicate that women in other countries, both more and less advanced than the United States, and even American "career" women, are less likely to experience this emotional rejection of pregnancy. Depression at pregnancy may be "normal" for the housewife-mother in the era of the feminine mystique, but it is not normal to motherhood. As Ruth Benedict said, it is not biological necessity, but our culture which creates the discomforts, physical and psychological, of the female cycle. See her *Continuities and Discontinuities in Cultural Conditioning*.

10. See William J. Goode, *After Divorce*, Glencoe, Ill., 1956.

11. A. C. Kinsey, *et al.*, *Sexual Behavior in the Human Male*, Philadelphia and London, 1948, p. 259, pp. 585–588.

12. The male contempt for the American woman, as she has molded herself according to the feminine mystique, is depressingly explicit in the July, 1962 issue of *Esquire*, "The American Woman, A New Point of View." See especially "The Word to Women—'No'" by Robert Alan Aurthur, p. 32. The sexlessness of the American female sex-seekers is eulogized by Malcolm Muggeridge ("Bedding Down in the Colonies," p. 84): "How they mortify the flesh in order to make it appetizing! Their beauty is a vast industry, their enduring allure a discipline which nuns or athletes might find excessive. With too much sex to be sensual, and too ravishing to ravish, age cannot wither them nor custom stale their infinite monotony."

13. Kinsey, *et al.*, *Sexual Behavior in the Human Male*, p. 631.

14. See Donald Webster Cory, *The Homosexual in America*, New York, 1960, preface to second edition, pp. xxii ff. Also Albert Ellis, *op. cit.*, pp. 186–190. Also Seward Hiltner, "Stability and Change in American Sexual Patterns," in *Sexual Behavior in American Society*, Jerome Himelhoch and Sylvia Fleis Fava, eds., New York,

1955, p. 321.

15. Sigmund Freud, *Three Contributions to the Theory of Sex*, New York, 1948, p. 10.

16. Kinsey, *et al.*, *Sexual Behavior in the Human Male*, pp. 610 ff. See also Donald Webster Cory, *op. cit.*, pp. 97 ff.

17. Birth out of wedlock increased 194 per cent from 1956 to 1962; venereal disease among young people increased 132 per cent. (*Time*, March 16, 1962).

18. Kinsey, *et al.*, *Sexual Behavior in the Human Male*, pp. 348 ff., 427–433.

19. Kinsey, *et al.*, *Sexual Behavior in the Human Female*, pp. 293, 378, 382.

20. Clara Thompson, "Changing Concepts of Homosexuality in Psychoanalysis" in *A Study of Interpersonal Relations, New Contributions to Psychiatry*, Patrick Mullahy, ed., New York, 1949, pp. 218 f.

21. Erich Fromm, "Sex and Character: the Kinsey Report Viewed from the Standpoint of Psychoanalysis," in *Sexual Behavior in American Society*, p. 307.

22. Carl Binger, "The Pressures On College Girls Today," *Atlantic Monthly*, February, 1961.

23. Sallie Bingham, "Winter Term," *Mademoiselle*, July, 1958.

Chapter 12. PROGRESSIVE DEHUMANIZATION: THE COMFORTABLE CONCENTRATION CAMP

1. Marjorie K. McCorquodale, "What They Will Die for in Houston," *Harper's*, October, 1961.

2. See David Riesman, *The Lonely Crowd;* also Erich Fromm, *Escape From Freedom*, New York and Toronto, 1941, pp. 185–206. Also Erik H. Erikson, *Childhood and Society*, p. 239.

3. David Riesman, introduction to Edgar Friedenberg's *The Vanishing Adolescent*, Boston, 1959.

4. Harold Taylor, "Freedom and Authority on the Campus," in *The American College*, pp. 780 ff.

5. David Riesman, introduction to Edgar Friedenberg's *The Vanishing Adolescent*.

6. See Eugene Kinkead, *In Every War But One*, New York, 1959. There has been an attempt in recent years to discredit or soft-pedal these findings. But a taped record of a talk given before the American Psychiatric Association in 1958 by Dr. William Mayer, who

had been on one of the Army teams of psychiatrists and intelligence officers who interviewed the returning prisoners in 1953 and analyzed the data, caused many pediatricians and child specialists to ask, in the words of Dr. Spock: "Are unusually permissive, indulgent parents more numerous today—and are they weakening the character of our children?" (Benjamin Spock, "Are We Bringing Up Our Children Too 'Soft' for the Stern Realities They Must Face?" *Ladies' Home Journal,* September, 1960.) However unpleasantly injurious to American pride, there must be some explanation for the collapse of the American GI prisoners in Korea, as it differed not only from the behavior of American soldiers in previous wars, but from the behavior of soldiers of other nations in Korea. No American soldier managed to escape from the enemy prison camps, as they had in every other war. The shocking 38 per cent death rate was not explainable, even according to military authorities, on the basis of the climate, food, or inadequate medical facilities in the camps, nor was it caused by brutality or torture. "Give-up-itis" is how one doctor described the disease the Americans died from; they simply spent the days curled up under blankets, cutting down their diet to water alone, until they were dead, usually within three weeks. This seemed to be an American phenomenon. Turkish prisoners, who were also part of the UN force in Korea, lost no men by disease or starvation; they stuck together, obeyed their officers, adhered to health regulations, cooperated in the care of their sick, and refused to inform on one another.

7. Edgar Friedenberg, *The Vanishing Adolescent,* pp. 212 ff.

8. Andras Angyal, M.D., "Evasion of Growth," *American Journal of Psychiatry,* Vol. 110, No. 5, November, 1953, pp. 358–361. See also Erich Fromm, *Escape from Freedom,* pp. 138–206.

9. See Richard E. Gordon and Katherine K. Gordon, "Social Factors in the Prediction and Treatment of Emotional Disorders of Pregnancy," *American Journal of Obstetrics and Gynecology,* 1959, 77:5, pp. 1074–1083; also Richard E. Gordon and Katherine K. Gordon, "Psychiatric Problems of a Rapidly Growing Suburb," *American Medical Association Archives of Neurology and Psychiatry,* 1958, Vol. 79; "Psychosomatic Problems of a Rapidly Growing Suburb," *Journal of the American Medical Association,* 1959, 170:15; and "Social Psychiatry of a Mobile Suburb," *International Journal of Social Psychiatry,* 1960, 6:1, 2, pp. 89–99. Some of these findings were popularized in the composite case histories of *The Split Level Trap,* written by the Gordons in collaboration with Max Gunther (New York, 1960).

10. Richard E. Gordon, "Sociodynamics and Psychotherapy," *A.M.A. Archives of Neurology and Psychiatry,* April, 1959, Vol. 81, pp. 486–

503.

11. Adelaide M. Johnson and S. A. Szurels, "The Genesis of Anti-social Acting Out in Children and Adults," *Psychoanalytic Quarterly*, 1952, 21:323–343.

12. *Ibid.*

13. Beata Rank, "Adaptation of the Psychoanalytical Technique for the Treatment of Young Children with Atypical Development," *American Journal of Orthopsychiatry*, XIX, 1, January, 1949.

14. *Ibid.*

15. *Ibid.*

16. Beata Rank, Marian C. Putnam, and Gregory Rochlin, M.D., "The Significance of the 'Emotional Climate' in Early Feeding Difficulties," *Psychosomatic Medicine*, X, 5, October, 1948.

17. Richard E. Gordon and Katherine K. Gordon, "Social Psychiatry of a Mobile Suburb," *op. cit.*, pp. 89–100.

18. *Ibid.*

19. Oscar Sternbach, "Sex Without Love and Marriage Without Responsibility," an address presented at the 38th Annual Conference of The Child Study Association of America, March 12, 1962, New York City (mimeo ms.).

20. Bruno Bettelheim, *The Informed Heart—Autonomy in a Mass Age*, Glencoe, Ill., 1960.

21. *Ibid.*, pp. 162–169.

22. *Ibid.*, p. 231.

23. *Ibid.*, pp. 233 ff.

24. *Ibid.*, p. 265.

Chapter 13. THE FORFEITED SELF

1. Rollo May, "The Origins and Significance of the Existential Movement in Psychology," in *Existence, A New Dimension in Psychiatry and Psychology*, Rollo May, Ernest Angel and Henri F. Ellenberger, eds., New York, 1958, pp. 30 f. (See also Erich Fromm, *Escape from Freedom*, pp. 269 ff.; A. H. Maslow, *Motivation and Personality*, New York, 1954; David Riesman, *The Lonely Crowd*.)

2. Rollo May, "Contributions of Existential Psychotherapy," in *Existence, A New Dimension in Psychiatry and Psychology*, p. 87.

3. *Ibid.*, p. 52.

4. *Ibid.*, p. 53.

5. *Ibid.*, pp. 59 f.

6. See Kurt Goldstein, *The Organism, A Holistic Approach to Biology Derived From Pathological Data on Man*, New York and Cincinnati, 1939; also *Abstract and Concrete Behavior*, Evanston,

Ill., 1950; *Case of Idiot Savant* (with Martin Scheerer), Evanston, 1945; *Human Nature in the Light of Psychopathology*, Cambridge, 1947; *After-Effects of Brain Injuries in War*, New York, 1942.

7. Eugene Minkowski, "Findings in a Case of Schizophrenic Depression," in *Existence, A New Dimension in Psychiatry and Psychology*, pp. 132 f.

8. O. Hobart Mowrer, "Time as a Determinant in Integrative Learning," in *Learning Theory and Personality Dynamics*, New York, 1950.

9. Eugene Minkowski, *op. cit.*, pp. 133–138:

We think and act and desire beyond that death which, even so, we could not escape. The very existence of such phenomena as the desire to do something for future generations clearly indicates our attitude in this regard. In our patient, it was this propulsion toward the future which seemed to be totally lacking. . . . In this personal impetus, there is an element of expansion; we go beyond the limits of our own ego and leave a personal imprint on the world about us, creating works which sever themselves from us to live their own lives. This accompanies a specific, positive feeling which we call contentment—that pleasure which accompanies every finished action or firm decision. As a feeling, it is unique. . . . Our entire individual evolution consists in trying to surpass that which has already been done. When our mental life dims, the future closes in front of us . . .

10. Rollo May, "Contributions of Existential Psychotherapy," pp. 31 f. In Nietzsche's philosophy, human individuality and dignity are "given or assigned to us as a task which we ourselves must solve"; in Tillich's philosophy, if you do not have the "courage to be," you lose your own being; in Sartre's, you *are* your choices.

11. A. H. Maslow, *Motivation and Personality*, p. 83.

12. A. H. Maslow, "Some Basic Propositions of Holistic-Dynamic Psychology," an unpublished paper, Brandeis University.

13. *Ibid.*

14. A. H. Maslow, "Dominance, Personality and Social Behavior in Women," *Journal of Social Psychology*, 1939, Vol. 10, pp. 3–39; and "Self Esteem (Dominance-Feeling) and Sexuality in Women," *Journal of Social Psychology*, 1942, Vol. 16, pp. 259–294.

15. A. H. Maslow, "Dominance, Personality and Social Behavior in Women," *op. cit.*, pp. 3–11.

16. *Ibid.*, pp. 13 f.

17. *Ibid.*, p. 180.

18. A. H. Maslow, "Self-Esteem (Dominance-Feeling) and Sexuality in Women," pp. 288. Maslow points out, however, that women with "ego insecurity" pretended a "self-esteem" they did not actually have. Such women had to "dominate," in the ordinary sense, in their sexual relations, to compensate for their "ego insecurity"; thus, they were either castrative or masochistic. As I have pointed out, such

women must have been very common in a society which gives women little chance for true self-esteem; this was undoubtedly the basis of the man-eating myth, and of Freud's equation of femininity with castrative penis envy and/or masochistic passivity.

19. A. H. Maslow, *Motivation and Personality*, pp. 200 f.
20. *Ibid.*, pp. 211 f.
21. *Ibid.*, pp. 214.
22. *Ibid.*, pp. 242 f.
23. *Ibid.*, pp. 257 f. Maslow found that his self-actualizing people "have in unusual measure the rare ability to be pleased rather than threatened by the partner's triumphs. . . . A most impressive example of this respect is the ungrudging pride of such a man in his wife's achievements even where they outshine his." (*Ibid.*, p. 252).
24. *Ibid.*, p. 245.
25. *Ibid.*, p. 255.
26. A. C. Kinsey, *et al.*, *Sexual Behavior in the Human Female*, pp. 356 ff.; Table 97, p. 397; Table 104, p. 403.

Decade of Birth vs. Percentage of Marital Coitus Leading to Orgasm.

	In First yr. of Marriage, per cent of females			
	Decade of Birth			
% of Marital Coitus with Orgasm	Before 1900	1900–1909	1910–1919	1920–1929
None	33	27	23	22
1–29	9	13	12	8
30–59	10	22	15	12
60–89	11	11	12	15
90–100	37	37	38	43
Number of cases	331	589	834	484

	In Fifth yr. of Marriage, per cent of females			
	Decade of Birth			
% of Marital Coitus with Orgasm	Before 1900	1900–1909	1910–1919	1920–1929
None	23	17	12	12
1–29	14	15	13	14
30–59	14	13	16	19
60–89	12	13	17	19
90–100	37	42	42	36
Number of cases	302	489	528	130

27. *Ibid.*, p. 355.
28. See Judson T. Landis, "The Women Kinsey Studied," George
    Simpson, "Nonsense about Women," and A. H. Maslow and James
    M. Sakoda, "Volunteer Error in the Kinsey Study," in *Sexual Be-
    havior in American Society*.
29. Ernest W. Burgess and Leonard S. Cottrell, Jr., *Predicting Success
    or Failure in Marriage*, New York, 1939, p. 271.
30. A. C. Kinsey, *et al.*, *Sexual Behavior in the Human Female*, p. 403.
31. Sylvan Keiser, "Body Ego During Orgasm," *Psychoanalytic Quart-
    erly*, 1952, Vol. XXI, pp. 153–166:

Individuals of this group are characterized by failure to develop adequate
egos. . . . Their anxious devotion to, and lavish care of, their bodies belies
the inner feelings of hollowness and inadequacy. . . . These patients have
little sense of their own identity and are always ready to take on the personality of someone else. They have few personal convictions, and yield
readily to the opinions of others. . . . It is chiefly among such patients that
coitus can be enjoyed only up to the point of orgasm. . . . They dared not
allow themselves uninhibited progression to orgasm with its concomitant
loss of control, loss of awareness of the body, or death. . . . In instances of
uncertainty about the structure and boundaries of the body image, one
might say that the skin does not serve as an envelope which sharply defines
the transition from the self to the environment; the one gradually merges
into the other; there is no assurance of being a distinct entity endowed
with the strength to give of itself without endangering one's own integrity.

32. Lawrence Kubie, "Psychiatric Implications of the Kinsey Report,"
    in *Sexual Behavior in American Society*, pp. 270 ff:

This simple biologic aim is overlaid by many subtle goals of which the
individual himself is usually unaware. Some of these are attainable; some
are not. Where the majority are attainable, then the end result of sexual
activity is an afterglow of peaceful completion and satisfaction. Where, however, the unconscious goals are unattainable, then whether orgasm has occurred or not, there remains a post-coital state of unsated need, and sometimes of fear, rage or depression.

33. Erik H. Erikson, *Childhood and Society*, pp. 239–283, 367–380. See
    also Erich Fromm, *Escape from Freedom* and *Man for Himself*; and
    David Riesman, *The Lonely Crowd*.
34. See Alva Myrdal and Viola Klein (*Women's Two Roles*), who
    point out that the number of American women now working out-
    side the home seems greater than it is because the base from which
    the comparison is usually made was unusually small: a century ago
    the proportion of American women working outside the home was
    far smaller than in the European countries. In other words, the
    woman problem in America was probably unusually severe because
    the displacement of American women from essential work and

identity in society was far more drastic—primarily because of the extremely rapid growth and industrialization of the American economy. The women who had grown with the men in the frontier days were banished almost overnight to *anomie*—which is a very expressive sociological name for that sense of nonexistence or non-identity suffered by one who has no real place in society—when the important work left the home, where they stayed. In contrast, in France where industrialization was slower, and farms and small family-size shops are still fairly important in the economy, women a century ago still worked in large numbers—in field and shop—and today the majority of French women are not full-time house-wives in the American sense of the mystique, for an enormous number still work in the fields, in addition to that one out of three who, as in America, work in industry, sales, offices, and professions. The growth of women in France has much more closely paralleled the growth of the society, since the proportion of French women in the professions has doubled in fifty years. It is interesting to note that the feminine mystique does not prevail in France, to the extent that it does here; there is a legitimate image in France of a feminine career woman and feminine intellectual, and Frenchmen seem responsive to women sexually, without equating femininity either with glorified emptiness or that man-eating castrative mom. Nor has the family been weakened—in actuality or mystique—by women's work in industry and profession. Myrdal and Klein show that the French career women continue to have children—but not the great number the new educated American housewives produce.

35. Sidney Ditzion, *Marriage, Morals and Sex in America, A History of Ideas*, New York, 1953, p. 277.
36. William James, *Psychology*, New York, 1892, p. 458.

Chapter 14. A NEW LIFE PLAN FOR WOMEN

1. See "Mother's Choice: Manager or Martyr," and "For a Mother's Hour," *New York Times Magazine*, January 14, 1962, and March 18, 1962.
2. The sense that work has to be "real," and not just "therapy" or busywork, to provide a basis for identity becomes increasingly explicit in the theories of the self, even when there is no specific reference to women. Thus, in defining the beginnings of "identity" in the child, Erikson says in *Childhood and Society* (p. 208):

The growing child must, at every step, derive a vitalizing sense of reality from the awareness that his individual way of mastering experience (his ego synthesis) is a successful variant of a group identity and is in accord with its space-time and life plan.

In this children cannot be fooled by empty praise and condescending encouragement. They may have to accept artificial bolstering of their self-esteem in lieu of something better, but their ego identity gains real strength only from wholehearted and consistent recognition of real accomplishment —i.e., of achievement that has meaning in the culture.

3. Nanette E. Scofield, "Some Changing Roles of Women in Suburbia: A Social Anthropological Case Study," transactions of the New York Academy of Sciences, Vol. 22, 6, April, 1960.
4. Polly Weaver, "What's Wrong with Ambition?" *Mademoiselle*, September, 1956.
5. Edna G. Rostow, "The Best of Both Worlds," *Yale Review*, March, 1962.
6. Ida Fisher Davidoff and May Elish Markewich, "The Postparental Phase in the Life Cycle of Fifty College-Educated Women," unpublished doctoral study, Teachers College, Columbia University, 1961. These fifty educated women had been full-time housewives and mothers throughout the years their children were in school. With the last child's departure, the women suffering severe distress because they had no deep interest beyond the home included a few whose actual ability and achievement were high; these women had been leaders in community work, but they felt like "phonies," "frauds," earning respect for "work a ten-year-old could do." The authors' own orientation in the functional-adjustment school makes them deplore the fact that education gave these women "unrealistic" goals (a surprising number, now in their fifties and sixties, still wished they had been doctors). However, those women who had pursued interests—which in every case had begun in college—and were working now in jobs or politics or art, did not feel like "phonies," or even suffer the expected distress at menopause. Despite the distress of those who lacked such interests, none of them, after the child-bearing years were over, wanted to go back to school; there were simply too few years left to justify the effort. So they continued "woman's role" by acting as mothers to their own aged parents or by finding pets, plants, or simply "people as my hobby" to take the place of their children.
 The interpretation of the two family-life educators—who themselves became professional marriage counselors in middle age—is interesting:

For those women in our group who had high aspirations or high intellectual endowment or both, the discrepancy between some of the values stressed in our success-and-achievement oriented society and the actual opportunities open to the older, untrained women was especially disturbing.

. . . The door open to the woman with a skill was closed to the one without training, even if she was tempted to try to find a place for herself among the gainfully employed. The reality hazards of the work situation seemed to be recognized by most, however. They felt neither prepared for the kind of job which might appeal to them, nor willing to take the time and expend the energy which would be required for training, in view of the limited number of active years ahead. . . . The lack of pressure resulting from reduced responsibility had to be handled. . . . As the primary task of motherhood was finished, the satisfactions of volunteer work, formerly a secondary outlet, seemed to be diminishing. . . . The cultural activities of the suburbs were limited. . . . Even in the city, adult education . . . seemed to be "busy work," leading nowhere. . . .

Thus, some women expressed certain regrets: "It is too late to develop a new skill leading to a career." "If I had pursued a single line, it would have utilized my potential to the full."

But the authors note with approval that "the vast majority have somehow adjusted themselves to their place in society."

Because our culture demands of women certain renunciations of activity and limits her scope of participation in the stream of life, at this point being a woman would seem to be an advantage rather than a handicap. All her life, as a female, she had been encouraged to be sensitive to the feelings and needs of others. Her life, at strategic points, had required denials of self. She had had ample opportunities for "dress rehearsals" for this latest renunciation . . . of a long series of renunciations begun early in life. Her whole life as a woman had been giving her a skill which she was now free to use to the full without further preparation . . .

7. Nevitt Sanford, "Personality Development During the College Years," *Journal of Social Issues*, 1956, Vol. 12, No. 4, p. 36.

8. The public flurry in the spring of 1962 over the sexual virginity of Vassar girls is a case in point. The real question, for the educator, would seem to me to be whether these girls were getting from their education the serious lifetime goals only education can give them. If they are, they can be trusted to be responsible for their sexual behavior. President Blanding indeed defied the mystique to say boldly that if girls are not in college for education, they should not be there at all. That her statement caused such an uproar is evidence of the extent of sex-directed education.

9. The impossibility of part-time study of medicine, science, and law, and of part-time graduate work in the top universities has kept many women of high ability from attempting it. But in 1962, the Harvard Graduate School of Education let down this barrier to encourage more able housewives to become teachers. A plan was also announced in New York to permit women doctors to do their

psychiatric residencies and postgraduate work on a part-time basis, taking into account their maternal responsibilities.

10. Virginia L. Senders, "The Minnesota Plan for Women's Continuing Education," in "Unfinished Business—Continuing Education for Women," *The Educational Record*, American Council on Education, October, 1961, pp. 10 ff.

11. Mary Bunting, "The Radcliffe Institute for Independent Study," *Ibid.*, pp. 19 ff. Radcliffe's president reflects the feminine mystique when she deplores "the use the first college graduates made of their advanced educations. Too often and understandably, they became crusaders and reformers, passionate, fearless, articulate, but also, at times, loud. A stereotype of the educated women grew up in the popular mind and concurrently, a prejudice against both the stereotype and the education." Similarly she states:

That we have not made any respectable attempt to meet the special educational needs of women in the past is the clearest possible evidence of the fact that our educational objectives have been geared exclusively to the vocational patterns of men. In changing that emphasis, however, our goal should not be to equip and encourage women to compete with men. . . . Women, because they are not generally the principal breadwinners, can be perhaps most useful as the trail blazers, working along the bypaths, doing the unusual job that men cannot afford to gamble on. There is always room on the fringes even when competition in the intellectual market places is keen.

That women use their education today primarily "on the fringes" is a result of the feminine mystique, and of the prejudices against women it masks; it is doubtful whether these remaining barriers will ever be overcome if even educators are going to discourage able women from becoming "crusaders and reformers, passionate, fearless, articulate,"—and loud enough to be heard.

12. *Time*, November, 1961. See also "Housewives at the $2 Window," *New York Times Magazine*, April 1, 1962, which describes how babysitting services and "clinics" for suburban housewives are now being offered at the race tracks.

13. See remarks of State Assemblywoman Dorothy Bell Lawrence, Republican, of Manhattan, reported in the *New York Times*, May 8, 1962. The first woman to be elected a Republican district leader in New York City, she explained: "I was doing all the work, so I told the county chairman that I wanted to be chairman. He told me it was against the rules for a woman to hold the post, but then he changed the rules." In the Democratic "reform" movement in New York, women are also beginning to assume leadership posts

commensurate with their work, and the old segregated "ladies' auxiliaries" and "women's committees" are beginning to go.

14. Among more than a few women I interviewed who had, as the mystique advises, completely renounced their own ambitions to become wives and mothers, I noticed a repeated history of miscarriages. In several cases, only after the woman finally resumed the work she had given up, or went back to graduate school, was she able to carry to term the long-desired second or third child.

15. American women's life expectancy—75 years—is the longest of women anywhere in the world. But as Myrdal and Klein point out in *Women's Two Roles*, there is increasing recognition that, in human beings, chronological age differs from biological age: "at the chronological age of 70, the divergencies in biological age may be as wide as between the chronological ages of 50 and 90." The new studies of aging in humans indicate that those who have the most education and who live the most complex and active lives, with deep interests and readiness for new experience and learning, do not get "old" in the sense that others do. A close study of 300 biographies (See Charlotte Buhler, "The Curve of Life as Studied in Biographies," *Journal of Applied Psychology*, XIX, August, 1935, pp. 405 ff.) reveals that in the latter half of life, the person's productivity becomes independent of his biological equipment, and, in fact, is often at a higher level than his biological efficiency—that is, *if the person has emerged from biological living*. Where "spiritual factors" dominated activity, the highest point of productivity came in the latter part of life; where "physical facts" were decisive in the life of an individual, the high point was reached earlier and the psychological curve was then more closely comparable to the biological. The study of educated women cited above revealed much less suffering at menopause than is considered "normal" in America today. Most of these women whose horizons had not been confined to physical housekeeping and their biological role, did not, in their fifties and sixties feel "old." Many reported in surprise that they suffered much less discomfort at menopause than their mothers' experience had led them to expect. Therese Benedek suggests (in "Climacterium: A Developmental Phase," *Psychoanalytical Quarterly*, XIX, 1950, p. 1) that the lessened discomfort, and burst of creative energy many women now experience at menopause, is at least in part due to the "emancipation" of women. Kinsey's figures seem to indicate that women who have by education been emancipated from purely biological living, experience the full peak of sexual fulfillment much later in life than had been expected, and in fact, continue to experience it through the forties and past meno-

pause. Perhaps the best example of this phenomenon is Colette—that truly human, emancipated French woman who lived and loved and wrote with so little deference to her chronological age that she said on her eightieth birthday: "If only one were 58, because at that time one is still desired and full of hope for the future."

Index

445